Collins

M000227180

WATERWAYS GUIDE 2

Severn, Avon & Birmingham

▌CONTENTS

Map data

Published by Nicholson
An imprint of HarperCollins Publishers
Westerhill Road, Bishopbriggs, Glasgow G64 2QT
www.harpercollins.co.uk

Waterways guides published by Nicholson since 1969
This version first published by Nicholson and Ordnance Survey 1997
New editions published by Nicholson 2000, 2003, 2006, 2009, 2012, 2014, 2015, 2018

Wildlife text from *Collins Complete Guide to British Wildlife* and *Collins Wild Guide*.

This product uses map data licensed from Ordnance Survey
© Crown copyright and database rights (2017) Ordnance Survey (100018598)

The representation in this publication of a road, track or path is no evidence of the existence of a right of way.

Researched and written by Jonathan Mosse

The publishers gratefully acknowledge the assistance given by Canal & River Trust and their staff in the preparation of this guide. Grateful thanks are also due to the Environment Agency, members of the Inland Waterways Association, and CAMRA representatives and branch members.

Photographs reproduced by kind permission of: Jonathan Mosse; p14, p35, p46, p101, 107, p111, p141, p189, p196: Shutterstock; p15–35, p25, p29, p66, p81, p108, p127: Alamy; p36–65, p57, p67–71, p72–105, p106-129, p131-139, p136, p140-153, p146, p153, p154-177, p159, p166, p178-195: Paul Huggins (paulhugginsphotography.com); p122

Every care has been taken in the preparation of this guide. However, the Publisher accepts no responsibility whatsoever for any loss, damage, injury or inconvenience sustained or caused as a result of using this guide.

HarperCollins does not warrant that any website mentioned in this title will be provided uninterrupted, that any website will be error free, that defects will be corrected, or that the website or the server that makes it available are free of viruses or bugs. For full terms and conditions please refer to the site terms provided on the website.

A catalogue record for this book is available from the British Library

Printed in China by RR Donnelley APS Co Ltd

ISBN 978-0-00-825801-6

10 9 8 7 6 5 4

MIX
Paper from
responsible sources

FSC
www.fsc.org

FSC™ C007454

This book is produced from independently certified FSC™ paper to ensure responsible forest management.

For more information visit: www.harpercollins.co.uk/green

■ INTRODUCTION

Wending their quiet way through town and country, the inland navigations of Britain offer boaters, walkers and cyclists a unique insight into a fascinating, but once almost lost, world. When built this was the province of the boatmen and their families, who lived a mainly itinerant lifestyle: often colourful, to our eyes picturesque but, for them, remarkably harsh. Transporting the nation's goods during the late 1700s and early 1800s, negotiating locks, traversing aqueducts and passing through long narrow tunnels, canals were the arteries of trade during the initial part of the industrial revolution.

Then the railways came: the waterways were eclipsed in a remarkably short time by a faster and more flexible transport system, and a steady decline began. In a desperate fight for survival canal tolls were cut, crews toiled for longer hours and worked the boats with their whole family living aboard. Canal companies merged, totally uneconomic waterways were abandoned, some were modernised but it was all to no avail. Large scale commercial carrying on inland waterways had reached the finale of its short life.

At the end of World War II a few enthusiasts roamed this hidden world and harboured a vision of what it could become: a living transport museum which stretched the length and breadth of the country; a place where people could spend their leisure time and, on just a few of the wider waterways, a still modestly viable transport system.

The restoration struggle began and, from modest beginnings, Britain's inland waterways are now seen as an irreplaceable part of the fabric of the nation. Long-abandoned waterways, once seen as an eyesore and a danger, are recognised for the valuable contribution they make to our quality of life, and restoration schemes are integrating them back into the network. Let us hope that the country's network of inland waterways continues to be cherished and well-used, maintained and developed as we move through the 21st century.

If you would like to comment on any aspect of the guides, please write to Nicholson Waterways Guides, Collins, Westerhill Road, Bishopbriggs, Glasgow G64 2QT or email nicholson@harpercollins.co.uk.

Also available:

Collins **NICHOLSON**

Waterways guides and map

1   **Grand Union, Oxford & the South East**

3   **Birmingham & the Heart of England**

4   **Four Counties & the Welsh Canals**

5   **North West & the Pennines**

6   **Nottingham, York & the North East**

7   **River Thames & the Southern Waterways**

Norfolk Broads

Inland Waterways Map of Great Britain   3

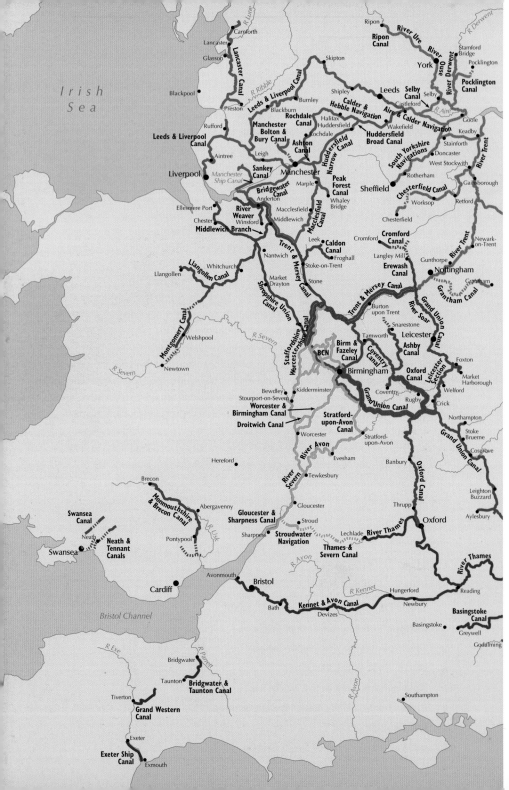

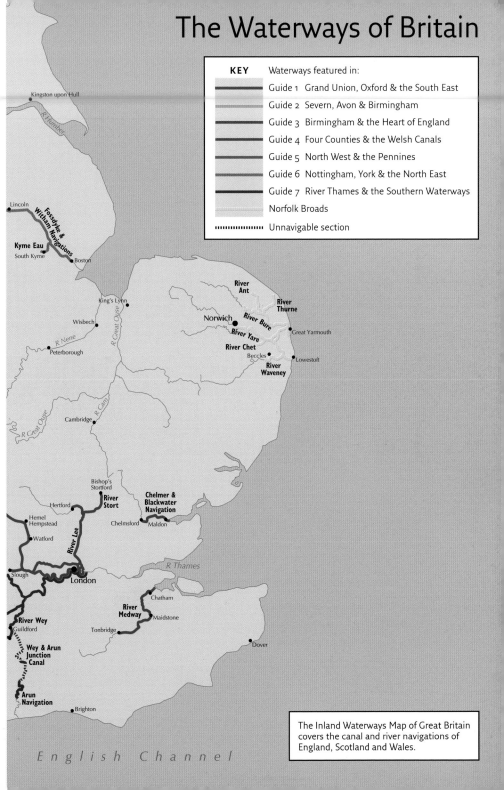

The Waterways of Britain

KEY Waterways featured in:

Guide 1 Grand Union, Oxford & the South East
Guide 2 Severn, Avon & Birmingham
Guide 3 Birmingham & the Heart of England
Guide 4 Four Counties & the Welsh Canals
Guide 5 North West & the Pennines
Guide 6 Nottingham, York & the North East
Guide 7 River Thames & the Southern Waterways
Norfolk Broads
·················· Unnavigable section

The Inland Waterways Map of Great Britain covers the canal and river navigations of England, Scotland and Wales.

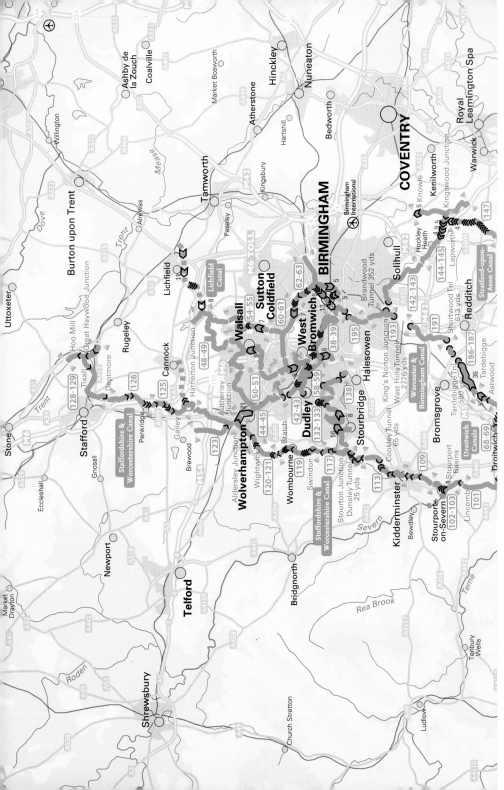

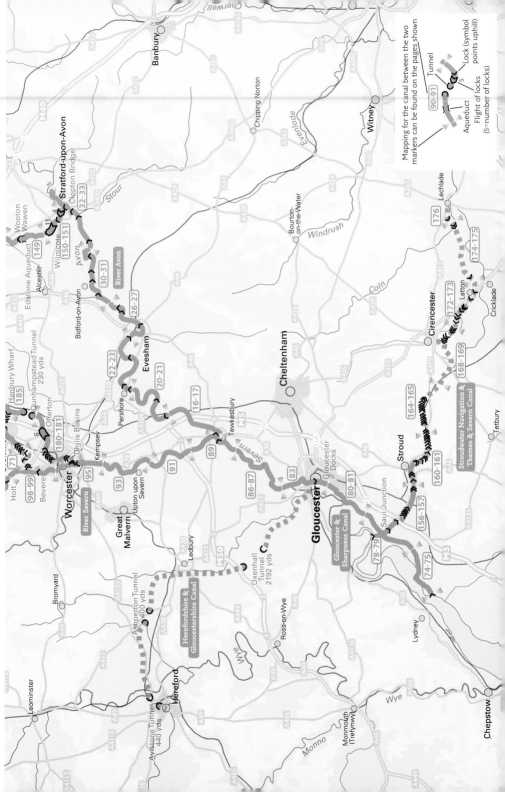

Mapping for the canal between the two
markers can be found on the pages shown

90-91 Tunnel

5 Lock (symbol
points uphill)

Aqueduct

Flight of locks
(5=number of locks)

Banbury

Chipping Norton

Witney

Stratford-upon-Avon

Clopton Bridge **32-33**

Wooton
Wawen

Edstone Aqueduct **149**

Wilmcote **150-151**

Alcester

Stour

Bourton-
on-the-Water

Windrush

Lechlade **176**

Avon

Bidford-on-Avon **30-31**

26-27

River Avon

Latton **174-175**

Coln

172-173

Cricklade

Hanbury Wharf **185**

Dunhampstead Tunnel
230 yds

Offerton **180-181**

Diglis Basins

Evesham **22-23**

20-21

Pershore

16-17

Cirencester **168-169**

Tetbury

164-165

**Stroudwater Navigation &
Thames & Severn Canal**

71

98-99

180-181

Bevere

Holt

Worcester **95**

River Severn

Kempsey

Upton upon
Severn

93

91

Great
Malvern

89

Tewkesbury

Severn

86-87

83

Stroud **160-161**

Saul Junction

156-157

Cheltenham

Gloucester Docks

Gloucester

**Gloucester &
Sharpness Canal** **80-81**

78-79

74-75

Ledbury

**Herefordshire &
Gloucestershire Canal**

Oxenhall
Tunnel
2192 yds

Ross-on-Wye

Lydney

Bromyard

Ashperton Tunnel
400 yds

Aylstone Tunnel
440 yds

Hereford

Wye

Leominster

Monmouth
(Trefynwy)

Monno

Wye

Chepstow

INTRODUCTION

Boaters, walkers, fishermen, cyclists and gongoozlers (on-lookers) all share in the enjoyment of our quite amazing waterway heritage. Canal & River Trust (CRT) and the Environment Agency, along with other navigation authorities, are empowered to develop, maintain and control this resource. It is to this end that a series of guides, codes, and regulations have come into existence over the years, evolving to match a burgeoning – and occasionally conflicting – demand. Set out in this section are key points as they relate to everyone wishing to enjoy the waterways.

The *Boater's Handbook* is available from all navigation authorities. It contains a complete range of safety information, boat-handling know-how, warning symbols and illustrations, and can be downloaded from www.canalrivertrust.org. uk/boating/navigating-the-waterways/boaters-handbook. It is complemented by this excellent video relating specifically to safe lock operation: www.youtube.com/watch?v=3UIW7VotJpM.

CONSIDERATE BOATING

Considerate Boating gives advice and guidance to all waterway users on how to enjoy the inland waterways safely and can be downloaded from www.canalrivertrust.org.uk/boating/navigating-the-waterways/considerate-boating. It is also well worth visiting www.considerateboater.com. These publications are also available from the Customer Services Team which is staffed *Mon–Fri, 08.00–18.00*. The helpful staff will answer general enquiries and provide information about boat licensing, mooring, boating holidays and general activities on the waterways. They can be contacted on 0303 040 4040; customer. services@canalrivertrust.org.uk; Canal & River Trust, Head Office, First Floor North, Station House, 500 Elder Gate, Milton Keynes MK9 1BB. Visit www.canalrivertrust.org.uk for up to date information on almost every aspect of the inland waterways from news and events to moorings.

Emergency Helpline Available from Canal & River Trust outside normal office hours on weekdays and throughout weekends. If lives or property are at risk or there is danger of serious environmental contamination then contact 0800 47 999 47 immediately for emergency help.

ENVIRONMENT AGENCY

The Environment Agency (EA) manages around 600 miles of the country's rivers, including the Thames and the River Medway. For general enquiries or to obtain a copy of the *Boater's Handbook*, contact EA Customer Services on 03708 506 506; enquiries@environment-agency.gov.uk. To find out about their work nationally (or to download a copy of the *Handbook)* and for lots of other useful information, visit www.gov.uk/government/organisations/environment-agency. The website www.visitthames.co.uk provides lots on information on boating, walking, fishing and events on the river.

Incident Hotline The EA maintain an Incident Hotline. To report damage or danger to the natural environment, damage to structures or water escaping, telephone 0800 80 70 60.

LICENSING – BOATS

The majority of the navigations covered in this book are controlled by CRT and the EA and are managed on a day-to-day basis by local Waterway Offices (you will find details of these in the introductions to each waterway). All craft using the inland waterways must be licensed and charges are based on the dimensions of the craft. In a few cases, these include reciprocal agreements with other waterway authorities (as indicated in the text). CRT and the EA offer an optional Gold Licence which covers unlimited navigation on the waterways of both authorities. Permits for permanent mooring on CRT waterways are issued by CRT.

Contact Canal & River Trust Boat Licensing Team on 0303 040 4040; www.canalrivertrust. org.uk/boating/licensing; Canal & River Trust Licensing Team, PO Box 162, Leeds LS9 1AX.

For the Thames and River Medway contact the EA. River Thames: 0118 953 5650; www.gov.uk/government/organisations/environment-agency; Environment Agency, PO Box 214, Reading RG1 8HQ. River Medway: 01732 223222 or visit the website.

BOAT SAFETY SCHEME

CRT and the EA operate the Boat Safety Scheme – boat construction standards and regular tests required by all licence holders on CRT and EA waterways. A Boat Safety Certificate (for new boats, a Declaration of Conformity), is necessary to obtain a craft licence. CRT also requires proof of insurance for Third Party Liability for a minimum of £2,000,000 for powered boats. The scheme is gradually being adopted by other waterway authorities. Contact details are: 0333 202 1000; www.boatsafetyscheme.org; Boat Safety Scheme, First Floor North, Station House, 500 Elder Gate, Milton Keynes MK9 1BB. The website offers useful advice on preventing fires and avoiding carbon monoxide poisoning.

TRAINING

The Royal Yachting Association (RYA) runs one and two day courses leading to the Inland Waters Helmsman's Certificate, specifically designed for novices and experienced boaters wishing to cruise the inland waterways. For details of RYA schools, telephone 023 8060 4100 or visit www.rya.org.uk. The practical course notes are available to buy. Contact your local boat clubs, too. The National Community Boats Association (NCBA) run courses on boat-handling and safety on the water. Telephone 0845 0510649 or visit www.national-cba.co.uk.

LICENSING - CYCLISTS

You no longer require a permit to cycle on those waterways under the control of Canal & River Trust. However, you are asked to abide by the ten point Greenway Code for Towpaths available at www.canalrivertrust.org.uk/see-and-do/cycling which also provides a wide range of advice on cycling beside the waterways. Cycling along the Thames towpath is generally accepted, although landowners have the right to request that you do not cycle. Some sections of the riverside path, however, are designated and clearly marked as official cycle ways. No permits are required but cyclists must follow London's Towpath Code on Conduct at all times.

TOWPATHS

Few, if any, artificial cuts or canals in this country are without an intact towpath accessible to the walker at least and the Thames is the only river in the country with a designated National Trail along its path from source to sea (for more information visit www.nationaltrail.co.uk). However, on some other river navigations, towpaths have on occasion fallen into disuse or, sometimes, been lost to erosion. The indication of a towpath in this guide does not necessarily imply a public right of way or mean that a right to cycle along it exists.

Horse riding and motorcycling are forbidden on all towpaths.

INDIVIDUAL WATERWAY GUIDES

No national guide can cover the minutiae of detail concerning every waterway, and some CRT Waterway Managers produce guides to specific navigations under their charge. Copies of individual guides (where available) can be obtained from the relevant CRT Waterway Office or downloaded from www.waterscape.com/things-to-do/boating/guides. Please note that times – such as operating times of bridges and locks – do change year by year and from winter to summer. For free copies of a range of helpful leaflets for all users of the River Thames – visit www.visitthames.co.uk/about-the-river/publications.

STOPPAGES

CRT and the EA both publish winter stoppage programmes which are sent out to all licence holders, boatyards and hire companies. Inevitably, emergencies occur necessitating the unexpected closure of a waterway, perhaps during the peak season. You can check for stoppages on individual waterways between specific dates on www.canalrivertrust.org.uk/notices/winter, lockside noticeboards or by telephoning 0303 040 4040; for stoppages and river conditions on the Thames, visit www.gov.uk/river-thames-conditions-closures-restrictions-and-lock-closures or telephone 0845 988 1188.

NAVIGATION AUTHORITIES AND WATERWAYS SOCIETIES

Most inland navigations are managed by CRT or the EA, but there are several other navigation authorities. For details of these, contact the Association of Inland Navigation Authorities on 0844 335 1650 or visit www.aina.org.uk. The boater, conditioned perhaps by the uniformity of our national road network, should be sensitive to the need to observe different codes and operating practices.

The Canal & River Trust is a charity set up to care for England and Wales' legacy of 200-year-old waterways, holding them in trust for the nation forever, and is linked with an ombudsman. CRT has a comprehensive complaints procedure and a free explanatory leaflet is available from Customer Services. Problems and complaints should be addressed to the local Waterway Manager in the first instance. For more information, visit their website.

The EA is the national body, sponsored by the Department for Environment, Food and Rural Affairs, to manage the quality of air, land and water in England and Wales. For more information, visit its website.

The Inland Waterways Association (IWA) campaigns for the use, maintenance and restoration of Britain's inland waterways, through branches all over the country. For more information, contact them on 01494 783453; iwa@waterways.org.uk; www.waterways.org.uk; The Inland Waterways Association, Island House, Moor Road, Chesham HP5 1WA. Their website has a huge amount of information of interest to boaters, including comprehensive details of the many and varied waterways societies.

STARTING OUT

Extensive information and advice on booking a boating holiday is available from the Inland Waterways Association, www.visitthames.co.uk and www.canalrivertrust.org.uk/boating/boat-trips-and-holidays. Please book a waterway holiday from a licensed operator – this way you can be sure that you have proper insurance cover, service and support during your holiday. It is illegal for private boat owners to hire out their craft. If you are hiring a holiday craft for the first time, the boatyard will brief you thoroughly. Take notes, follow their instructions and do ask if there is anything you do not understand. CRT have produced a 40 min DVD which is essential viewing for newcomers to canal or river boating. Available to view free at www.canalrivertrust.org.uk/boatersdvd or obtainable (charge) from the CRT Customer Service Centre 0303 040 4040; www.canalrivertrust.org.uk/shop.

PLACES TO VISIT ALONG THE WAY

This guide contains a wealth of information, not just about the canals and rivers and navigating on them, but also on the visitor attractions and places to eat and drink close to the waterways. Opening and closing times, and other details often change; establishments close and new ones open. If you are making special plans to eat in a particular pub, or visit a certain museum it is always advisable to check in advance.

MORE INFORMATION

An internet search will reveal many websites on the inland waterways. Those listed below are just a small sample:

National Community Boats Association is a national charity and training provider, supporting community boat projects and encouraging more people to access the inland waterways. Telephone 0845 0510649; www.national-cba.co.uk.

National Association of Boat Owners is dedicated to promoting the interests of private boaters on Britain's canals and rivers. Visit www.nabo.org.uk.

www.canalplan.org.uk is an online journey-planner and gazetteer for the inland waterways. **www.canals.com** is a valuable source of information for cruising the canals, with loads of links to canal and waterways related websites. **www.ukcanals.net** lists services and useful information for all waterways users.

GENERAL CRUISING NOTES

Most canals and rivers are saucer shaped, being deepest at the middle. Few canals have more than 3-4ft of water and many have much less. Keep to the centre of the channel except on bends, where the deepest water is on the outside of the bend. When you meet another boat, keep to the right, slow down and aim to miss the approaching craft by a couple of yards. If you meet a loaded commercial boat keep right out of the way and be prepared to follow his instructions. Do not assume that you should pass on the right. If you meet a boat being towed from the bank, pass it on the outside. When overtaking, keep the other boat on your right side.

Some CRT and EA facilities are operated by pre-paid cards, obtainable from CRT and EA regional and local waterways offices, lock keepers and boatyards. Weekend visitors should purchase cards in advance. A handcuff/anti-vandal key is commonly used on locks where vandalism is a problem. A watermate/sanitary key opens sanitary stations, waterpoints and some bridges and locks. Both keys and pre-paid cards can be obtained via CRT Customer Service Centre.

Safety

Boating is a safe pastime. However, it makes sense to take simple safety precautions, particularly if you have children aboard.

- Never drink and drive a boat – it may travel slowly, but it weighs many tons.
- Be careful with naked flames and never leave the boat with the hob or oven lit. Familiarise yourself and your crew with the location and operation of the fire extinguishers.

- Never block ventilation grills. Boats are enclosed spaces and levels of carbon monoxide can build up from faulty appliances or just from using the cooker.
- Be careful along the bank and around locks. Slipping from the bank might only give you a cold-water soaking, but falling from the side of, or into a lock is more dangerous. Beware of slippery or rough ground.
- Remember that fingers and toes are precious! If a major collision is imminent, never try to fend off with your hands or feet; and always keep hands and arms inside the boat.
- Weil's disease is a particularly dangerous infection present in water which can attack the central nervous system and major organs. It is caused by bacteria entering the bloodstream through cuts and broken skin, and the eyes, nose and mouth. The flu-like symptoms occur two-four weeks after exposure. Always wash your hands thoroughly after contact with the water. Visit www.leptospirosis.org for details.

Speed

There is a general speed limit of 4 mph on most CRT canals and 5 mph on the Thames. There is no need to go any faster – the faster you go, the bigger a wave the boat creates: if your wash is breaking against the bank, causing large waves or throwing moored boats around, slow down. Slow down also when passing engineering works and anglers; when there is a lot of floating rubbish on the water (try to drift over obvious obstructions in neutral); when approaching blind corners, narrow bridges and junctions.

Mooring

Generally you may moor where you wish on CRT property, as long as you are *not causing an obstruction*. Do not moor in a winding hole or junction, the approaches to a lock or tunnel, or at a water point or sanitary station. On the Thames, generally you have a right to anchor for 24 hours in one place provided no obstruction is caused, however you will need explicit permission from the land owner to moor. There are official mooring sites along the length of the river; those provided by the EA are free, the others you will need to pay for. Your boat should carry metal mooring stakes, and these should be driven firmly into the ground with a mallet if there are no mooring rings. Do not stretch mooring lines across the towpath and take account of anyone who may walk past. Always consider the security

of your boat when there is no one aboard. On tideways and commercial waterways it is advisable to moor only at recognised sites, and allow for any rise or fall of the tide.

Bridges

On narrow canals slow down well in advance and aim to miss one side (usually the towpath side) by about 9 inches. *Keep everyone inboard when passing under bridges and ensure there is nothing on the roof of the boat that will hit the bridge.* If a boat is coming the other way, the craft nearest to the bridge has priority. Take special care with moveable structures – the crew member operating the bridge should be strong and heavy enough to hold it steady as the boat passes through.

Going aground

You can sometimes go aground if the water level on a canal has dropped or you are on a particularly shallow stretch. If it does happen, try reversing *gently*, or pushing off with the boat hook. Another method is to get your crew to rock the boat from side to side using the boat hook, or move all crew to the end opposite to that which is aground. Or, have all crew leave the boat, except the helmsman, and it will often float off quite easily.

Tunnels

Again, ensure that everyone is inboard. Make sure the tunnel is clear before you enter, and use your headlight. Follow any instructions given on notice boards by the entrance.

Fuel

Diesel can be purchased from most boatyards and some CRT depots. To comply with HMRC regulations you must declare an appropriate split between propulsion and heating so that the correct level of VAT can be applied. However, few boatyards stock petrol. Where a garage is listed under a town or village's facilities petrol (and DERV) are available.

Water

It is advisable to top up daily.

Pump out

Self-operated pump out facilities are available at a number of locations on the waterways network. These facilities are provided by CRT and can be operated via a 25-unit prepayment card. Details of how to buy a pump out card either

11

online, by phone or in person are available from www.canalrivertrust.org.uk. The cards provide for one pump out or 25 units of electricity. Cards can be obtained from CRT Waterway Offices, some Marinas and boatyards, shops and cafés.

Boatyards
Hire fleets are usually turned around at a weekend, making this a bad time to call in for services.

VHF Radio
The IWA recommends that all pleasure craft navigating the larger waterways used by freight carrying vessels, or any tidal navigation, should carry marine-band VHF radio and have a qualified radio operator on board. In some cases the navigation authority requires craft to carry radio and maintain a listening watch. Two examples of this are for boats on the tidal River Ouse wishing to enter Goole Docks and the Aire & Calder Navigation, and for boats on the tidal Thames, over 45ft, navigating between Teddington Lock and Limehouse Basin. VHF radio users must have a current operator's certificate. The training is not expensive and will present no problem to the average inland waterways boater. Contact the RYA (see Training) for details.

PLANNING A CRUISE
Don't try to go too far too fast. Go slowly, don't be too ambitious, and enjoy the experience. Mileages indicated on the maps are for guidance only. A *rough* calculation of time taken to cover the ground is the lock-miles system:

Add the number of *miles* to the number of *locks* on your proposed journey, and divide the resulting figure by three. This will give you an approximate guide to the number of *hours* your travel will take.

TIDAL WATERWAYS
The typical steel narrow boat found on the inland waterways is totally unsuitable for cruising on tidal estuaries. However, the adventurous will inevitably wish to add additional 'ring cruises' to the more predictable circuits of inland Britain. Passage is possible in most estuaries if careful consideration is given to the key factors of weather conditions, tides, crew experience, the condition of the boat and its equipment and, perhaps of overriding importance, the need to take expert advice.

In many cases it will be prudent to employ the skilled services of a local pilot. Within the text, where inland navigations connect with a tidal waterway, details are given of sources of advice and pilotage. It is also essential to inform your insurance company of your intention to navigate on tidal waterways as they may very well have special requirements or wish to levy an additional premium. This guide is to the inland waterways of Britain and therefore recognizes that tideways – and especially estuaries – require a different approach and many additional skills. We do not hesitate to draw the boater's attention to the appropriate source material.

LOCKS AND THEIR USE
A lock is a simple and ingenious device for transporting your craft from one water level to another. When both sets of gates are closed it may be filled or emptied using gates, or ground paddles, at the top or bottom of the lock. These are operated with a windlass. On the Thames, the locks are manned all year round, with longer hours from April to October. You may operate the locks yourself at any time.

If a lock is empty, or 'set' for you, the crew open the gates and you drive the boat in. If the lock is full of water, the crew should check first to see if any boat is waiting or coming in the other direction. If a boat is in sight, you must let them through first: do not empty or 'turn' the lock against them. This is not only discourteous, and against the rules, but wastes precious water.

In the diagrams the *plan* shows how the gates point uphill, the water pressure forcing them together. Water is flooding into the lock through the underground culverts that are operated by the ground paddles: when the lock is 'full', the top gates (on the left of the drawing) can be opened. One may imagine a boat entering, the crew closing the gates and paddles after it.

In the *elevation*, the bottom paddles have been raised (opened) so that the lock empties. A boat will, of course, float down with the water. When the lock is 'empty' the bottom gates can be opened and the descending boat can leave.

Remember that when going *up* a lock, a boat should be tied up to prevent it being thrown about by the rush of incoming water; but when going *down* a lock, a boat should never be tied up or it will be left high and dry.

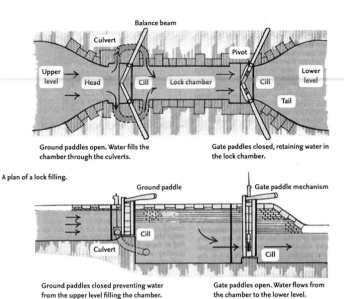

Balance beam

Culvert

Pivot

Upper level → Head Cill Lock chamber → Cill Lower level

Tail

Ground paddles open. Water fills the chamber through the culverts.

Gate paddles closed, retaining water in the lock chamber.

A plan of a lock filling.

Ground paddle

Gate paddle mechanism

Cill

Culvert

Cill

Ground paddles closed preventing water from the upper level filling the chamber.

Gate paddles open. Water flows from the chamber to the lower level.

An elevation of a lock emptying.

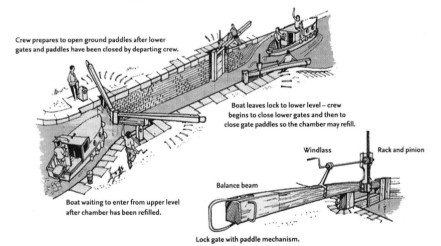

Crew prepares to open ground paddles after lower gates and paddles have been closed by departing crew.

Boat leaves lock to lower level – crew begins to close lower gates and then to close gate paddles so the chamber may refill.

Windlass

Rack and pinion

Balance beam

Boat waiting to enter from upper level after chamber has been refilled.

Lock gate with paddle mechanism.

- Make safety your prime concern. *Keep a close eye on young children.*
- Always take your time, and do not leap about.
- Never open the paddles at one end without ensuring those at the other end are closed.
- Keep to the landward side of the balance beam when opening and closing gates. Whilst it may be necessary to put your back behind the balance beam to gain a better purchase when starting to close a gate, always move to the correct position as soon as possible.

- Never leave your windlass slotted onto the paddle spindle – it will be dangerous should anything slip.
- Keep your boat away from the top and bottom gates to prevent it getting caught on the gate or the lock cill.
- Never drop the paddles – always wind them down.
- Be wary of fierce *top gate* paddles, especially in wide locks. Operate them slowly, and close them if there is *any* adverse effect.
- Always follow the navigation authority's instructions, where given on notices or by their staff.

13

Moored in Evesham on the River Avon

RIVER AVON

MAXIMUM DIMENSIONS	Avon Navigation Trust
Length: 70'	Mill Wharf, Mill Lane, Wyre Piddle,
Beam: 13' 6" – reducing on Upper Avon	Pershore, Worcs. WR10 2JF
(above Evesham) – being 12' 9" at Bidford Bridge	01386 552517; emergency number 0300 999 2010;
at normal river levels.	office@avonnavigationtrust.org
Draught	www.avonnavigationtrust.org
– Lower Avon: 4'	
– Upper Avon: 3'	**MILEAGE**
Headroom	*Avon Lock, TEWKESBURY to:*
– Lower Avon: 10' (at normal river levels)	Pershore Lock: 14½ miles
– Upper Avon: 8' (at normal river levels)	Evesham Lock: 25¾ miles
	Bidford Bridge: 32¼ miles
Electric power lines and telephone wires cross the	*Tramway Bridge, STRATFORD:* 42¼ miles
river at a height approaching 30' above normal	Alveston Weir: 45½ miles
summer levels. A sensible allowance must be made	Locks: 17
for mast height etc when navigating in semi-flood	Remember that the river is not under the jurisdiction
conditions and for the possibility of flash discharge.	of Canal & River Trust therefore water points may not
	be of a standard design.

Rising at Welford on the Leicestershire and Northampton boundary and joining the River Severn at Tewkesbury, the River Avon was first made navigable to Stratford by William Sandys of Fladbury during the period 1635-9, with authority to extend eventually to Warwick, Coventry and beyond. In 1717 the ownership of the river was split into the Upper and Lower Avon, the dividing line being the tail of Evesham Weir. Following several changes in ownership, the upper river was purchased by the Oxford, Worcester and Wolverhampton (OWW) Railway. By refusing tolls they avoided the obligation to maintain the river and as a result within ten years it was in a ruinous state. By 1875 all traffic on the Upper Avon had ceased.

Although deteriorating gradually, the Lower Avon did remain navigable to Pershore until it was bought, for £1500, by C.D. Barwell OBE in 1950. At this time the Lower Avon Navigation Trust was formed and restoration began, with navigation being restored to the Bridge Inn, Offenham by June 1964. In July of that year, the southern section of the Stratford-on-Avon Canal from Kingswood Junction to Stratford was also re-opened, making the restoration of the Upper Avon the next logical step. But with no right of access to the river, a non-effective navigation authority, all but three of the weirs collapsed and the locks in complete ruin, it seemed an all but impossible task.

The Upper Avon Navigation Trust was formed in 1965 and in 1969, under the leadership of David Hutchings MBE, work began. An appeal was made to raise £375,000 and eventually over a third of this sum was given by one anonymous donor. Despite enormous difficulties, the upper river was officially opened by HM Queen Elizabeth the Queen Mother on 1 June 1974. A truly magnificent achievement for private initiative and volunteer labour.

In January 2010 the Upper and Lower Avon Navigation Trusts amalgamated to form a new independent charitable navigation authority, the Avon Navigation Trust (ANT).

CRUISING ON THE AVON

This is a river navigation and can present problems to those more accustomed to the still waters of the canals. On the lower reaches just 36 hours of summer rain can make passage difficult – the pull upstream of the weirs increases, cross-currents below the weirs become fierce and the water piles up as it rushes through narrow bridge-holes. River Watch is an important initiative by ANT to better inform users of the state of the river, accessible via their website. ANT also publish a comprehensive guide to the river which, amongst many other things, sets out the the Rules and regulations for the navigation – see page 17, Navigational Notes for further details.

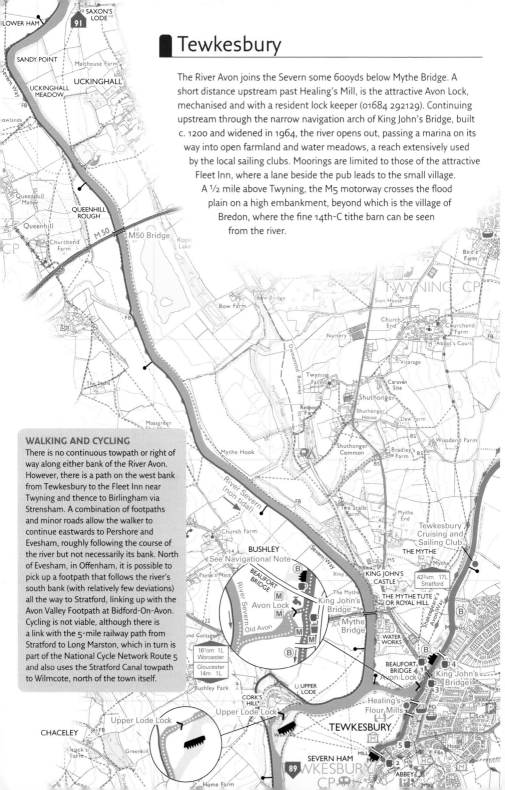

Tewkesbury

The River Avon joins the Severn some 600yds below Mythe Bridge. A short distance upstream past Healing's Mill, is the attractive Avon Lock, mechanised and with a resident lock keeper (01684 292129). Continuing upstream through the narrow navigation arch of King John's Bridge, built c. 1200 and widened in 1964, the river opens out, passing a marina on its way into open farmland and water meadows, a reach extensively used by the local sailing clubs. Moorings are limited to those of the attractive Fleet Inn, where a lane beside the pub leads to the small village. A ½ mile above Twyning, the M5 motorway crosses the flood plain on a high embankment, beyond which is the village of Bredon, where the fine 14th-C tithe barn can be seen from the river.

WALKING AND CYCLING

There is no continuous towpath or right of way along either bank of the River Avon. However, there is a path on the west bank from Tewkesbury to the Fleet Inn near Twyning and thence to Birlingham via Strensham. A combination of footpaths and minor roads allow the walker to continue eastwards to Pershore and Evesham, roughly following the course of the river but not necessarily its bank. North of Evesham, in Offenham, it is possible to pick up a footpath that follows the river's south bank (with relatively few deviations) all the way to Stratford, linking up with the Avon Valley Footpath at Bidford-On-Avon. Cycling is not viable, although there is a link with the 5-mile railway path from Stratford to Long Marston, which in turn is part of the National Cycle Network Route 5 and also uses the Stratford Canal towpath to Wilmcote, north of the town itself.

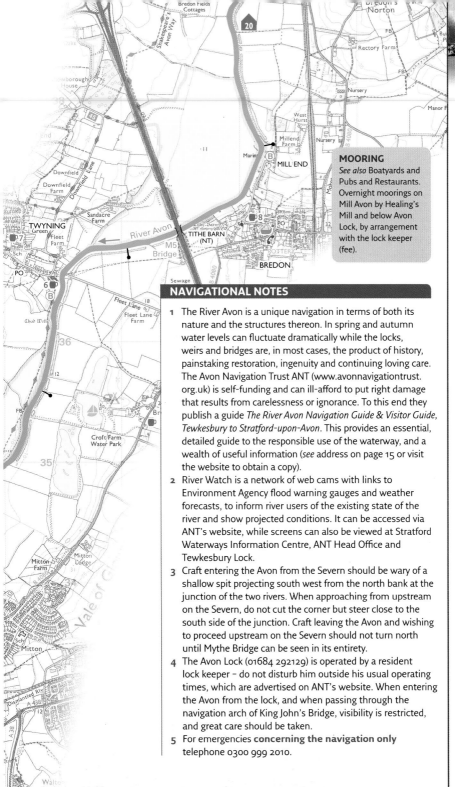

MOORING

See also Boatyards and Pubs and Restaurants. Overnight moorings on Mill Avon by Healing's Mill and below Avon Lock, by arrangement with the lock keeper (fee).

NAVIGATIONAL NOTES

1 The River Avon is a unique navigation in terms of both its nature and the structures thereon. In spring and autumn water levels can fluctuate dramatically while the locks, weirs and bridges are, in most cases, the product of history, painstaking restoration, ingenuity and continuing loving care. The Avon Navigation Trust ANT (www.avonnavigationtrust.org.uk) is self-funding and can ill-afford to put right damage that results from carelessness or ignorance. To this end they publish a guide *The River Avon Navigation Guide & Visitor Guide, Tewkesbury to Stratford-upon-Avon*. This provides an essential, detailed guide to the responsible use of the waterway, and a wealth of useful information (*see* address on page 15 or visit the website to obtain a copy).

2 River Watch is a network of web cams with links to Environment Agency flood warning gauges and weather forecasts, to inform river users of the existing state of the river and show projected conditions. It can be accessed via ANT's website, while screens can also be viewed at Stratford Waterways Information Centre, ANT Head Office and Tewkesbury Lock.

3 Craft entering the Avon from the Severn should be wary of a shallow spit projecting south west from the north bank at the junction of the two rivers. When approaching from upstream on the Severn, do not cut the corner but steer close to the south side of the junction. Craft leaving the Avon and wishing to proceed upstream on the Severn should not turn north until Mythe Bridge can be seen in its entirety.

4 The Avon Lock (01684 292129) is operated by a resident lock keeper – do not disturb him outside his usual operating times, which are advertised on ANT's website. When entering the Avon from the lock, and when passing through the navigation arch of King John's Bridge, visibility is restricted, and great care should be taken.

5 For emergencies **concerning the navigation only** telephone 0300 999 2010.

17

Boatyards

®**Tewkesbury Marina** Bredon Road, Tewkesbury GL20 5BY (01684 293737; www.tewkesbury-marina. co.uk). ☗☗⚒P D Pump out, gas, overnight mooring, long-term mooring, winter storage, 6 tonne gantry crane, slipway, small chandlery, boat sales, toilets, showers, launderette, solid fuel, WiFi. ®**Bredon Marina** Dock Lane, Bredon, Tewkesbury GL20 7LG (01684 773166/07811 458335; www.bredonmarina.co.uk). Gas, boat sales, moorings, crane, repairs, chandlery, slipway, showers, toilets. Boat surveys and boat safety examiner. ®**Twyning Park River Moorings** Fleet Road, Tewkesbury GL20 6DG (01684 301425/07879 040101; www.twyningpark.com/the-river-moorings.html). Daily, overnight, short- and long-term moorings.

● **Tewkesbury**
Glos. All services (station distant). A historic town at the junction of the rivers Avon and Severn, with many attractive and ancient buildings to see, chief among these being, of course, the abbey. One of the more unusual aspects of Tewkesbury is the great number of tiny alleys leading off the main street that is the backbone of the town. These alleys yield tempting views of discreet cottages, gardens, back walls and private yards. One of these – Baptist Chapel Court – leads to the old chapel, built around 1655. This tiny, simple building and its little burial ground reflect well the modest aspirations of the minority Baptist movement. There are many other buildings of great interest throughout Tewkesbury, chiefly of the half- timbered variety, with overhanging gables. Some have curious names like House of the Nodding Gables and Ancient Grudge. There is also a liberal scattering of historic pubs, notably the Hop Pole Inn (associated with Dickens' *Pickwick Papers*) and the Bell hotel, an Elizabethan building which was Abel Fletcher's home in the book *John Halifax, Gentleman*.
Tewkesbury Abbey Church Street, Tewkesbury GL20 5RZ (01684 850959; www.tewkesburyabbey.org.uk). This superb building is cathedral-like in proportions and is generally reckoned to be one of the finest Norman churches in the country. It is contemporary with Gloucester Cathedral, and has the same type of vast cylindrical arches the length of the nave. This massive scale is repeated throughout the building: the beautifully decorated central tower, 46ft square and over 130ft high, is the largest Norman tower in existence. The recessed arch that frames the mighty west window is over 60ft high. The abbey's interior is no less splendid than the exterior, and contains interesting monuments, notably the Despencer and Beauchamp tombs. The abbey, which was completed c.1120, was part of a Benedictine monastery until this was threatened with dissolution by King Henry VIII in 1539. The townspeople bought the Abbey – for £453 – to save it from demolition, and it became the town's parish church. *Open all year Mon-Sat 08.30-17.30 (Wed & Fri 07.30) & Sun 07.30-18.00).* The Abbey Shop is *open Mon-Sun 09.30-16.30 (Sun 12.30)* and the Tea Room is *open Mon-Sun 10.45-13.45 & Sun 12.30-16.00. Daily summer* tower tours.
The Abbey Cottages Church Street. The most unusual buildings in Tewkesbury must surely be the row of medieval shops near the abbey. These 25 cottages were rescued from dereliction and threatened demolition when it was realised that they are unique in this country. As built, in about 1450, they were made of wattle and daub in a heavy timber framework. The ground floor consisted of trodden earth, the windows had no glass, and there was no chimney in the roof – the smoke from the fireplace escaped through a hole under the eaves. The shutters covering the big window facing the street folded down to form a shop counter. One of the houses has been restored to this original state (*see* Merchant's House below) and may be visited; the others have been modified to provide pleasantly discreet modern houses. This restoration won a Civic Trust award.
Abbey Gatehouse Church Street, Tewkesbury. Another worthy building, rescued by the Landmark Trust and given a new lease of life as holiday accommodation. For details of how to become a temporary gate keeper, telephone (01628 825925 or visit www.landmarktrust.org.uk).
Cascades Leisure Pool Oldbury Road, Tewkesbury GL20 5DN (01684 293740; www.tewkesbury.gov.uk). The usual mix of water-based fun.
Croft Farm Water Park Bredon's Hardwick, Tewkesbury GL20 7EE (01684 772321; www.croftfarmleisure. co.uk). Follow track and footpath south east from the bank opposite Twynning. Husky dog rides, canoeing, windsurfing and sailing facility offering tuition and hire of craft, wetsuits and buoyancy aids. Also camping. *Open daily in summer 08.30-17.00 & winter Mon-Fri 08.30-16.30. Closed Jan.* Fishing and a wide variety of birdlife. Clubhouse, café and shop. Charge.
John Moore Countryside Museum 41 Church Street, Tewkesbury GL20 5SN (01684 297174; www.johnmooremuseum.org). Established in the memory of a local conservationist, the museum features a wide range of indigenous animals and birds, hand tools, wildlife sculptures, temporary exhibitions and live animal days. Set in a delightful 15th-C timber-framed merchant's cottage and garden. Shop. *Open Apr-Oct, Tue-Sat and B Hols 10.00-13.00 and 14.00-17.00 & Nov-Mar at the same times on Sat; School Hols and B Hols.* Charge.
A few doors away is
The Merchant's House (Little Museum) 45 Church Street, Tewkesbury GL20 5SN. Showing the construction of a medieval merchant's shop and house, with many original features and copies of medieval furniture. *Opening times* as per Countryside Museum.
30 & 32 St Mary's Lane Tewkesbury. Rare survivors of framework knitters' cottages from a previous era of prosperity within the town. Stocking makers worked at home at frames lit by the long, airy windows on the first floor. The quality of the construction of these houses suggests that the living was a decent one. These represent another rescue on the part of the Landmark Trust and a means by which the visitor can linger longer in the town. Details as per Abbey Gatehouse.
Roses Theatre Sun Street, Tewkesbury GL20 5NX (01684 295074; www.rosestheatre.org). Lively focus for the arts

in Tewkesbury offering a mix of music, theatre, cinema and workshops for all ages and tastes.

Tewkesbury Museum 64 Barton Street, Tewkesbury ● GL20 5PX (01684 292901; www.tewkesburymuseum. org). A small, child friendly museum in a delightfully irregular timber-framed house. Displays of local history, costumes and furniture. Also a large model of the Battle of Tewkesbury. *Open Mar-Sep, Mon-Fri 13.00-16.00 & Sat-Sun 11.00-16.00; Oct-Feb, Sat-Mon 11.00-15.00.* Free.

Tewkesbury Mop Fair takes place *9-10 Oct every year*, except when that date falls on a Sunday. A mop fair and one of the oldest in the country, it used to be held at the monastery gate.

Battle of Tewkesbury 4 May 1471
The penultimate battle in the Wars of the Roses, fought to the south of the town, where the Lancastrians, under Queen Margaret's commanders Somerset, Wenlock and Devonshire were defeated by Edward IV's Yorkists under Edward, Gloucester and Hastings.

Tourist Information Centre
100 Church Street, Tewkesbury GL20 5AB (01684 855040; www.visittewkesbury.info). *Open Apr-Oct, Mon-Sat 10.00-16.00; Nov-Apr, Mon, Tue, Fri & Sat 10.00-16.00.*

● **Twyning**
Glos. PO, tel, stores, off-licence. In the main this attractive habitation is arranged around a most spacious village green with a small lane leading down to the river.

● **Bredon**
Worcs PO, tel, stores, off-licence, greengrocer, bakery. A substantial and attractive village with many fine timbered buildings. Close to the river is a 14th-C tithe barn (GL20 7EG, 01452 814213; www.nationaltrust. org.ul/bredon-barn), 124ft long and once one of the best preserved in the country, where grain – paid as taxes to the church – was stored. Severely damaged by fire, it has now been rebuilt. The Church of St Giles has a vaulted Norman porch, and dates from c.1180 – it was mentioned by John Masefield in 'All the land from Ludlow Town to Bredon Church's spire'. Bredon Hill, which dominates the river for several miles, rises to 961ft some 3 miles to the north east – it is said that eight or more counties can be seen from its summit on a fine day. On the southern slope is an 18th-C castellated folly, Bell's Castle, and on the top is a 2nd-C BC hill fort containing Parson's Folly, a prominent tower built in the late 18th C. The hill was celebrated in A. E. Housman's *A Shropshire Lad*.

Bredon Pottery Main Road, Bredon, Tewksbury GL20 7Lw (01684 773417; www.bredonpottery.co.uk). A husband and wife team producing a range of decorated earthenware pottery for use in the house, kitchen, conservatory and garden. *Open Tue-Sat 10.00-18.00.*

Pubs and Restaurants (pages 16-17)

There are many pubs and hotels in Tewkesbury, including:

🍺 1 **The Boat House** King John's Island, Mythe Road, Tewkesbury GL20 6EB (01684 275714; www. theboathousepub.co.uk). Good value food – available *daily 12.00-22.00 (Sun 21.00)* – served from a varied menu, by attentive, friendly staff in a welcoming modern pub/restaurant, with a large riverside terrace. Family-friendly, Wi-Fi. *Open daily 11.00-23.00.*

🍺✕ 2 **The Bell** 52 Church Street, Tewkesbury GL20 5SA (01684 293293; www.oldenglishinns. co.uk/tewkesbury). 12th-C inn opposite the abbey, complete with 500-year-old wall carvings, serving real ale. Bar snacks and a full restaurant menu available *daily 11.00-22.00.* Children welcome *until 20.30*; dogs welcome in bar and lounge area only. Garden. Wi-Fi. B&B.

🍺 3 **The Olde Black Bear** 68 High Street, Tewkesbury GL20 5BJ (01684 292202). In existence since 1308 and said to be the oldest inn in Gloucestershire. Real ale and bar meals served in a dining area that was once stables *daily 12.00-21.00.* Garden, dog- and family-friendly. Real fires and mooring. B&B. *Open 11.00-23.00.*

🍺 4 **The White Bear** Bredon Road, Tewkesbury GL20 5BU (01684 296614; www.famouswhitebear.co.uk). CAMRA Pub of the Year winner three years running. An excellent selection of real ales dispensed in a basic single-bar pub. Real draught cider and traditional pub games. Dog- and family-friendly. Garden and Wi-Fi. Live music *Sun 16.00-19.00. Open 10.00-00.00.*

🍺 5 **The Royal Hop Pole Hotel** 94 Church Street, Tewkesbury GL20 5RS (01684 278670; www. jdwetherspoon.com/pubs/all-pubs/england/ gloucestershire/the-royal-hop-pole-tewkesbury). Historic, town-centre hotel *open daily 07.00-23.00,* serving a wide selection of real ales and inexpensive food. Family-friendly, large-screen TV, real fires and Wi-Fi. B&B.

🍺✕ 6 **The Fleet Inn** Fleet Lane, Twyning GL20 6FL (01684 274020; www.thefleetattwyning.co.uk). Busy, friendly pub dispensing real ale together with food served *Mon-Fri L and E; Sat-Sun 12.00-21.30 (Sun 21.00).* Dogs and children welcome. Moorings, garden, *regular* live music, real fires and Wi-Fi. *Open 12.00-23.00.*

🍺 7 **The Village Inn** Twyning Green, Twyning GL20 6DF (01684 293500; www.thevi.co.uk). Real ales and food available *Mon-Thu 17.00-21.00 & Fri-Sun 12.00-14.00.* Family-friendly, garden, traditional pub games, real fires and skittle alley. *Open Mon-Thu 17.00-23.00 & Fri-Sun 12.00-23.00.*

🍺 8 **The Cross Keys Inn** Bredon's Hardwick GL20 7EE (01684 772626). Follow track and footpath south east on bank opposite Twyning. Freehouse. Real ale served in a friendly two-roomed village local. Extensive pie menu. Dog- and child-friendly. Garden, traditional pub games, live music, real fires and sports TV. Quiz *Tue. Open Mon-Thu E & Fri-Sun L and E.*

19

Eckington

The river is wide to Strensham Lock and is used extensively by the unusually named Severn Sailing Club. Below the lock a pipe bridge carries the Coventry Water Main over the navigation, and beyond this the weir spills into the river, creating a very strong cross current when there is fresh water in the river. The river now starts to meander around Eckington village, passing under a railway bridge carrying the main Penzance to Aberdeen line before reaching Eckington Bridge, a six-arched and irregular 16th-C structure still in good condition. Above the bridge, the river meanders beside the ever-present Bredon Hill, turning a full 180 degrees at the Swan's Neck. Nafford Lock adjoins the wilderness of Nafford Island, a nature reserve, and a path leads from here to Birlingham, 1 mile to the north west. The swing bridge across the lock must be left closed on leaving. The path over the sluice leads to Eckington, Woollas Hall and Great Comberton but, alas, there are no moorings by the lock, the next being those at Comberton Quay. The village of Nafford was obliterated some 300 years ago by a landslide on Bredon Hill. There is little to see from the river until Pershore.

- **Strensham**
  Worcs. Birthplace of Samuel Butler (1612–80), verse satirist and secretary to Judge Thomas Jeffrey, who lived in the 16th-C house by the well-sited Church of St Philip and St James, which has a painted gallery and two fine brasses of the Russells, once the Lords of the Manor. The key is kept at the farm.
- **Eckington**
  Worcs. Tel, stores, off-licence.
  A dormitory village of little interest except for Holy Trinity Church, which dates from the 12th C, and three pubs. Walk from Strensham Lock or Eckington Bridge.
  Woollas Hall A mile south of Nafford Lock. Elizabethan manor house with a three-storey porch, now divided into flats. Beyond the hall a track climbs to the summit of Bredon Hill.
  Great Comberton
  Worcs. Tel. One of the timeless small villages which surround Bredon Hill – Little Comberton, Bricklehampton and especially Elmley Castle, with its half-timbered cottages and Church of St Mary containing fine 17th-C monuments, are worth visiting.

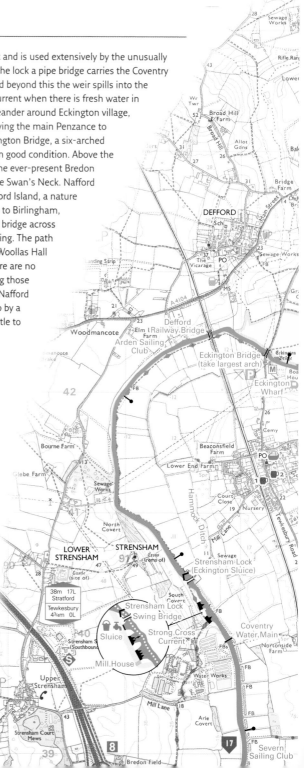

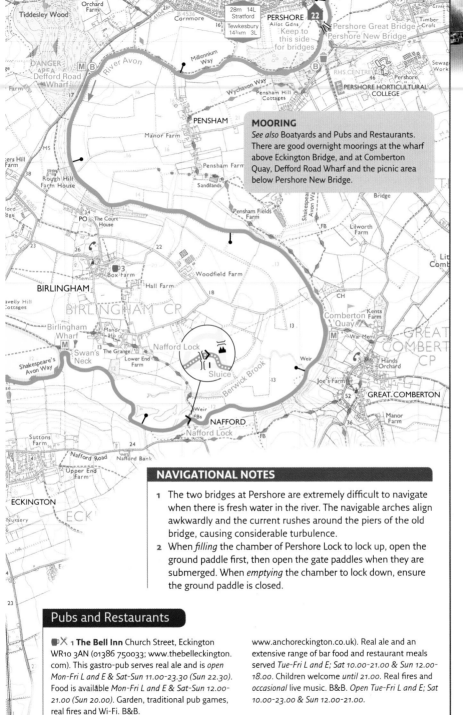

MOORING

See also Boatyards and Pubs and Restaurants.
There are good overnight moorings at the wharf
above Eckington Bridge, and at Comberton
Quay, Defford Road Wharf and the picnic area
below Pershore New Bridge.

NAVIGATIONAL NOTES

1 The two bridges at Pershore are extremely difficult to navigate
when there is fresh water in the river. The navigable arches align
awkwardly and the current rushes around the piers of the old
bridge, causing considerable turbulence.
2 When *filling* the chamber of Pershore Lock to lock up, open the
ground paddle first, then open the gate paddles when they are
submerged. When *emptying* the chamber to lock down, ensure
the ground paddle is closed.

Pubs and Restaurants

🍺✕ 1 **The Bell Inn** Church Street, Eckington
WR10 3AN (01386 750033; www.thebelleckington.
com). This gastro-pub serves real ale and is *open
Mon-Fri L and E & Sat-Sun 11.00-23.30 (Sun 22.30).*
Food is available *Mon-Fri L and E & Sat-Sun 12.00-
21.00 (Sun 20.00).* Garden, traditional pub games,
real fires and Wi-Fi. B&B.

🍺✕ 2 **The Anchor Inn** Cotheridge Lane, Eckington
WR10 3BA (01386 750356;

www.anchoreckington.co.uk). Real ale and an
extensive range of bar food and restaurant meals
served *Tue-Fri L and E; Sat 10.00-21.00 & Sun 12.00-
18.00.* Children welcome *until 21.00.* Real fires and
occasional live music. B&B. *Open Tue-Fri L and E; Sat
10.00-23.00 & Sun 12.00-21.00.*

Also try: 🍺 3 **The Swan Inn** Church Street,
Birlingham WR10 3AQ (01386 750485;
www.theswaninn.co.uk).

Wyre Piddle

There is now a hydro-electric turbine incorporated in the weir at Pershore Lock, with the intake marked with a barrage 100yds or so to the east of the navigation, above the lock itself. The reach between the locks at Pershore and Wyre Piddle is the shortest on the navigation, being just 1 mile. There is a *water point, sewerage disposal* (both free) *and a pump out facility* (fee) at Pershore Recreation Ground moorings. Wyre Mill, called by the traveller Charles Showell 'the ugliest, of which the Avon is ashamed', is now a sailing and social club. The lock is diamond-shaped, the last of its kind on the river. Approaching from downstream the weir creates a strong cross current, especially after prolonged rain. Wyre Piddle (the Piddle Brook runs behind the village) spreads around the outside of a wide bend, with gardens down to the river, and the Anchor Inn provides a useful mooring for patrons. The villages then skirt the flood plain of the Avon, and there is little to

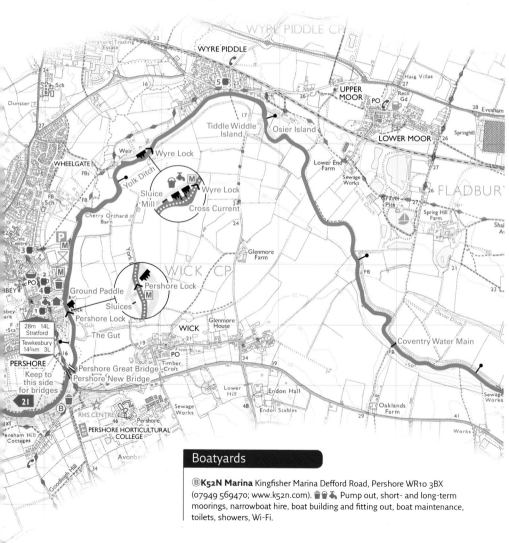

Boatyards

Ⓑ**K52N Marina** Kingfisher Marina Defford Road, Pershore WR10 3BX (07949 569470; www.k52n.com). 🎁🏆🔧 Pump out, short- and long-term moorings, narrowboat hire, boat building and fitting out, boat maintenance, toilets, showers, Wi-Fi.

see except for the wild life – those interested in herons will be particularly pleased. Beyond the Coventry Water Main Bridge the village of Cropthorne sits on higher ground to the south east. Below Jubilee Bridge are the remains of the last flash lock on the river, dismantled in 1961. The approach channel below Fladbury Lock is extremely narrow and steep sided, with restricted vision. The lock walls narrow towards the base and this should be borne in mind when two craft lock down together. The beautiful Fladbury Mill overlooks the weir – it was in use as recently as 1930, and ferry wires, **difficult to see from upstream**, stretch across the weir stream. On the north side, beyond the railway bridge carrying the main London to Hereford line, is Evesham golf course. Above Craycombe Turn are extensive woodlands, while to the south lie the inevitable water meadows, with few buildings or roads near the river. There is another handsome mill at Chadbury Lock, which was restored in 1952–3, the first major project carried out by the Lower Avon Navigation Trust, who were helped by the Royal Engineers.

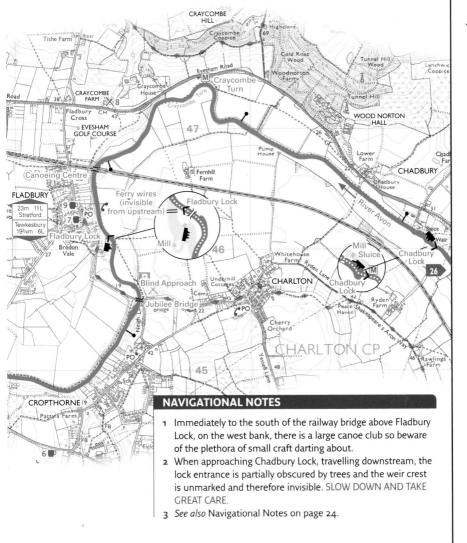

NAVIGATIONAL NOTES

1 Immediately to the south of the railway bridge above Fladbury Lock, on the west bank, there is a large canoe club so beware of the plethora of small craft darting about.

2 When approaching Chadbury Lock, travelling downstream, the lock entrance is partially obscured by trees and the weir crest is unmarked and therefore invisible. SLOW DOWN AND TAKE GREAT CARE.

3 *See also* Navigational Notes on page 24.

1 All the locks on the river are wide locks, and those on the Upper Avon once demonstrated considerable ingenuity in the recycling of gates and paddle gear from other canals and rivers – as a consequence some of the locks were difficult to operate, and required a good deal of physical strength. Since 1995 all locks have new gear and have been re-gated.

2 Those accustomed to the cosy informality and go as you please atmosphere of the narrow canals will find more restrictions on the river. There is no continuous towpath and, therefore, no right to land and moor as one pleases. Many villages are sited back from the river, away from the floods, and the scenery is generally that of quiet water meadows with prolific bird life.

3 The Avon Navigation Trust is a charity relying, in some instances, on volunteers. Boat crews can help them to keep down their costs by observing their rules and requests. They should also be acquainted with the relevant by-laws, and ensure that their craft is equipped with such items as an anchor made off to a chain and warp, a bow fender and so on.

4 Remember that sailing and canoe clubs operate on the river and on meeting a sailing boat maintain a fixed speed and a steady course on the right-hand side of the channel. Maximum speed (over the bed of the river) – 6 mph downstream and 4 mph upstream.

5 Watch out for anglers, and slow down.

6 Keep off private land and well away from weirs. Slow down when approaching locks or blind corners – especially through bridges.

7 Moor only at recognised sites, moor economically, and be prepared to breast up (moor side-by-side) where this does not obstruct traffic. Moorings – marked [M] on the maps – can be limited at the height of the season.

MOORING

See also Pubs and Restaurants. The recreation ground moorings above Pershore Lock are convenient for the town, and thus very popular. There is a *water point together with sewage disposal* (both free) *and pump out facilities* (fee) here. There are also limited *moorings* below the lock and at the *picnic area* downstream of the new bridge. There are overnight moorings in the weir stream at Wyre Lock and at Craycombe Turn.

● **Pershore**
Worcs. All services and swimming baths by the river.
A busy market town with many well-kept Georgian buildings, set among fruit farms and market gardens. The fine 6-arched 14th-C bridge over the Avon no longer carries traffic – a 3-arched structure built in 1928 now takes the load. The abbey, now the Parish Church of Holy Cross, was built on the site of a wooden building erected in AD689 by King Oswald. This was replaced in AD983 by a new building commissioned by Ethelwold, and again by a later Norman building, finally consecrated in 1239. In 1288 a fire destroyed part of the Abbey (and a large part of the town) resulting in much rebuilding before the dissolution in 1539. Restoration was by Scott 1862–5. Of the original Norman building, the nave, crossing and transepts survive. The Church of St Andrew, very close by, is now a community centre. Perrott House in Bridge Street was built in 1760 by George Perrott, when he purchased the Lower Avon Navigation.
Pershore Heritage Centre Town Hall, 34 High Street, Pershore WR10 1DS (01386 561342;

www.pershoreheritage.co.uk). Staffed and run entirely by volunteers whose aim is to preserve, promote and exhibit items of local public interest. Telephone for *opening times.*
Tourist Information Centre Town Hall, 34 High Street, Pershore WR10 1DS (01386 556591; www. visitpershoreco.uk). *Open Mon-Thu 09.00-17.00.*
● **Wyre Piddle**
Worcs. Tel. A straggling village, now bypassed by the main road, with no public mooring. The church has a Norman chancel arch and font, and an Early English bellcote. There is a shop at Lower Moor, east of The Anchor Inn.
● **Cropthorne**
Worcs. An attractive village of thatch and timbers on the Spring blossom route. Much local fruit and vegetable produce is sold from small roadside stalls in this area.
● **Charlton**
Worcs. Tel.
● **Fladbury**
Worcs. Tel. A picturesque village of half-timbered

houses and cottages around a square, once the home of William Sandys, who began making the Avon navigable in 1636. The Church of St John Baptist has a fine 14th-C rib-vaulted porch and contains some fine brasses to John Throckmorton and his wife. About 1 mile to the north east is Craycombe House, built c.1791 by George Byfield for George Perrott and later restored by the author Francis Brett Young, who lived here from 1932 until he went to South Africa after World War II.

Wood Norton Above the north bank below Chadbury Lock. Once the seat of the Duc d'Aumale and later the Duc d'Orleans, pretender to the throne of France, it now houses an engineering school run by the BBC, who have built some incongruous modern buildings to accompany the mansion.

PLANT LIFE
The River Avon is one of England's most famous chalk rivers and supports rare habitats and species, including populations of Atlantic salmon, brook and sea lamprey and water voles and otters. The presence of non-native invasive plants is a significant threat, as it is on other inland waterways. *Japanese knotweed* is fast growing, to over 10 feet in height, quick to colonise riverbanks, roadsides and other wayside places. Large, triangular leaves are borne on red, zigzag stems. Loose spikes of white flowers arise from leaf bases and appear August-October. Once established, populations are extremely persistent, can survive severe floods and are difficult and expensive to eradicate. If you spy what you think is Japanese knotweed, please inform the Environment Agency (www.environment-agency.gov.uk) or the appropriate waterway authority!

Pubs and Restaurants (pages 22-23)

1 The Miller's Arms 8 Bridge Street, Pershore WR10 1AT (01386 553864; www.millersarmspershore.co.uk). Bustling pub patronised by the town's younger clientele, dispensing real ale and serving food *Wed-Sat 12.00-14.00 & Sun 13.00-16.00*. Live music *Fri* and sports TV. *Open Mon-Fri L and E & Sat-Sun 12.00-00.00.*

2 The Angel Inn 9 High Street, Pershore WR10 1AF (01386 552046; www.angelpershore.co.uk). Real ale and food – made from local produce from their own farm – served *daily from 21.00 Mon-Thu; 21.30 Fri-Sat & 20.30 Sun.* Riverside garden, children welcome. Moorings and Wi-Fi. B&B. *Open 08.00 until late.*

3 The Pickled Plum 135 High Street, Pershore WR10 1EQ (01386 556645; www.pickledplum.co.uk). Justifiably popular pub serving a wide range of real ales and ciders. Appetising, home-cooked food from local sources is available *Mon-Fri L and E; Sat 12.00-21.00 & Sun 12.00-16.00.* Quiz *Sun* and *regular* live music. *Open 12.00-23.00 (Fri-Sat 00.00).*

4 The Star Inn 23 Bridge Street, Pershore WR10 1AJ (01386 561356; www.starinnatpershore.co.uk). Real ales in Pershore's oldest hostelry. Bar snacks and restaurant meals are available *daily from 12.00.* Well-behaved children and dogs welcome. Riverside garden. Mooring by arrangement. B&B. *Open Mon 10.00-20.00 & Tue-Sun 10.00-23.00.*

5 The Anchor Inn Main Road, Wyre Piddle, Pershore WR10 2JB (01386 244590; www.anchorinnpershore.co.uk). A good selection of real ales and ciders are dispensed in this Grade II listed, 17th-C pub. Food is available *daily 12.00-21.00 (Fri-Sat 22.00).* Dog- and family-friendly. Riverside garden and the only mooring for the village. Live music *Fri-Sun 19.00. Open 12.00-00.00 (Fri-Sat 01.00).*

6 The Bell Main Road, Cropthorne, Pershore WR10 3NE (01386 861860; www.thebellinncropthorne.co.uk). Food orientated pub serving real ale and meals *Mon-Fri L and E & all day at weekends.* Children welcome. Garden and Wi-Fi. *Closed Mon & Tue out of season* so telephone for opening hours before visiting.

7 The Chequers Inn Chequers Lane, Fladbury WR10 2PZ (01386 860276; www.chequersinnfladbury.com). Dating from 1372 and adjacent to the village green, this friendly village pub serves real ales and ciders, together with appetising food sourced locally. Garden, real fires and Wi-Fi. B&B. *Open Mon-Thu L and E (not Mon L) & Fri-Sun 12.00-00.00.*

8 Café Craycombe Evesham Road, Fladbury WR10 2QS (01386 860732). Just north of Fladbury and Evesham golf course. Home-made local food for *breakfast and L.* Snacks, delicious cakes and puddings. Wines and bottled beers. Parties catered for. *Open daily 10.00-16.00.*

Also try: **9 The Anchor** Anchor Lane, Fladbury WR10 2PY (01386 860391; www.anchorfladbury.co.uk).

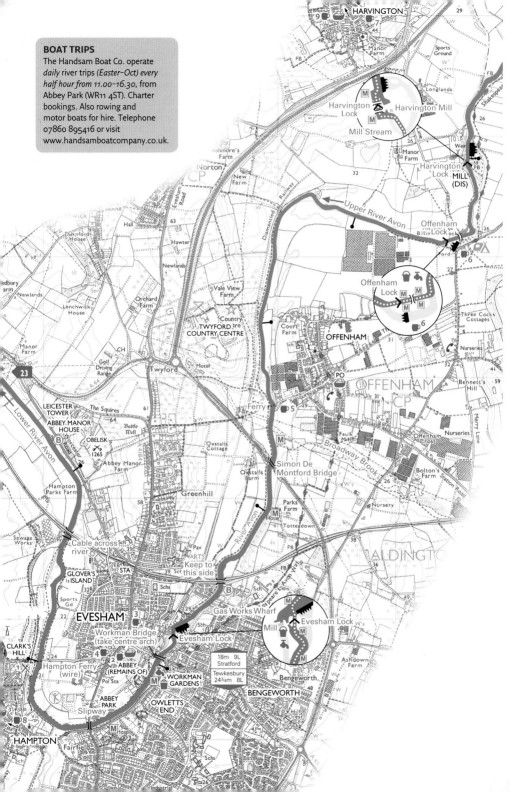

BOAT TRIPS
The Handsam Boat Co. operate *daily* river trips *(Easter–Oct)* every half hour from 11.00–16.30, from Abbey Park (WR11 4ST). Charter bookings. Also rowing and motor boats for hire. Telephone 07860 895416 or visit www.handsamboatcompany.co.uk.

Evesham

Beyond Chadbury Lock, the river passes the Abbey Manor House and a boatyard, before passing through Evesham in a wide loop. There is no longer a pump out facility upstream of the railway bridge. The Avon Navigation Trust has, however, installed new facilities at Strensham, Pershore and Evesham. Care should be taken approaching Hampton Ferry, where a wire stretches across the river – this will be lowered when the ferry man hears three long blasts of your horn. Gas is available here (01386 442458; www.hamptonferry.co.uk) sold *09.00-17.00 daily*. Above the ferry to the west is Clarke's Hill, where the monks of Evesham once grew vines. Beyond the A435 road bridge the Abbey Public Park opens out to the north, with riverside gardens giving way to the borough and Trust moorings and Workman Gardens to the east, below the handsome Workman Bridge, built in 1856. After passing through the centre arch of the bridge, you will see the lock to the left past the old mill stream. This marks the old boundary between the Lower and Upper Navigation. Evesham Lock (01386 446511) is now boater operated and there is a *water point* and *sewerage disposal facility* downstream of the lock. Craft should keep well away from the weir above the lock, passing close to the boatyard on the opposite bank. The river is then once again in open country, entering the Vale of Evesham, a major fruit and vegetable growing area. Offenham Lock was the first of the new Upper Avon locks, built in the winter of 1969. The unusual (and supposedly) flood-proof lock keeper's hut – the Offenham Light – is a more recent addition and has remained empty since inundation by the floods of 2007! The new lock cut joins the river at right angles, and care should be exercised when rejoining the main course. Harvington Lock soon follows, overlooked by Harvington Mill, disused since the turn of the century, together with the old lock, now used as a dry dock. The steep ridge of Cleeve Hill closes from the south to a virtual cliff at the water's edge below Cleeve Prior.

Boatyard

Ⓑ**Sankey Marine** Worcester Road, Evesham WR11 4TA (01386 442338; www.sankeymarine. co.uk). Below the Abbey Manor House. ⚓ Gas, overnight mooring, long-term mooring, winter storage, slipway, chandlery, boat sales, engine and boat repairs, crane, hull blasting and painting, toilets, showers, bar.

Ⓑ**Evesham Marina** Kings Road, Evesham WR11 3XZ (01386 768500; www.eveshammarina. co.uk). ⚓⚓ Pump out, gas, overnight mooring, long-term mooring, winter storage, slipway, crane (30 ton), boat sales, boat building, engine repairs, covered and heated wet dock, DIY facilities, chandlery.

THE LEAM LINK

For more than 30 years the Avon Navigation Trust (and its predecessors) has administered, financed, maintained and developed the river for the considerable benefit of the local community. It is, arguably, the most popular section of the Avon ring – made up of almost equal lengths of canal and river – and its charms and facilities are well documented in the *ANT Guide* (a copy of which can be obtained from the address on page 15).

To further enhance the value of the Upper Avon for its wide diversity of users, ANT has supported a proposal to construct a navigable link connecting the Grand Union Canal and the River Leam, between Leamington and Warwick. This scheme displays great sensitivity in its enhancement of a wide range of wildlife habitats, whilst at the same time providing increased leisure opportunities to walkers, fishermen, boaters and cyclists alike. The proposal makes imaginative use of natural features and materials to open up a waterway, not only as a potential link between existing river and canal systems but, just as importantly, as a series of environmentally-rich, managed and secure sites attracting wildlife to the River Leam.

The proposed structures – in the form of locks (four in total), islands, dams and bypass channels – are designed to create adjoining wetlands which will be complemented by a series of silt banks, reeds and sedges, hardwood copses and hedge planting. Thus birds, fish and mammals, either low in numbers or non-existent at present, will be attracted back to an area which the inevitable urban growth has gradually depleted.

In the initial phase of work, the plan is to connect the Grand Union Canal, east of Leamington Spa, with the River Leam via two locks. A further two locks along the river will be constructed to maintain navigable levels before the Leam meets the River Avon north of Warwick. This would, in turn, enable pleasure craft to access these two historic towns, providing attractive moorings. Longer term plans envisaged a scheme to improve the Upper Avon as a navigation between Warwick and Stratford-upon-Avon, thereby opening up a further wide range of leisure possibilities.

Abbey Manor House The Squires, Evesham WR11 4TB (01386 442437; www.westwingabbeymanor.blogspot.com). 1 mile above Chadbury Lock, on the north bank, c.1840. An obelisk in the grounds overlooks the site of the Battle of Evesham, 4 August 1265, when Simon de Montfort and his rebel barons were defeated by the Royalists under Prince Edward, resulting in some 4000 deaths. Another memorial, the Leicester Tower, built c.1840, is visible in the woodland. B&B is available in the West Wing.

● **Hampton**
Worcs. *PO, tel, stores, off-licence, fish & chips.* Overlooking the river and Evesham, the village was once a thriving market gardening centre. There is a useful *farm shop* (01386 41540) and the welcoming *store* and *newsagent* (01386 47777) is *open Mon-Sat 08.00-20.00 & Sun 09.00-13.00.*

● **Evesham**
Worcs. *All services including laundrette.* A town which owes the major part of its prosperity to the fruit and vegetable growing in the Vale of Evesham – in the spring a mass of blossom, and in the autumn rich in local produce. All that remains of the once-important Benedictine abbey, founded in AD714 by Bishop Egwin and dissolved by Henry VIII in 1539, is the fine timbered gatehouse, a detached bell tower (1533) and a few ruins. Close by there are elegant Georgian buildings and half-timbered houses, Booth Hall (late 15th-C) being a fine example. Close to the bell tower are two notable churches – St Lawrence (16th-C) and All Saints (12th-C). There is an annual regatta on *Spring Bank Holiday.*

Almonry Heritage Centre Abbey Gate, Evesham WR11 4BG (01386 446944; www.almonryevesham. org). 14th-C building, once the home of the Almoner at Evesham Abbey, it now houses artefacts, exhibitions and information detailing events from the rich history of the area. A superb example of Early English architecture with its warren of rooms. Attractive and peaceful garden. *Opening as per the Tourist Information Centre. Last admission 16.30.* Charge.

Arts Centre Victoria Avenue, Evesham WR11 4QH (01386 48883; www.eveshamartscentre.co.uk). 300-seat theatre presenting music, drama, dance, etc.

Evesham River Festival (theeveshamriverfestival.uk) *Held annually over the second weekend in Jul.* Further details from the website or the Tourist Information Centre.

Evesham Vale Light Railway The Valley Evesham, Twyford, Evesham WR11 4TP (01386 422282; www.evlr.co.uk). Narrow gauge steam railway running through the 130 acre Country Park. Restaurant and shop. *Open weekends 10.30-17.00 (16.00 in winter) & daily during school holidays and half terms.* Charge.

The Valley Evesham Twyford, Evesham WR11 4TP (01386 298026; www.thevalleyshopping. co.uk). Shopping, garden centre, the Evesham Vale Light Railway and the Ark Animal Sanctuary. Also restaurant and Visitor Centre. *Open Mon-Sat 09.00-17.30 & Sun 10.30-16.30.*

Tourist Information Centre The Almonry Heritage Centre, Abbey Gate, Evesham WR11 4BG (01386 446944; www.almonryevesham.org). *Open all year,*

Mon–Sat 10.00-1700; also Sun, Mar–Oct 14.00-17.00. Closed Wed Nov–Feb. Guided walks around the town start from here May–Sep, Tue 14.30. Free.
● **Offenham**
Worcs. PO, tel, stores, off-licence, home-bakery. Twelve centuries ago this was the headquarters of Offa, King of Mercia; today it is one of the few English villages (together with Welford) to possess a maypole. The village has grown considerably, and of the original Church of St Mary and St Milburga only the tower remains.

● **Middle Littleton**
Worcs. Walk east from the Fish at Offenham to see the tithe barn (WR11 5LN, 01905 371006, www.nationaltrust.org.uk, open Apr–Oct) thought to have been built by John de Ombersley, Abbot of Evesham from 1367 to 1377. Nearby is the 17th-C manor house and St Nicholas's Church.
● **Harvington**
Worcs. Tel, stores, off-licence. A typical half-timbered, black and white Worcestershire village.

WILDLIFE
In England, otter populations have been found in almost twice as many areas as they were 10 years ago. Persecution from fishing interests, hunting and habitat destruction from rapid industrialisation caused a serious decline and otter populations disappeared completely from much of England in the 1960s and 70s. The World Wide Fund for Nature and Worcestershire Wildlife Trust are working on a section of the River Avon to provide suitable habitats for otters moving through the district. Otters are superbly adapted to their amphibious lifestyle – dives may last for several minutes. They feed mainly on fish.

MOORING
See also Boatyards and Pubs and Restaurants. Upstream of Abbey Bridge the waterside moorings on the right bank, provided by the Trust, are free as are the extensive borough moorings by Workman Gardens. Weir Meadow Caravan Park (01386 442417), between Workman Bridge and the lock, has overnight moorings (by prior arrangement) with full facilities for craft up to 24ft long above Evesham Lock (fee). There are free overnight moorings at Offenham Lock and Harvington Lock.

Pubs and Restaurants (pages 26-27)

✗♑ 1 **Raphaels** Hampton Ferry, Boat Lane, Evesham WR11 4BP (01386 45460; www.hamptonferry.co.uk). Award-winning restaurant with full bar facilities. Sun carvery L and E. Children welcome, as are dogs in riverside garden. Moorings and slipway. Toilets, showers, laundry facilities and gas. Open daily 09.00-20.00 (Sat-Sun 08.00).
🍺 2 **The Red Lion** 6 Market Pace, Evesham WR11 4RW (01386 761688). Re-opened after 100 years, this no-nonsense, welcoming, town-centre hostelry serves an excellent selection of real ales and real ciders. Traditional pub games, dog- and family-friendly, Wi-Fi. No electronic machines or TVs. Open Mon-Sat 11.00-23.00 (Fri-Sat 00.00) & Sun 12.00-22.30.
🍺 3 **The Old Swanne Inn** 66 High Street, Evesham WR11 4HG (01386 442650; www.jdwetherspoon.com/pubs/all-pubs/england/worcestershire/the-old-swanne-inne-evesham). Imposing town-centre pub serving real ales, open daily 08.00-00.00 (Fri-Sat 01.00). Food available from breakfast until 22.00. Children welcome, large screen TV, outside seating and Wi-Fi.
🍺 4 **Ye Olde Red Horse** 17 Vine Street, Evesham WR11 4RE (01386 442784; yeolderedhorsebedandbreakfast.co.uk). This timber-framed, Black & White pub dispenses real ales and real ciders and serves food Mon-Thu L and E & Sat-Sun 12.00-15.00. Family- and dog-friendly, garden.

Traditional pub games, real fires, sports TV and Wi-Fi. B&B. Open Mon-Sat 10.00-23.00 (Fri-Sat 00.00) & Sun 12.00-23.00.
🍺 5 **The Bridge Inn** Boat Lane, Offenham WR11 8QZ (01386 446565). Real ale and real cider, together with bar snacks. Children and dogs welcome. Riverside seating and moorings. Open daily 11.00-23.00.
🍺 6 **The Fish and Anchor** Offenham WR11 8QT (01386 40374; www.thefishandanchor.co.uk). Friendly, welcoming pub serving real ale and good value food Mon-Fri L and E; Sat 12.00-20.00 & Sun 12.00-18.30. Large garden and moorings nearby. Camping. Open Mon-Sat 12.00-23.00 (Sat 00.00) & Sun 12.00-22.00.
🍺✗ 7 **The Coach and Horses** Station Road, Harvington WR11 8NJ (01789 772420; www.coachandhorsesharvington.co.uk). Traditional country pub and restaurant serving real ale and offering good value food Mon-Sat E & Sun 12.00-15.00. Dog- and child-friendly, garden. Traditional pub games, real fires, Wi-Fi and live music Tue. Open Mon-Fri L and E & Sat-Sun 12.00-00.00 (Sun 23.30).

Also try: 🍺 8 **The Cider Mill** Pershore Road, Evesham WR11 2NA (01386 442014) and 🍺✗ 9 **The Golden Cross** 97 Village Street, Harvington WR11 8PQ (01386 871900; goldencrossharvington.co.uk).

Bidford-on-Avon

The river now heads north away from Marlcliff Hill, entering Warwickshire and approaching Bidford-on-Avon with its splendid old bridge. The village makes an excellent stopping place for a good range of *shops and takeaways*, although mooring can be difficult at peak times of the year. Proceeding upstream, craft should follow the narrower right-hand channel below Bidford Grange – there were once two mills and a lock here, but now nothing remains. Beyond is the new Bidford Grange Lock, built in the winter of 1970. The navigation flows through attractive meadowland, and pleasant orchards announce the village of Welford-on-Avon and Welford Lock, completed in July 1971. The river meanders round the village, passing a fine Victorian house inappropriately adorned with a modern chimney, before the multi-arched Binton Bridges and the Four Alls pub are reached. Weston-on-Avon lies to the south on a very attractive stretch of deep water with many trees lining the banks.

Pubs and Restaurants

🍺 1 **The Kings Arms** Bidford Road, Cleeve Prior WR11 8LQ (01789 773335; www.thekingsarmsevesham.co.uk). Comfortable, well-patronised village local serving real ales and home-cooked food *daily L and E*. Dogs and children welcome. Garden, real fires and Wi-Fi. *Open Mon E, Tue-Sat 12.00-23.30 & Sun 12.00-19.00*.

✗🍷 2 **The Bridge Riverside Eaterie** 53 High Street, Bidford-on-Avon B50 4BG (01789 773700; www.thebridgeatbidford.com). Modern British restaurant serving food *L and E (not Sun E)*. Children welcome. Outside seating. Moorings. *Open Mon-Sat L and E & Sun 12.00-15.00*.

🍺✗ 3 **The Frog** 65 High Street, Bidford-on-Avon B50 4BG (01789 772369; www.thefrogbidford.com). Welcoming pub, selling real ale. Food is available *daily 12.00-15.00* in bar and restaurant – booking advisable. Riverside balcony, garden, newspapers, Wi-Fi and Mooring. Quiz *Thu. Open Mon E & Tue-Sun 12.00-00.00*.

🍺✗ 4 **Cottage of Content** 15 Welford Road, Barton B50 4NP (01789 772279; www.cottage-a-real-pub.co.uk). Picturesque 15th-C pub, with a riverside garden, dispensing real ales and bar and restaurant meals *L and E*, *daily*. Dogs welcome. Campsite, showers and toilets. *Open 12.00-00.00*.

🍺✗ 5 **The Four Alls** Binton Road, Welford-on-Avon CV37 8PW (01789 751470; www. thefourallswelfordonavon.co.uk). Riverside pub and restaurant, serving real ale. Food available *Mon-Thu 12.00-20.00 & Fri-Sun 11.00-20.00 (Sun 19.00)*, garden. Children's play area. Darts, pool table and dominoes. Overnight mooring by arrangement.

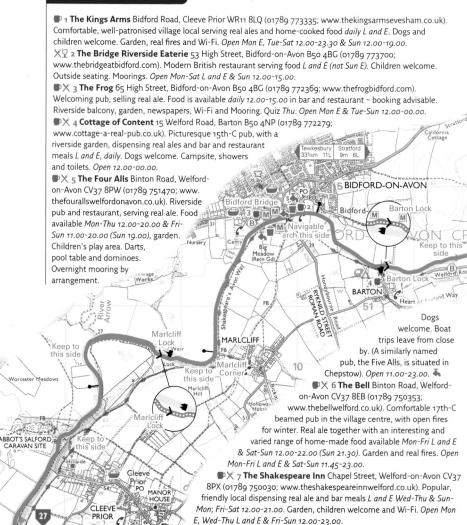

Dogs welcome. Boat trips leave from close by. (A similarly named pub, the Five Alls, is situated in Chepstow). *Open 11.00-23.00*.

🍺✗ 6 **The Bell** Binton Road, Welford-on-Avon CV37 8EB (01789 750353; www.thebellwelford.co.uk). Comfortable 17th-C beamed pub in the village centre, with open fires for winter. Real ale together with an interesting and varied range of home-made food available *Mon-Fri L and E & Sat-Sun 12.00-22.00 (Sun 21.30)*. Garden and real fires. *Open Mon-Fri L and E & Sat-Sun 11.45-23.00*.

🍺✗ 7 **The Shakespeare Inn** Chapel Street, Welford-on-Avon CV37 8PX (01789 750030; www.theshakespeareinnwelford.co.uk). Popular, friendly local dispensing real ale and bar meals *L and E Wed-Thu & Sun-Mon; Fri-Sat 12.00-21.00*. Garden, children welcome and Wi-Fi. *Open Mon E, Wed-Thu L and E & Fri-Sun 12.00-23.00*.

NAVIGATIONAL NOTES

1 The downstream approach to Marlcliff Lock can be shallow, particularly when turning into the lock cut.
2 The navigational channel under Bidford Bridge is through the southern-most arch.
3 On the sharp bend, west of Binton Bridges, the channel is in the centre of the river and not to the outside.

● **Cleeve Prior**
Worcs. PO box, tel, garage. The early origins of the village, as a Saxon and Medieval farming community, are clearly illustrated in the presence of numerous farm buildings from the 16th to 19th centuries. There is a useful farm shop close to the river (07795 447184).

● **Bidford-on-Avon**
Warwicks. PO, tel, stores, butcher, chemist, bank, off-licence, takeaways, hardware & DIY, baker, fish & chips, garage. The irregular-arched bridge was built in 1482 by the monks of Alcester, near the site of a Roman ford which was finally removed in 1970. The village has an excellent delicatessen and bakery, selling a tempting array of home-made pies, which is to be found not far from the bridge.

● **Barton**
Warwicks. Tel. A charming, sleepy little village strung out along a winding back road. At Barton moorings (07500 700718; www.bartonmoorings.com) there is *gas, a slipway, solid fuel, camping and short-term moorings* available.

● **Welford-on-Avon**
Warwicks. Tel, stores, off-licence, butcher, garage.

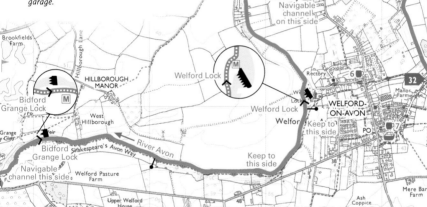

MOORING

See also Pubs and Restaurants. Overnight moorings are available, for a fee, at Abbots Salford Caravan Site (unfortunately on the opposite bank to Cleeve Prior), and at Marlcliff Lock (free). The free public moorings at Bidford are very good, but limited in number. There is a single mooring available at Bell Court on the town side, and more at Bidford Boats, both for a fee. The Frog pub also has public moorings. Upstream, at Barton, there are free overnight moorings in the lock cut. There are also free overnight moorings at Bidford Grange Lock, Welford Lock, Welford (no access to village), and below Binton Bridges (access to Welford) for a fee.

Boatyards

Ⓑ**Bidford Boat Services** Riverside House, 4 The Pleck, Bidford-on-Avon B50 4BB (01789 773205; 07796 520825; http://www.bidfordboats.co.uk). 🛉🔧D Pump out (and mobile pump outs) day boat hire (including narrowboats) long-term mooring, winter storage, slipway, boat sales and repairs, boat fit outs and upgrades, dry dock, welding, blacking, chandlery, engine repairs and servicing, DIY facilities. *Emergency call-out.*

31

Stratford-upon-Avon

Stan Glover Lock was built in spring 1971 – there are free overnight moorings here, but a sign informs 'sorry, no shop, no pub'. A little further upstream the River Stour joins the Avon from the south. The disused railway bridge here once carried the line from Stratford to Gloucester. Weir Brake Lock, which takes its name from the wooded bank to the south east of the river, was completed early in 1973; the weir was completed a few months later. Immediately beyond the new bypass bridge is the deep Colin P. Witter Lock, reinforced by a series of rectangular steel girder frames to overcome the high ground pressures and overlooked by a monument to celebrate the reopening of the navigation.

On sunny summer weekends the lockside is thick with gongoozlers (onlookers) enjoying the river,

MOORING

See also Boatyards. There are overnight moorings at Stan Glover Lock, Weir Brake Lock, below Colin P. Witter Lock, by the recreation ground opposite the theatre, in the Stratford Canal Basin and at the Old Bathing Place, 3/4 mile above Clopton Bridge.

	Tewkesbury	Stratford
	39¾m 15L	3m 2L

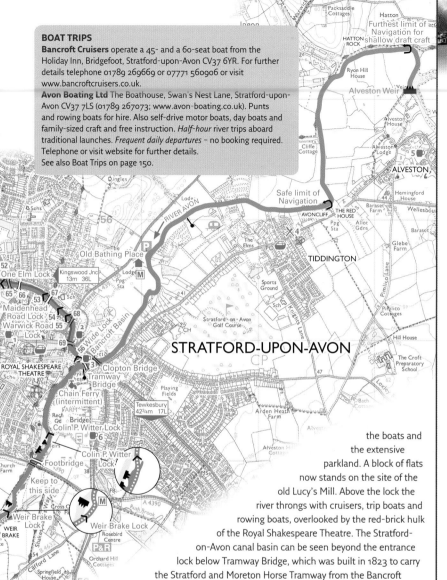

BOAT TRIPS

Bancroft Cruisers operate a 45- and a 60-seat boat from the Holiday Inn, Bridgefoot, Stratford-upon-Avon CV37 6YR. For further details telephone 01789 269669 or 07771 560906 or visit www.bancroftcruisers.co.uk.

Avon Boating Ltd The Boathouse, Swan's Nest Lane, Stratford-upon-Avon CV37 7LS (01789 267073; www.avon-boating.co.uk). Punts and rowing boats for hire. Also self-drive motor boats, day boats and family-sized craft and free instruction. *Half-hour river trips aboard traditional launches. Frequent daily departures* – no booking required. Telephone or visit website for further details.
See also Boat Trips on page 150.

the boats and the extensive parkland. A block of flats now stands on the site of the old Lucy's Mill. Above the lock the river throngs with cruisers, trip boats and rowing boats, overlooked by the red-brick hulk of the Royal Shakespeare Theatre. The Stratford-on-Avon canal basin can be seen beyond the entrance lock below Tramway Bridge, which was built in 1823 to carry the Stratford and Moreton Horse Tramway from the Bancroft basin to Shipston-on-Stour. It is now a footbridge. The 14-arched road bridge was built c.1480 by Sir Hugh Clopton, once Lord Mayor of London, and was widened in 1814. The surroundings become quieter as the river gently winds to its effective head of navigation by the Red House, although shallow-draught craft may proceed to just below Alveston Weir. Proposals have been put forward to extend navigation to Leamington Spa and in conjunction with the River Leam and four locks, link into the Grand Union Canal. However, a public enquiry rejected the idea, for the time being at least.

NAVIGATIONAL NOTES

When approaching Weir Brake Lock coming downstream, keep to the south east side of the river and look out for the lock cut on your left.

- **Luddington**
  Warwicks. It is thought that Shakespeare may have been married here, in a church now replaced by a more recent building.
- **Stratford-upon-Avon**
  Warwicks. All services. Tourism has been established for a very long time in Stratford. It was in 1789 that the first big celebrations in William Shakespeare's honour were organised by the actor David Garrick. They are now held annually on St George's Day (23 April), which is believed to have been Shakespeare's birthday. An annual Mop Fair on 12 October reminds the visitor that Stratford was already well-established as a market town long before Shakespeare's time. Indeed the first grant for a weekly market was given by King John in 1196. Today, Stratford is well used to the constant flow of charabancs and tourists, ancient charm vying with the expected commercialism that usually mars popular places like this. There are wide streets of endless low, timbered buildings that house dignified hotels and antique shops; plenty of these are also private houses. On the river, hired punts and rowing boats jostle each other while people picnic in the open parkland on the banks. The Royal Shakespeare Theatre, opened in 1932, is on an enviable site beside the Avon. Its massive industrial-style building, designed by Elizabeth Scott to replace an earlier theatre, destroyed by fire in 1926, is being re-developed by the theatre company. More in keeping with the historic Shakespearian tradition is the delightful Swan Theatre, risen phoenix-like from the ashes of the original building, thanks to the exceptional generosity of a single benefactor – for a long time anonymous. Attached to the main building, this theatre has a simple charm echoing the 16th-C Globe Playhouse.

Shakespeare Birthplace Trust Stratford-upon-Avon (01789 204016; www.shakespeare.org.uk). This Trust was founded in 1847 to look after the five buildings most closely associated with Shakespeare; four of these are in Stratford (listed below) and the other is Mary Arden's Cottage at Wilmcote (*see page 148*). Admission charge to each building. *The summer season is mid Mar–mid Oct. An all-inclusive ticket is available covering either the in-town properties, or all five Shakespeare Houses.*

Shakespeare's Birthplace Henley Street CV37 6QW (01789 204016/201822; www.shakespeare.org.uk). An early 16th-C half-timbered building containing books, manuscripts and exhibits associated with Shakespeare and rooms furnished in period style. Gardens. Next door is the Shakespeare Exhibition *open daily (except Xmas day) Apr-Oct 09.00-17.00 & Nov-Mar 10.00-16.00.* Charge.

Hall's Croft Old Town CV37 6BG (01789 292107; www.shakespeare.org.uk). A Tudor house and garden complete with period furniture – the home of Shakespeare's daughter Susanna and her husband Dr John Hall. *Open daily (except Xmas & Boxing days) Apr-Oct 10.00-17.00 & Nov-Mar 11.00-16.00.* Charge.

Nash's House and New Place Chapel Street CV37 6EP. (01789 292325; www.shakespeare.org.uk). The foundations of Shakespeare's last home set in a replica of an Elizabethan garden. *Open daily (except Xmas & Boxing days) Apr-Oct 10.00-17.00 & Nov-Mar 11.00-16.00.* Charge.

Anne Hathaway's Cottage Cottage Lane, Shottery CV37 9HH (01789 292100; www.shakespeare.org.uk). 1 mile west of Stratford. Dating from the 15th C this fine thatched farmhouse was once the home of Anne Hathaway before she married William Shakespeare in 1582. Her family, yeoman farmers, remained in occupation until 1892, when the cottage was purchased by the Shakespeare Birthplace Trust. The rooms retain their original features. The cottage was badly damaged by fire in 1969, but has since been completely restored. It has a mature, typically English garden, and long queues of visitors in the summer. *Open daily (except Xmas & Boxing days) Apr-Oct 09.00-17.00 & Nov-Mar 10.00-16.00.* Charge.

Royal Shakespeare Theatre (Tickets 0844 800 1110; www.rsc.org.uk). The home of the Royal Shakespeare Company, which produces Shakespeare plays to a very high standard *Apr–Dec every year.* The first theatre in Stratford was a temporary octagon built for Garrick's festival in 1769. A permanent theatre was not erected until 1827, with a library and art gallery being added in 1881.

Stratford-upon-Avon Butterfly Farm Swan's Nest Lane CV37 7LS (01789 299288; www.butterflyfarm.co.uk). Just south of the Tramway Bridge. Rainforest growth, fish pools and waterfalls, hundreds of butterflies and fascinating insects. For the not-so-squeamish there is Arachnoland, where you can view deadly insects (in perfect safety). Adventure playground, gift shop and refreshments. *Open 10.00-18.00 (17.00 in winter).* Charge.

Stratford Waterways Information Centre aboard *William James,* Bancroft Basin, Stratford-upon-Avon CV37 6YS (07584 086321; www.avonnavigationtrust.org/index.php?id=141). A wide range of boater and tourist information is available from the Avon Navigation Trust's boat moored in Bancroft Basin. Also licenses for the River Avon and the canal system, gifts, souvenirs and a meeting room for hire. *Open daily Apr-Oct 08.00-17.00.*

Holy Trinity Church Old Town CV37 6BG (01789 266316; www.stratford-upon-avon.org). Attractively situated among trees overlooking Colin P. Witter lock on the River Avon. Mainly of the 15th C but the spire was rebuilt in 1763. William Shakespeare is buried in the chancel. His tomb bears a curse against anyone who dares to disturb it.

Tourist Information Centre Bridgefoot CV37 6GW (01789 264293; www.discover-stratford.com). A mine of information, and lots of guide books and souvenirs for sale. *Open Mon-Sat 09.00-17.30 & Sun 10.00-16.00.*

- **Tiddington**
  Warwicks. PO, stores, takeaway, off-licence, greengrocer.

Boatyards

There are trip boats and many rowing and motor boats for hire in Stratford-upon-Avon. *See page 33.*

ⓑ**Stratford Marina** Clopton Bridge, Stratford-upon-Avon CV37 6YY (01789 269977). 🚿 Pump out, slipway, long-term mooring, short-term mooring.

ⓑ**The Chandlery** Stratford Marina, Clopton Bridge, Stratford-upon Avon CV37 6YY (01789 269977; www.avonboatingservices.co.uk/the-chandlery). 🏠🚿 Pump out, electric hook-up, outboard centre and engineering, well-stocked chandlery, boat building, boat services and boat safety examinations.

ⓑ**Excellence Afloat at Valley Cruises** Valley Wharf Western Road, Stratford-upon-Avon CV37 0AH (02476 393333; www.valleycruises. co.uk). WSDE Pump out, gas, solid fuel, boat hire, wet dock, boat and engine repairs, overnight and long-term moorings, chandlery (consumables), boat fitting out, books, maps and gifts, Barrus agent.

Festival time on the River Avon near the Royal Shakespeare Theatre, Stratford-upon-Avon

Pubs and Restaurants (pages 32–33)

There are numerous restaurants, snack bars, fast-food outlets and pubs in Stratford-upon-Avon.

🍺 1 **The Stratford Alehouse** 12B Greenhill Street, Stratford-upon-Avon CV37 6LF (07746 807966; thestratfordalehouse.com). Totally devoid of gaming machines and loud music, this small, family-run pub serves superb real ales, ciders and wines. Dog-friendly and newspapers. Folk club *1st & 3rd Wed of month* with live music *every Wed and most Sun*. *Open Mon-Sat 13.00-23.00 & Sun 14.00-20.00.*

🍺✕ 2 **The Pen & Parchment Hotel** Bridgefoot CV37 6YY (01789 297697; www.oldenglishinns. co.uk/our-locations/the-pen-and-parchment-stratford-upon-avon). This is a pleasant beamy pub in a listed building. Good selection of real ale. Wide range of bar and restaurant meals available *daily, L and E*. There are outside seats surrounded by tubs of flowers, where you can watch the tourist sightseeing buses depart. Children welcome. Wi-Fi. B&B. *Open 11.00-23.00.*

🍺 3 **Cox's Yard** Bridgefoot CV37 6YY (01789 404600; www.coxsyard.com). Pub, restaurant, theatre and teashop, this 'total leisure experience' offers food *all day, every day*, together with a selection of real ales. Children welcome, outside seating area. *Regular* live music events. *Open Mon-Sat 12.00-23.00 (Fri-Sat 00.00) & Sun 12.00-22.30).*

✕🍷 4 **Connolly's Tapas Bar** 25 Main Street, Tiddington CV37 7AN (01789 204712; www. connollystapasbar.co.uk). Family owned restaurant, fully licensed bar and deli serving fresh and locally sourced food in a relaxed and friendly atmosphere. Hearty breakfasts, takeaway coffee, sandwiches, tapas-style dishes and main courses; full complement of deli foods. *Open Wed-Sat 10.00-23.00 & Tue 10.00-15.00.*

🍺✕ 5 **The Ferry Inn** Ferry Lane, Alveston CV37 7QX (01789 269883; www.theferryalveston.co.uk). Comfortable dining pub serving real ale and home-cooked meals using locally sourced produce. Meals available *Tue-Sun, L and E (not Sun E)*. *Open Tue-Fri L and E, Sat 12.00-23.00 & Sun 12.00-17.00.*

Also try: 🍺 6 **Old Tramway Inn** 91 Shipston Road, Stratford-upon-Avon CV37 7LW (01789 297593; www.theoldtramwayinn.co.uk)

WALKING AND CYCLING

The Stratford Greenway is a linear country park, almost five miles long, following the old Honeybourne Railway Line and providing a traffic-free walking and cycling route, together with two picnic sites. It starts immediately to the south of Colin P. Witter Lock, finishing in Long Marston and interlinks with other riverside footpaths which can be used to form a number of circular walks. *See also* Walking & Cycling on page 153 and visit Country Parks Information Service at www.warwickshire.gov.uk.

BIRMINGHAM CANAL NAVIGATIONS (BCN) – MAIN LINE

MAXIMUM DIMENSIONS
Length: 70'
Beam: 7' 0"
Headroom: 6' 6"

MANAGER
0303 040 4040
enquiries.westmidlands@canalrivertrust.org.uk

MILEAGES

Birmingham Canal new main line
BIRMINGHAM Gas Street to:
SMETHWICK JUNCTION (old main line): 2⁷/8 miles
BROMFORD JUNCTION: 4⁷/8 miles
PUDDING GREEN JUNCTION
(Wednesbury Old Canal): 5⁵/8 miles
TIPTON FACTORY JUNCTION
(old main line): 8³/4 miles
DEEPFIELDS JUNCTION
(Wednesbury Oak loop): 10 miles
(Bradley Workshops: 2¹/4 miles)
HORSELEY FIELDS JUNCTION
(Wyrley & Essington Canal): 13 miles
Wolverhampton Top Lock: 13¹/2 miles
ALDERSLEY JUNCTION
(Staffordshire & Worcestershire Canal): 15¹/8 miles
Locks: 24

Birmingham Canal old main line
SMETHWICK JUNCTION to:
SPON LANE JUNCTION: 1¹/2 miles
OLDBURY JUNCTION
(Titford Canal, 6 locks): 2¹/2 miles
BRADESHALL JUNCTION
(Gower Branch, 3 locks): 3¹/2 miles
Aqueduct over Netherton Tunnel Branch: 4³/8 miles
TIPTON JUNCTION (Dudley Canal): 5¹/2 miles
FACTORY JUNCTION (new main line): 6 miles
Locks: 9

Netherton Tunnel Branch
WINDMILL END JUNCTION to:
DUDLEY PORT JUNCTION: 2⁷/8 miles
No Locks

Wednesbury Old Canal
PUDDING GREEN JUNCTION to:
RYDER'S GREEN JUNCTION: 5/8 mile
No locks

Walsall Canal
RYDER'S GREEN JUNCTION to:
Ryder's Green Bottom Lock: ¹/4 mile
DOEBANK JUNCTION: 1³/8 miles
WALSALL JUNCTION: 6⁷/8 miles
Locks: 8

Walsall Branch Canal
WALSALL JUNCTION to:
BIRCHILLS JUNCTION (Wyrley &
Essington Canal): 7/8 mile
Locks: 8

Wyrley & Essington Canal
HORSELEY FIELDS JUNCTION to:
SNEYD JUNCTION: 6¹/4 miles
BIRCHILLS JUNCTION (Walsall Branch Canal): 8 miles
PELSALL JUNCTION (Cannock Extension): 12⁷/8 miles
Norton Canes Docks: 11¹/2 miles
CATSHILL JUNCTION: 15³/8 miles
OGLEY JUNCTION (Anglesey Branch): 16³/8 miles
Anglesey Basin and Chasewater: 1¹/2 miles
No locks

Daw End Branch
CATSHILL JUNCTION to:
LONGWOOD JUNCTION (Rushall Top Lock): 5¹/4 miles
No locks

Rushall Canal
LONGWOOD JUNCTION to:
RUSHALL JUNCTION: 2³/4 miles
Locks: 9

Tame Valley Canal
DOEBANK JUNCTION to:
RUSHALL JUNCTION: 3¹/2 miles
Perry Barr Top Lock: 5¹/2 miles
SALFORD JUNCTION: 8¹/2 miles
Locks: 13

The Birmingham Canal Company was authorised in 1768 to build a canal from Aldersley on the Staffordshire & Worcestershire Canal to Birmingham. With James Brindley as engineer the work proceeded quickly. The first section, from Birmingham to the Wednesbury collieries, was opened in November 1769, and the whole 22½-mile route was completed in 1772. It was a winding, contour canal, with 12 locks taking it over Smethwick, and another 20 (later 21) taking it down through Wolverhampton to Aldersley Junction. As the route of the canal was through an area of mineral wealth and developing industry, its success was immediate. Pressure of traffic caused the summit level at Smethwick to be lowered in the 1790s (thus cutting out six locks – three on either side of the summit), and during the same period branches began to reach out towards Walsall via the Ryder's Green Locks, and towards Fazeley. Out of this very profitable and ambitious first main line there grew the Birmingham Canal Navigations, more commonly abbreviated to BCN.

As traffic continued to increase so did the wealth of the BCN. The pressures of trade made the main line at Smethwick very congested and brought grave problems of water supply. Steam pumping engines were installed in several places to recirculate the water, and the company appointed Thomas Telford to shorten Brindley's old main line. Between 1825 and 1838 he engineered a new main line between Deepfields and Birmingham, using massive cuttings and embankments to maintain a continuous level. These improvements not only increased the amount of available waterway (the old line remaining in use), but also shortened the route from Birmingham to Wolverhampton by 7 miles.

Railway control of the BCN meant an expansion of the use of the system, and a large number of interchange basins were built to promote outside trade by means of rail traffic. This was of course quite contrary to the usual effect of railway competition upon canals. Trade continued to grow in relation to industrial development and by the end of the 19th C it was topping 8½ million tons per annum. A large proportion of this trade was local, being dependent upon the needs and output of Black Country industry. After the turn of the century this reliance on local trade started the gradual decline of the system as deposits of raw materials became exhausted. Factories bought from further afield and developed along the railways and roads away from the canals. Yet as late as 1950 there were over a million tons of trade and the system continued in operation until the end of the coal trade in 1967 (although there was some further traffic for the Birmingham Salvage Department), a pattern quite different from canals as a whole. Nowadays there is no recognisable commercial traffic – a dramatic contrast to the roaring traffic on the newer Birmingham motorways.

As trade declined, so parts of the system fell out of use and were abandoned. In its heyday in 1865, the BCN comprised over 160 miles of canal. Today just over 100 miles remain, and much has been done in recent years to tidy these up. This is now having a noticeable effect. Where once there were the old and run-down relics of industry, there is now much new housing, and stylish industrial estates. Of course some of the older vestiges of industry can still be found, and we hope that their most charming manifestations are kept for future generations to see and enjoy. But overall (and noting the exceptions and inevitable run-down areas) it is a fascinating environment. Just do not treat it like the remoter parts of Cheshire and Shropshire – it will always be subjected to the stresses of inner-city life, and you must always exercise caution. But it remains an area of retreat for the harassed city dweller and a new area of exploration for the canal traveller.

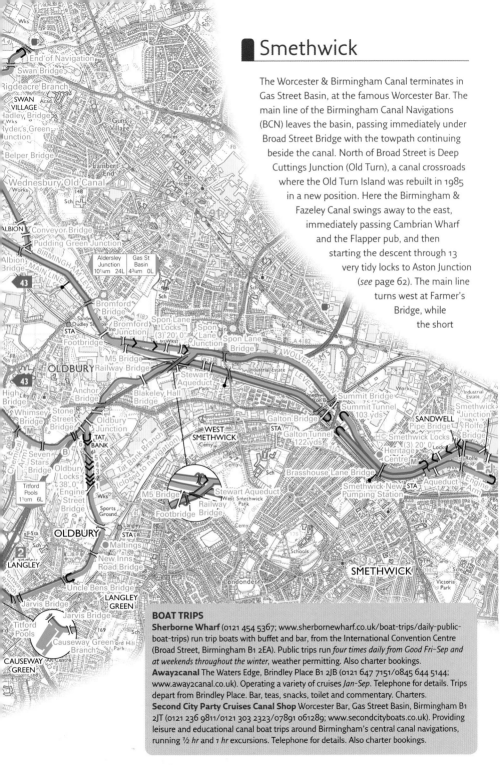

Smethwick

The Worcester & Birmingham Canal terminates in Gas Street Basin, at the famous Worcester Bar. The main line of the Birmingham Canal Navigations (BCN) leaves the basin, passing immediately under Broad Street Bridge with the towpath continuing beside the canal. North of Broad Street is Deep Cuttings Junction (Old Turn), a canal crossroads where the Old Turn Island was rebuilt in 1985 in a new position. Here the Birmingham & Fazeley Canal swings away to the east, immediately passing Cambrian Wharf and the Flapper pub, and then starting the descent through 13 very tidy locks to Aston Junction (*see* page 62). The main line turns west at Farmer's Bridge, while the short

	Aldersley Junction	Gas St Basin
	10¼m 24L	4¾m 0L

BOAT TRIPS

Sherborne Wharf (0121 454 5367; www.sherbornewharf.co.uk/boat-trips/daily-public-boat-trips) run trip boats with buffet and bar, from the International Convention Centre (Broad Street, Birmingham B1 2EA). Public trips run *four times daily from Good Fri–Sep and at weekends throughout the winter, weather permitting.* Also charter bookings.
Away2canal The Waters Edge, Brindley Place B1 2JB (0121 647 7151/0845 644 5144; www.away2canal.co.uk). Operating a variety of cruises *Jan–Sep.* Telephone for details. Trips depart from Brindley Place. Bar, teas, snacks, toilet and commentary. Charters.
Second City Party Cruises Canal Shop Worcester Bar, Gas Street Basin, Birmingham B1 2JT (0121 236 9811/0121 303 2323/07891 061289; www.secondcityboats.co.uk). Providing leisure and educational canal boat trips around Birmingham's central canal navigations, running ½ hr and 1 hr excursions. Telephone for details. Also charter bookings.

Oozell's Street loop goes to the south, quickly disappearing behind new apartments. This loop, which now houses a boatyard and moorings, and the others further along, are surviving parts of Brindley's original contour canal, now known as the Birmingham Canal Old Main Line. The delays caused by this prompted the Birmingham Canal Company to commission Telford to build a straighter line, the Birmingham Canal New Main Line. This was constructed between 1823 and 1838, and when completed reduced Brindley's old 22½-mile canal to 15 miles. The Oozell's Street loop reappears from the south, and then, after two bridges, the Icknield Port loop leaves to the south. This loop acts as a feeder from Rotton Park Reservoir and rejoins after ¼ mile at another canal crossroads – the Winson Green or Soho loop, which leaves the main line opposite the Icknield Port loop. This last loop is the longest of the three, running in a gentle arc for over a mile before rejoining the main line again. It was the only loop to have a towpath throughout its length until the recently completed towpath on the Oozell's Street loop. At its eastern end is Hockley Port, formerly railway-owned but now used for residential moorings. There are houseboats, a community hall, dry docks and workshops. The main line continues towards Smethwick Junction. Here there is a choice of routes: Brindley's old main line swings to the right, while Telford's new main line continues straight ahead – the old line is the more interesting of the two. The two routes run side by side, but the old line climbs to a higher level via the three Smethwick Locks. Here there were two flights of locks side by side. Beyond the junction, Telford's new line enters a steep-sided cutting. This 40ft-deep cutting enabled Telford to avoid the changes in level of the old line and thus speed the flow of traffic. The two routes continue their parallel courses, the one overlooking the other, until the lower line passes under the Telford Aqueduct. This elegant single span cast iron structure carries the Engine Arm, a short feeder canal that leaves the old line, crosses the new line and then turns back to the south for a short distance. There is a *laundry* in the *facilities block* here. This arm is named after the first Boulton & Watt steam pumping engine to be bought by the Birmingham Canal Company. This continued to feed the old summit level for 120 years. It was then moved to Ocker Hill for preservation and demonstrations, until the 1950s, when it was finally retired. The sides of the cutting are richly covered with wild flowers

and blackberry bushes, and the seclusion of the whole area has turned it into an unofficial nature reserve. The old pumping station at Brasshouse Lane has been restored after years of disuse as part of the new Galton Valley Canal Park development. A Tangyes Engine has been installed to replace the original. The New Main Line continues through natural wilderness to Galton Tunnel. Telford's Galton Bridge crosses the cutting in one magnificent 150ft cast iron span. This bridge is preserved as an ancient monument. The old and the new Birmingham canal lines continue their parallel course, and soon the pleasant semi-rural isolation of the cutting ends, to be replaced by a complex meeting of three types of transport system. The M5 motorway swings in from the east, carried high above the canal on slender concrete pillars; the railway stays close beside Telford's new line; and the canals enter a series of junctions that seem to anticipate modern motorway practice. The new line leaves the cutting and continues in a straight line through industrial surroundings. It passes under Stewart Aqueduct and then reaches Bromford Junction. Here a canal sliproad links the old and the new lines via the three Spon Lane Locks, joining the new at an angle from the east. Note the unusual split bridge at Spon Lane top lock, which was rebuilt in 1986. The old line swings south west following the 473ft contour parallel to the M5, crossing the new line on Stewart Aqueduct. Thus canal crosses canal on a flyover. Spon Lane Locks, the linking sliproad, survive unchanged from Brindley's day and are among the oldest in the country. The old and the new lines now follow separate courses. The old line continues below the motorway to Oldbury Locks Junction. Here the short Titford Canal climbs away to the south via the six Oldbury Locks; this canal serves as a feeder from Titford Pools to Rotton Park Reservoir. After the junction the old line swings round to the north west and continues on a parallel course to the new line once again. After Bromford Junction the new line continues its straight course towards Wolverhampton. At Pudding Green Junction the main line goes straight on; the Wednesbury Old Canal forks right to join the Walsall Canal, which in turn joins the Tame Valley Canal at Doebank Junction.

WALKING AND CYCLING

Much of Birmingham's 100-mile network of canals offers excellent opportunities for walkers and cyclists, and provides the chance to explore a side of the city well away from the obvious tourist attractions and close to the area's industrial roots. From a more formal approach, Birmingham is a crossroads for the National Cycle Network with Route 5 approaching from Kings Norton via Worcester & Birmingham Canal. Route 81 follows the Birmingham Level Main Line from the city to Wolverhampton, to eventually head into Mid Wales. Several excellent routes lead out from the city centre along traffic-free or contraflow cycle lanes. Further details are available from www.sustrans.org.uk/ncn/map/themed-routes-o/urban-adventures/top-cycle-routes-and-around-birmingham and by visiting http://bhamcyclerevolution.org.uk. On the Mainline the south side tow path is no longer usable between Rolfe Bridge and Bromford Junction.

NAVIGATIONAL NOTES

Since the Titford Canal is the highest level on the BCN, it is advisable to telephone the Canal & River Trust Waterway Office (0303 040 4040; enquiries.westmidlands@canalrivertrust.org.uk) to check that there is adequate water before you visit the canal. You will need a standard T-shaped water conservation key (aka 'handcuff key') for Oldbury Locks in order to access this canal.

Boatyards

Ⓑ**Sherborne Wharf** Sherborne Street, Birmingham B16 8DE (0121 455 6163/0121 454 5367; www.sherbornewharf.co.uk). On the Oozell's Street Loop. 🛥🛥⚓D E Pump out, gas, day-hire boats, overnight mooring, long-term mooring, wet docks, dry dock, winter storage, chandlery, boat repairs, engine repairs, welding, fabrication, crane, books, maps and gifts, DIY facilities, electrical hook-up, solid fuel, toilets, showers, laundrette, Wi-Fi, large supermarket nearby. *Emergency call out. Open 7 days.*

● **The Titford Canal**

Built in 1837 as part of the original Birmingham Canal scheme, acting as a feeder to Spon Lane, the Titford Canal served Causeway Green. This must have been a very busy canal in its heyday, with many branches, wharves and tramways connecting it to the surrounding mines and engineering works. Today it survives in shortened form and has the distinction of being the highest navigable part of the BCN, with a summit level above Oldbury Locks of 511ft. The locks are sometimes referred to as the Crow – a branch which left the canal above the third lock and served the alkali and phosphorus works of a local industrialist and benefactor Jim Crow. The last surviving recirculatory pumphouse can be seen by the top lock. The building has been completely restored and is now the home of the Birmingham Canal Navigation Society (01902 788441; www.bcnsociety.com). The waterway terminates at the wide expanse of water of Titford Pools.

Tourist Information Centre *see* page 66.

Pubs and Restaurants (pages 38–39)

In a large city such as Birmingham there are many fine pubs and restaurants. As a result of the development of the area adjoining the canal, between Gas Street Basin and Cambrian Wharf, there are now approaching two dozen eating and drinking establishments. This choice is further expanded by walking south along Broad Street, from Broad Street Bridge, at Gas Street Basin. However beyond the canalside the enterprising boater (walker and cyclist) might like to seek out some of the City's more diverse hostelries:

📖 **1 The Flapper** Cambrian Wharf, Kingston Row, Birmingham B1 2NU (0121 236 2421; www.theflapper.co.uk). Student-type pub majoring on bottled beers, cocktails and music. Canalside terrace seating. *Open Mon–Thu & Sun 16.00–23.00 and Fri–Sat 12.00–01.00.*

📖 **2 The Brasshouse** 44 Broad St, Birmingham B1 2HP (0121 633 3383; www.brasshousebirmingham.co.uk). Busy, modern pub serving *all day* breakfasts and good value bar meals, together with real ales. *Fri and Sat* night discos. Children allowed *until 18.00* if eating. Wi-Fi. *Open daily from 08.00 'til late.*

📖 **3 The Prince of Wales** 84 Cambridge St, Birmingham B1 2NP (0121 643 9460). Popular hostelry situated behind the NIA and ICC serving real ales and inexpensive food *Tue–Sat 12.00-20.00.* Dogs welcome and live music *Sun 16.00-19.00. Open daily from 11.00 (Sun 12.00) 'til late.*

📖 **4 The Old Contemptibles** 176 Edmund St, Birmingham B3 2HB (0121 200 3310; www.nicholsonspubs.co.uk/theoldcontemptiblesedmundstreetbirmingham). Close to Snow Hill Station. This comfortable, wood-panelled pub serves a good selection of real ales (nation-wide micro-breweries being well represented) and excellent food *Mon–Fri 11.00-22.00, Sat 12.00-22.00 & Sun 12.00-18.00.* Pump clips carry tasting notes and you can sip before you buy. Also real cider. *Open Mon–Sat 11.00 'til late (Sat 12.00) & Sun 12.00-18.00.*

📖 **5 The Figure of Eight** 236-239 Broad St, Birmingham B1 2HG (0121 633 0917; www.jdwetherspoon.co.uk/home/pubs/the-figure-of-eight). Sensibly priced real ale in a pub handy for Gas Street Basin. Disabled access and outside seating. Wi-Fi. *Open all day from 07.00* serving breakfast and food *all day.*

📖 **6 The Wellington** 37 Bennett's Hill, Birmingham B2 5SN (0121 200 3115; www.thewellingtonrealale.co.uk). Busy, CAMRA award-winning pub, with up to 17 hand pumps and a choice of real ciders. No food but customers are welcome to consume their own on the crockery provided. Also foreign bottled beers. Traditional pub games, garden, newspapers, sports TV and Wi-Fi. *Open 10.00-00.00.*

📖 **7 The Post Office Vaults** 84 New St, Birmingham B2 4BA (0121 643 7354; www.postofficevaults.co.uk). Close to New Street Station. Wide range of real ales, ciders and perries available *daily 11.00-23.00 (Fri-Sat 00.00).* Also well over 300 foreign bottled beers to choose from. Free bar billiards, dog-friendly, newspapers and Wi-Fi.

📖 **8 The Old Joint Stock** 4 Temple Row, Birmingham B2 5NY (0121 200 1892; www.oldjointstock.co.uk). Real ales and tasty food is served *Mon–Sat 08.00-11.00 and 12.00-22.00 & Sun 10.00-16.00* in an elaborately decorated, Grade II listed, Victorian building. Once a joint stock bank, there is now a theatre upstairs. Outside seating, children welcome, traditional pub games, newspapers and Wi-Fi. Live jazz *Sun. Open Mon–Sat 08.00-23.00 & Sun 09.00-18.00.*

📖 **9 The Old Royal**, 53 Church St, Birmingham B3 2DP (0121 200 3841; www.theoldroyalbirmingham.co.uk). Serving real ales and traditional pub food (including breakfast) *all day* from behind an elegant city centre façade. Sports TV and Wi-Fi. *Open daily 10.00-23.00 (Sat–Sun 12.00).*

📖 **10 The Shakespeare** 21 Lower Temple St, Birmingham B2 4JD (0121 616 2196; www.nicholsonspubs.co.uk/theshakespearelowertemplestreetbirmingham). Beside New Street Station. Attractively refurbished Victorian pub serving real ales and cider, together with quality pub food *daily from 10.00-22.00. Open Mon–Sat 10.00-23.00 (Fri-Sat 00.00) & Sun 10.00-22.30.*

See also page 195.

Dudley

At Bradeshall Junction the Gower Branch links the two lines, descending to the lower level of the new line through three locks. To the south west of Tipton Junction is the branch leading to the Black Country Museum and the Dudley Tunnel. This branch connects with the Dudley Canal, the Stourbridge Canal, and thus with the Staffordshire & Worcestershire Canal. The old line turns north at the junction, rejoining the new line at Factory Junction. At Albion Junction the Gower Branch turns south to join the old line at Bradeshall. At Dudley Port Junction the Netherton Tunnel Branch joins the main line. The Netherton Tunnel Branch goes through the tunnel to Windmill End Junction (note the west side towpath through the tunnel is closed); from here boats can either turn south down the old Dudley Canal to Hawne Basin, or west towards the Stourbridge Canal, and thus to the Staffordshire & Worcestershire Canal. North of Dudley Port the new line crosses a main road on the Ryland Aqueduct. Continuing its elevated course the new line reaches Tipton, where there are *moorings* with *shops* close by, and a small basin. The new line climbs the three Factory Locks and immediately reaches Factory Junction, where the old line comes in from the south.

Pubs and Restaurants

📮 1 **The Old Court House** 57 Lower Church Lane, Tipton DY4 7PE (0121 520 2865). North east of Dudley Port Station. Food available *L and E, daily* in a pub that used to be the holding cells for the police station across the road. Children and dogs welcome. Outside seating, traditional pub games, newspapers, sports TV and Wi-Fi. *Open Mon-Thu E & Fri-Sun 12.00-01.30 (Sun 23.30).*

📮✕ 2 **The Bottle & Glass Inn** Black Country Living Museum, Tipton Road, Dudley DY1 4SQ (0121 557 9643; www.bclm.co.uk/locations/bottle-and-glass-inn/28.htm#.WZBUXK2ZMUE). Real ale in a wonderful old pub, moved to the site. Snacks available *all day. Open daily 10.00-17.00.* More substantial refreshment available in the nearby 📮✕ **Gongoozler Restaurant** (0121 520 3200) and 1930s fish & chip shop.

📮✕ 3 **Mad O'Rourke's Pie Factory** 50 Hurst Lane, Tipton DY4 9AB (0121 557 1402; www.madorourkes.com). Quirky, popular eatery renowned for its world-famous Desperate Dan cow pies,, serving real ales,

real cider and food *daily 12.00-21.30 (Sun 21.00).* Sun *L* carvery. Garden, family-friendly, real fires and Wi-Fi. Live music *Fri & Sat.* B&B. *Open Mon-Sat 11.00-23.00 & Sun 12.00-22.30.*

📮 4 **The Tamebridge** 45 Tame Road, Tipton DY4 7JA (0121 557 2496). Friendly, welcoming family pub serving a changing range of real ales. Garden, dog- and family-friendly. *Monthly* live music. Real fires, sports TV and Wi-Fi. *Open 12.00-23.00.*

📮 5 **The New Inn** 35 Ward Street, Coseley WV14 9LQ (01902 670669). Friendly pub dispensing real ale and bar snacks. Family-friendy. Traditional pub games, real fires and Wi-Fi. *Open Mon-Fri E (Fri 15.00) & Sat-Sun 12.00-00.00 (Sun 22.30).*

Also try: 📮 6 **The Barge & Barrel** Factory Road, Tipton DY4 9AJ (0121 520 6962; thebargeandbarreltipton.weebly.com).

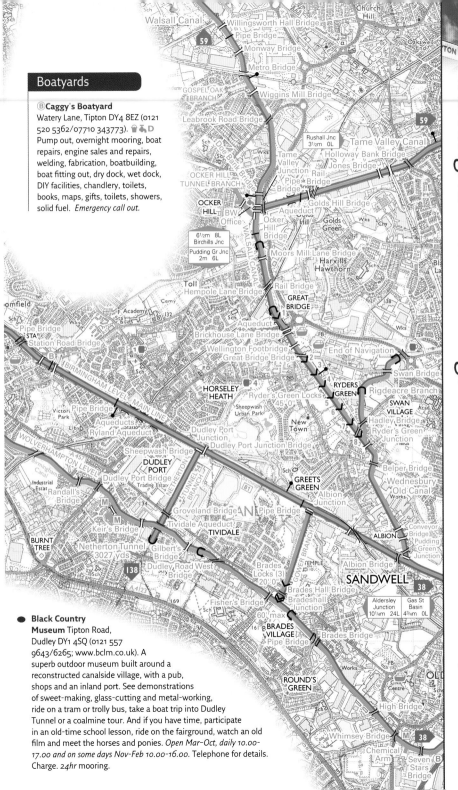

Boatyards

ⒷCaggy's Boatyard
Watery Lane, Tipton DY4 8EZ (0121 520 5362/07710 343773). 🛒♿D Pump out, overnight mooring, boat repairs, engine sales and repairs, welding, fabrication, boatbuilding, boat fitting out, dry dock, wet dock, DIY facilities, chandlery, toilets, books, maps, gifts, toilets, showers, solid fuel. *Emergency call out.*

● **Black Country Museum** Tipton Road, Dudley DY1 4SQ (0121 557 9643/6265; www.bclm.co.uk). A superb outdoor museum built around a reconstructed canalside village, with a pub, shops and an inland port. See demonstrations of sweet-making, glass-cutting and metal-working, ride on a tram or trolly bus, take a boat trip into Dudley Tunnel or a coalmine tour. And if you have time, participate in an old-time school lesson, ride on the fairground, watch an old film and meet the horses and ponies. *Open Mar-Oct, daily 10.00-17.00 and on some days Nov-Feb 10.00-16.00.* Telephone for details. Charge. *24hr mooring.*

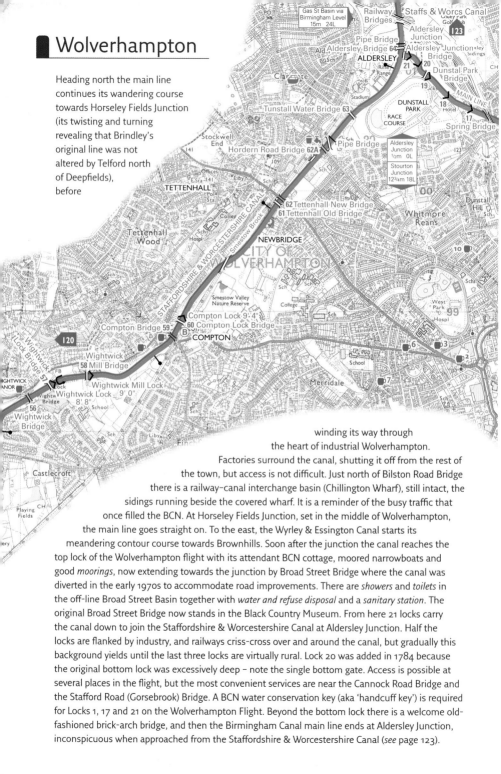

Wolverhampton

Heading north the main line continues its wandering course towards Horseley Fields Junction (its twisting and turning revealing that Brindley's original line was not altered by Telford north of Deepfields), before

winding its way through the heart of industrial Wolverhampton. Factories surround the canal, shutting it off from the rest of the town, but access is not difficult. Just north of Bilston Road Bridge there is a railway-canal interchange basin (Chillington Wharf), still intact, the sidings running beside the covered wharf. It is a reminder of the busy traffic that once filled the BCN. At Horseley Fields Junction, set in the middle of Wolverhampton, the main line goes straight on. To the east, the Wyrley & Essington Canal starts its meandering contour course towards Brownhills. Soon after the junction the canal reaches the top lock of the Wolverhampton flight with its attendant BCN cottage, moored narrowboats and good *moorings*, now extending towards the junction by Broad Street Bridge where the canal was diverted in the early 1970s to accommodate road improvements. There are *showers* and *toilets* in the off-line Broad Street Basin together with *water and refuse disposal* and a *sanitary station*. The original Broad Street Bridge now stands in the Black Country Museum. From here 21 locks carry the canal down to join the Staffordshire & Worcestershire Canal at Aldersley Junction. Half the locks are flanked by industry, and railways criss-cross over and around the canal, but gradually this background yields until the last three locks are virtually rural. Lock 20 was added in 1784 because the original bottom lock was excessively deep – note the single bottom gate. Access is possible at several places in the flight, but the most convenient services are near the Cannock Road Bridge and the Stafford Road (Gorsebrook) Bridge. A BCN water conservation key (aka 'handcuff key') is required for Locks 1, 17 and 21 on the Wolverhampton Flight. Beyond the bottom lock there is a welcome old-fashioned brick-arch bridge, and then the Birmingham Canal main line ends at Aldersley Junction, inconspicuous when approached from the Staffordshire & Worcestershire Canal (*see page 123*).

NAVIGATIONAL NOTES

1 A standard T-shaped water conservation (aka 'handcuff key') is needed to operate Tipton Factory Locks.
2 Bradeshall Bridge, on the Gower Branch (page 43) has an air draught of 6' 6".

51

Wyrley & Essington Canal

Wood End
Sch

Wards Bridge
Nordley
Hill

WEDNESFIELD
Pinfold Bridge
FIEL
M

New
Cross
Hospital

Church Bridge

Rookery Bridge

Wednesfield Junction
New Cross Bridge

Wednesfield Junction

Site of
Bentley Canal

New Bentley
Bridge

HEATH
TOWN

Heath Town Bridge

Neachells

Industri

WYRLEY & ESSINGTON CANAL

LEISURE
POOL

Gorsebrook Bridge
14
16 15 13
Pipe Bridge
12
Stour Valley Viaduct
11
Fox's Lane Bridge
10
9
Jordans Bridge
8
7
Wolverhampton
Locks
(21) 132' 0"
6
5
Cannock Road Bridge
4   Springfield
3
Deans Road Bridge
2
1
Rail Bridge
Little's Lane Bridge
B
M
Broad Street Bridge
Civic
Centre
9
M
STA
5   4
8
Mill Street Bridge
M
Horseley Fields Bridge
Rail Bridge
Walsall Street Bridge
Pipe Bridge
Chillington Wharf
Bilston Road Bridge

8m 0L
Birchills Jnc

WOLVERHAMPTON

Swan Garden Bridge
Horseley Fields Junction

WOLVERHAMPTON LEVEL

P&R

East Park
Speedway Stadium

Molineux
Stadium

Trading
Estate

Cable Street
Bridge

Pipe Bridge
Dixon Street Bridge

MONMORE
GREEN

Stow
Heath
College

Priestfield

Rough
Hills

Catchems Corner
Bridge

Freezeland
Sch

Pipe Bridges

MAIN LINE

Jibbet Lane Bridge

Millfields Bridge

Ettingshall

Works

MILLFIELDS

Lan

WOLVERHAMPTON LEVEL

5m 21L
Aldersley
Junction

Gas St
Basin
10m 3L

SPRING
VALE

42 Ladymoor

LADYMOOR
Highfields Road
Bridge

72B
Deepfields Junction

Pubs and Restaurants (pages 44–45)

In a town such as Wolverhampton there are many pubs to choose from. Below are a selection for the enterprising to seek out:

▶ 1 **The Lych Gate Tavern** 44 Queen Square, Wolverhampton WV1 1TX (01902 399516; lychgatetavern.co.uk). With its 16th-C timber-framed interior and an early 18th-C Georgian façade, this pub is one of the city's oldest buildings, now dispensing an ever-changing range of real ales and real cider. Home-made cobs available or bring your food. Terrace, newspapers, real fires and Wi-Fi. *Open 11.00–23.00 (Fri-Sat 00.00).*

▶ 2 **The Clarendon** 38 Chapel Ash, Wolverhampton WV3 0TN (01902 420587; www.clarendonhotelpub. co.uk). Banks brewery tap serving real ale and food *daily 12.00–21.00 (Sun 19.00). Thu & Fri* live music. Dog- and family-friendly, outside seating. *Sun* quiz, sports TV and Wi-Fi. *Open Mon-Sat 11.30–23.00 (Fri-Sat 23.30) & Sun 12.00–22.30.*

▶ 3 **The Combermere Arms** 90 Chapel Ash, Wolverhampton WV3 0TY (01902 421880). Real ale served in a terraced house look-alike: both cosy and intimate. Renown for the tree growing in the gents lavatory! Open fires, a family room and outdoor drinking area. Sports TV and newspapers. Food available *Tue-Fri L. Open Mon-Thu L and E & Fri-Sun 12.00–00.00 (Sun 22.30).*

▶ 4 **The Great Western** Sun Street, Wolverhampton WV10 0DJ (01902 351090; www. holdensgreatwesternwolverhampton.co.uk). Real ale, railway memorabilia and good local cooking *L (not Sun).* Dog- and family-friendly, outside seating. Real fires, sports TV and Wi-Fi. *Open 11.00–23.00.*

▶ 5 **The Posada** 48 Lichfield Street, Wolverhampton WV1 1DG (07967 185830). Grade II listed building with its striking tiled frontage. A good range of real ales. Outdoor drinking area. Family-friendly, sports TV and Wi-Fi. *Open Mon-Sat 12.00–23.00 (Fri-Sat 00.10) & Sun 12.00–22.30.*

▶ 6 **The Royal Oak** 70 Compton Rd, Wolverhampton WV3 9PH (01902 422845; royaloakwolverhampton. co.uk). Traditional, single-room, community pub serving real ales and fresh cobs. Live music *Fri & Sat.* Outside seating, family- and dog-friendly. Newspapers, sports TV and Wi-Fi. *Open Mon-Sat 11.00–23.00 (Fri-Sat 00.00) & Sun 12.00–23.00).*

▶ 7 **The Chindit Inn** 113 Merridale Rd, Wolverhampton WV3 9SE (07986 773487; www. thechindit.co.uk). Originally built as an off-licence, this 1950's hostelry serves a good range of real ales. Outdoor drinking area, children welcome *until 19.00.* Live music *Fri & Tue.* Traditional pub games, sports TV and Wi-Fi. *Open Mon-Fri L and E, Sat 12.00–00.00 & Sun 14.00–23.00.*

▶ 8 **The Moon Under Water** 53-55 Lichfield Street, Wolverhampton WV1 1EQ (01902 422447; www. jdwetherspoon.co.uk/home/pubs/the-moon-under-water-wolverhampton). Situated in the ground floor of the former Co-op building this busy city centre pub serves real ales and food *all day* including breakfast. Children welcome. *Open all day from 07.00.* Wi-Fi.

▶ 9 **The Hogs Head** 186 Stafford St, Wolverhampton WV1 1NA (01902 717955; www.craft-pubs.co.uk/ hogsheadwolverhampton). CAMRA award-winning pub serving a range of real ales (including beers from local micro-breweries) and real cider. Food is available *daily 10.00–22.00.* Outdoor drinking area. Quiz *Wed.* Children welcome *until 21.00* if eating. Pool, sports TV and Wi-Fi. *Open daily 10.00–00.00 (Fri 01.00 & Sun 00.20).*

▶ 10 **The Stile Inn** 3 Harrow St, Wolverhampton WV1 4PB (01902 425336). Friendly Victorian, street-corner hostelry serving real ales and food (including Polish dishes) *daily 12.00–20.30 (Fri-Sat 21.30).* Child- and dog-friendly, outside drinking area. Traditional pub games, newspapers, sports TV and Wi-Fi. *Open daily 11.30–23.00 (Fri 00.00 & Sat 01.00).*

Boatyards

ⓑ**Oxley Marina** The Wharf, Oxley Moor Road, Wolverhampton WV10 6TZ (01902 789522; www.oxleymarina.co.uk). 🚿🛒D Pump out, gas, overnight and day boat hire, over night and long-term mooring, slipway, solid fuel, winter storage, lifting facility, DIY facilities, boat sales and repairs, engine sales and repairs, welding and fabrication, toilets, car parking, *emergency call out.* Licensed bar *evenings and at weekends.* Snacks.

Broad Street Basin

Brownhills

The Wyrley & Essington Canal meanders quietly through suburbs, passing an useful general store at Teece's Bridge. At Pelsall Junction, amidst the flat grassy expanse of Pelsall Wood, the Cannock Extension Canal leaves to the north. This waterway was built between 1858 and 1863 and once connected with the Staffordshire & Worcestershire Canal. The old basins just before the present terminus used to serve the Brownhills Colliery. It is wholly rural until the boatyards are reached, and is well worth the short diversion – indeed there is a pub 50yds from the terminus (across a very busy road). The section to the north of Watling Street was closed in 1963 due to subsidence. It was apparently quite a spectacular length, with massive embankments and vast brick overflow weirs. About 70 boats were left for scrap when it was abandoned. The main line continues on its eccentric course through fields, factories and houses until it approaches the wharf at Brownhills, now a tidy public area with a large *supermarket*, *market place* and *shops* within easy reach. The Daw End Branch begins south of Catshill Junction – it was built in 1803 to carry lime from the workings around Daw End and Hay Head – and although constructed originally as a contour canal following the 473ft line, mining and subsidence have frequently left it in a very high, exposed position. This is immediately apparent when approaching Walsall Wood Bridge, a good stop for *shops and a post office*. The Anglesey Branch, which heads off east at Catshill Junction, last carried coal from the Cannock Mines in 1967, so those who make this worthwhile diversion may be surprised to find that the route is extremely rural, with open country to the north. An elegant cast iron bridge spans Ogley Junction, where the main line of the Wyrley & Essington once descended through locks to join the Coventry Canal at Huddlesford Junction; the route, abandoned in 1954, is now the subject of an energetic restoration campaign. What was once just a feeder from Chasewater now passes through sandy heathland to pass under the new M6 Toll motorway before terminating at Anglesey Basin, a wide expanse where there are still the remains of loading chutes to be seen. Note the fine overflow weir, and the octagonal valve house high up on the dam. Chasewater Park is just a short walk from here.

Pelsall North Common Walsall Countryside Services (01922 459813; www.walsall.gov.uk). Originally rough grazing, much of the common was consumed by a great ironworks between 1832 and 1888, which employed 100 people from Pelsall village. Eventually iron prices fell, and the company went into liquidation, with the works being demolished in the late 1920s. A large machine, known as 'the cracker', was used to break up the mounds of foundry waste, and this gave the common its local nickname 'the cracker'. This machine was disposed of shortly after World War II. The common covers 137 acres, 92 of which, north of the canal, are designated a local nature reserve. There are areas of valuable lowland heath, pools containing mallard, snipe and mute swans, and many lime-loving plants in the west. Bright green and blue emperor dragonflies can be seen near the canal in summer.

Chasewater Built as a canal feeder reservoir, and so efficient was it that at one time its owners, the Wyrley & Essington Canal Company, sold its water to other companies. Just after building, in 1799, the dam collapsed, pouring a torrent of water across Watling Street and into the River Tame at Tamworth. Meadows were left strewn

with gravel, and some livestock was drowned, but luckily little other damage was caused. The dam was rebuilt, faced with stone, and has remained stoically intact ever since. Note the fine octagonal valve house, built in the same style as the once common BCN toll houses.

Chasewater Country Park Pool Road, near Brownhills WS8 7NL (01543 370607; www.lichfielddc.gov.uk). A 700-acre park where there is rich bird life, fishing and nature trails to enjoy. Sailing and power boating on the reservoir are for clubs only, but you can, of course, always watch. *Open daily.*

Chasewater Steam Railway Chasewater Country Park, Pool Road, near Brownhills WS8 7NL (01543 452623; www.chasewaterrailway. co.uk). At Brownhills West Station. A preserved section of the Cannock Chase & Wolverhampton Railway, built originally to carry coal from Cannock Chase. Now a fine selection of steam, diesel and even a petrol locomotive are maintained here, together with an assortment of rolling stock. Museum and café. Trains run *weekends Apr-Sep & Sun Oct-Nov* (check *website for steaming days*); *Santa Specials at Xmas*. Telephone or visit website for details.

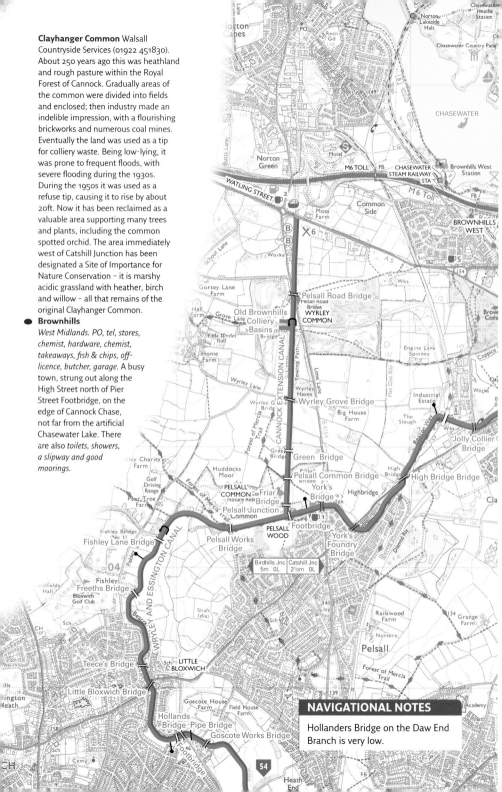

Clayhanger Common Walsall Countryside Services (01922 451830). About 250 years ago this was heathland and rough pasture within the Royal Forest of Cannock. Gradually areas of the common were divided into fields and enclosed; then industry made an indelible impression, with a flourishing brickworks and numerous coal mines. Eventually the land was used as a tip for colliery waste. Being low-lying, it was prone to frequent floods, with severe flooding during the 1930s. During the 1950s it was used as a refuse tip, causing it to rise by about 20ft. Now it has been reclaimed as a valuable area supporting many trees and plants, including the common spotted orchid. The area immediately west of Catshill Junction has been designated a Site of Importance for Nature Conservation – it is marshy acidic grassland with heather, birch and willow – all that remains of the original Clayhanger Common.

● **Brownhills**
West Midlands. PO, tel, stores, chemist, hardware, chemist, takeaways, fish & chips, off-licence, butcher, garage. A busy town, strung out along the High Street north of Pier Street Footbridge, on the edge of Cannock Chase, not far from the artificial Chasewater Lake. There are also *toilets, showers, a slipway and good moorings.*

Birdhills Jnc	Catshill Jnc
5m 0L	2½m 0L

NAVIGATIONAL NOTES

Hollanders Bridge on the Daw End Branch is very low.

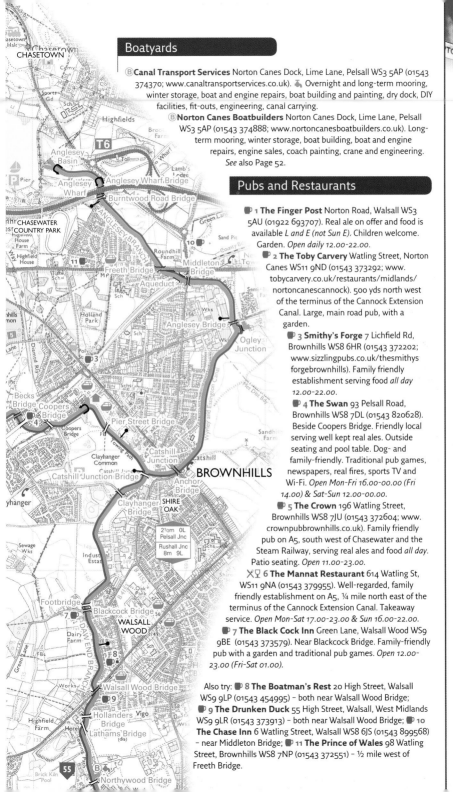

Boatyards

ⒷCanal Transport Services Norton Canes Dock, Lime Lane, Pelsall WS3 5AP (01543 374370; www.canaltransportservices.co.uk). ⚓ Overnight and long-term mooring, winter storage, boat and engine repairs, boat building and painting, dry dock, DIY facilities, fit-outs, engineering, canal carrying.

ⒷNorton Canes Boatbuilders Norton Canes Dock, Lime Lane, Pelsall WS3 5AP (01543 374888; www.nortoncanesboatbuilders.co.uk). Long-term mooring, winter storage, boat building, boat and engine repairs, engine sales, coach painting, crane and engineering. See also Page 52.

Pubs and Restaurants

🍺 1 The Finger Post Norton Road, Walsall WS3 5AU (01922 693707). Real ale on offer and food is available L and E (not Sun E). Children welcome. Garden. Open daily 12.00-22.00.

🍺 2 The Toby Carvery Watling Street, Norton Canes WS11 9ND (01543 373292; www.tobycarvery.co.uk/restaurants/midlands/nortoncanescannock). 500 yds north west of the terminus of the Cannock Extension Canal. Large, main road pub, with a garden.

🍺 3 Smithy's Forge 7 Lichfield Rd, Brownhills WS8 6HR (01543 372202; www.sizzlingpubs.co.uk/thesmithys forgebrownhills). Family friendly establishment serving food all day 12.00-22.00.

🍺 4 The Swan 93 Pelsall Road, Brownhills WS8 7DL (01543 820628). Beside Coopers Bridge. Friendly local serving well kept real ales. Outside seating and pool table. Dog- and family-friendly. Traditional pub games, newspapers, real fires, sports TV and Wi-Fi. Open Mon-Fri 16.00-00.00 (Fri 14.00) & Sat-Sun 12.00-00.00.

🍺 5 The Crown 196 Watling Street, Brownhills WS8 7JU (01543 372604; www.crownpubbrownhills.co.uk). Family friendly pub on A5, south west of Chasewater and the Steam Railway, serving real ales and food all day. Patio seating. Open 11.00-23.00.

✕🍽 6 The Mannat Restaurant 614 Watling St, WS11 9NA (01543 379955). Well-regarded, family friendly establishment on A5, ¼ mile north east of the terminus of the Cannock Extension Canal. Takeaway service. Open Mon-Sat 17.00-23.00 & Sun 16.00-22.00.

🍺 7 The Black Cock Inn Green Lane, Walsall Wood WS9 9BE (01543 373579). Near Blackcock Bridge. Family-friendly pub with a garden and traditional pub games. Open 12.00-23.00 (Fri-Sat 01.00).

Also try: 🍺 8 The Boatman's Rest 20 High Street, Walsall WS9 9LP (01543 454995) – both near Walsall Wood Bridge; 🍺 9 The Drunken Duck 55 High Street, Walsall, West Midlands WS9 9LR (01543 373913) – both near Walsall Wood Bridge; 🍺 10 The Chase Inn 6 Watling Street, Walsall WS8 6JS (01543 899568) – near Middleton Bridge; 🍺 11 The Prince of Wales 98 Watling Street, Brownhills WS8 7NP (01543 372551) – ½ mile west of Freeth Bridge.

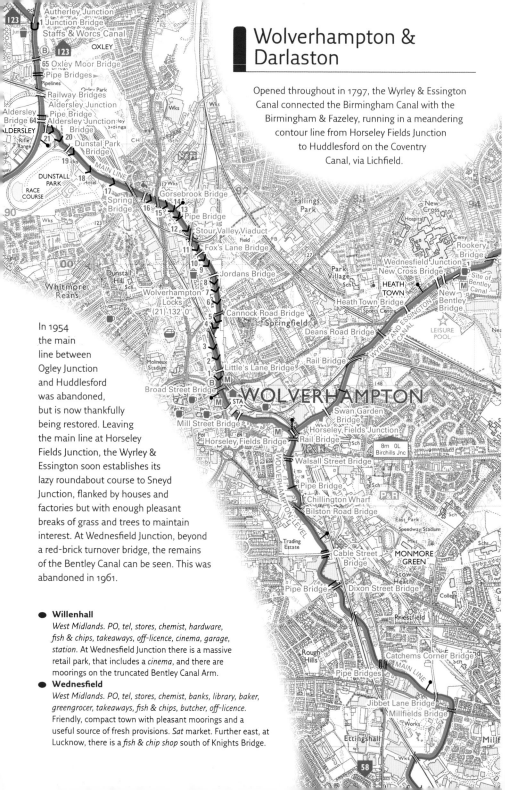

Wolverhampton & Darlaston

Opened throughout in 1797, the Wyrley & Essington Canal connected the Birmingham Canal with the Birmingham & Fazeley, running in a meandering contour line from Horseley Fields Junction to Huddlesford on the Coventry Canal, via Lichfield.

In 1954 the main line between Ogley Junction and Huddlesford was abandoned, but is now thankfully being restored. Leaving the main line at Horseley Fields Junction, the Wyrley & Essington soon establishes its lazy roundabout course to Sneyd Junction, flanked by houses and factories but with enough pleasant breaks of grass and trees to maintain interest. At Wednesfield Junction, beyond a red-brick turnover bridge, the remains of the Bentley Canal can be seen. This was abandoned in 1961.

● **Willenhall**
West Midlands. PO, tel, stores, chemist, hardware, fish & chips, takeaways, off-licence, cinema, garage, station. At Wednesfield Junction there is a massive retail park, that includes a cinema, and there are moorings on the truncated Bentley Canal Arm.

● **Wednesfield**
West Midlands. PO, tel, stores, chemist, banks, library, baker, greengrocer, takeaways, fish & chips, butcher, off-licence. Friendly, compact town with pleasant moorings and a useful source of fresh provisions. Sat market. Further east, at Lucknow, there is a fish & chip shop south of Knights Bridge.

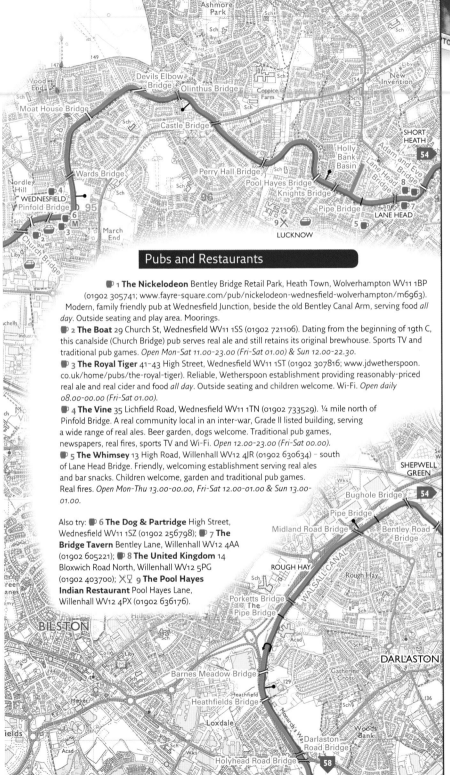

Pubs and Restaurants

🍺 1 **The Nickelodeon** Bentley Bridge Retail Park, Heath Town, Wolverhampton WV11 1BP (01902 305741; www.fayre-square.com/pub/nickelodeon-wednesfield-wolverhampton/m6963). Modern, family friendly pub at Wednesfield Junction, beside the old Bentley Canal Arm, serving food *all day*. Outside seating and play area. Moorings.

🍺 2 **The Boat** 29 Church St, Wednesfield WV11 1SS (01902 721106). Dating from the beginning of 19th C, this canalside (Church Bridge) pub serves real ale and still retains its original brewhouse. Sports TV and traditional pub games. *Open Mon-Sat 11.00-23.00 (Fri-Sat 01.00) & Sun 12.00-22.30.*

🍺 3 **The Royal Tiger** 41-43 High Street, Wednesfield WV11 1ST (01902 307816; www.jdwetherspoon. co.uk/home/pubs/the-royal-tiger). Reliable, Wetherspoon establishment providing reasonably-priced real ale and real cider and food *all day*. Outside seating and children welcome. Wi-Fi. *Open daily 08.00-00.00 (Fri-Sat 01.00).*

🍺 4 **The Vine** 35 Lichfield Road, Wednesfield WV11 1TN (01902 733529). ¼ mile north of Pinfold Bridge. A real community local in an inter-war, Grade II listed building, serving a wide range of real ales. Beer garden, dogs welcome. Traditional pub games, newspapers, real fires, sports TV and Wi-Fi. *Open 12.00-23.00 (Fri-Sat 00.00).*

🍺 5 **The Whimsey** 13 High Road, Willenhall WV12 4JR (01902 630634) – south of Lane Head Bridge. Friendly, welcoming establishment serving real ales and bar snacks. Children welcome, garden and traditional pub games. Real fires. *Open Mon-Thu 13.00-00.00, Fri-Sat 12.00-01.00 & Sun 13.00-01.00.*

Also try: 🍺 6 **The Dog & Partridge** High Street, Wednesfield WV11 1SZ (01902 256798); 🍺 7 **The Bridge Tavern** Bentley Lane, Willenhall WV12 4AA (01902 605221); 🍺 8 **The United Kingdom** 14 Bloxwich Road North, Willenhall WV12 5PG (01902 403700); ✗🍴 9 **The Pool Hayes Indian Restaurant** Pool Hayes Lane, Willenhall WV12 4PX (01902 636176).

Walsall Canal

Beyond Foresters Bridge and the railway viaduct the Anson Branch used to fork off north east – this once connected with the Bentley Canal, which in turn joined the Wyrley & Essington. Now the Walsall Canal is up on an embankment, crossing James Bridge Aqueduct (dated 1797), very exposed but with fine views over distant housing, a car breaker's yard and a cemetery. The M6 motorway zooms overhead. You pass the new ornate gateway to Sister Dora Gardens before reaching Walsall Junction, where the Town Arm branches off below the locks, and it is worth the short diversion to visit the fine new *pub* and the art gallery. New *shops* are within a stone's throw of the basin. Walsall Locks climb away north, enclosed by tall buildings – note especially Albion Flour Mill, dated 1849, with its covered loading bay, at lock 7. Once again traditional paddle gear and big wooden balance beams contribute to the enjoyment of the flight – at the top lock look out for the old Boatman's Rest, opposite Thomas's Wharf. Note also the toll office and BCN house no. 206 here. A *pub* and a *shop* are close by. The canal then makes for Birchills Junction, passing the old brick arch of Raybolds Bridge on the way.

Boatyards

Ⓑ **Aldridge Marina** Brickyard Road, Aldridge WS9 8SR (01922 743874; www.krhardy.co.uk). 🛢 🚽 ⚓ Refurbished marina, pump out, secure long-term mooring, winter storage, toilets.

Goscote

The Wyrley & Essington Canal continues its eccentric course around Rough Wood to join the M6 motorway for a short while, but this is thankfully soon left well behind as Edwards Bridge is approached. At Sneyd Junction the main line turns sharp right under the bridge. Ahead, beyond the derelict lock, the old Wyrley Branch once linked with coal workings and the Essington Branch, at 533ft above sea level the highest point reached on the BCN. It was never successfully operated due to water supply problems. Beyond the wharf buildings and crane the canal makes its journey through Leamore to Birchills Junction, where the Walsall Canal leaves to the south, and the Wyrley & Essington continues, passing factories and car parks. These soon give way to neat rows of suburban houses, and then finally the canal is in open country.

Daw End Branch

Continuing south, the Daw End Branch of the Wyrley & Essington now finds itself high up on an embankment with very deep clay pits either side, some now partially flooded and landscaped, some still being worked. These dramatic surroundings give way to light industry and new housing, which in turn are followed by a surprisingly rural area which is to last until Walsall's smarter suburbs are reached. There is a remarkable stone cottage and red-brick arch at Brawn's Bridge; these red-brick arches then appear regularly, enhancing the canal's remote quality. At Longwood Junction the main line of the Daw End Branch used to continue to Hay Head – this is now abandoned and forms part of a nature reserve *(see Page 52)*. Longwood Boat Club have their moorings at the junction, and their club house is in an old canal building next to BCN house no. 93 at the top lock. With pretty gardens, the whole makes for a charming canal scene. Longwood Boat Club has a useful information board at the top lock.

Longwood Junction

Leaving Longwood the character of the route south changes to that of a straight modern canal, revealing that the traveller is now on the Rushall Canal; this was built in 1847 to connect the Daw End Branch with the Tame Valley Canal in order to capture the coal trade from Cannock Mines. After the top two locks the canal passes a golf course; beyond Sutton Road Bridge the banks are lined with canalside gardens, and the towpath is overhung with willow, flowering currant and berberis. There is a children's play-park at Gillity Bridge. Another golf course accompanies the route through the next flurry of locks on this long, drawn-out flight, and still the surroundings are wholly amenable. This is truly a fine length of urban canal, which would stand comparison with many others in the country.

The New Art Gallery Walsall Gallery Square, Walsall WS2 8LG (01922 654400; www.thenewartgallery.org.uk). At the end of the Walsall Town Arm. Features the Garman Ryan Collection of works by artists such as Picasso, Van Gogh, Constable and Sir Jacob Epstein, plus feature exhibitions. *Open Tue-Sat 10.00-17.00 & Sun 12.00-16.00. Closed B Hols*. Shop. Free.

Walsall Leather Museum Littleton Street West, Walsall WS2 8EQ (01922 721153; www.walsall.gov.uk/leathermuseum). A short walk north east of the Town Arm. For two centuries Walsall has been the centre of British saddlery and leathergoods, and indeed a hundred or so companies still trade, producing wallets, purses, belts, bridles and saddles. Here you can see craftsmen at work, and perhaps even have a try yourself. There are also plenty of leathergoods for sale. *Open Tue-Sat 10.00-17.00*.

Rough Wood Chase Walsall Countryside Services (0121 360 9464; www.walsall.gov.uk). In the 12th C Rough Wood was part of Bentley Hay, a district of Cannock Forest. Deer were hunted here, in what was a Royal Forest, until the 1500s when the king ordered all the trees to be felled. Coal was found here in the 1700s, and this was transported by canal to the furnaces of the Black Country. It used to be loaded onto boats by Bentley Wharf Bridge. Today Rough Wood contains fine stands of oak, which in turn support vast numbers of insects, upon which a great variety of birds feed.

Park Lime Pits Walsall Countryside Services (01922 451238; www.walsall.gov.uk). Some 200 years ago this area was a thriving lime quarry, the lime being used as flux in the production of iron. Blocks of limestone were taken to the canal in trucks, to be transported to the furnaces of the Black Country.

It is also possible that the Romans may have used stone from here in the building of Watling Street. When quarrying ended some 150 years ago the old workings were landscaped, beech trees were planted and the quarries filled with water. These pools now support coot, moorhen and other waterfowl. Daubenton's bats fly over the water at dusk. Limestone spoil heaps support plants such as burnet-saxifrage and potentilla.

Lime Pits Farm Walsall Countryside Services (01922 451238; www.walsall.gov.uk). This farm adjoins the reserve, and is a pioneering project which is endeavouring to combine nature conservation with productive farming. Follow the trail to see wheat and barley growing, with Jersey cows producing milk. The cattle drink from ponds which also support a variety of birds and insects. There is a wildflower hay meadow, small fields and rich hedgerows, protected from pesticides and fertilisers. Trees have been planted in field corners to provide both shelter and wildlife habitats. *If you visit, please do not leave the marked trail. This is a working farm.*

Hay Head Wood Walsall Countryside Services (01922 451238; www.walsall.gov.uk). Another limestone area, with evidence of mine shafts dating from the late 18th C still visible. The lime from here was found to be suitable for cement production, and much was used in the construction of canal buildings. The pond was once an arm of the canal, built to transport limestone from the mines, and the remains of old wharf buildings can still be made out. Follow the trail *Apr-Jun* and you will see (and smell) wild garlic, as well as dog's mercury, a plant which loves the lime. Old oak woods support varied birds and insects, and occasionally kingfishers and herons are seen in the remains of the old canal basin.

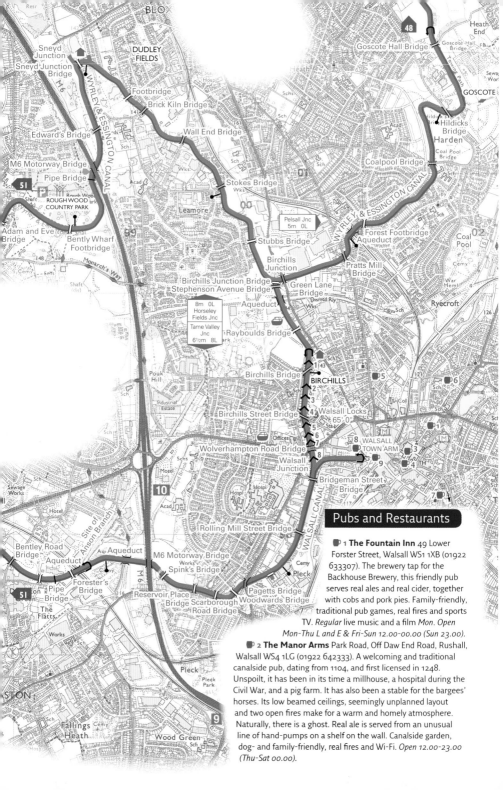

BLO

DUDLEY FIELDS

Sneyd Junction
Sneyd Junction Bridge

Footbridge
Brick Kiln Bridge

Edward's Bridge

M6 Motorway Bridge
Pipe Bridge

51

ROUGH WOOD COUNTRY PARK

Leamore

Adam and Eve Bridge

Bently Wharf Footbridge

Wall End Bridge

Stokes Bridge

Stubbs Bridge

Birchills Junction

Birchills Junction Bridge
Stephenson Avenue Bridge

Aqueduct

8m 0L
Horseley Fields Jnc

Tame Valley Jnc
6½m 8L

Rayboulds Bridge

Pouk Hill

Birchills Bridge

Birchills Street Bridge

Wolverhampton Road Bridge

Walsall Junction

Bentley Road Bridge

Aqueduct

M6 Motorway Bridge
Spink's Bridge

51
Pipe Bridge
Forester's Bridge

Reservoir Place
Scarborough Road Bridge
Pagetts Bridge
Woodwards Bridge

Rolling Mill Street Bridge

10

9

48

Goscote Hall Bridge

GOSCOTE

Hildicks Bridge Harden

Coalpool Bridge

WYRLEY & ESSINGTON CANAL

Pelsall Jnc
5m 0L

Forest Footbridge
Aqueduct

Pratts Mill Bridge

Green Lane Bridge

Dismtd Rly

Ryecroft

Coal Pool

BIRCHILLS

Walsall Locks

65' 0"

WALSALL TOWN ARM

Bridgeman Street Bridge

Pubs and Restaurants

🍺 1 **The Fountain Inn** 49 Lower Forster Street, Walsall WS1 1XB (01922 633307). The brewery tap for the Backhouse Brewery, this friendly pub serves real ales and real cider, together with cobs and pork pies. Family-friendly, traditional pub games, real fires and sports TV. *Regular* live music and a film *Mon. Open Mon-Thu L and E & Fri-Sun 12.00-00.00 (Sun 23.00).*

🍺 2 **The Manor Arms** Park Road, Off Daw End Road, Rushall, Walsall WS4 1LG (01922 642333). A welcoming and traditional canalside pub, dating from 1104, and first licensed in 1248. Unspoilt, it has been in its time a millhouse, a hospital during the Civil War, and a pig farm. It has also been a stable for the bargees' horses. Its low beamed ceilings, seemingly unplanned layout and two open fires make for a warm and homely atmosphere. Naturally, there is a ghost. Real ale is served from an unusual line of hand-pumps on a shelf on the wall. Canalside garden, dog- and family-friendly, real fires and Wi-Fi. *Open 12.00-23.00 (Thu-Sat 00.00).*

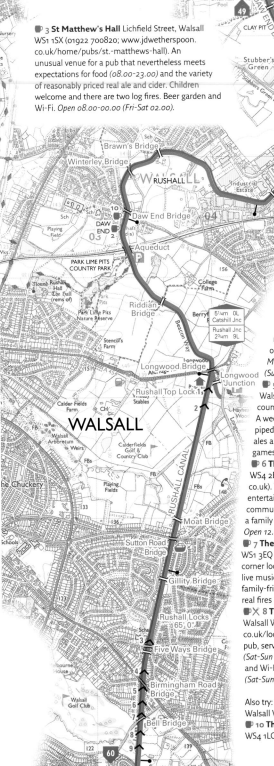

3 St Matthew's Hall Lichfield Street, Walsall WS1 1SX (01922 700820; www.jdwetherspoon. co.uk/home/pubs/st.-matthews-hall). An unusual venue for a pub that nevertheless meets expectations for food (*08.00-23.00*) and the variety of reasonably priced real ale and cider. Children welcome and there are two log fires. Beer garden and Wi-Fi. *Open 08.00-00.00 (Fri-Sat 02.00).*

4 The Black Country Arms High Street, Town Centre, Walsall WS1 1QW (01922 640588; www. blackcountryarms.co.uk). Set in an imposing Grade II listed building, dating from 1627, this hostelry serves up to 16 real ales (many from micro-breweries) and real cider. Food is served *Sun-Mon L & Tue-Sat 11.00-19.30 (Sat 12.00)* including a popular traditional *Sun* roast (booking advisable). Children welcome, outside seating, newspapers and Wi-Fi. *Open Mon-Fri (Fri 00.00) & Sat-Sun 12.00-00.00 (Sun 23.00).*

5 The Pretty Bricks 5 John Street, Walsall WS2 8AF (01922 612553; www.black countryales.co.uk/the-pubs/the-pretty-bricks). A wee Victorian gem: cosy, inviting, free from piped music and dispensing a wide range of real ales and real cider. Real fires, traditional pub games and dog-friendly. *Open daily 12.00-23.00.*

6 The Butts Tavern 44 Butts Street, Walsall WS4 2BJ (01922 629332; www.buttstavern. co.uk). Traditional pub games, a *Tue* quiz and live entertainment on *Fri & Sat* nights. This welcoming, community pub serves real ales. Patio seating and a family room. Traditional pub games and sports TV. *Open 12.00-00.00 (Sat-Sun 11.00).*

7 The White Lion 150 Sandwell Street, Walsall WS1 3EQ (07746 219452). Impressive Victorian, street corner local serving real ales and real cider. Regular live music and a small walled garden. Dog- and family-friendly. Traditional pub games, newspapers, real fires and Wi-Fi. *Open 12.00-00.00 (Sat-Sun 11.00).*

8 The Waterfront Wolverhampton Street, Walsall WS2 8DH (01922 616382; www.hungryhorse. co.uk/locations/waterfront-1). Newly-built, chain pub, serving real ale and food *daily 11.00-22.00 (Sat-Sun 10.00).* Outside seating, family-friendly and Wi-Fi. Mooring nearby. *Open 11.00-23.00 (Sat-Sun 10.00).*

Also try: **9 The Red Lion** 69 Park Street, Walsall WS1 1NW (01922 622380) and **10 The Boathouse** Park Road, Walsall WS4 1LG (01922 615032).

Great Bridge

The Walsall Canal runs from Ryder's Green Junction to Birchills Junction, connecting with the Tame Valley and Wyrley & Essington Canals. Its construction to Walsall was completed in 1799, with the link with the Wyrley & Essington being made via eight locks in 1841. The Wednesbury Old Canal was opened prior to this, in 1769, and still provides the vital link with the Walsall Canal. These two canals are still industrialised, and as such they give some impression of what the BCN was like in its heyday. The Wednesbury Old Canal leaves the main line at Pudding Green Junction under a flurry of bridges and hemmed in by factories. Immediately after Ryder's Green Junction, where the shortened Ridgeacre Branch heads half-a-mile to the north, eight locks descend to Doebank Junction. Access to shops is easily made by walking west from Great Bridge Bridge. Hempole Lane Bridge is one of the few BCN bridges dated in Roman numerals – MDCCCXXV – 1825, and just beyond here is the Ocker Hill Tunnel Branch. This once fed water to the Wednesbury Oak Loop via six pumping engines, a tunnel and shafts. The branch has been tidied up, and is used for long-term moorings (so don't take your boat in!). Black and white cast iron bridges mark the junction with the Tame Valley Canal, and just beyond here the canal reaches what is left of the Gospel Oak Branch (no navigation). This whole area is now quite smart, with Holyhead and Darlaston Bridges looking particularly attractive.

The Wednesbury Oak Loop

This was the original course of the Old Main Line which followed a contour route around Coseley Hill, and was bypassed in 1837 with the building of Coseley Tunnel. Leaving the main line at Deepfields Junction, the canal passes through what was once a mining area, now landscaped and with wide views to south and north. Beyond Pothouse Bridge, land which at one time reverberated to the sound of iron making is now grassy fields, accompanying the waterway on its last 1/4 mile to the terminus at the Canal & River Trust Regional Workshop. It is to this maintenance yard, where lock gates and boats are made and repaired, that the remaining section of the loop owes its survival. There is now little trace of the length which once connected to the Walsall and Tame Valley canals via the Bradley Locks Branch, although plans are afoot to reinstate this link. Please DO NOT take your boat right to the end outside working hours.

CARING FOR BODY AND SOUL

The Walsall Iron Company's works once stood close to the canal at Birchalls, not far from the Boatman's Rest, which now houses the Birchills Canal Museum. A furnace in the works, loaded with more molten metal than was prudent, exploded on 15 October 1875, showering 17 men with molten metal and burning them badly. Three of the unfortunate victims jumped into the canal in an effort to find relief. Although lovingly nursed by Sister Dora (Dorothy Pattison), only two survived the incident, making it one of Walsall's worst industrial accidents.

Sister Dora, who died three years later, became famous in the area for her nursing skills, and did much to reduce the death rate from industrial accidents, giving Walsall a better track record in this respect than many of the London teaching hospitals. She came from Yorkshire in 1865, taking charge of Walsall's first hospital and soon gaining a reputation as a civilian Florence Nightingale.

The Boatman's Rest was one of three such institutions operated by the Incorporated Seamen and Boatman's Friend Society – the other two, at Gas Street Basin and Hednesford, have now been demolished. Caring for the physical and spiritual needs of the boatmen, the halls offered religious services, a clubroom (with no alcohol), overnight accommodation, letter writing and a semblance of education for the boat children. Stables were also provided for the horses.

Hall Green

Opened in 1844 to overcome the long delays which were occurring at Farmer's Bridge Locks, the canal is typified by its direct course, deep cuttings and high embankments. The 3½ mile section between Doebank Junction and Rushall Junction has the distinction of being the dreariest on the whole BCN. For those who would choose to stop along here, there are *shops, takeaways and fish & chips* in the area south of Hately Heath Aqueduct and Crankhall Lane Bridge. There is also a large *hardware and DIY* emporium immediately north of Holloway Bank Bridge.

Ryder's Green Locks, Walsall Canal

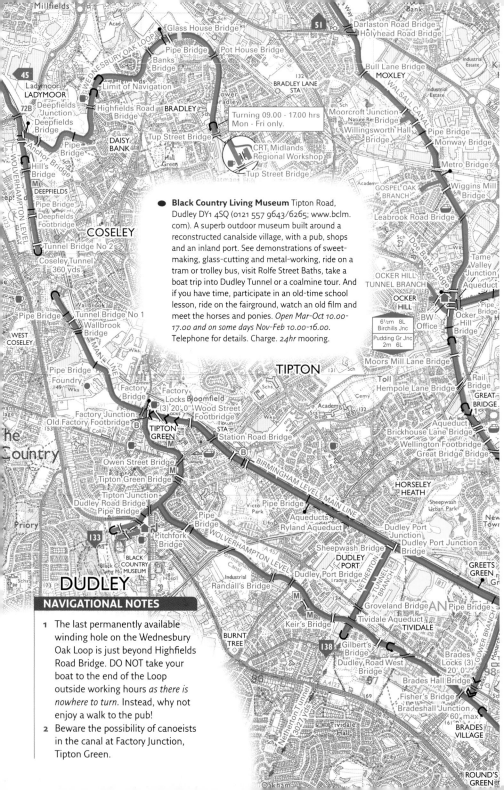

Black Country Living Museum Tipton Road, Dudley DY1 4SQ (0121 557 9643/6265; www.bclm. com). A superb outdoor museum built around a reconstructed canalside village, with a pub, shops and an inland port. See demonstrations of sweet-making, glass-cutting and metal-working, ride on a tram or trolley bus, visit Rolfe Street Baths, take a boat trip into Dudley Tunnel or a coalmine tour. And if you have time, participate in an old-time school lesson, ride on the fairground, watch an old film and meet the horses and ponies. *Open Mar-Oct 10.00-17.00 and on some days Nov-Feb 10.00-16.00.* Telephone for details. Charge. *24hr* mooring.

Turning 09.00 - 17.00 hrs Mon - Fri only.

NAVIGATIONAL NOTES

1 The last permanently available winding hole on the Wednesbury Oak Loop is just beyond Highfields Road Bridge. DO NOT take your boat to the end of the Loop outside working hours *as there is nowhere to turn.* Instead, why not enjoy a walk to the pub!

2 Beware the possibility of canoeists in the canal at Factory Junction, Tipton Green.

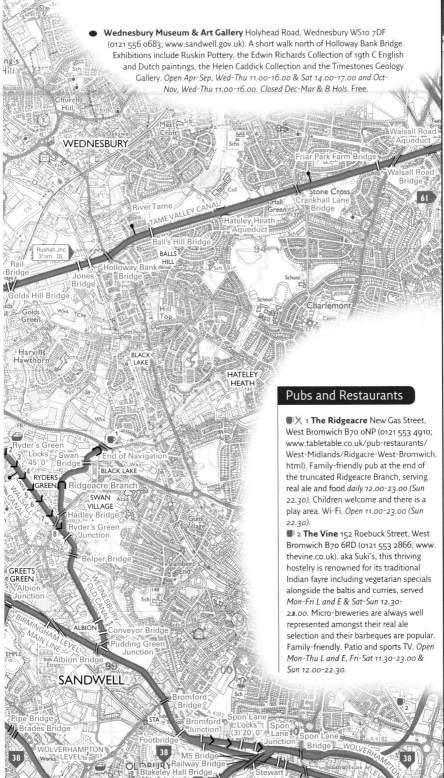

● **Wednesbury Museum & Art Gallery** Holyhead Road, Wednesbury WS10 7DF (0121 556 0683; www.sandwell.gov.uk). A short walk north of Holloway Bank Bridge. Exhibitions include Ruskin Pottery, the Edwin Richards Collection of 19th C geology and Dutch paintings, the Helen Caddick Collection and the Timestones Geology Gallery. *Open Apr-Sep, Wed-Thu 11.00-16.00 & Sat 14.00-17.00 and Oct-Nov, Wed-Thu 11.00-16.00. Closed Dec-Mar & B Hols. Free.*

Walsall & Tame Valley

Pubs and Restaurants

🍺✕ **1 The Ridgeacre** New Gas Street, West Bromwich B70 0NP (0121 553 4910; www.tabletable.co.uk/pub-restaurants/West-Midlands/Ridgacre-West-Bromwich.html). Family-friendly pub at the end of the truncated Ridgeacre Branch, serving real ale and food *daily 12.00-23.00 (Sun 22.30)*. Children welcome and there is a play area. Wi-Fi. *Open 11.00-23.00 (Sun 22.30)*.

🍺 **2 The Vine** 152 Roebuck Street, West Bromwich B70 6RD (0121 553 2866; www.thevine.co.uk). aka Suki's, this thriving hostelry is renowned for its traditional Indian fayre including vegetarian specials alongside the baltis and curries, served *Mon-Fri L and E & Sat-Sun 12.30-22.00*. Micro-breweries are always well represented amongst their real ale selection and their barbeques are popular. Family-friendly. Patio and sports TV. *Open Mon-Thu L and E, Fri-Sat 11.30-23.00 & Sun 12.00-22.30.*

59

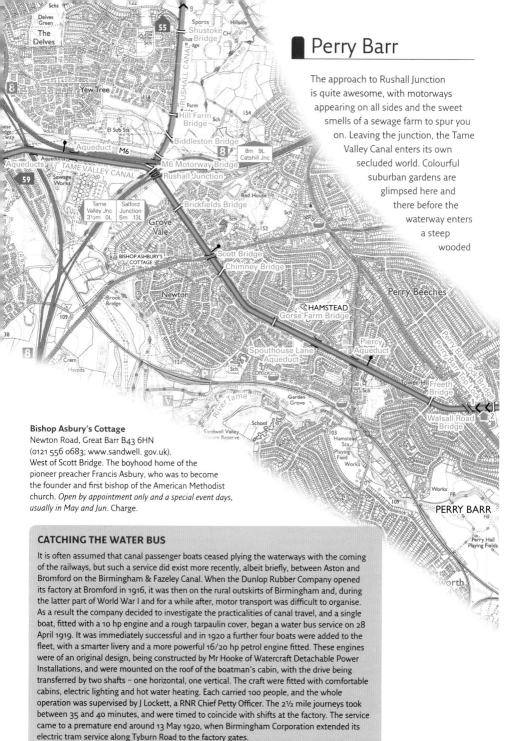

Perry Barr

The approach to Rushall Junction
is quite awesome, with motorways
appearing on all sides and the sweet
smells of a sewage farm to spur you
on. Leaving the junction, the Tame
Valley Canal enters its own
secluded world. Colourful
suburban gardens are
glimpsed here and
there before the
waterway enters
a steep
wooded

Bishop Asbury's Cottage
Newton Road, Great Barr B43 6HN
(0121 556 0683; www.sandwell. gov.uk).
West of Scott Bridge. The boyhood home of the
pioneer preacher Francis Asbury, who was to become
the founder and first bishop of the American Methodist
church. *Open by appointment only and a special event days,
usually in May and Jun.* Charge.

CATCHING THE WATER BUS

It is often assumed that canal passenger boats ceased plying the waterways with the coming
of the railways, but such a service did exist more recently, albeit briefly, between Aston and
Bromford on the Birmingham & Fazeley Canal. When the Dunlop Rubber Company opened
its factory at Bromford in 1916, it was then on the rural outskirts of Birmingham and, during
the latter part of World War I and for a while after, motor transport was difficult to organise.
As a result the company decided to investigate the practicalities of canal travel, and a single
boat, fitted with a 10 hp engine and a rough tarpaulin cover, began a water bus service on 28
April 1919. It was immediately successful and in 1920 a further four boats were added to the
fleet, with a smarter livery and a more powerful 16/20 hp petrol engine fitted. These engines
were of an original design, being constructed by Mr Hooke of Watercraft Detachable Power
Installations, and were mounted on the roof of the boatman's cabin, with the drive being
transferred by two shafts – one horizontal, one vertical. The craft were fitted with comfortable
cabins, electric lighting and hot water heating. Each carried 100 people, and the whole
operation was supervised by J Lockett, a RNR Chief Petty Officer. The 2½ mile journeys took
between 35 and 40 minutes, and were timed to coincide with shifts at the factory. The service
came to a premature end around 13 May 1920, when Birmingham Corporation extended its
electric tram service along Tyburn Road to the factory gates.

cutting crossing by the high modern Scott Bridge, and the more agreeable Chimney Bridge, a footbridge supported on substantial brick pillars. Emerging from the cutting, the traveller then finds himself on a high embankment, with wide views all around; two aqueducts are crossed. By the second, Piercy, there are *shops, fish & chips, takeaways, garages, a chemist, off-licence and a station* all to the south of the navigation. Again the canal enters a deep cutting, this time through sandstone some 200 million years old, and propped up here and there with brickwork. After passing the handsome brick arch of Freeth Bridge, Perry Barr Top Lock is reached, set between a fine red-brick BCN house (no. 86), old stables and the Gauging Weir House. The lock flight straggles along the canal, and passes through an area of private back gardens, public open spaces and sports fields. Little industry intrudes, although the M6 motorway crosses twice. There are *petrol station*s by College Bridge Road where industrial premises begin to close in. The Tame Valley Canal joins the Birmingham & Fazeley and Grand Union canals under 'Spaghetti Junction' motorway interchange, where cast iron towpath bridges are dwarfed by flyovers, making a strangely mesmeric scene in complete and utter contrast to the tranquillity of the canals hidden below. A unique experience. If cycling, it is best to use the southern towpath between Brookvale Road Bridge and Rushall Junction on the NCN 5.

Pubs and Restaurants

🍺 1 **The Safe Harbour** Moor Lane, Witton B6 7AE (0121 331 4071). Near Moor Lane Bridge, and known locally as 'the Diggers', due to its proximity to the vast cemetery close-by. This old-fashioned community pub has a garden and offers darts and pool. *Open Mon-Thu 12.00-23.00 (Thu 00.00) & Fri-Sun 11.00-01.00 (Sun 23.00).*

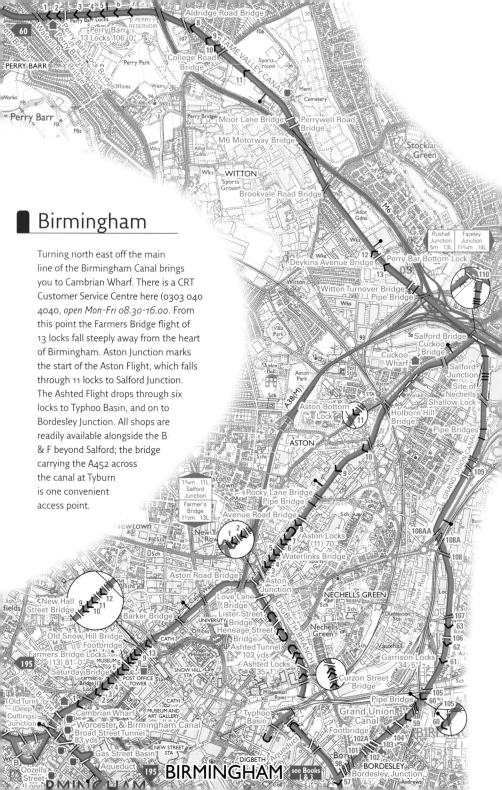

Birmingham

Turning north east off the main line of the Birmingham Canal brings you to Cambrian Wharf. There is a CRT Customer Service Centre here (0303 040 4040, open Mon-Fri 08.30-16.00. From this point the Farmers Bridge flight of 13 locks fall steeply away from the heart of Birmingham. Aston Junction marks the start of the Aston Flight, which falls through 11 locks to Salford Junction. The Ashted Flight drops through six locks to Typhoo Basin, and on to Bordesley Junction. All shops are readily available alongside the B & F beyond Salford; the bridge carrying the A452 across the canal at Tyburn is one convenient access point.

Ackers Adventure Activity Centre Golden Hillock Road, Small Heath, Birmingham B11 2PY (0121 772 5111; www.ackers-adventure.co.uk). Alongside the Grand Union canal at Small Heath. This non-profit making charity, run for the benefit of the community, offers a wide range of outdoor activities for all ages and abilities – everything from skiing and snowboarding to climbing, canoeing, archery and operating four-wheel-drive vehicles. Also a nature area. Charge. Telephone for further details.

Aston Hall Trinity Road, Aston, Birmingham B6 6JD (0121 348 8100; www.birminghammuseums. org.uk/aston). Built between 1618 and 1635, this one of the last great houses to be constructed in the spectacular Jacobean style and is decorated and furnished to reflect the lifestyle of a wealthy gentleman. There is the 136' Long Gallery and a magnificent carved oak staircase. It has been home to Charles I (albeit for a single night) and James Watt junior, son of the famous steam engineer. Drinks, snacks and souvenirs. *Open Tue-Sun & B Hol Mon 11.00-16.00. Closed 23rd Dec-2nd Jan.* Garden and grounds free. House charge.

Aston Villa Stadium Tours Aston Villa Football Club, Villa Park, Birmingham B6 6HE (0333 323 1874; www.avfc.co.uk). A chance to take a look behind the scenes of one of the world's oldest football clubs. Tours take place throughout the week – telephone for further details.

Barber Institute of Fine Arts The University of Birmingham, Edgbaston, Birmingham B15 2TS (0121 414 7333; www.barber.org.uk). A fine collection, donated to the university complete with the impressive gallery building, and embracing works of art from Old Masters through to modern paintings, drawings and sculpture, including major works by Bellini, Poussin, Rubens, Gainsborough, Rossetti, Monet, Degas and Magritte. There really is something here for everyone. Also a regular programme of exhibitions, concerts, lectures and events. *Open Mon-Fri 10.00-17.00 & Sat-Sun 11.00-17.00.* Free (donations welcome).

BBC Birmingham Level 10, The Mailbox, Birmingham B1 1RF (0370 901 1227; www.bbc.co.uk/showsand tours). A chance to visit the BBC's Birmingham home and see where famous radio and television programmes are made. Home to *The Archers* and *Gardeners' World* to name but two. Take a peek into the television production gallery and a trip down memory lane with the Time Tunnel. Hands-on displays and exhibits. Shop. Visitor Centre *open daily 10.00-17.00 (Sun 11.00).* Free. Pre-booked 1½ hr tours available *Tue-Wed & Sat 10.30-13.00* – telephone 0121 567 6888. Charge.

Pubs and Restaurants

🍺 1 **The Flapper** Cambrian Wharf, Kingston Row, Birmingham B1 2NU (0121 236 2421; www.theflapper.co.uk). Student-type pub majoring on bottled beers, cocktails and music. Canalside terrace seating. *Open Mon-Thu & Sun 16.00-23.00 and Fri-Sat 12.00-01.00.*

🍺 2 **The Malt House** 75 King Edwards Road, Brindley Place B1 2NX (0121 633 4171; www.greeneking-pubs.co.uk/pub/malt-house-birmingham/p0937). Overlooking Deep Cuttings Junction, this pub serves real ale and food *12.00-21.00 daily.* Children welcome, outside seating. Sports TV and Wi-Fi. *Open 11.00-23.00 (Fri-Sat 00.00).*

See also entries for Pubs and Restaurants on page 41

Birmingham Back to Backs 50–54 Inge Street/55–63 Hurst Street, Birmingham B5 4TE (0121 666 7671; www.nationaltrust.org.uk/birmingham-back-to-backs). A fully restored example of Birmingham's back-to-back housing that was once built by the thousand to accommodate Britain's rapidly rising population in industrial towns. This project gives you the chance to experience the lives of the people who lived and worked here through four different decades between 1840 and 1977. Culture, religion and profession are reflected in the interior design of the houses. *Open Tue–Sun, varying times.* Telephone for details. Limited capacity so booking (0121 666 7671) recommended. Charge.

Birmingham Botanical Gardens and Glasshouses Westbourne Road, Edgbaston, Birmingham B15 3TR (0121 454 1860; www.birminghambotanicalgardens.org.uk). Fifteen acres of beautiful gardens and four exotic glasshouses together with the National Bonsai Collection and a range of colourful birds and wildfowl. Gallery, sculptures and playground. Gift shop, plant sales and tearoom. *Summer Sun* bands and concerts. *Open daily May–Sep 10.00–18.00 & Oct–Apr 10.00–17.00 (or dusk).* Charge.

Birmingham Hippodrome Theatre Hurst Street, Birmingham B5 4TB (0844 338 5000; www.birminghamhippodrome.com). Home to the Birmingham Royal Ballet and DanceXchange. Having undergone a multi-million pound refurbishment in 2001, this is one of the city's most exciting and vibrant theatres and attracts some of the best ballets, musicals, operas and pantomimes.

Birmingham Museum and Art Gallery Chamberlain Square, Birmingham B3 3DH (0121 348 8034; www.birminghammuseums.org.uk/bmag). This magnificent building houses one of the world's finest collections of Pre-Raphaelite art and is home to extensive collections of ceramics, archaeology, sculpture and social history. There is the newly opened Waterhall Gallery of modern art and an elegant Edwardian tearoom. *Open daily 10.00–17.00 (Fri 10.30).* Free.

Birmingham Wildlife Conservation Park Pershore Road, Birmingham B5 7RL (0121 464 8728; www.birmingham.gov.uk/info/50042/birmingham_wildlife_conservation_park/329/birmingham_wildlife_conservation_park). An ideal place to introduce children to wildlife in the form of otters, foxes, lynx, fallow deer, harvest mice and snowy owls amongst over 130 British and European species. This award-winning centre is set in six and a half acres and has a visitor centre and café. *Open Apr–Oct, daily 10.00–17.00 & Nov–Mar, Sun 10.00–16.00.* Charge.

Birmingham Repertory Theatre Broad Street Birmingham B1 2EP (0121 236 4455; www.birmingham-rep.co.uk). One of Britain's most successful producing theatres with an excitingly innovative programme featuring both classic and contemporary plays and dance staged in the main 850 seat auditorium and in The Door – a 140 seat studio theatre dedicated to new writing.

Birmingham Tours run a variety of guided walks (including children's walks and a Tolkien Trail). For more details telephone or visit the website (0121 427 2555/07805 115998; www.birmingham-tours.co.uk).

For the less athletic there is also a bus-borne version of the Tolkien Trail available by visiting www.bmag.org.uk.

Blakesley Hall Blakesley Road, Yardley, Birmingham B25 8RN (0121 348 8120; www.bmag.org.uk/blakesley-hall). One of the few surviving examples of a timber-framed farmhouse left in the city, this delightfully restored building is home to a wealth of 17th-C domestic oak furniture, a bed chamber with original Elizabethan painted walls and a traditional herb garden. Café. *Open Tue–Sun & B Hol Mon 11.00–16.00.* Charge for house; gardens and grounds free.

Bowlplex Ladywood, Middleway, Birmingham B16 8LP (0844 477 0491; www.bowlplex.co.uk/our-centres/birmingham_city_centre). Total entertainment in a family-friendly environment where all ages feel at home. *Open Mon–Fri 11.00–23.00 (Fri 00.00) & Sat–Sun 10.00–00.00 (Sun 23.00).* Charge.

Cadbury World Linden Road, Birmingham B30 2LU (0844 880 7667; www.cadburyworld.co.uk). The ultimate chocoholic's dream come true – the chance to see it; feel it, smell it and taste it and then do it all over again. Restaurant, shops, snack bar, picnic and play areas. *Open all year, daily.* Opening times vary, so telephone for details. Charge.

Castle Bromwich Hall Gardens Trust Chester Road, Castle Bromwich B36 9BT (0121 749 4100; www.cbhgt.org.uk). Ten acres of walled gardens restored to their 18th-C splendour – an oasis of tranquility with historic plants, vegetables and fruits and a holly maze. Refreshments, gift shop and plant sales. *Open Apr–Oct Mon–Fri 11.00–16.00 & Sat–Sun and B Hols 12.30–16.30. Telephone for out of season opening times.* Charge.

The Digbeth Branch This leaves the Birmingham & Fazeley main line at Aston Junction, and descends through six locks to Typhoo Basin, where it meets the former Warwick & Birmingham Canal, which became part of the Grand Union Canal when the GUC Company was formed in 1929. There was a stop lock – called Warwick Bar – at the junction by Bordesley Basin. One of the lesser-known tunnels on the canal system is on the Digbeth Branch – the Ashted.

The Drum 144 Potters Lane, Aston, Birmingham B6 4UU (0121 333 2400; www.the-drum.org.uk). Europe's first arts centre dedicated to African, Asian and Caribbean arts and culture. A top venue for live jazz outside London and also featuring comedy, dance and drama.

Dudley Zoological Gardens 2 Broadway, Dudley, Birmingham DY1 4QF (01384 215313; www.dudleyzoo.org.uk). Lions, tigers, snakes and spiders and the Discovery Centre for a close encounter with a wide range of cuddly (and not-so-cuddly) beasts. Train, fairground rides and adventure playground. Restaurant and picnic area. *Open Summer 10.00–17.00, winter 10.00–16.00. Last admission 1 hour before closing.* Charge.

The Jewellery Quarter Birmingham (www.jewelleryquarter.net). This is a fascinating part of the city which, as its name suggests, defines the historic area devoted to the manufacture of all forms of human adornment. The quarter includes jewellers and manufacturers of jewellery, a museum (*see below*), several pavement trails and an information centre at Vyse Street. Clocks and watches also figure, both large and small.

Galton Valley Canal Heritage Centre 152
Brasshouse Lane, Smethwick, Birmingham B66 1BA
(0121 556 0683; www.culture24.org.uk/am60421).
Lying at the heart of the area's canal system, the
centre has examples of the work of Telford, Brindley
and Smeaton along with many examples of the
industrial architecture of the period. It offers an
introduction to the valley, its canal system, wildlife
and industrial history. Also access to the Smethwick
Pumping Engine (*see below*). *Telephone for opening
times.* Free.

The Glee Club The Arcadian, 70 Hurst Street,
Birmingham B5 4TD (0871 472 0400; www.glee.
co.uk/birmingham). The Midland's premier comedy
and live music venue: comedy *every Thu, Fri & Sat*;
music *on selected nights*. Bar and restaurant.
Charge.

Grand Prix Karting Birmingham Wheels,
1 Adderley Road South, Birmingham B8 1AD
(0121 327 7700; www.grandprixkarting.co.uk).
Karting for eight year olds upwards. Arrive and drive
and experience a stark contrast with the waterways.
Office *open 10.00–23.00.* Charge.

Historic Buildings For historic buildings in and
around Birmingham contact: Historic England (0370
333 0607; historicengland.org.uk) the National Trust
(0344 800 1895; www.nationaltrust.org.uk).

Lapworth Museum of Geology The Aston Webb
Building, Birmingham University, Edgbaston,
Birmingham B15 2TT (0121 414 7294/6751;
www.birmingham.ac.uk/facilities/lapworth-
museum). The museum holds one of the most
extensive collections of fossils, minerals and rocks in
the Midlands and is named after Charles Lapworth,
an influential geologist in the late 19th and early
20th centuries.The mineral specimens include many
rare and beautiful examples displaying stunning
colours and crystal shapes. *Open Mon–Fri 09.00–
17.00 & Sat–Sun 12.00–17.00.* Free.

MAC Midlands Art Centre Cannon Hill Park,
Birmingham B12 9QH (0121 446 3232;
www.macarts.co.uk). Arts centre offering varied
exhibitions and performances. Café.

Museum of the Jewellery Quarter 75–79 Vyse
Street, Birmingham B18 6HA (0121 348 8140; www.
birminghammuseums.org.uk/jewellery). Walk north
west from Summer Row, below lock 1, to the
Jewellery Quarter. A museum built in a 100-year-old
jeweller's workshop. See craftsmen at work. *Open
Tue–Sat and B Hol Mons 10.30–17.00.* Charge.

National Sea Life Centre The Waters Edge,
Brindley Place, Birmingham B1 2HL (0871 423 2110;
www.visitsealife.com/birmingham). Over 3,000
British marine and freshwater creatures to see and
the chance to discover a tropical paradise in the heart
of the city. Walk through a transparent underwater
tube with sharks swimming around you, and visit the
'wreck' of the Titanic. There is a daily programme of
talks and feeding demonstrations to provide visitors
with a deeper understanding of the marvels of the
marine world. Restaurant and shop. *open daily from
10.00. Closing times vary* so telephone or visit website
for details. Charge.

New Alexander Theatre, Suffolk Street
Queensway, Birmingham B5 4DS (0844 871 7627;
www.birminghamtheatres.com/newalexandra.
htm). One of the top touring theatres in the country
featuring a wide range of entertainment from West
End musicals to comedies and concerts.

The Pen Museum Unit 3, The Argent Centre,
60 Frederick Street, Hockley, Birmingham B1 3HS
(0121 236 9834; penmuseum.org.uk). This museum
celebrates Birmingham's pre-eminent position as
the centre of the world's pen manufacture for well
over a century. Demonstrations and displays. *Open
Mon–Sat 11.00–16.00, Sun 13.00–16.00.* Free
(donations welcome).

Royal Birmingham Society of Artists' Gallery
4 Brook Street, St Paul's, Birmingham B3 1SA
(0121 236 4353; www.rbsa.org.uk). A lively and
inspiring art gallery with regular exhibitions of
contemporary paintings and sculpture and a craft
gallery selling designer jewellery, ceramics and glass.
Bistro-style café. *Open Mon–Fri 10.30–17.30, Sat
10.30–17.00, Sun 13.00–17.00.* Free.

St Chad's Cathedral St Chad's Queensway,
Birmingham B4 6EU (0121 236 2251;
www.stchadscathedral.org.uk). Designed in Gothic
revival style by Pugin in 1841, this was the first
Catholic Cathedral to be erected in England since
the Reformation. It possesses a large collection of
medieval artifacts and carvings, largely assembled
by Pugin himself, and a unique collection of stained
glass, metalwork and vestments made by John
Hardman and Co., a world-famous firm based in the
Jewellery Quarter. *Open Mon–Fri 07.00–17.00, Sat
from 07.00 & Sun 07.00–15.00.*

St Martin's-in-the-Bullring Bull Ring,
Birmingham B5 5BB (0121 600 6020; www.bullring.
org). Birmingham's parish church, cleaned and
somewhat incongrously rising phoenix-like as the
focal point of the 21st-C Bull Ring Shopping Centre.

St Paul's Church St Paul's Square, Birmingham
B3 1QZ (0121 236 7858; www.stpaulsjq.church).
Built in 1779 and centrepiece of the Georgian St
Paul's Square, this Grade I jewel features a painted
window, by Benjamin West, showing the conversion
of St Paul. *Open Tue–Thu 10.00–15.00 & for the 10.30
Sun* service.

St Philip's Cathedral Colmore Row, Birmingham
B3 2QB (0121 262 1840; www.birminghamcathedral.
com). Walk south east from Saturday Bridge.
Completed in 1725, Birmingham Cathedral is one of
the most beautiful historic buildings in the city
centre and is famous for its four Pre-Raphaelite
stained-glass windows by Sir Edward Burne-Jones.
Look out for the canal scene on the altar fall,
depicting a canal boat, a lock and a bridge. One of
the clergy's vestments also depicts Smethwick
Pumping Station. *Open Mon–Fri 07.30–17.00 &
Sat–Sun 08.30–17.00 (Sun 08.10).* Free (donations
welcome).

Sarehole Mill Cole Bank Road, Hall Green,
Birmingham B13 0BD (0121 348 8160; www.
birminghammuseums.org.uk/sarehole). One of two
working watermills left in Birmingham, Sarehole
Mill has been in existence for over 450 years and

today visitors can view the waterwheel, grinding stones and agricultural machinery all integral to the building. Also carpenters' workshop display. This building was a childhood haunt of J.R.R. Tolkien and inspirational for *The Hobbit* and *Lord of the Rings*. Café and shop. *Open Wed-Sun & B Hol Mon 11.00-16.00. Grounds free; Mill charge.*

Selly Manor Museum Maple Road, Bournville, Birmingham B30 2AE (0121 472 0199; www.sellymanormuseum.org.uk). The chance to visit two of Birmingham's oldest buildings on one site: Selly Manor, a Tudor manor house and home to a stunning collection of furniture dating from 1500-1750; and Minworth Greaves, a medieval hall house of cruck-frame construction. Both are set in a delightful period garden. *Open mid Jan-mid Dec, Tue-Fri 10.00-17.00; Easter-Sep, also Sat, Sun & B Hol Mons 14.00-17.00. Charge.*

Smethwick New Pumping Station Brasshouse Lane, Smethwick, Birmingham B66 1BA (0121 556 0683; www.sandwell.gov.uk). Restored to full working order, this is the engine that lifts water from the Telford New Mainline Canal up to the old Brindley-built Woverhampton Level. The pump house itself was built in 1892. Access via the nearby Galton Valley Canal Heritage Centre.

Soho House Soho Avenue, off Soho Road, A41 Handsworth, Birmingham B18 5LB (0121 348 8150; www.birminghammuseums.org.uk/soho). This was the elegant Georgian home of the industrialist and entrepreneur Matthew Boulton from 1766 until 1809 and also the favourite meeting place of the Lunar Society whose members included Darwin, Watt and Priestley: they met on the night of the full moon to enable them to find their way home by moonlight. Soho House reflects the inventiveness of its owner with an early form of central heating, flushing toilets and furniture to his own design. Displays also tell the story of the Soho Mint. Gift shop, garden and tearoom. *Open Wed-Thu & 1st Sun of month 11.00-16.00. Also some B Hol Mon.* Gardens and grounds free, House charge.

Symphony Hall Broad Street, Birmingham B1 2EA (0121 780 3333; www.thsh.co.uk). One of the UK's top concert halls and home to the City of Birmingham Symphony Orchestra. Symphony Hall offers a diverse programme of world class music making including jazz, folk, rock and pop as well as stand-up comedy.

Thinktank Millennium Point, Curzon Street, Birmingham B4 7XG (0121 348 8000; www.birminghammuseums.org.uk/thinktank). Walk west from Curzon Street Bridge on the Digbeth Branch. A science centre with ten galleries spread over four floors: a unique opportunity to immerse yourself in an awe-inspiring world. Over 200 interactive exhibits, where you can, for example, try an operation or drive a digger, and see a Spitfire and a Hurricane, along with a steam locomotive and a racing car. Also an IMAX cinema. *Open daily 10.00-17.00. Last admissions 16.00.* Restaurant, shop. Charge.

The Transport Museum Chapel Lane, Wythall, Worcs. B47 6JX (01564 826471; www.wythall.org.uk). One of the largest collections of preserved buses and coaches in the UK. Also extensive collection of restored battery-electric vehicles. Classic bus rides, exhibitions, miniature steam railway, shop and café. *Open Easter-Oct, Sat, Sun & B Hol Mons 11.00-16.30. Also Jun-Aug Wed.* Charge. Direct bus service from Birmingham.

Travel Information For national bus enquiries contact Traveline on 0871 200 2233; www.traveline.info. For national rail enquiries telephone 03457 48 49 50; www.nationalrail.co.uk. For local travel information telephone 0345 303 6760; www.networkwestmidlands.com). For cheaper national rail travel visit new.trainsplit.com.

Walking in Birmingham There are several walking guides to the city available from the TIC (see below) which promote healthy activity alongside the opportunity to explore the City. Visit www.birmingham.gov.uk/info/20177/sport_health_and_wellbeing/847/walking_and_jogging_routes_in_birmingham for additional information. See also visitbirmingham.com/travel/maps-guides).

Winterbourne House and Garden 58 Edgbaston Park Road, Birmingham B15 2RT (0121 414 3003; www.winterbourne.org.uk). Six-acre Edwardian garden on the Birmingham University Edgbaston Campus with rare horticultural features. Over 1500 plant species including National Historic Rose Collection laid out in herbaceous borders, water gardens, herb gardens and arboretum. *Open Apr-Oct, Mon-Fri 10.00-17.30; Sat-Sun 11.00-17.30 & Nov-Mar Mon-Fri 10.00-16.00; Sat-Sun 11.00-16.00. Closed for 4 weeks over Xmas.* Charge.

Tourist Information Centre Birmingham Central Library, Chamberlain Square, Birmingham B3 3HQ (0844 888 3883; visitbirmingham.com). *Open Mon-Fri 10.00-18.00 & Sat 09.00-17.00.* Also at New Street Station, Birmingham B2 4DB. *Open Mon-Sat 09.00-17.00 & Sun + B Hol 10.00-16.00.*

WILDLIFE

Daubenton's Bat is a medium-sized bat (wingspan 23-27cm) with comparatively short ears. Frequently associated with water and seen flying low over lakes, ponds and canals just as dusk is falling. Also feeds along woodland rides. Chirps can be heard by those with good hearing. In summer, roosts, sometimes in colonies, in hollow trees and tunnel entrances. In winter, hibernates in caves, mines and cellars. Widespread and fairly common in Britain. Daubenton's Bat is found in Park Lime Pits, Walsall (*see page 53*).

DROITWICH CANALS

MAXIMUM DIMENSIONS

Droitwich Barge Canal
either Length: 61' 0"
    Beam: 14' 0"*
or   Length: 71' 6"
    Beam: 7' 0"
Draught: 3' 6"
Headroom: 8' 0"
*N.B. There is a restricted width of 7' 0" for all craft through Bridge 15 on the approach to Droitwich.

Droitwich Junction Canal
Length: 71' 6"
Beam: 7' 0"
Draught: 2' 6"
Headroom: 6' 5"*
*N.B. The headroom through the M5 culvert can vary according to the flow of the Body Brook which enters the canal above the motorway. When the brook is in spate the headroom through the culvert can be reduced significantly.

MILEAGE

River Severn to:
Ladywood Lock: 2¾ miles
Barge Lock, Droitwich: 5¾ miles
Hanbury Wharf (junction with Worcester & Birmingham Canal): 7¼ miles
Locks: 16

MANAGER

0303 040 4040
enquiries.southwalessevern@canalrivertrust.org.uk

The Droitwich canals are unique in this country in that they owe their existence to salt: coal came into the town by barge to boil the salt pans, while the finished product left by the same means. Authorised in 1768, engineered by James Brindley (although pressure of other work meant he was rarely present) and opened on 12th March 1771, the Droitwich Barge Canal was one of the earliest canals built. In reality much of the detailed design work fell to his assistant Robert Whitworth while the resident engineer was John Priddy. As with many canals that were branches of existing river navigations, it was built to a wide gauge which allowed river craft – such as Severn Trows and Wych Barges - to use it, transporting salt directly to the port of Bristol. The Droitwich Junction Canal, which connected Droitwich to the Worcester & Birmingham Canal and the new salt works at Stoke was completed in 1852, well after the period of canal mania, and at the start of the railway age. In 1874 the Droitwich canals and the Worcester & Birmingham Canal were bought by the Sharpness New Docks Company, who then owned a through route to Birmingham but, despite considerable improvements, including dredging, these acquisitions never earned enough to even repay the interest on their mortgage. Traffic dwindled, with the last boat navigating the Barge Canal in 1918, while a load of bricks from the Hanbury Brickworks is reputed to have been the final cargo on the Junction Canal, carried in the mid 1920s. The entire route was finally abandoned by Act of Parliament in 1939. The Droitwich Canals Trust Ltd was established in 1973, with the objective of restoring navigation to the town from both the River Severn and the Worcester & Birmingham Canal. Early work was concentrated on the Barge Canal, for which it held the lease and much progress was made due to the unstinting efforts of volunteers, the Inland Waterways Association, government grants and from contributions made by local firms and from fund raising events. In all some 300,000 tons of mud was removed from the canal to be spread on local fields! From 1998 onwards attention was focused on the Junction Canal and within three years the first three locks were restored with the aid of a grant from the Inland Waterways Association. 2001 saw the formation of the Droitwich Canals Restoration Partnership who succeeded in raising the £11.5 million needed to complete restoration from Advantage West Midlands and the Heritage Lottery Fund. The two canals were finally opened on 1st July 2011.

Hawford Junction

With the restoration of the Droitwich Canals now complete, Hawford Junction has once again become a scene of activity, with craft diverting off the natural course of the Severn to explore the meandering, river-like course of the canal to Droitwich, or completing (if they are no more than 7ft beam) a 22-mile cruising ring encompassing the Worcester & Birmingham Canal and the River Severn. The waterway is entered through the two Hawford Locks, which were considered at the time to be one of canal engineer James Brindley's finest works. There is a *caravan and camping site* here, with a nearby *boatyard* accessed from the River Severn via one of its tributaries, the Salwarpe. Beyond, the navigation continues on its extravagant way, passing Mildenham and Porter's Locks before beginning its ascent of the four Ladywood Locks. Linacre Bridge 3 is worthy of close examination, since it is a rare surviving example of one of Brindley's original structures. Also look out for the 15th C timber-framed manor house of Salwarpe Court just past Bridge 7 on the south bank, a building that very much characterises this area.

NAVIGATIONAL NOTES

1. The River Salwarpe is navigable with care to George Judge's boatyard for craft of around 30ft and drawing less than 2ft 6ins of water (and who have a valid reason to visit). Craft over 30ft long will be unable to turn.
2. When the River Severn floods water will enter the pound between Hawford Locks 1 &

2 so boaters should moor above Hawford Top Lock 2.
3. See Navigational Notes on page 82 for information on navigating the River Severn including lock opening times.

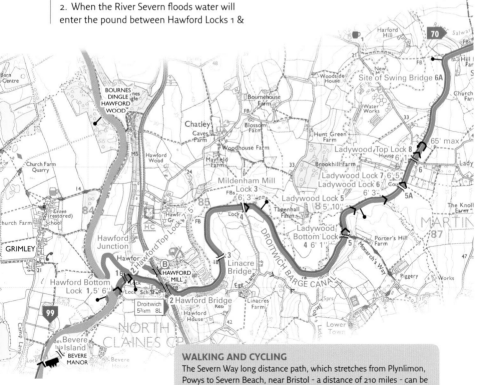

WALKING AND CYCLING
The Severn Way long distance path, which stretches from Plynlimon, Powys to Severn Beach, near Bristol - a distance of 210 miles - can be joined near Hawford Junction.

Boatyards

Ⓑ**Mill House Caravan & Camping Site** Mill House, Hawford WR3 7SE (01905 451283; www.millhousecaravanandcamping.co.uk). A pleasant site right by the canal and at the limit of navigation on the River Salwarpe. *Open Apr–Oct*. Gas, toilets, showers, shop and café (*weekend* café serving takeaway breakfasts). Wi-Fi and fishing available.

Ⓑ**Mill House Boatyard** Mill House, Hawford WR3 7SE (01905 451283; www.millhousecaravanandcamping.co.uk). Just east of the A449 bridge on the River Salwarpe. Gas, winter storage, crane, boat sales and repairs, boat fitting out, DIY facilities, chandlery, provisions and café *weekends during camping season*, toilets, showers, camping and caravan site. There are no visitor moorings and craft over 26ft *cannot turn*.

Pubs and Restaurants (pages 68–71)

🍺✕ **1 The Hadley Bowling Green** Hadley Heath, Droitwich WR9 0AR (01905 620294; www.thehadleybowlinggreen.com). Either follow the road north from Ladywood Top Lock 8 or the footpath west of the bend opposite Hill End Farm. Acclaimed for its friendly welcome and excellent home-made food (*available Mon-Sat L and E & Sun 12.00-20.00*) this pub also dispenses a broad range of real ales. Children welcome inside and in the garden alongside the oldest crown bowling green in the country. Wi-Fi. B&B. *Open Mon-Sat 11.30-23.00 & Sun 12.00-20.00*.

🍺✕ **2 The Copcut Elm** Worcester Road, Copcut, Droitwich WR9 7JA (01905 778845; www.hungryhorse.co.uk/index.php/pub-finder/details/copcut-elm-droitwich). Large roadhouse pub serving real ale and food *all day, every day*. Family-friendly, garden. Traditional pub games (pool) sports TV and Wi-Fi. *Open Sun-Tue 11.00-23.00 & Wed-Sat 11.00-00.00*.

🍺 **3 The Star & Garter** 13 High Street, Droitwich WR9 8EJ (01905 770234). Friendly local serving real ale. Children welcome, traditional pub games and Wi-Fi. *Open daily 11.00-00.00 (Sun 22.30)*.

🍺 **4 The Railway Inn** Kidderminster Road, Droitwich WR9 9AY. (01905 771578). There is lots of railway memorabilia in this pub, which serves real ale and food *L*. Children welcome. First floor terrace garden.

🍺 **5 The Talbot Hotel** 19 High Street, Droitwich WR9 8EJ (01905 773871). Cosy, traditional pub in a 17th-C Grade II listed building serving a wide range of real ales and real cider. Pie-based menu available *Mon-Sun 12.00-20.00 (Sun 17.00)*. Dog- and child-friendly (*until 19.00*). Traditional pub games, real fires and Wi-Fi. *Open 11.30-23.00 (Fri-Sat 23.30)*.

🍺 **6 The Barley Mow** 1-3 Hanbury Street, Droitwich WR9 8PL (01905 773248). 1930s Tudor-style pub serving real ale. Children and dogs welcome. Pub games and real fires. Canalside seating and patio. *Open 11.00-23.00 (Sun 22.30)*.

✕♀ **7 Portofino** 6 Worcester Road, Droitwich WR9 8AB (01905 794799; www.fortofinodroitwich.co.uk). Real Italian cooking served in light, airy surroundings amidst a welcoming, friendly atmosphere. Good, relatively inexpensive wine list. *Open Tue-Sun L and E*. Booked parties welcome.

🍺✕ **8 The Old Cock Inn** 77 Friar Street, Droitwich WR9 8EQ (01905 770754; www.oldcockinn.co.uk). First licensed in 1712, the ecclesiastical window was taken from nearby St Nicholas church after it was destroyed in the 18th C. The carved head is thought to represent Judge Jeffries, with a frog emerging from his mouth. All this notwithstanding you can enjoy real ales, real cider and food *L and E Tue-Sun*. Dog- and family-friendly, patio seating. Real fires and Wi-Fi. *Open Mon E & Tue-Sun 12.00-23.00 (Fri-Sat 00.00)*.

🍺 **9 The Hop Pole** 40 Friar Street, Droitwich WR9 8ED (01905 770155). Welcoming community pub serving a wide range of real ales and homemade food *12.00-14.00 daily*. Children welcome, outside seating. *Regular* live music, traditional pub games and newspapers. *Open 12.00-23.00 (Sun 22.30)*.

🍺✕ **10 The Gardeners Arms** Vines Lane, Droitwich WR9 8LU (01905 772936; www.pubfoodhotelnatureadventureholidayscanaldroitwicheurope.co.uk). Popular canalside pub *open all day* serving real ales and ciders together with a wide range of inexpensive food. Beer garden, dog- and child-friendly. Traditional pub games, real fires and Wi-Fi. *Open Mon-Sat 11.00-23.00 & Sun 12.00-22.30*.

🍺✕ **11 The Eagle & Sun** Hanbury Wharf, Hanbury Rd, Droitwich WR9 7DX (01905 799266; www.eagleandsundroitwich.com). Busy pub, overlooking Hanbury Junction, serving real ales and a selection of inexpensive, fixed price menus *daily 12.00-21.00 (Sun 20.30)*. Children welcome. Canalside seating. Mooring close by – use the Droitwich Canal. *Open 10.00-23.00 (Sun 22.30)*.

Droitwich

Ladywood Lock 8 is finely reached, although the even spread of the flight means the climb is far from arduous. A pretty lock cottage, enlivened with plantings of colourful flowers, compliments the tidy, black and white painted lock, composing the archetypal English canal scene. Heading east, the navigation approaches the town, passing through countryside that is surprisingly peaceful bearing in mind the close proximity of Worcester. This stretch takes the waterway through Salwarpe and Vines Park into the centre of Droitwich and the Barge Canal Lock, once its terminus. It is a fine example of the way in which an artificial waterway, mellowed with time and heavy use, adds a unique character to the surrounding urban environment. People come to the park to picnic by the canal, walk, jog or simply go about their daily business, connected to an industrious past and a better, cleaner future. It is now just two miles, along the Junction Canal, to Hanbury Junction with the initial section of the navigation diverted to negotiate the motorway, using the culvert originally constructed for the Body Brook when the M5 was built. The waterway begins a steady climb, first through two single locks, followed by the newly constructed staircase, before finally regaining its original bed and the three locks that lead to the junction with the Worcester & Birmingham Canal.

Boatyards

Ⓑ**Droitwich Spa Marina** Hanbury Road, Droitwich Spa WR9 7DU (07970 626807; www.droitwichspamarina. co.uk). 🛈🛒🚿 D Pump-out, gas, short & long term mooring, solid fuel, cranage facilities, hard standing & winter storage, DIY facilities, slipway, laundrette, toilets, showers, dog washing facility. *Open daily 10.00-16.00.*

Ⓑ**Bridge 35** Chandlers Unit 3, Canal Village, Hanbury Wharf Droitwich WR9 7DU (07748 408245). D Gas, chandlery, refreshments, ice cream. *Open Thu-Tue 09.00-17.00 (Sun 10.00).*

WALKING AND CYCLING
The well maintained towpath makes an excellent walk from Hawford Junction to Hanbury Junction. Cyclists will find the ride east from Ladywood Locks relatively easy going.

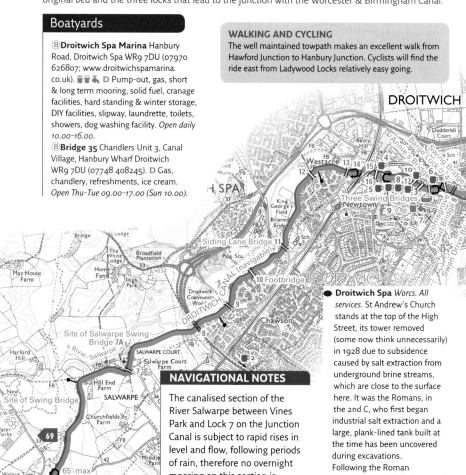

NAVIGATIONAL NOTES

The canalised section of the River Salwarpe between Vines Park and Lock 7 on the Junction Canal is subject to rapid rises in level and flow, following periods of rain, therefore no overnight mooring on this section is allowed.

● **Droitwich Spa** *Worcs. All services.* St Andrew's Church stands at the top of the High Street, its tower removed (some now think unnecessarily) in 1928 due to subsidence caused by salt extraction from underground brine streams, which are close to the surface here. It was the Romans, in the 2nd C, who first began industrial salt extraction and a large, plank-lined tank built at the time has been uncovered during excavations. Following the Roman abandonment of Britain around AD410, the Angles and Saxons gradually spread west, and salt production increased, only to face disaster during the 7th or 8th C, when flooding spread vast quantities of silt and clay across the salt wells. But their economic importance was demonstrated with the clearance of the wells and reinforcement of the flood defences.

By the 8th C, under the control of the Mercian kings, the town was known as 'Saltwic', and the salt wells were considered one of the wonders of Britain. A complete network of routes, or 'saltways', radiated from the town.

Salt was extracted from brine ($2^1/_2$ pounds of salt in each gallon of water, a concentration ten times that of sea water) by boiling in pans, and as a consequence vast quantities of timber was felled for fuel, even though coal was available from the 14th C. The result of all this burning and boiling was terrible pollution, but still salt production continued to increase and, in spite of a set-back during the Civil War, it rose to 3,000 tons per annum

the Royal Brine Baths in Queen Street in 1836, and this was soon followed by further baths and some fine hotels. Salt production finally ended in Droitwich in 1922, although pumping at Stoke Prior continued, causing serious subsidence in the town until that in turn ceased. The last of the original brine baths, St Andrew's, closed on Christmas Eve in 1975, but new baths were opened in 1984. A replica brine pit, and other remains of the salt industry, can be seen in Vines Park, by the canal.

Droitwich was also known nationally, and internationally, for its powerful long-wave transmitter, which was built here in 1933. Marked on the dial of wireless sets (as they were then known) as 'Droitwich 1,500 metres', transmissions began on 6 September 1934. During World War II the transmitter was initially used to broadcast to occupied Europe, and later used to jam signals to enemy aircraft. Today it broadcasts Radio 4 long wave, the World Service and Radio 5.

Radiating the friendly atmosphere typical of a small West Midland town, most of historic Droitwich lies to the south of the canal, in an area enclosed by Saltway, and is easily explored.

Tourist Information & Heritage Centre St Richard's House, Victoria Square, Droitwich WR9 8DS (01905 774312; www.visit worcestershire.org). The Heritage Centre opened in 1980 and is housed on the former Brine Baths site, first established in the 1880s. There is a fascinating small museum devoted to the salt industry, and other exhibits illustrate the history of the BBC transmitting station. Extremely friendly and helpful. *Open Mon-Sat 10.00-16.00 (Sat 13.30). Closed Sun & B Hol Mon.*

St Andrew's Church High Street, Droitwich WR9 8DY (01905 794952; www.droitwichparish.org.uk). The structure of the church was greatly affected by subsidence due to salt extraction, with the result that the tower was dismantled in 1928, and the bells removed to the north aisle. Built around 1310 on the site of an earlier church destroyed by a fire in 1290, which also laid waste to most of the rest of the town, only the base of the tower and the plinth of the chancel survived. If you are lucky you might be offered a short guided tour of the church.

in the late 1600s, and increased further when the town's monopoly on production ended and many private wells opened. When steam engines were introduced to drive pumps in the 18th C, production soared to 15,000 tons each year. Factories built in the 19th C exploited production, which peaked at an astonishing 120,000 tons per annum.

Around this time the major salt producer was John Corbett, a philanthropist who decided to move his salt production to Stoke Prior, on the Worcester & Birmingham Canal, and transformed Droitwich into a spa town following the realisation of the therapeutic qualities of salt water in the 1830s. He opened

GLOUCESTER & SHARPNESS CANAL AND RIVER SEVERN

GLOUCESTER & SHARPNESS CANAL

MAXIMUM DIMENSIONS
Length: 240'
Beam: 30'
Draught: 10'
Headroom: 105'

SPEED LIMIT
Gloucester & Sharpness Canal: 6 mph

MILEAGE
SHARPNESS Lock to:
Purton: 1½ miles
Saul Junction: 8 miles
GLOUCESTER Lock: 16½ miles

Locks: 2

RIVER SEVERN

MAXIMUM DIMENSIONS
Gloucester to Worcester
Length: 135'
Beam: 21'
Draught: 6'
Headroom (at low summer level): 24' 6"

Worcester to Stourport
Length: 90'
Beam:19'
Draught: 6' (in low rainfall and with silting, this can be reduced to less than 5' in places during the summer)
Headroom (at low summer level): 20'

SPEED LIMIT
River Severn Navigation: 6 mph heading upstream – 8 mph heading downstream

MILEAGE
GLOUCESTER Lock to:
Ashleworth: 5 miles
Haw Bridge: 8¼ miles

TEWKESBURY Junction with River Avon: 13 miles
Upton upon Severn: 19 miles

DIGLIS Junction with Worcester & Birmingham Canal: 29 miles
Holt Fleet: 36 miles

STOURPORT Junction with Staff & Worcs Canal: 43 miles

Locks: 5

MANAGER
0303 040 4040
enquiries.southwalessevern@canalrivertrust.org.uk
Out of hours waterway-related emergencies
0800 4799947

The River Severn has always been one of the principal navigations in England. Its great length has made it an important trade artery since the medieval period. With its tributary, the Avon, it cuts deep into the heart of England, linking the iron and coal fields with the Bristol Channel and the British coastal trade. By using the Severn, boats of a considerable size could sail into the Midlands, and into Wales as far as Welshpool. However, the navigation, especially above Worcester, was always difficult, owing to currents, shoals and the demands of water supply for milling, etc.

As boats increased in size, and the cargoes became heavier, the navigational problems increased. The larger boats in common use in the 18th C could rarely sail higher than Bewdley, and so by the end of the century this inland port was beginning to lose its significance. At the same time the sandbanks and shifting shoals in the Gloucester area were seriously affecting the trade on the river as a whole. In order for the river to survive as a viable trade route, it became necessary for drastic improvements to be made. Various Acts were passed to ensure the maintenance of the towing path, although the Severn maintained its tradition of using gangs of men to bow-haul boats until well into the 19th C. In 1803 over 150 men were still employed in what Telford called 'this barbarous and expensive slave-like office' on the section between Bewdley and Coalbrookdale.

The demands of increasing navigation, and the spread of canals in the West Midlands (the Staffordshire & Worcestershire Canal linked the Severn with Birmingham and the rest of the network was opened in 1772) led to the passing of an Act in 1793 that authorised a canal to be built from Berkeley Pill to Gloucester. Work began on Gloucester Docks in 1794, and over the next few years 5½ miles of canal were cut. Shortage of money then caused work to be stopped, and so the canal remained useless and incomplete. In 1817 Telford was commissioned by the government to report on the feasibility of the canal, with particular reference to the maintenance of navigation on the Severn. He reported in favour of continuing and completing the canal, but recommended that it should run to Sharpness instead of to Berkeley. The government put up the money for the canal, mainly to relieve acute problems of unemployment, and after considerable delays the Gloucester & Sharpness Canal was opened throughout in 1827.

Some of the structural problems were caused by the decision to build the canal to ship standard. At the time of opening, this was the broadest, deepest canal in the world. But, although it greatly increased the cost, this far-sighted decision has ensured that the canal remains in use, and even today Sharpness Dock is still a commercial port. Once the canal was completed, considerable dredging works and improvements became necessary to maintain the navigation of the upper Severn to Worcester and Stourport. This work, carried out extensively since the formation of the Severn Commission in 1842, included the building of locks and weirs, and the canalisation of parts of the river. The links with the Midlands canal network helped the Severn to flourish, and railway competition increased rather than decreased the traffic both in the docks and on the ship canal. In 1874 Sharpness docks were enlarged and modernised, to handle ships of up to 1000 tons. The same year the Gloucester & Berkeley Canal Company leased the Worcester & Birmingham Canal, to maintain their hold on the trade routes to the Midlands. By 1888 the Severn had a minimum depth of over 6ft, and in most places the depth was 8–9ft. Trade continued to thrive, and the recession in the 1920s was soon overcome by the rapidly growing oil traffic which became the mainstay of the river. The CRT Waterway Office publish an excellent guide, giving detailed information on both the canal and river, obtainable from the manager above.

Sharpness

The Gloucester & Sharpness Ship Canal, which was built to bypass the dangerous winding stretch of the tidal River Severn between these two places, has its southern terminus at Sharpness, where there are docks and a large lock up from the Severn. The Gloucester & Sharpness Canal is nowadays the only navigable route between the Severn estuary and the Severn Navigation above Gloucester, so all boats heading upstream must pass through Sharpness Lock and Docks. It should be noted that the entrance to the lock dries out completely at low water, so boats heading in from the estuary should time their arrival for 1 hour before high water, notifying Sharpness in advance. The best time to arrive at the lock is about 2 hours before high water when locking down, and 1 hour before high water when locking up. (**It cannot be stressed too strongly** that craft should **not** attempt to arrive at Sharpness too early – i.e. *more than one hour before high water*). It is unlikely that any boat arriving after high water will be locked in, leaving a choice between an extremely unpleasant 12 hours in the estuary, or a return voyage to Portishead. (The lock is normally operated *2¹/₂ hours before, up until high water*). CRT maintain free visitor moorings on the canal outside the docks, which are available for 48 hours. It is important to give prior notice of one's intentions to Sharpness pier head staff (VHF channel 13 or 01453 511968) who can be contacted within a core operating period of *5 hours before high water to 1 hour after high water*. *Boaters not equipped with VHF marine band radio should carry a mobile phone.* Craft wishing to use the lock must also book the dock bridges with Sharpness pier head staff *24 hours in advance*. The Low Level Bridge must be swung for all craft; the High Level Bridge has an air draught of approx 16' 6" – it is important to state whether this bridge is required to be operated. Boaters wishing to proceed down the Severn estuary from Sharpness are advised not to do so without a pilot (*see* Navigational Note 1 on page 76). It is important to keep to the marked channel, and the tide runs extremely fast.

WALKING AND CYCLING

To make a worthwhile circular trip it is feasible to catch a train between Cam & Dursley station (approximately 1¼ miles east of Patch Bridge) and Gloucester. For those with more stamina, Cam & Dursley station can also be accessed from Sharpness via lanes through the villages of Wanswell, Halmore and Gossington: a distance of approximately 5 miles through delightfully peaceful country lanes. Trains run roughly every 2 hours. Telephone 08457 484950 for train times.

Immediately above the lock are Sharpness Docks, which handle ships from Europe, North Africa, Scandinavia and the Mediterranean, making them a busy area. Pleasure boats are encouraged to move on quickly through the two swing bridges out of the docks and onto the ship canal itself. Just north of the swing bridges is an arm off to the west (diesel for sale): this leads to a tidal basin which is now, unfortunately, disused. However the length of the arm leading to it is used for permanent and temporary pleasure craft moorings, and there is a small boatyard at the end of it. It is a fascinating place to walk round and see the tidal Severn flowing strongly at the foot of the stone walls. Across the river is the tree-lined west bank of the river, only ½ a mile across at this point. A railway line runs along the bottom of the hills. However, the old 22-arched railway bridge that used to cross the river just north of here has been completely demolished, and only the merest traces of some of the stone piers can be seen at low water. The bridge was badly damaged one foggy night in November 1959, when a vessel collided with it; the bridge then stood with a hole in the middle until it was demolished and the iron girders sold to – of all places – Chile, where they now form a road-carrying viaduct. Along the main line of the canal, the circular stone structure is all that remains of the railway's swing bridge over the canal. One mile from Sharpness Docks, the canal is lined with trees on each side – an uncharacteristically river-like stretch that is belied by the occasional

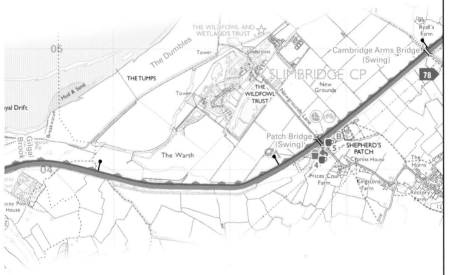

glimpse of the Severn flowing alongside. Old timber ponds open off the canal to the right. Timber was stored afloat here in the round. A curve leads to the village of Purton and its two swing bridges: the Upper Bridge is remotely operated. The Lower Bridge keeper can be contacted on 01453 811384 (there are also disabled moorings here). The navigation snakes through the village, passing the large waterworks before settling down to a steady course of wide, straight reaches. It traverses a quiet, green and predictably flat landscape that is well studded with trees and always bounded to the north by saltings and the mud-flats of the Severn estuary – which is here much wider than at Sharpness. At Patch Bridge (01453 890324) there is a striking wooden sculpture and two pubs; this is the best access point to the Slimbridge Wildfowl Trust (see page 77).

1 The Severn Estuary is rightly regarded as no place for the inexperienced inland boater. However, safe passage is perfectly feasible for craft properly prepared and equipped for a short sea voyage and with a crew familiar with these waters, or with a qualified Severn Pilot. Pilotage can be arranged by contacting Amalgamated Gloucester Pilots 07774 226143; www.gloucesterpilots.co.uk/services/leisure who are also an excellent source of guidance and advice. Safety Guidance Notes for Small Boat Passage of the Severn Estuary are available by sending a large SAE to: The Harbourmaster, Sharpness Port Authority, Sharpness Dock, Berkeley, Glos. GL13 9UD or by visiting www. gloucesterharbourtrustees.org.uk.

2 Once through the docks and onto the canal, remember that this is a commercial waterway; moor only at recognised sites: Old Arm, Sharpness; Purton Lower Bridge; Patch Bridge; Fretherne Bridge; Sandfield Bridge; Saul Junction Bridge; Sellars Bridge; Romans Quay; Bakers Quay; Gloucester Docks.

3 The mechanical swing bridges are manned as per the lock operating times on the River Severn (see Navigational Note 3, page 82). Last boat admitted *10 minutes before closing time*. Some bridges can be navigated, closed, by low air draught craft. All bridges are guarded by traffic lights and **under no circumstances** should you proceed without a green light.

4 Gloucester Lock and some bridge keepers operate a listening watch on marine band VHF channel 74. It is not necessary to contact each bridge or lock unless you are delayed, or have an emergency.

5 CRT insist on boats being licensed before entry to Sharpness Lock from the River Severn is permitted.

6 The canal is closed to navigation *on some days over Xmas and New Year.*

● **Sharpness**

Glos. PO, tel. Stores and garage distant. Sharpness exists only for its docks, old and new warehouses and ever-changing display of foreign ships. It has a strange atmosphere and an interesting situation beside the River Severn. The Severn is wide here, and wild: the tidal range at Sharpness is believed to be the third biggest in the world (only the Bay of Fundy, sandwiched between Nova Scotia and New Brunswick, and the Bay of Mont St Michel have a greater range) and the current is swift, especially when accompanied by the high winds that often race up the estuary from the sea. Across the water is the hilly Forest of Dean, with a main railway line running almost along the shore. It is only half a mile away, but it could as well be another country, so remote does it seem. In terms of population, Sharpness is very strung out; here and there is a row of terraced cottages, inhabited mainly by dock workers. Along the lockside – the focus of the docks – are the buildings housing the offices of various shipping firms and the British Waterways Harbourmaster (01453 310832). The annual tonnage currently handled here is approximately 600,000 tons, with cargoes consisting mainly of animal feedstuffs, grain, fertilisers, coal, cement and scrap metal, coming from Europe, the Mediterranean, North Africa and Scandinavia. Ships handled average 3,000 tons dead weight, with 5,000 tons being the maximum: the limiting dimensions of the entrance lock are 55ft beam by 21ft 6in draught. An interesting development at Sharpness is the privatisation of the dock's operation, which should result in a significantly increased traffic flow through the port. However, BW remain as the port authority. Traffic along the canal is now limited to approximately half a dozen shipping movements a year – a coaster collecting bulky distillation plant and water separation units from a manufacturer on the outskirts of Gloucester.

● **Purton**

Glos. Tel. A tiny village of lean, modest houses. It derives an unusual charm from being bisected by the Ship Canal. The canal is not particularly wide here, and to have a large coaster quietly throbbing past these diminutive dwellings seems an incredible distortion of scale. There used to be a ford for cattle across the river nearby – the herdsman had to judge the time to cross the treacherous river to within a few minutes. Just outside Purton, a huge waterworks has been built for the city of Bristol, where up to 24 million gallons of water can be drawn daily from the Ship Canal, purified and pumped through a 4ft pipeline down to Bristol for drinking purposes. Small reservoirs have been constructed on the other side of the canal: these will provide a temporary feed if and when a monitoring device beside the canal nearer Gloucester indicates that the water is too heavily polluted to draw on.

● **Shepherd's Patch**

Glos. This little settlement existed long before the canal: it used to be where the shepherds watched over their flocks grazing the Severn estuary. There is a pub here and youth hostel.

**Slimbridge Wildfowl and Wetland Trust
(WWT)** Shepherd's Patch, Slimbridge GL2 7BT
(01453 891900; www.wwt.org.uk; www.wwt.org.
uk/wetland-centres/slimbridge). Conveniently
situated just half a mile north west of the canal
at Patch Bridge, WWT Slimbridge is well worth
visiting. Close to the River Severn, apart from
containing the largest collection of captive
wildfowl in the world (182 species), the grounds
and adjacent reserve attract many thousands of
migrant birds – Bewick's Swans, White-fronted
Geese and all kinds of ducks and waders.
Visitors are able to walk around the grounds
and study and feed the inhabitants, which
are fascinating for their variety, quantity and
behaviour. WWT also incorporates an important
research establishment that studies all aspects
of wildfowl, with special reference to ecological
trends. It also plays an important role in the
defence of the various species from extinction
and can already be credited with the rescue of
several important species. Restaurant, gift, book
and children's shops, exhibitions and binocular

hire, children's activities. No dogs. *Open daily Apr-
Oct 09.30-17.30 & Nov-Mar 09.30-17.00 (except
Xmas day)*. Canoe Safari available *Easter-Sep
11.00-16.00 (and some winter weekends)* subject to
weather. Charge. Full disabled access including
wheelchair loan.

WALKING AND CYCLING

The towpath is passable for walkers and
cyclists along the Gloucester & Sharpness
Canal from Sharpness Old Arm to Llanthony
Bridge. North of Gloucester there is an
established footpath from Maisemore to
Tewkesbury on the west bank, and from
Gloucester to Tewkesbury (the Severn Way)
on the east bank. A length of the 128-mile
Gloucester, Bristol and Newbury section
of the National Cycle Network Route 41
uses the towpath between Slimbridge
and Frampton. Bicycles can be hired from
Slimbridge Boat Station (01453 899190).

Boatyards

Ⓑ**Sharpness Shipyard** Sharpness Docks GL13
9UD (01453 811261; www.sharpnessshipyard.com).
Overnight mooring, long-term mooring, winter
and long-term storage, crane (18 tons), engine
sales, DIY facilities, general marine engineering
facilities and electrical services.

Ⓑ**Sharpness Marina** Floating Yacht Services
Store, The Old Dock, Sharpness GL13 9UN (01453
811476; www.sharpnessmarina.co.uk). 🔧 **D**

Gas, overnight and long-term mooring, winter
storage, chandlery, boat building and fitting out,
charts, toilets, shower,laundrette, solid fuel.
Ⓑ**Slimbridge Boat Station** Shepherds Patch,
Slimbridge GL2 7BP (01453 899190). 🔧 Pump
out, gas, narrowboat hire, day boat hire, winter
storage, chandlery, maps, books, gifts, café, cycle
hire and spares, toilet.

Pubs and Restaurants (pages 74-75)

🍺 1 **The Pier View Hotel** 34 Oldminster Road,
Sharpness GL13 9NA (01453 811255). East of dock
area, in centre of village serving real ale and real
cider. Excellent food available *L and E (not Sun E)*.
Garden and traditional pub games. B&B. *Open
daily L and E.*

🍺✕ 2 **The Lammastide Inn** Old Brookend,
Berkeley GL13 9SF (01453 811337; www.
lammastideinn.co.uk). 1 mile east of Sharpness
at Old Brookend, near Berkeley. Comfortable,
welcoming pub dispensing a variety of real ales
and real cider. Also a wide range of good value
for money food *Tue-Sat L and E & Sun 12.00-
20.00*. Excellent *Sunday* roasts. Children and dogs
welcome. Large enclosed garden with swings and
climbing frame. *Open Mon-Fri L and E & Sat-Sun
12.00-00.00.*

🍺 3 **The Berkeley Arms** Purton, near Berkeley
GL13 9HU (01453 811262). 150yds from the lower
bridge. Situated beside the river with an excellent
view along it. This is a completely unspoilt,
no-nonsense rural pub, having all the appearance
of a private house. Real ale, good conversation and

absolutely no electronic intrusion. Real fires and
outside seating. *Open during the summer months
Mon-Sun 19.00-22.00 & Sat-Sun 12.00-14.00.*
The pub *is only open if the gate is open!*

🍺✕ 4 **The Tudor Arms** Shepherd's Patch,
Slimbridge GL2 7BP (01453 890306; www.
thetudorarms.co.uk). Large, country pub (once a
smallholding, then a beer and cider house for the
canal-constructing Irish navvies) serving real ales
and real cider. Food is available *daily 12.00-21.00*.
Dog- and child-friendly, garden. Traditional pub
games, newspapers and Wi-Fi. B&B. *Open Mon-
Fri 11.00-23.00 & Sun 12.00-22.30.*

🍺✕ 5 **The Black Shed** Shepherd's Patch,
Slimbridge GL2 7BP (01453 890609). Former
munitions hut, and now a listed building, this
friendly canalside café/bar/shop serves hot and
cold snacks and real ale. There is also a floating
pizza boat moored outside, together with craft
workshops inside. Newspapers and occasional
live music. Dogs welcome. Boat trips, cycle hire
and **D**. *Open daily 09.00-16.00 (Fri-Sat 23.30) but
check opening times.*

Saul Junction

The Ship Canal continues towards Gloucester, with the spacious Severn estuary over to the west. Swing bridges punctuate the canal and at almost every bridge is a bridge keeper's cottage (Cambridge Arms Bridge – 01453 890272, Junction Bridge – 01452 740444). These cottages are peculiar to the Gloucester & Sharpness Canal and have great charm – they are only small single-storey buildings, but each one has a substantial classical façade with fluted Doric columns and a pediment. At Cambridge Arms Bridge there is an unnavigable arm which feeds the canal with water from the Cotswolds. At Frampton on Severn the church is passed on the east side, then after a long straight the navigation bends to the north east. Trees encroach here on one side, and several bridges lead past scattered houses to Saul Junction where the Cotswold Canals Trust's Visitor Centre *provides information, complimentary refreshment, boat trips and a useful range of services including a laundry.* Over to the east the great Cotswold scarp marches parallel to the canal.

RIVER SEVERN (tidal)

CROWN POINT

Framilode Lock 13
Court Farm
76
Framilode Bridge
Baldwins
FRAMILODE
3
UPPER FRAMILODE
Saul Bridge
Moor Street Bridge
STROUDWATER NAVIGATION
Glebe Farm
Passage Road
Moor Street
SAUL
Junction Bridge
Square Covert
Stroudwater Lock 12 (dis)
Junction'l (Swing)
FRETHERNE WITH SAUL CP
CCT Visitor Centre
Farm
Whitminster House
Sandfield Bridge (Swing)
5
Marina
Malthouse Farm
M
Walk Bridge
Well
Oatfield
Whitminster Farm Bridge
Dunstalls Wood
Sewage Works
Dunstalls
Fretherne Bridge (Swing)
MS
B
Sch
12
Hock Ditch
Saul Lodge
P
2
Saul Warth
Manor Farm
PO
FRAMPTON ON SEVERN
The Green
FRAMPTON COURT
Works
12
1
Townfield Farm
CP Bdy
Mean High Water

10m 1L
Gloucester
Sharpness
6½m 0L

Splatt Bridge (Swing)
Frampton Pill
FRAMPTON BREAKWATER
CHURCH END
THE SPLATT
Oak Wood
Nebrow Hill
The M
Ryall's Farm
MIDDLE POINT BREAKWATER
9
WILDFOWL AND WETLANDS TRUST
Underpass
SLIMBRIDGE CP
Cambridge Arms Bridge (Swing)
75
Cambridge Arm (unnavigable feeder)
Severn Way
THE GLOUCESTER AND SHARPNESS CANAL

WALKING AND CYCLING

An excellent circular walk, starting at Saul Junction, takes you along the footpath following the River Frome to Framilode. Thence via the minor road to Epney, turning right to Parkend Bridge, before returning along the Canal towpath. Highly regarded hostelries mark two out of the three turning points!

See also **Walking and Cycling** on page 158 – Stroudwater Navigation

BOAT TRIPS

The Cotswold Canals Trust (www. cotswoldcanals.com) run two trip boats on this side of the Cotswolds: *nb Endeavour* from Saul Junction (01453 752568) and *nb Perseverance* from the Operations Wharf, on the towpath side of the canal, just west of Ebley Cloth Mills Bridge. *Nb Perseverance* operates *Apr-Sep, Sun & B Hol Mon 12.00-16.30* and *nb Endeavour* operates *Apr-Sep, Sat throughout the year 12.00-16.30*. No booking is required for public trips. Both craft can be booked *throughout the year* for private charter *on those days when not allocated* for public trips by telephoning 01453 752568.

Boatyards

ⒷACP Fuels Ltd Frampton on Severn Industrial Park, Bridge Road, Frampton on Severn GL2 7HE (01452 741821; www. johnstonfuels.co.uk). **D** Gas.

ⒷR.W. Davis & Son Junction Dry Dock, Saul GL2 7LA (01452 740233; www. rwdavis.co.uk). Long-term mooring, winter storage, crane (10 tons), dry dock, boat building and fitting out, boat and engine sales and repairs (including wooden boat repairs), shot blasting, foam insulation spraying, modest chandlery stocking nautical antiques, solid fuel nearby.

ⒷSaul Junction Marina Church Lane, Frampton on Severn GL2 7JY (01452 740043; www.saulmarina.co.uk). 🛆🛆🪣🛆**D** Pump-out, gas, slipway, boat sales, chandlery, coal, wood, launderette, toilets, showers, CRT licences, Wi-Fi.

● **Cotswold Canals Trust Visitor Centre** The Canal Towpath, Church Lane, Saul GL2 7LA (07854 026504; www.cotswoldcanals.com). A mine of information on all things to do with the ambitious restoration project that sits under the Cotswold Canals umbrella. Find out more about the Phased approach to breathing new life into the Stroudwater Navigation and the Thames & Severn Canal, and see where current progress has reached. Complimentary tea, coffee, hot chocolate and Severn Bore timetables. Children actively engaged and outside seating. Toilets and showers. Shop selling ice cream, soft drinks, confectionary, books, maps and gifts. *Open summer, Sat 12.30-17.00; Sun and B Hols 10.00-17.00 & winter Sat, Sun and B Hols 12.30-16.00 and whenever the green flag is flying.* Also pump-out cards, Watermate keys and laundry tokens for sale.

● **Frampton on Severn**
Glos. PO, tel, stores, garage. A beautiful linear village notable mainly for its green, which is about 100yds wide and fully half a mile long. The Church of St Mary at the south end of the village, near the canal, is mainly of the 14th C. Shop and PO *open daily 07.00-19.00 (Sun 17.00).*
Frampton Court Frampton on Severn GL2 7EP (01452 740268; www.framptoncourtestate.co.uk/tours. htm). This Grade I listed Georgian Mansion (1731-3) set in its 1500 acre estate, faces the village green and has attractive gardens, a Gothic orangery (1745) and an octagonal dovecote. Tours, by appointment only, can be arranged for groups of 10 or more.

BOAT TRIPS
The Willow Trust 11A Whiteway Court, Whiteway Farmhouse, Cirencester GL7 7BA (01285 651661; www.willowtrust.org). The Trust, a charitable organisation founded in 1989, operates 2 purpose-built boats (carrying up to 30 people) from Saul Junction (GL2 7LA) for seriously ill and disabled children and adults giving them the opportunity to enjoy a day afloat totally free of charge. Telephone or visit the website for further details.

Pubs and Restaurants

🍺✕ 1 **The Three Horseshoes** The Green Avenue, Frampton on Severn GL2 7DY (01452 742100; www.threehorseshoespub.co.uk). Real village pub dispensing real ale and cider and serving food *L and E*. Children and dogs welcome, outside seating and boules. *Regular* live music, traditional pub games, newspapers and real fires. *Open Mon-Fri L and E & Sat-Sun 11.30-01.00 (Sun 22.00).*

🍺✕ 2 **The Bell Inn** The Green, Frampton on Severn GL2 7EP (01452 740346; www.thebellatframpton. co.uk). Village inn offering warmth and hospitality beside the longest village green in England, together with an excellent selection of real ales and regional ciders. Home-cooked English country food using local produce served *L and E*. Children and dogs welcome in prescribed areas. Traditional pub games and real fires. B&B. *Open L and E.*

🍺✕ 3 **The Ship Inn** Framilode, Saul GL2 7LH (01452 740260; www.shipinnframilode.co.uk). An easy walk west from Saul Junction, along the bed of the Stroudwater Navigation, beside the River Frome. An excellent hostelry serving real ales, together with an interesting selection of food *L and E*. Large garden with children's play area. Traditional pub games and real fires. B&B. *Open Tue-Sat L and E (not Tue L) & Sun 12.00-19.00.*

🍺 4 **The Anchor** Epney GL2 7LN 01452 740433). Beside the River Severn, dispensing real ales and good food *daily L and E* – homemade pies a speciality. Children welcome inside, dogs outside on a chain. Large garden. Very busy *in the summer. Open daily L and E.*

✕ 5 **The Stables Café** Sandfield Bridge, Canal Bank, Saul GL2 7LA (01452 741965; www. thestablescafe.co.uk). Once a stables catering for canal horses, this establishment now serves breakfasts *until 11.30*; lunches using fresh, locally sourced ingredients and a selection of homemade cakes, tea and coffee. Children welcome. Garden and terrace. *Open daily 09.00-16.30 (Sat & Sun 17.00).*

See also **Pubs and Restaurants** on page 158 – Stroudwater Navigation

Hardwicke

Heading more or less north from Parkend, the canal continues through undramatic country, which is slightly wooded. There are no villages on this section, but several farms are situated near the canal. Towards Sellars Bridge (01452 720251), the navigation enters a cutting for the first time since Sharpness. There is a *pub* by this bridge, and just to the north is a disused oil wharf for small ships. This was the furthest (northernmost) point which the oil traffic reached on the navigation once carrying had ceased on the river – originally as far as Stourport in barges – but this is all finished now. North of Quedgeley Wharf the canal approaches the River Severn (hidden behind a flood bank and far narrower up here than downstream); turning sharply eastward, the canal reaches Rea Bridge.

NAVIGATIONAL NOTES

The three bridges, Sellars, Rea and Sims have a greater headroom (over 7ft) than the others on the Gloucester & Sharpness Canal. Boats normally used on the narrow canals will find no difficulty in getting under these bridges without them being opened, although they do o at their own risk. Boats *should not* pass under these bridges without receiving a green light from the keeper.

Boatyards

Ⓑ**A & D Marine Services** Hempsted Dry Dock, 338 Bristol Road, Gloucester GL2 5DH (415430/07540 383150; www.admarineservices.co.uk). Boat sales and repairs, engine sales and repairs (inboard and outboard), dry dock, mechanical and electrical engineering, fabrication and welding, hull coatings, DIY facilities, extensive chandlery, books and maps. *Open Mon-Fri 09.00-17.30 & Sat 09.00-13.00.*

Pubs and Restaurants

🍺 1 **The Pilot Inn** Sellars Road, Hardwicke GL2 4QD (01452 720252; www.pilotinn.com). Canalside, at Sellars Bridge, Hardwicke. Traditional pub serving meals *L and E*. Real ales. Nooks, crannies and open fires. Children welcome; dogs in garden only. Garden with excellent view overlooking the ship canal. *Regular* live music. *Open daily 11.30-23.00.*

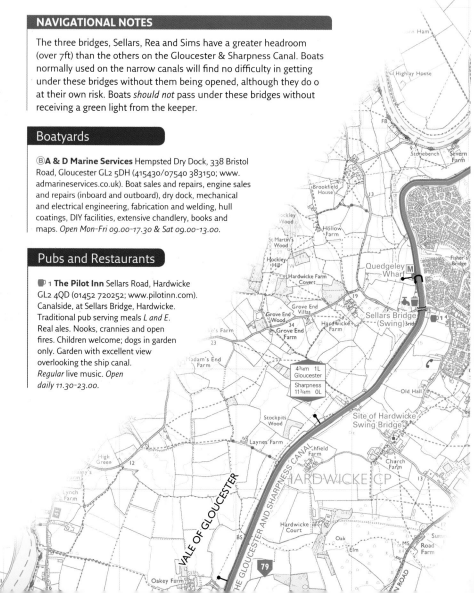

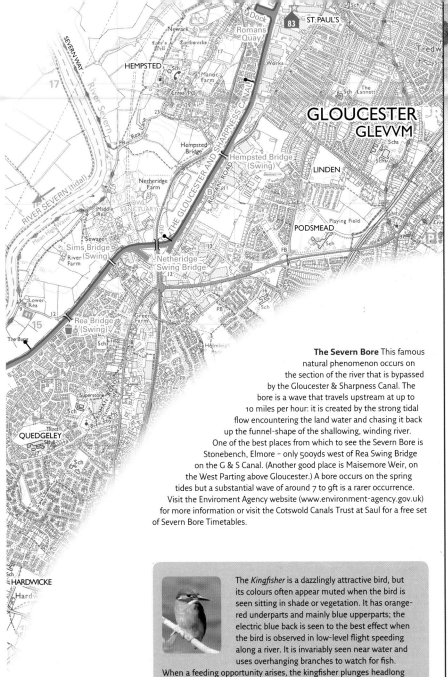

GLOUCESTER
GLEVVM

The Severn Bore This famous natural phenomenon occurs on the section of the river that is bypassed by the Gloucester & Sharpness Canal. The bore is a wave that travels upstream at up to 10 miles per hour: it is created by the strong tidal flow encountering the land water and chasing it back up the funnel-shape of the shallowing, winding river. One of the best places from which to see the Severn Bore is Stonebench, Elmore – only 500yds west of Rea Swing Bridge on the G & S Canal. (Another good place is Maisemore Weir, on the West Parting above Gloucester.) A bore occurs on the spring tides but a substantial wave of around 7 to 9ft is a rarer occurrence. Visit the Enviroment Agency website (www.environment-agency.gov.uk) for more information or visit the Cotswold Canals Trust at Saul for a free set of Severn Bore Timetables.

The *Kingfisher* is a dazzlingly attractive bird, but its colours often appear muted when the bird is seen sitting in shade or vegetation. It has orange-red underparts and mainly blue upperparts; the electric blue back is seen to the best effect when the bird is observed in low-level flight speeding along a river. It is invariably seen near water and uses overhanging branches to watch for fish. When a feeding opportunity arises, the kingfisher plunges headlong into the water, catching its prey in its bill: the fish is swallowed whole. Kingfishers nest in holes excavated in the river bank.

81

▌Gloucester

At Rea Bridge the canal enters a cutting and at Sims Bridge describes a sharp double bend soon to pass under the new Netheridge swing bridge, from which one emerges into a completely different landscape: the quiet countryside has disappeared, its place taken by a mix of industrial works and new residential development. The Ship Canal, strangely enough, has never played a large part in the generation of wealth that this industry represents, but north of Hempsted Bridge (01452 521880) there was a large timber wharf for discharging ships bringing imported wood. Further north there was an oil dock, a grain silo and a general cargo quay. Ahead is Gloucester, and the extensive docks that are laid out virtually in the town centre. These are superb docks, for all around are great warehouses ranged along the quays. Boatmen wishing to moor here – the best place for visiting Gloucester – should go to the office by the lock and seek advice from the CRT lock keeper. Gloucester Lock (VHF channel 74 or 01452 310832) marks the northern end of the Gloucester & Sharpness Canal, and lowers boats back into the River Severn, reminding one that the ship canal is well above the river level. It has to be kept filled with water by pumping up from the river. No boats should follow the river to the south west at the tail of Gloucester Lock, for Llanthony Lock is closed and only a weir awaits them. North of Gloucester Lock, the river is bounded on the town side by a high quay, with moorings more suitable for larger vessels than for motor cruisers. Gloucester gaol was nearby. Proceeding upstream, boatmen will find themselves on a dull length of river, narrow and hemmed in by high banks. A sharp bend requires a careful lookout; beyond it are road and rail bridges. The river winds along in its own isolated way, flanked mainly by trees. At one point it approaches a minor road; the former pub here is now a private house. Further upstream is the junction with the big western channel of the Severn, whose separate course between here and Gloucester explains the narrowness of the navigation channel. There is in fact a lock (Maisemore Lock, now closed) just 300yds along the western channel of the Severn. This is a relic of the days before the Ship Canal was built; it used to give access from the upper Severn to the Herefordshire & Gloucestershire Canal (now undergoing restoration, *see* page 104), which joined the Severn near Gloucester.

NAVIGATIONAL NOTES

1   Gloucester Lock Bridge, Hempsted Bridge and Llanthony Bridge (01452 312143) will not be opened for pleasure craft during peak road traffic flows *08.20–09.00 and 16.30–17.30*. This does not apply to *weekends and B Hols.*
2   As with all river navigations, the Severn must be treated with respect, especially after periods of prolonged rain, when the current increases. If you are in any doubt regarding your safety on the river, moor up out of the main stream and seek expert advice.
3   All locks on the River Severn are manned. They are open: *Nov–Mar 08.00–16.00; Apr, May & Oct 08.00–18.00; Jun–Sep 08.00–19.00. Last boat admitted 15 mins before lock closes. These dates are approximate and can vary from year to year.* Contact Gloucester Lock (VHF channel 74 or 01452 310832) for further details. Do not enter a lock unless the green light is showing.
4   Boaters are strongly advised to radio or telephone Gloucester Lock when heading downstream approaching the Upper Parting so that i) the lock can be made ready for them if available and ii) they can be advised of any large vessels that they may encounter in the somewhat narrow East Channel.
5   When approaching Gloucester Docks downstream on the River Severn slow right down and take extreme care especially if the current is flowing strongly. Tie up to the chains fitted along the quay with your stern rope first.
6   Gloucester Docks is a *48hr* visitor mooring only. Safety ladders must not be obstructed by moored craft at any time.

BOAT TRIPS

Gloucester Narrowboats
Gloucester Docks, Gloucester
GL1 2DN (07774 464555; www.
gloucesternarrowboats.co.uk).
Day- and holiday-hire narrowboats
available *Mar–Oct*. 45-min boat
trips and pre-booked tea cruises.
Open daily 09.00–17.00. Also BSC
examiner.

Gloucester Leisure Cruises
Gloucester Waterways Museum,
Llanthony Warehouse, The Docks,
Gloucester GL1 2EH (01452
318200; www.gloucesterwater
waysmuseum.org.uk). Boat trips
and boat hire. *Boadicea II*, one of
the Little Ships of Dunkirk, offers
45-minute cruises, Easter–Oct, on
the Gloucester & Sharpness Canal.
King Arthur, with her panoramic
saloon, offers longer scheduled
cruises (canal/river) throughout
the year; available also for private
charter. Both vessels have toilet
and commentary facilities.
Departures from Merchants Quay,
Gloucester Docks *12.00* & *13.30*.

Boatyards

Ⓑ **T. Nielsen & Co** The
Shipyard, Gloucester
Docks, Gloucester
GL1 2EH (01452 301117;
www.tnielsen.co.uk).
Winter storage, crane
(9 ton), boat repairs
(specialising in wooden
boats), boat building and
fitting out, dry dock (170ft).
Ⓑ **Victoria Basin
Moorings** The Docks,
Gloucester GL1 2LG (01225
424301; www.bwml.co.uk/
marinas/victoria_basin).
🏠🚿E. Short- and
long-term moorings

Map labels

Long Reach
86
Mussel End
SANDHURST
Singleton Farm
Tarrent
The Reddin
Gardiner's Farm
Home Farm
Maisemore Park
SEVERN WAY
MAISEMORE CP
Maisemore Weir
(limit of tideway
except Spring tides)
Weir
Maisemore
Lock (dis)
MAISEMORE
UPPER PARTING
Abloads Court
Gloucester
Broadboard Brook
LONGFORD
Queen's Dyke
Longford
River Severn
(East Channel)
NTL
Maisemore
Bridge
Cross
Three Choirs
Way
MAISEMORE HAM
82
45
Channel
Walham
A 40
Hotel
Hospl
Frogcastle
Farm
Vale of Gloucester
Persh Farm
River Severn – tidal
We (West Channel)
River Leadon
81
20
Wye
(site of)
ALNEY ISLAND
Walham Bridge
River Twyver
Start of Herefordshire and
Gloucestershire Canal
(Under Restoration)
See Page 104
Site of Over Basin
and Lock
Over Bridge
8
Pope's Pool Cottages
Telford's Bridge
OVER
MS
W 14
Viaduct
TOWN HAM
Black Bridge
St Oswalds Park
KINGSHOLM
Works
Schs
14m 1L
Tewkesbury
POOL MEADOW
PORT HAM
Sharpness
16½m 1L
hard's
Westgate
Bridges
LOWER PARTING
Electricity
Tr OXLEASE
Station
Oxlease
MUS
CATH
Shire Hall
STA
7
9
GLOUCESTER DOCKS
COMMERCIAL ROAD
WEST QUAY
Main Basin
Victoria Basin
Long Term Moorings
Automatic Pumps
Keep Clear
River Severn
Lint
Far
M
M
B
M
Barge Arm
National Waterways
Museum
BAKERS QUAY
LLANTHONY ROAD
Gloucester & Sharpness Canal
CASTLE and
MEADS serve
Castle
Meads
Meadow
CATH
HM Prison
MUS
MUS
Gloucester Lock
Gloucester Lock
Bridge
Docks
5
4
6
Llanthony Pontoons
Sanitary station and pumpout,
toilets and showers.
CRT permanent and Visitor pontoon moorings
(limit of tideway
except Spring tides)
PRIORY
(REMS OF)
(rems of)
High Orchard
Gloucester
Quays
Llanthony Bascule Bridge
The Park
10
High Orchard Bridge
Superst
FB
Newark
81
Dock
Romans Quay
ST. PAUL'S

GLOUCESTER 83

Gloucester

Glos. All services. Now a busy manufacturing town and commercial centre, Gloucester was once the Roman colony of Glevum. The town was laid out in a cross plan, with north, south, east and west gates. This geography still survives, if only in name. Traces of Roman habitation are much more difficult to find than in other Roman towns in Britain, but when the Bell Hotel was being demolished in recent years, excavations revealed 1000 sq ft of paved courtyard, believed to be the site of the Roman forum. There are a few interesting old buildings in the town centre, notably the 12th-C Fleece Hotel and numbers 11–15 Southgate, but otherwise the town centre is of less interest than one might expect. However the glorious cathedral provides an oasis of peace and beauty in the town. The other area of real interest is the docks; many of the splendid warehouses only just escaped demolition in a less enlightened time.

Bus Enquiries (01452 418630; www.travelinesw.com).
Cathedral College Green, Gloucester GL1 2LX (01452 528095; www.gloucestercathedral.org.uk). Founded as an abbey in 1089 by Abbot Serlo, this splendid building is essentially Norman, but extensive remodelling of the choir and transepts between 1330 and 1370 shows fine examples of early Perpendicular architecture. But perhaps the most interesting part of the present building is the adjacent cloisters: they feature the earliest known fan-vaulting (mid-14th C). Coffee shop and guided tours.
City Museum & Art Gallery Brunswick Road GL1 1HP (01452 396131; www.gloucester.gov.uk). Exhibits of furniture, glass, silver, costumes and coins; also local archaeology, geology and natural history. *Open all year, Tue–Sat 10.00–17.00.* Charge. Joint ticket with Folk Museum available.
Dean Forest Railway Forest Road, Lydney GL15 4ET (01594 845840; 24 hr information line 01594 843423; www.deanforestrailway.co.uk). A living memory in steam of all those branch lines that used to serve small local communities and currently open for 4½ miles between Lydney (mainline connection) and Parkend. Cafés and shops. The railway operates a mix of steam and diesel traction *throughout the year.* Telephone or visit website for more information.
Eastgate Viewing Chamber Eastgate, Gloucester GL1 1PU (01452 396131; www.thecityofgloucester.co.uk). Access to the medieval east gate of the city and original city walls. *Open for pre-booked tours (via the Museum) Apr–Sep Sat.* Charge.
Gloucester Docks These extensive docks close to the centre of Gloucester are, to many people, really much more interesting than the town itself. They are at the north end of the Gloucester & Sharpness Ship Canal, where it locks down into the Severn, and were built around 1827. Imported timber and grain are two of the main cargoes that used to be brought up here – they arrived mostly in big barges from ports down the Bristol Channel. The seven-storey dock warehouses are magnificent. For details of guided walks – to both the Docks and the City – visit www.thecityofgloucester. co.uk/things-to-do/walks-and-tours or download the

App via www.thecityofgloucester.co.uk/things-to-do/ gloucester-walking-tours-app-p1990243.
Gloucester Life Museum 99-103 Westgate Street GL1 2PG (01452 396868; www.gloucester.gov.uk). Fine collection of local history and bygones: there is a whole section on the River Severn, its vessels and the salmon and eel fishing industries that it once supported. Also schoolroom, shoemaker's, carpenter's and wheelwright's workshops. Dairy, toys and games and model steam engines. *Opening as for City Museum & Art Gallery.* Charge. Joint pass with City Museum available.
Gloucester Waterways Museum Llanthony Warehouse, The Docks, Gloucester GL1 2EH (0303 040 4040; www.canalrivertrust.org.uk/gloucester-waterways-museum). Journey the waterways of Britain. Unravel the 200-year story of inland waterways through touch, working models and archive film. Board historic boats moored at the two quaysides. Specialist book/gift shop stocked with traditional Roses & Castles painted ware. *Open daily throughout year, 11.00–16.00 (Jul–Aug 10.30–17.00. Last admission 1 hour before closing.* Charge. Joint ticket for museum and boat trip.
Guildhall Arts Centre 23 Eastgate Street, Gloucester GL1 1NS (01452 503050; venues.gloucester.gov.uk/ freetime/guildhall). Lively, friendly venue for an imaginative range of theatre, music, dance, films and visual arts. Licensed bar and snacks.
House of The Tailor of Gloucester 9 College Court, Gloucester GL1 2NJ (01452 422856; www. thecityofgloucester.co.uk/things-to-do/beatrix-potters-house-of-the-tailor-of-gloucester-p136633). Tiny shop and museum in the home that Beatrix Potter chose for her tailor in the famous story *The Tailor of Gloucester. Open Mon–Sat 10.00-16.30 & Sun 12.00-16.00.* Free (donations appreciated).
Jet Age Museum Meteor Business Park, Cheltenham Road East, Gloucester GL2 9QL (01452 260078; www. jetagemuseum.org). Home to a unique collection of historic aircraft and artefacts charting the history of Gloucestershire's rich aviation heritage. Café, shop and play plane. *Open Sat-Sun & B Hols 10.00-16.00. Also Wed during school Hols.* Free. (donations appreciated).
Nature in Art Wallsworth Hall, Twigworth, Gloucester GL2 9PA (01452 731422; www.thecityofgloucester.co. uk/things-to-do/nature-in-art-p139873). On the main A38. Dedicated to all forms of art – from any period, in any medium – inspired by nature. A grand diversity of artists and a collection that is continually changing and developing. Gift shop and coffee shop serving home-made snacks, meals and drinks. *Open Tue–Sun and B Hol Mon 10.00-17.00. Closed 24-26 Dec.* Charge. Bus service to the entrance gate then ½ mile walk.
Soldiers of Gloucestershire Gloucester Docks, Gloucester GL1 2HE 01452 522682; www. soldiersofglos.com). The story of Gloucestershire's two regiments told with photographs, reconstructed scenes and displays of uniforms, medals, etc. An altogether more lively experience than many of its ilk. Teashop and gift shop. *Open daily 10.00-17.00 (closed over Xmas period).* Charge.

Tourist Information Centre
28 Southgate Street Gloucester (01452 396572; www.thecityofgloucester.co.uk/explore/tourist-information-centre). *Open Mon-Sat 09.30-17.00 (Sun 10.00)*.
The Wharf House Over Canal Basin, Over, Gloucester GL2 8DB (01452 332900; www.thewharfhouse.co.uk). Opposite Telford's Bridge, on the West Severn Channel. This is the culmination of the largest all-volunteer canal restoration project in the UK in 2000 when the original basin – connecting the Herefordshire and

Gloucester Canal with the River Severn – was re-discovered, excavated and returned to water. Subsequently this replacement Wharf House has been built and the shell fitted out, again, almost entirely by volunteer labour to provide a Visitor Centre that explores 750 years of the Leadon Valley including the Roman Vineyards, Civil War, willow growing and basketry, to the ongoing restoration of the Canal. Tearooms, restaurant and shop promoting the talents of local artists and crafts people. *Open daily 10.00-17.00*. Free. B&B. For further details of restoration progress visit www.h-g-canal.org.uk.

Pubs and Restaurants (pages 83)

✗ 1 **Café on the Cut** The Barge Arm, Gloucester Docks, Gloucester GL1 2DN (07914 172610; cafeonthecut.co.uk). Experience breakfast and lunch, or tea and cake, inside a narrowboat. A unique, friendly and cosy meeting place serving free-range foods and scrummy cakes. This eclectic café serves locally sourced foods and runs on solar energy. Tapas nights and high teas: bookings taken for 5-11 people. Mediterranean meze in summer, nourishing hot food in winter – everything from a quiche to a cassoulet! Vegetarian, gluten-free and vegan options; allergies and food intolerances catered for. *Open Wed-Mon 10.30-17.00 & winter Wed-Sun. Also B Hols and festivals*.

🍺 2 **The Dick Whittington** 100 Westgate Street, Gloucester GL1 2PE (01452 502039; www.thedickwhittington.co.uk). Ancient hostelry commemorating the city's most famous son serving real ales and food *Mon-Sat 12.00-21.00; Sun L and E*. Beer garden, dog-friendly and Wi-Fi. *Open Mon-Sat 11.00-00.00 (Fri-Sat 02.00) & Sun 12.00-23.00*.

🍺✗ 3 **The Linden Tree** 73-75 Bristol Road, Gloucester, GL1 5SN (01452 527869; www.lindentreegloucester.co.uk). A warm, welcoming and homely community pub serving real ales and generous portions of homemade food *Mon E, Tue-Fri L and E & Sat-Sun L*. Children welcome, outside seating. Traditional pub games, real fires and Wi-Fi. B&B. *Open Mon E, Tue-Thu L and E, Fri-Sat 11.30-23.30 & Sun 12.00-23.00*.

🍺 4 **The Tall Ship** 134 Southgate Street, Gloucester GL1 2EX (01452 522793). Real ale, light meals and seafood specials. Student and *L* seafood specials. Beer garden, family-friendly and traditional pub games. *Open 11.00-23.00*.

✗🍷 5 **Topoly's** 49 Southgate Street, Gloucester GL1 1TX (01452 331062; www.topolys.co.uk). Good value Italian food served in a friendly, family-run, welcoming restaurant close to the docks. All your favourite Italian dishes free from the chain-run, fast food format. *Open daily L and E* (booking advisable *E*).

🍺 6 **The Whitesmiths Arms** 81 Southgate Street, Gloucester GL1 1UR (01452 312947). Traditional pub dispensing real ales and named after nautical metalworkers. Food available *Mon-Fri*. Family-friendly, large garden. Real fires and traditional pub games. *Open 11.00-23.00*.

🍺✗ 7 **The New Inn Hotel** 16 Northgate Street, Gloucester GL1 1SF (01452 522177). Fine old Grade I listed building that has been restored as a superb example of a medieval, galleried inn. A restaurant, coffee shop and three bars surround the cobbled courtyard and real ales are available, together with real cider. Food is served *L and E*. Children welcome, outside seating and pub games. B&B. *Open 11.00-23.00*.

✗ 8 **The Wharf House Over** Gloucester GL2 8DB (01452 332900; www.thewharfhouse.co.uk). Well worth making the effort to visit and enjoy the newly restored canal basin, an exciting daytime and evening restaurant menu prepared from fresh local produce and the Visitor Centre which explores 750 years of history in the Leadon Valley. Everything from salads and sandwiches to a 3-course lunch or mouth- watering evening meal. Children welcome. Tea rooms *open daily 10.00-17.00* & restaurant *(prior booking only) open 19.30-last orders 21.30*. B&B.

Also try: 🍺 9 **The Regal** 33 St Aldate Street, Gloucester GL1 1RP (01452 332344; www. jdwetherspoon.com/pubs/all-pubs/england/gloucestershire/the-regal-gloucester) and 🍺 10 **The Nelson Inn** 166 Southgate Street, Gloucester GL1 2EX (01452 307398).

Haw Bridge

Leaving the junction (known as the Upper Parting) of the east and west channels of the River Severn, from this point northwards the river is predictably wider. Its character changes very little in all its journey to Stourport – most of the way it is lined by trees and high banks. The surrounding countryside is quite pretty but because of the banks, the boater will see little except for the occasional hills. The walker along the banks is luckier in having good views of the river and the surrounding countryside. Away from the centre the river is often extremely shallow; there are anyway limited mooring places, so access to the villages on either side is restricted. After a series of long reaches, the spire of Ashleworth Church appears on the left side as the river bends to the east towards the hills that rise steeply from the river bank. There are visitor *moorings* on the west bank, just upstream of the *pub*. The main hill here is Wainlode Hill, which reaches a height of almost 300ft. The silted-up lock on the east bank is the entrance to the former Coombe Hill Canal, now partly restored, but land-locked. The modern bridge to the north is Haw Bridge. There are *pubs* and visitor *moorings* on the west bank, downstream of the bridge. Navigators should keep away from the east bank near this bridge – there is a submerged obstruction. The river winds through an S-bend, passing a riverside pub and a line of hills to the east; then it straightens out somewhat as it heads for Tewkesbury. Yet another riverside *pub*, the Yew Tree Inn, is passed – a half-sunk barge serves as a mooring. A sailing club is based here. Opposite is Odda's Chapel, but access is difficult because of the rocky banks.

NAVIGATIONAL NOTES

Because of Wainlode Hill's susceptibility to erosion by the river, old barges have been sunk in the river near the south east bank, in order to protect it. All boats should keep to the north side of the river to avoid the hulks. The area is marked by posts.

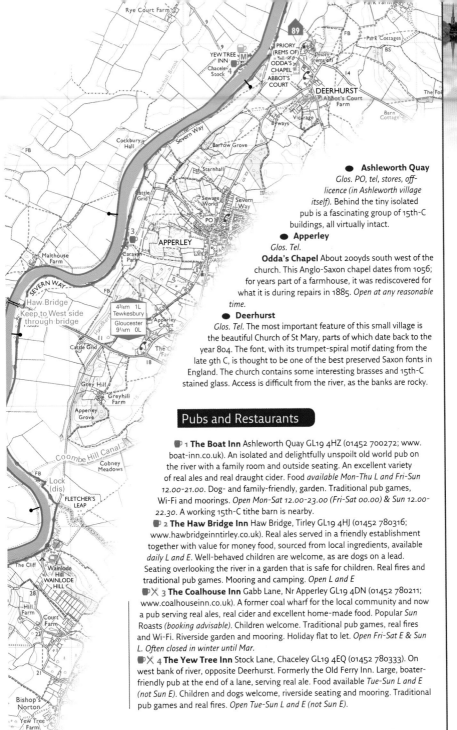

● **Ashleworth Quay**
*Glos. PO, tel, stores, off-
licence (in Ashleworth village
itself).* Behind the tiny isolated
pub is a fascinating group of 15th-C
buildings, all virtually intact.

● **Apperley**
Glos. Tel.
Odda's Chapel About 200yds south west of the
church. This Anglo-Saxon chapel dates from 1056;
for years part of a farmhouse, it was rediscovered for
what it is during repairs in 1885. *Open at any reasonable
time.*

● **Deerhurst**
Glos. Tel. The most important feature of this small village is
the beautiful Church of St Mary, parts of which date back to the
year 804. The font, with its trumpet-spiral motif dating from the
late 9th C, is thought to be one of the best preserved Saxon fonts in
England. The church contains some interesting brasses and 15th-C
stained glass. Access is difficult from the river, as the banks are rocky.

Pubs and Restaurants

📖 1 **The Boat Inn** Ashleworth Quay GL19 4HZ (01452 700272; www.
boat-inn.co.uk). An isolated and delightfully unspoilt old world pub on
the river with a family room and outside seating. An excellent variety
of real ales and real draught cider. Food *available Mon-Thu L and Fri-Sun
12.00-21.00.* Dog- and family-friendly, garden. Traditional pub games,
Wi-Fi and moorings. *Open Mon-Sat 12.00-23.00 (Fri-Sat 00.00) & Sun 12.00-
22.30.* A working 15th-C tithe barn is nearby.

📖 2 **The Haw Bridge Inn** Haw Bridge, Tirley GL19 4HJ (01452 780316;
www.hawbridgeinntirley.co.uk). Real ales served in a friendly establishment
together with value for money food, sourced from local ingredients, available
daily L and E. Well-behaved children are welcome, as are dogs on a lead.
Seating overlooking the river in a garden that is safe for children. Real fires and
traditional pub games. Mooring and camping. *Open L and E*

📖✕ 3 **The Coalhouse Inn** Gabb Lane, Nr Apperley GL19 4DN (01452 780211;
www.coalhouseinn.co.uk). A former coal wharf for the local community and now
a pub serving real ales, real cider and excellent home-made food. Popular *Sun*
Roasts *(booking advisable).* Children welcome. Traditional pub games, real fires
and Wi-Fi. Riverside garden and mooring. Holiday flat to let. *Open Fri-Sat E & Sun
L. Often closed in winter until Mar.*

📖✕ 4 **The Yew Tree Inn** Stock Lane, Chaceley GL19 4EQ (01452 780333). On
west bank of river, opposite Deerhurst. Formerly the Old Ferry Inn. Large, boater-
friendly pub at the end of a lane, serving real ale. Food available *Tue-Sun L and E
(not Sun E).* Children and dogs welcome, riverside seating and mooring. Traditional
pub games and real fires. *Open Tue-Sun L and E (not Sun E).*

Mythe Bridge

The river now passes another *pub* with excellent CRT visitor *moorings*. One of the two channels of the Warwickshire Avon enters here from Tewkesbury: the Battle of Tewkesbury was fought just to the east of here in 1471. Marked by the abbey, Tewkesbury can be seen to the north east, but the Severn sweeps round to the west of the town, leaving an enormous expanse of flat, empty meadow between them. Upper Lode Lock (01684 293138) is well concealed on a corner between the weir and a backwater. (The weir is, incidentally, the highest point to which normal spring tides flow.) Upstream of the lock is a junction with the main (navigable) course of the River Avon – boats heading for the Lower and Upper Avon navigations should turn east here, as should boats intending to visit Tewkesbury. Beware of the shallow spit projecting south west from the tip of the of the junction – see Navigational Notes on page 17. Continuing up the Severn, one reaches the single 170ft-span of the cast iron Mythe Bridge over the river, built by Thomas Telford in 1828. Steep wooded hills rise on the east bank by this bridge, but the river bears off to the north west and soon leaves them behind. Its character remains virtually unchanged – it is lined by high banks and trees, untouched by villages or towns, and seemingly isolated from the countryside that its wide course divides so effectively.

THE RIVER AVON IN TEWKESBURY It is certainly worth turning off the Severn into the River Avon – this is the way to Tewkesbury, Evesham and Stratford-upon-Avon. Boaters not wishing to buy the short-term pass on to the Lower Avon Navigation may tie up just below the old Healing's Flour Mill to visit Tewkesbury (charge), but those who decide to go through the pretty Avon Lock (operated by a lock keeper – 01684 292129) will find it a worthwhile diversion. *See* page 18 and the River Avon section for all details and boatyard services in the town.

SEVERAL SEVERN CROSSINGS

For thousands of years the river has been a barrier to communication. It has served both as a defence, keeping one marauding horde from the throats of another, and as a bar to pedestrian and road communication. Initially it was crossed via fords – or lodes as they were known locally – and by using tree trunks supported by stones on some of the upper, shallower reaches.

The first records of bridge building date from the 13th C when a flurry of fine structures, mainly of stone, were constructed in the pursuit of commerce. None have survived the vagaries of flood, war and the ravages of time. The most famous surviving bridge is at Coalbrookdale where Darby, a successful local ironmaster, built Ironbridge – opened in 1781 – to a design by Thomas Pritchard. Thomas Telford was responsible for many of the existing major crossings including Holt Fleet, Mythe and Over – just to the west of Gloucester – and now disused. Further upstream he constructed the cast iron Haw Bridge, inadvertently demolished by an oil barge in December 1958 when the river was in spate. Two other cast iron bridges, at Arley and Coalbrookdale, were built by John Fowler in the mid-19th C.

Spanning the non-tidal Severn, the more modern crossings are no more than utilitarian concrete affairs lacking the beauty and grace of their forebears but with one exception: Upton Bridge. This steel cantilever design, with a main span of 200' soaring gracefully over the river, was built by Worcester C.C. in 1940 and represents one of the last rivetted constructions to be built in England. It replaced an 1854 swing bridge sited approximately 100 yards downstream. Below Gloucester, the two tidal Severn crossings are not without style and an element of daring, although it is the aviator rather than the boater, who is best placed to appreciate their aesthetic appeal.

Pubs and Restaurants

▶✕ 1 **The Lower Lode** Forthampton GL19 4RE (01684 293224; www.lowerlodeinn.co.uk). 3/4 mile below Upper Lode Lock. 15th-C inn with excellent CRT visitor moorings close by. This pub, in a delightful riverside setting, dispenses a selection of real ales and bar snacks. The informal restaurant serving meals *L* and *E*, daily. Children welcome *until 21.00*; well-behaved dogs at all times. Food is available *all day during the summer* as are morning coffee and afternoon cream teas. Riverside gardens and slipway. Camping and day fishing. Tradition pub games and real fires. *Open Sun-Thu 12.00-00.00 & Fri-Sat 12.00-02.00.* The pub operates a ferry for walkers and cyclists *Easter-Sep, Tue-Sun 12.00-20.00* (07716 394704).

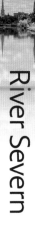

NAVIGATIONAL NOTES

There is regular aggregate traffic operating between Ripple Wharf and Ryall Wharf, a run of approximately two miles (*see* map on page 91). Keep a good lookout for barges and be prepared to move out of their way when fully loaded or manoeuvring at either wharf.

WALKING AND CYCLING

The Severn Way allows walkers to follow the entire 220-mile course of the river from the Bristol Channel to its source on Plynlimon. For the most part the path closely follows the navigation, moving from bank to bank as indicated on the mapping, only diverging where the right of way no longer exists or is uncertain. For a comprehensive guide to the complete route visit www.worcestershire.gov. uk/directory/37/walks_in_ worcestershire/category/112. Also available from good bookshops and TICs.

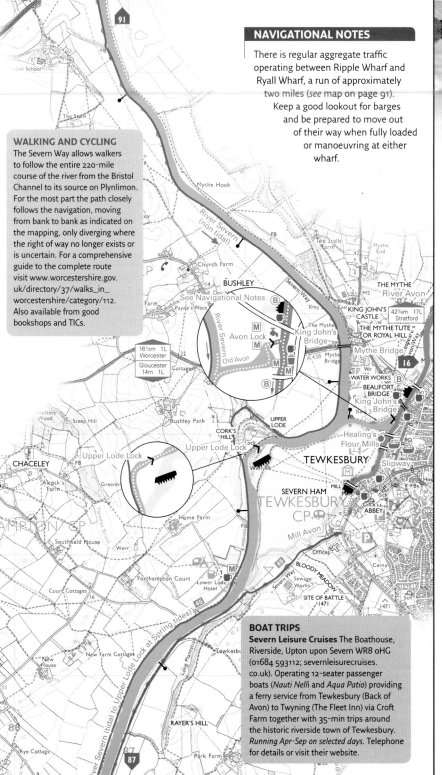

BOAT TRIPS

Severn Leisure Cruises The Boathouse, Riverside, Upton upon Severn WR8 0HG (01684 593112; severnleisurecruises. co.uk). Operating 12-seater passenger boats (*Nauti Nelli* and *Aqua Patio*) providing a ferry service from Tewkesbury (Back of Avon) to Twyning (The Fleet Inn) via Croft Farm together with 35-min trips around the historic riverside town of Tewkesbury. *Running Apr-Sep on selected days.* Telephone for details or visit their website.

Upton upon Severn

The River Severn continues on its predictable, undramatic course northwards, flanked by wooded banks that prevent any views of the countryside. There are few signs of habitation or human activity apart from boats and anglers. Between Ripple Wharf and a discharge point two miles upstream at Ryall, there is regular aggregate traffic so a careful lookout for barges should be maintained (*see* Navigational Notes on page 89). The significant-looking pipes sticking out of the ground on the east bank at this point betray the existence of an old underground oil depot, but it is now disused. A mile further on, the view improves as the old church tower at Upton upon Severn appears, followed by the graceful modern bridge and interesting waterfront of this attractive small town. Plenty of boats are moored here – there are visitor *moorings* on the west bank, just upstream of the bridge. Under an agreement with CRT *water, refuse and Elsan disposal* are provided by the boatyard on the east bank, downstream of the bridge. Leaving Upton, the river resumes its high-banked course through the countryside. On the west bank, but hardly visible from a boat, is the village of Hanley Castle.

Boatyards

Ⓑ**Upton Marina** East Waterside, Upton upon Severn WR8 0PB (01684 594287; www.tingdene-marinas.co.uk/marinas/upton-marina). 🛡🛡⚓D E Gas, overnight and long-term mooring, winter storage, slipway, 18 ton hoist, chandlery, books and maps, boat sales, toilets, showers, telephone. Licensed club. Wi-Fi.

NAVIGATIONAL NOTES

The rocks placed in the River Severn, near the Swan Hotel at Upton upon Severn, have been removed and the moorings here are now fully operational.

Pubs and Restaurants

🍺✕ 1 **The Railway Inn** Station Road, Ripple GL20 6EY (01684 592225; railwayinnatripple.co.uk). Follow the footpath into the village. Friendly village local dispensing real ale together with genuine home-cooked food *Tue–Sun L and E*. Dog- and child-friendly, garden. Traditional pub games and real fires. *Open Tue–Fri L and E and Sat–Sun 12.00-23.00 (Sun 21.30).*

🍺✕ 2 **Ye Olde Anchor Inn** 5 High Street, Upton upon Severn WR8 0HQ (01684 593735; www.anchorupton.co.uk). This pub is dated 1601 and was once the haunt of body snatchers. It now serves a range of guest real ales and bar meals *L, daily*. Patio seating, real fires and Wi-Fi. *Open Mon–Sat 12.00-23.00 (Fri-Sat 00.00) & Sun 12.00-22.30.*

✕♀ 3 **Pundits** 9 Old Street, Upton upon Severn WR8 0HN (01684 591022; www.pundits-upton.co.uk). Bangladeshi restaurant serving appetising food *daily* 17.30-23.30 (and *L* by prior arrangement). Children welcome. Garden seating *in summer*. Takeaway service.

🍺✕ 4 **The Swan Hotel** Waterside, Upton upon Severn WR8 0JD (01684 594948; www.theswanhotelupton.co.uk). Real ales and traditional

pub food available *L and E daily*. Real fires, patio seating and moorings. B&B. *Open Mon–Sat 11.00-22.30 (Fri-Sat 23.30) & Sun 12.00-22.30.*

✕♀ 5 **The Bell House** 9 New Street, Upton upon Severn WR8 0HP (01684 437090). Pretty 17th-C black and white tea shop and restaurant. *Open Wed & Sun-Mon 09.30-16.00 (Sun 15.00) & Thu-Sat 09.30-20.00* (often open later during festivals). Well-behaved dogs welcome.

🍺 6 **The Three Kings** 29 Church End, Hanley Castle WR8 0BL (01684 592686). In the village centre. An attractive 15th-C country pub, unspoilt by progress, run by the same family since 1911, serving a wide range of real ales and real draught cider. Bar snacks available *weekday L*. Well-behaved dogs and children welcome, garden. Traditional pub games and real fires. *Open L and E daily.*

Also try: 🍺 7 **The Plough Inn**, Waterside, Upton upon Severn WR8 0HY (01684 591198; youruptonuponsevern.co.uk/index.php/directory/riverside/the-plough-inn).

● **Ripple**
Worcs. Tel. Although set back from the river, Ripple is well worth a visit. It is a pretty village, the houses scattered irregularly along the road. The large church is very fine and dates almost entirely from the late 12th C. Only the chancel is late 13th-C. The central tower at one time had a spire. Inside are 15th-C choir stalls, carved with astrological symbols.

● **Upton upon Severn**
Worcs. PO, tel, stores, baker, hardware, bank, chemist, off-licence, takeaways, fish & chips, laundrette, garage. This delightful town is well provided with fascinating old timbered and early Georgian buildings, and it is doubly welcome for being situated on the river bank. The best area is nearest the river, where various pubs and venerable hotels beckon; nearby is the

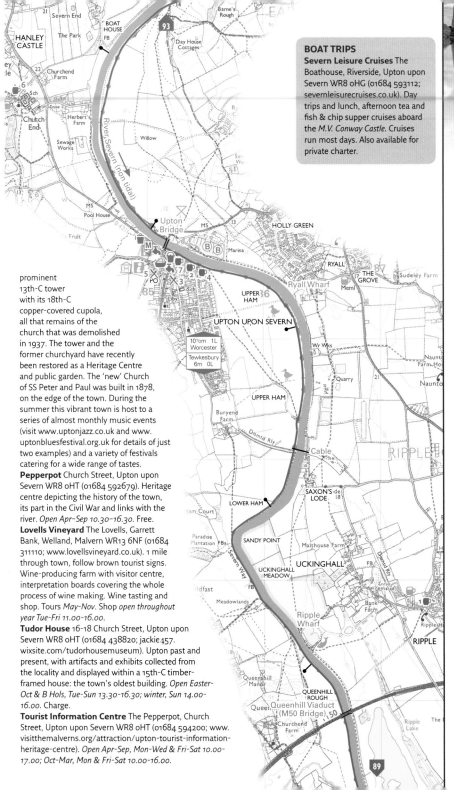

BOAT TRIPS

Severn Leisure Cruises The Boathouse, Riverside, Upton upon Severn WR8 0HG (01684 593112; severnleisurecruises.co.uk). Day trips and lunch, afternoon tea and fish & chip supper cruises aboard the *M.V. Conway Castle*. Cruises run most days. Also available for private charter.

prominent 13th-C tower with its 18th-C copper-covered cupola, all that remains of the church that was demolished in 1937. The tower and the former churchyard have recently been restored as a Heritage Centre and public garden. The 'new' Church of SS Peter and Paul was built in 1878, on the edge of the town. During the summer this vibrant town is host to a series of almost monthly music events (visit www.uptonjazz.co.uk and www.uptonbluesfestival.org.uk for details of just two examples) and a variety of festivals catering for a wide range of tastes.

Pepperpot Church Street, Upton upon Severn WR8 0HT (01684 592679). Heritage centre depicting the history of the town, its part in the Civil War and links with the river. *Open Apr–Sep 10.30–16.30.* Free.

Lovells Vineyard The Lovells, Garrett Bank, Welland, Malvern WR13 6NF (01684 311110; www.lovellsvineyard.co.uk). 1 mile through town, follow brown tourist signs. Wine-producing farm with visitor centre, interpretation boards covering the whole process of wine making. Wine tasting and shop. Tours *May-Nov.* Shop *open throughout year Tue-Fri 11.00–16.00.*

Tudor House 16-18 Church Street, Upton upon Severn WR8 0HT (01684 438820; jackie457. wixsite.com/tudorhousemuseum). Upton past and present, with artifacts and exhibits collected from the locality and displayed within a 15th-C timber-framed house: the town's oldest building. *Open Easter-Oct & B Hols, Tue-Sun 13.30-16.30; winter, Sun 14.00-16.00.* Charge.

Tourist Information Centre The Pepperpot, Church Street, Upton upon Severn WR8 0HT (01684 594200; www. visitthemalverns.org/attraction/upton-tourist-information-heritage-centre). *Open Apr-Sep, Mon-Wed & Fri-Sat 10.00-17.00; Oct-Mar, Mon & Fri-Sat 10.00-16.00.*

Severn Stoke

Beyond Hanley Castle, on the east bank, is a wooded ridge with a curious turreted house projecting from the trees. The village of Severn Stoke is to the east; it is reached by a lane from a jetty on the river. North from here is an enjoyably romantic stretch of river, where tall, steep red cliffs rise sharply from the water to over 100ft. Trees and shrubs struggle to grow from this treacherous slope, and somewhere hidden at the top is Rhydd Court. The steep hill recedes, allowing a large caravan site to nestle by the river. A scattering of bungalows appears; then the river leaves houses and hills and wanders off north east. Distantly, to the west, can be seen the grey lumps of the Malvern Hills. The river winds past the hamlet of Pixham, then the bold tower of Kempsey church appears on the east bank, and a line of moored boats betrays the presence of a *boatyard*. There are temporary *moorings* along here for visitors to the village. Upstream, the river straightens out as it makes for Worcester.

Boatyards

Ⓑ●✕**Seaborn Yacht Company** Court Meadow, Kempsey, Worcester WR5 3JL (01905 820295; www.seaborneleisure.co.uk). Long-term moorings, slipway, free house and restaurant, caravan park. Log cabins and lodges.

Pubs and Restaurants

●1 **The Walter de Cantelupe Inn** Main Road, Kempsey WR5 3NA (01905 820572; www. walterdecantelupe.co.uk). A small, intimate village inn with warm décor, offering reliable food, real ale and accommodation, 15 minutes' walk from the river. All food is made on the premises and this establishment is renowned for its hefty ploughman's lunch with local cheese and home-made pickle. Food is available *L and E Tue-Sat and Sun L*. Well-behaved children welcome – under 14's *until 20.15*. Dogs welcome, garden. Traditional pub games, newspapers, real fires, sports TV and Wi-Fi. B&B. *Open Tue-Sat & B Hol Mon L and E; Sun 12.00-21.00.*

●✕2 **The Huntsman Inn** Green Street, Kempsey, Worcester WR5 3QB (01905 820336). Real ales and home-cooked food *(Thu-Sat E & Sun L)* dispensed in a 300-year-old farmhouse with exposed beams. Child- and dog-friendly, garden. Traditional pub games and real fires. *Open Mon-Fri E & Sat-Sun 12.00-23.00.*

●✕3 **The Rose & Crown** Church Lane, Severn Stoke WR8 9JQ (01905 371249; rosecrownworcesterpub.co.uk). Traditional, black and white, village hostelry serving real ales, real cider and food *daily 12.00-22.00*. Dog- and family-friendly, beer garden. Traditional pub games, newspapers, real fires and Wi-Fi. *Open 11.30-23.00.*

●4 **The Anchor Inn** 69 Main Road, Kempsey, Worcester WR5 3NB (01905 820011; anchorkempsey. co.uk). Light, airy and friendly pub serving real ale, real cider and food *Mon-Fri L and E & Sat-Sun 12.00-21.00 (Sun 19.00)*. Garden with children's play equipment. Traditional pub games (including pool) sports TV and Wi-Fi. *Open Mon-Sat 12.00-23.00 (Fri-Sat 00.00) & Sun 12.00-22.30.*

● **Severn Stoke**
Worcs. Tel. The village is scattered along the main road, and has no real centre. The best part is near the pretty half-timbered pub with its rose garden. Nearby is the church with its curious 14th-C side tower.

● **Kempsey**
Worcs. PO, tel, stores, off-licence. A dull village in which acres of new housing have swamped the original settlement. One or two beautiful thatched cottages have survived to defy the invasion of modernity.

However, it is the church that should be visited, for the enormous scale of this building is matched by its interior grandeur. It was constructed to cater for the Bishop of Worcester and his huge retinue – the Bishop's Palace used to stand just a few yards west of the church. Hence the generous proportions of, especially, the chancel and sanctuary. Note the medieval glass in the Chancel. Both the post office and shop are *open daily 06.00-22.00 (Sun 07.00)*.

KEMPSEY

95

Priors Court
Pixham
Saint Cloud
MS
PIXHAM
LOWER HAM
Pixham Farm
19 Oaks
Frieze Wood
Clevelode Rough
CHAPELHILL ROUGH
Falconers Farm
Clevelode Farm
CLEVELODE
FB
Little Clevelode Farm
Portocks End
DRIPSHILL WOOD
Dripshill House
Dripshill Farm
Fowler's Farm
RHYDD
RHYDD GREEN
BS
Sch
The Rhydd Gardens
Square Plantation
CLIFFEY WOOD
BRICKPITS PLANTATION
Cliffey Farm
Hangman's Lane
Sink Covert
Northfield Farm
Northend Farm
Cross (rems of)
The Gorse
Merevale Farm
Long Covert

PO
Draycott
Bight Farm
Bannut Hill
Sewage Works
Old Road
Oak Farm
Draycott Villa
Baynhall
MS
Baynhall Farm
THE BOGS
Ashmoor Common
Clifton Court
Clifton Lower Farm
CLIFTON
MS
Naunton Farm
Clifton Arles
A 38
SEVERN STOKE
Sheepcote Farm
Sandford
Sandford Villa Farm
Sewage Works
Knights Hill
Hotel
PO
SEVERN STOKE
High House Farm
Severn Bank Wood
SEVERN BANK
Cattle Grids
CLIFF WOOD
Hollybeds Farm

River Severn

Severn W

7¾m 1L Worcester
Tewkesbury 8¾m 0L

91

93

Worcester

Soon the Severn narrows somewhat as a wooded ridge encroaches from the east. The Severn Motor Yacht Club is based here – it is well-named, for the cruisers moored along here are lavish and grand. There is a pub up among the trees near the club. The Battle of Worcester was fought in 1651 near where the little River Teme joins the Severn and 3/4 of a mile upstream are the paired Diglis Locks (01905 354280). Just above the locks is the terminal basin where the oil tankers used to come to unload before the traffic finished many years ago. A few hundred yards on the once thriving wharfs have been redeveloped for light industry and housing, followed by the two locks that lead into Diglis Basin (01905 358758) and the Worcester & Birmingham Canal (*see page 156*). Worcester Cathedral is well in view now; the big square tower commands the town and the riverside. Two other church towers contribute to the scene and the unspoilt nature of the west bank makes Worcester's riverside a pretty one. Anglers fish from a path along the east bank, seemingly just below the great west window of the cathedral, while fours and eights appear from rowing clubs. There are three bridges over the river in Worcester – a 5-arched stone road bridge and, just north of it, an imposing brick and iron railway viaduct and the Sabrina Footbridge. The best temporary *moorings* are above Diglis Lock and north of the railway bridge. The west bank is built up while the east bank is green and tree-lined, with the racecourse right by the river. At the city's northern boundary is a busy waterworks, contrasting with the bijou houses which adjoin it. Upstream of here the river moves out into pleasantly wooded country; the only trace of civilisation is the glimpse of the occasional farm and a pretty, secluded riverside *pub* with good *moorings*.

BOAT TRIPS
Severn Leisure Cruises The Boathouse, Riverside, Upton upon Severn WR8 0HG (01684 593112; severnleisurecruises.co.uk). Day trips and lunch, afternoon tea and fish & chip supper cruises aboard the *M.V. Conway Castle*. Cruises run most days. Also available for private charter.
Worcester Boat Trips 22 Portland Street, Worcester WR1 2NL (01905 814147; www.worcesterboattrips. co.uk). *45-min trips, departing on the hour –11.00-16.00* – from South Quay (WR1 2JN) aboard *The Earl*. Bar, tea, coffee and cake. Also *30-min* cocktail cruises, *departing every 45 min between 18.30 and dusk*. Telephone for seasonal timings.

Boatyards

Ⓑ**Diglis Basin Marina** Diglis Road, Worcester WR5 3BW (01905 356314; bwml.co.uk/diglis-basin-marina). 🛈🛠. Long-term and visitor moorings (contact in advance), boat sales, chandlery, toilets, showers. *Open Tue & Sun 09.00-12.00; Thu 09.00-15.00.*

Ⓑ**Grist Mill Boatyard** Diglis Basin, Diglis Dock Road, Worcester (01905 350814/07956 084107).

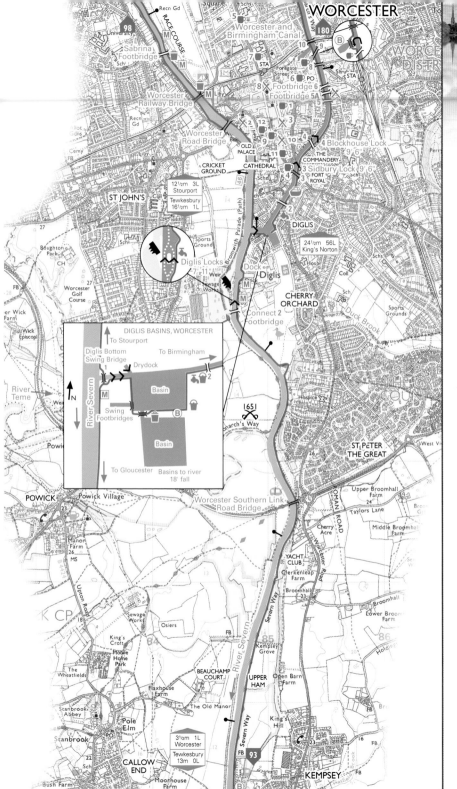

WORCESTER

98 University
Sabrina Footbridge
RACE COURSE
Worcester and Birmingham Canal
180

Recn Gd
Square
Schs
10
9

University
M
Foregate Street
STA
STA
8
Shrub's STA
PO
Footbridge 6
Footbridge 5A
7
6

Worcester Railway Bridge
M
Lib

Recn Gd
Recn Gd

Worcester Road Bridge
OLD PALACE

CRICKET GROUND
CATHEDRAL
Bromwich Parade (Path)

12½m 3L Stourport
Tewkesbury 16½m 1L

ST JOHN'S

Boughton Park
Cemy
FB
Worcester Golf Course
Sports Ground
Schs

Diglis Locks
7'11" Weir
Sewage Works

Wick Episcopal
River Teme
Weir

4 Blockhouse Lock 9' 6"
THE COMMANDERY
3 Sidbury Lock 9' 6"
FORT ROYAL

DIGLIS

24½m 56L King's Norton

Dock
Diglis

CHERRY ORCHARD

M
M

Connect 2 Footbridge

Hosp
Coll
Schs
Sports Grounds

DIGLIS BASINS, WORCESTER
To Stourport
Diglis Bottom Swing Bridge
Drydock
To Birmingham
Basin
M
N
River Severn
Swing Footbridges
B
Basin
To Gloucester
Basins to river 18' fall

Duck Brook

1651

Monarch's Way

Hospice

ST PETER THE GREAT
West Vi
26

POWICK
Powick Village
23
Manor Farm 26
MS
Upton Road

Worcester Southern Link Road Bridge
Upper Broomhall Farm
24
Taylors Lane
Middle Broomhall Farm
Cherry Acre
Lower Broomhall Farm

Sewage Works
Osiers
King's Croft
Mobile Home Park
The Wheatfields

K CP
18
84

YACHT CLUB
Clerkenleap Farm
Broomhall
23

FB
85
Kempsey Grove

BEAUCHAMP COURT
Flaxhouse Farm
The Old Manor

UPPER HAM
Open Barn Farm

Severn Way

86

Stanbrook Abbey
Pole Elm
Stanbrook
22
Schs

3½m 1L Worcester
Tewkesbury 13m 0L

Severn Way

King's Hill
23
FB

CALLOW END
Moorhouse Farm
Bush Farm

93
KEMPSEY

95

Battle of Worcester, 3 September 1651 On 22 August 1651, Charles Stuart (later Charles II), having been proclaimed king by the rebels at Scone, reached Worcester with his Scottish army of 17,000 men. The Roundhead General Lambert was sent off in pursuit with his northern cavalry, and captured the Severn Bridge at Upton upon Severn, cutting off Charles' retreat. Meanwhile, another army of 28,000 under Cromwell advanced on Worcester from Nottingham. Charles, realising that he would have to fight at Worcester, organised his defences around the rivers Severn and Teme. After receiving further reinforcements from Banbury, the Roundhead armies advanced across the Severn, using a pontoon made of boats; meanwhile their cavalry crossed by a ford south of Powick Bridge, on the Teme. Heavy fighting broke out, and Charles' Scottish infantry, taken by surprise, were soon driven back. Charles tried to redeem the battle by leading a brave charge out of the east gate of Worcester; supported by cavalry this might have succeeded, but by this time the Scottish cavalry had fled. Cromwell held his ground and forced the Royalists back into the town, killing many in the narrow streets. This Roundhead victory ended the Royalist hopes; Charles fled with a few followers, and after the famous Boscobel Oak episode he made his way back to France.

● **Worcester**

Worcs. All services. A bishopric was founded in the Saxon town of Wigorna Ceaster around the year 680, and a castle was built here following the Norman conquest. During the Civil War the city was the first to declare for Charles I, and the last place where the Royalists rallied around Charles II. They were subsequently defeated in 1651 by Cromwell's army. These days Worcester has plenty to offer the visitor, although the enjoyment is lessened by the constant flow of heavy traffic through the city. A railway bridge at Foregate Street does not intrude, for the girders are suitably decorated and trains are infrequent. However the best area is around Friar Street, and of course the splendid cathedral.

The Commandery Sidbury, Worcester WR1 2HU (01905 361821; www.worcestershire.gov.uk/museums/info/1/the_commandery). By Sidbury Lock. Founded as a small hospital just outside the city walls by Bishop Wulstan in 1085: from the 13th C the masters of the hospital were referred to as commanders, hence the building's name. The present timbered structure dates from the reign of Henry VII in the 15th C, and served as Charles II's headquarters before the Battle of Worcester in 1651. The glory of the building is the superb galleried hall with its ancient windows and Elizabethan staircase. The museum explains in detail various points of time in the building's history, including the monastic hospital and the Battle of Worcester. *Open Feb-Dec, Tue-Sat 10.00-17.00 & Sun 13.30-17.00.* Charge.

Diglis Basin This is a fascinating terminus at the junction of the River Severn and the Worcester & Birmingham Canal. It consists of basins, old warehouses and a dry dock, much of which has undergone considerable redevelopment. Commercial craft have been entirely replaced by a mixture of pleasure boats designed for narrow canals, rivers and the sea. The locks will take boats up to 72ft by 18ft 6in, although obviously only narrowboats can proceed along the canal. The locks are under the supervision of the basin attendant, who is available *from 08.00-19.30 (16.00 winter) with breaks for meals.* Craft are not permitted to use the locks outside these times. The CRT basin attendant can be contacted on (01905) 358758, or enquire through the Waterways Unit Office (0303 040 4040; enquiries.southwalessevern@canalrivertrust.org.uk). Near the first lock is a small pump-house that raises water from the river to maintain the level in the basin.

George Marshall Medical Museum Charles Hastings Education Centre, Worcester Royal Hospital, Worcester WR5 1DD (01905 760738; www.medicalmuseum.org.uk). Meet the past heros of medicine and see how its developing science has transformed our lives. *Open Mon-Fri 09.00-17.00.* Free. Regular bus service from Crowngate Bus Station

The Greyfriars Friar Street, Worcester WR1 2LZ (01905 23571; www.nationaltrust.org.uk/greyfriars-house-and-garden). Dating from 1480, this was once part of a Franciscan priory and is one of the finest half-timbered houses in the country. Charles II escaped from this house after the Battle of Worcester on 3 September 1651. It has a delightful walled garden. *Opening times vary* so visit the website or telephone for details.

The Guildhall High Street, Worcester WR1 2EY (01905 723471). Built in 1721-3 by a local architect, Thomas White, this building has a splendidly elaborate façade with statues of Charles I and Charles II on either side of the doorway and of Queen Anne on the pediment. It contains a fine assembly room.

Worcester Live Huntingdon Hall, Crowngate, Worcester WR1 3LD (01905 611427; www.worcesterlive.co.uk). For information on all events at the Swan Theatre, Huntingdon Hall, the Worcester Festival, as well as Shakespeare at The Commandery and the Historic Ghost Walk of Worcester.

Worcester Porcelain Museum Severn Street, Worcester WR1 2ND (01905 21247; www.museumofroyalworcester.org). Here, where it should be, is the most comprehensive collection of Worcester porcelain in the world, from 1751 to the present day. Visitor Centre. *Open Mar-Oct 10.00-17.00 & Nov-Feb 10.00-16.00.* Tours of the porcelain works. Shop. Charge.

Swan Theatre The Moors, Worcester WR1 3ED. Year-round drama, music and dance from local and national companies. *see* Worcester Live above.

Worcester Cathedral 8 College Yard, Worcester WR1 2LA (01905 732900; www.worcestercathedral.co.uk). An imposing building which dates from 1074 (when Bishop Wulstan started to rebuild the Saxon church), but has work representative of the five subsequent centuries. There is a wealth of stained glass and monuments to see – including the tomb of King John, which lies in the chancel. Carved out of Purbeck marble in 1216, this is the oldest royal effigy in England. When he was dying at Newark, King John demanded to be buried at Worcester Cathedral between two saints: but the saints have gone now. The best way into the cathedral is from the Close with its immaculate lawns and houses, passing through the cloisters where one may inspect five of the cathedral's old bells, two of which were cast in 1374. The gardens at the west end of the building look out over the Severn and on to the Malvern Hills – a particularly fine sight at sunset. Gift shop, tours and tearoom. *Open daily 07.30-18.00.* Donations. **The Three Choirs Festival** is held annually in rotation at the cathedrals of Worcester, Gloucester and Hereford, during the last week in *Aug.* This famous festival has inspired some fine music, one notable composer being Vaughan Williams. For further information about the festival, contact the Tourist Information Centre in any of the three cities.

Worcester City Art Gallery and Museum
Foregate Street, Worcester WR1 1DT (01905 25371; www.worcestershire.gov.uk/museums/info/2/city_art_gallery_and_museum). Opened in 1896, it contains collections of folk life material and natural history illustrating man and his environment in the Severn valley. In the Art Gallery are a permanent collection and loan exhibitions. Children's activities. Also the Worcestershire Soldier Gallery. Balcony Café. Open *Mon-Sat 10.30-16.30.* Free.
Tourist Information Centre The Guildhall, High Street, Worcester WR1 2EY (01905 726311; www.visitworcester.com). Enquire here about local guided walks (www. worcesterwalks.co.uk). *Open Mon-Sat 09.30-17.00; B Hols 10.00-16.00.*

Pubs and Restaurants (pages 95)

🍺 1 **The King Charles House** 29 New Street, Worcester WR1 2DP (01905 726100; www.thekingcharleshouse.com). King Charles is reputed to have escaped from here but, in pursuit of a more contemporary role, this timber-framed hostelry dispenses real ale, real cider and a predominantly pie-based menu *Mon-Fri L and E, Sat-Sun 12.00-21.00 (Sat 20.00).* Dog- and family-friendly. Traditional pub games, newspapers, real fires and Wi-Fi. Quiz *Tue. Open daily 11.30-23.00 (Fri-Sat 23.30).*

✕🍷 2 **Browns @ The Quay** 24 South Quay, Worcester WR1 2JJ (01905 25800; brownsworcester.co.uk). Trendy, contemporary riverside establishment, majoring on food, wine and cocktails. B&B. *Open Mon-Sat 10.00-23.00 (Fri-Sat 01.00) & Sun 10.00-20.00.*

✕🍷 3 **Saffrons Bistro** 15 New Street, Worcester WR1 2DP (01905 610505; saffronsbistro.co.uk). An internationally inspired menu in relaxed, pine-clad surroundings. Food is available *Mon-Sat L and E (booking advisable).* Children welcome. There are also over 60 gins to sample!

🍺✕ 4 **The Kings Head** 67 Sidbury, Worcester WR1 2HU (01905 726025; www.kingsheadsidbury.co.uk). Lockside, Sidbury Lock. Bar and restaurant serving modern British cooking – *daily 12.00-21.00 (Sun 20.00)* – along with real ales. Breakfast available *from 09.00 daily.* Courtyard seating beside the lock. Children and dogs welcome. Traditional pub games. *Open Mon-Sat 09.00-23.00 (Sat 00.00) & Sun 10.00-22.30.*

🍺 5 **The Dragon Inn** 51 The Tything, Worcester WR1 1JT (01905 25845; thedragoninnworcester.co.uk). Georgian building housing the Church End Brewery tap, serving both real ales and real cider. Pork pies and sausage rolls *always* available. Dog-friendly, patio. Traditional pub games, newspapers, real fires and Wi-Fi. *Open Mon-Thu E & Fri-Sun 12.00-23.00 (Sun 22.30).*

🍺 6 **The Firefly** 54 Lowesmoor, Worcester WR1 2SE (01905 616996). Once the old vinegar works manager's Georgian residence, this comfortable hostelry has its own micro-brewery and serves real ales and real ciders. Food is available *Mon-Fri L* and *E & Sat-Sun 12.00-21.00 (Sun 18.00).*

Beer garden, real fires and Wi-Fi. *Open Mon-Fri 12.00-00.00 (Thu-Fri 00.10) Sat 12.00-02.00 & Sun 12.00-23.00.*

🍺✕ 7 **The Postal Order** 18 Foregate Street, Worcester WR1 1DN (01905 22373; www.jdwetherspoon.com/pubs/all-pubs/england/worcestershire/the-postal-order-worcester). The old telephone exchange with the Wetherspoon treatment now connected to handpumps dispensing real ale, together with real cider. Popular with a wide-ranging clientele this pub serves reasonably priced food daily *08.00-23.00.* Family-friendly, sports TV and Wi-Fi. *Open 08.00-00.00 (Fri-Sat 01.00).*

✕ 8 **St Custards Café** 4 The Hopmarket, Worcester WR1 1DL (01905 26654). Excellent coffee, home-made snacks and meals. The chance to eat al fresco in a delightful courtyard. Children welcome. Quick and friendly service. *Open Mon 09.30-16.00, Tue-Sat 09.00-16.30*

🍺 9 **The Farriers Arms** 9 Fish Street (off High Street), Worcester WR1 2HN (01905 27569). Grade II listed building dispensing real ales. Old paintings promoting the Wychwood Brewery and outside seating. Traditional, home-made food available *Sun-Wed L* and *Thu-Fri E.* Dog- and family-friendly. Traditional pub games, newspapers, sports TV and Wi-Fi. B&B. *Open 12.00-23.00.*

✕🍷 10 **Thai Gallery Restaurant** 26–32 Friar Street, Worcester WR1 2LZ (01905 25451; www.thaigallery.co.uk/worcester). Tudor timber-framing. Thai food offered *Mon-Sun 17.30-23.00 (Sun 22.00).*

🍺✕ 11 **Ye Olde Talbot Hotel** Friar Street, Worcester WR1 2NA (01905 235730; www.oldenglishinns.co.uk/our-locations/the-ye-olde-talbot-worcester). This cosy, original coaching inn, dating back to the 13th C, is situated in the centre of the city, close to the Cathedral. Food available *daily 11.00-22.00.* Family-friendly, garden and Wi-Fi. *Open all day.*

🍺 12 **The Plough** 23 Fish Street, Deansway, Worcester WR1 2HN (01905 21381). Down to earth local set in an historic, listed building. Real ales, real cider and perry. Food available *Fri-Sun L.* Children and dogs welcome. Patio, traditional pub games and newspapers. *Open Mon-Sat 12.00-23.00 (Fri-Sat 23.30) & Sun 12.00-22.30.*

Grimley

Just upstream of the Camp House Inn is Bevere Lock (01905 640275), which is certainly one of the prettiest on the Severn. Half a mile north the little River Salwarpe and the restored Droitwich Barge Canal enter together from the east. The Salwarpe is navigable for craft up to 35ft as far as Judge's Boatyard at Hawford, but there are no visitors' moorings. The village of Grimley is at the end of a lane leading up from the river, but it is difficult to distinguish this track, and there are currently no official moorings. The river continues north west now, until Holt Castle is reached, a curious composite building overlooking the river. The Droitwich Barge Canal is an attractive rural waterway, which leaves the Severn ½ mile north east of Bevere Lock. Surveyed and built by James Brindley it goes to Droitwich – 6¾ miles and eight locks away. Linacre bridge is an original accommodation bridge constructed to a Brindley design. The navigation is then joined by the Droitwich Junction Canal, whose seven locks lead it a further 1½ miles to terminate in a junction with the Worcester & Birmingham Canal at Hanbury Wharf (*see* page 185). Both the Droitwich Canals had been derelict for most of the last century and we owe a large debt of gratitude to the late Max Sinclair, whose drive, commitment and vision – over a period of more than 30 years – made restoration possible. His efforts, which were recently recognised with an English Heritage Angel Award (for the best rescue of a historic building or site) are largely responsible for our renewed ability to enjoy this immensely attractive waterway: now an intrinsic part of a delightful 22-mile cruising ring.

● **Grimley**
Worcs. Tel. A small farming village close to, but hidden from, the river. The well-placed church has some Norman work, but has been heavily restored; it has a curious outside staircase by the door. Access from the river is not easy.

Boatyards

Ⓑ **George Judge** (see p69 entry)

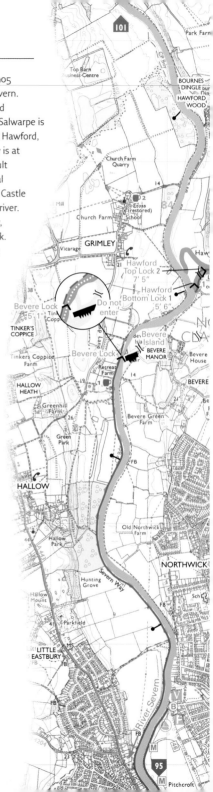

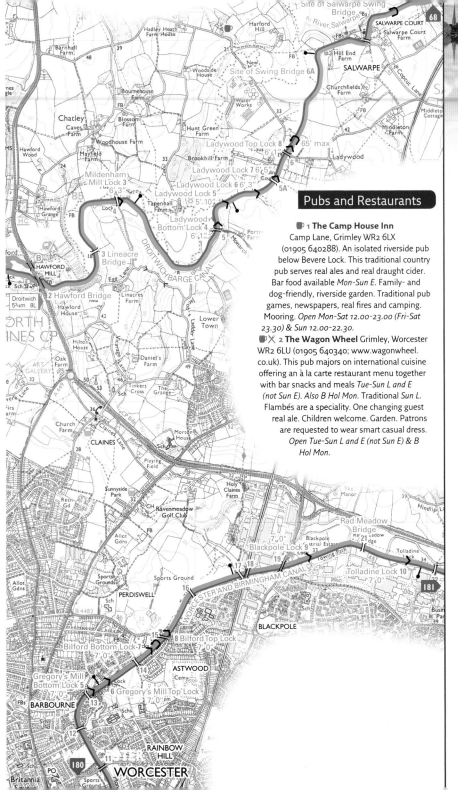

Pubs and Restaurants

▣ 1 The Camp House Inn
Camp Lane, Grimley WR2 6LX
(01905 640288). An isolated riverside pub
below Bevere Lock. This traditional country
pub serves real ales and real draught cider.
Bar food available *Mon–Sun E*. Family- and
dog-friendly, riverside garden. Traditional pub
games, newspapers, real fires and camping.
Mooring. *Open Mon-Sat 12.00-23.00 (Fri-Sat
23.30) & Sun 12.00-22.30.*

▣✗ 2 The Wagon Wheel Grimley, Worcester
WR2 6LU (01905 640340; www.wagonwheel.
co.uk). This pub majors on international cuisine
offering an à la carte restaurant menu together
with bar snacks and meals *Tue–Sun L and E
(not Sun E). Also B Hol Mon.* Traditional *Sun L.*
Flambés are a speciality. One changing guest
real ale. Children welcome. Garden. Patrons
are requested to wear smart casual dress.
*Open Tue-Sun L and E (not Sun E) & B
Hol Mon.*

Holt Fleet

Beside Holt Castle is the discreet tower of a small church, while further on is the delicate iron span of Holt Fleet Bridge. Above Holt Lock (01905 620218) steep wooded hills continue, rising straight up from the river bank. It is a pleasant scene, and there is a riverside *pub* nearby. The next few miles form an attractive reach, with tree-lined hills rising from the river banks first on one side, then on the other. Another riverside *hostelry* lies close by. The reach from Lenchford to Stourport is one of the most pleasant on the Severn. Unlike much of its journey further downstream, the river runs here through a well-defined valley, with steep rising ground never far away from either bank. The hills on the west bank are the more impressive and the more thickly wooded, although the old church at Shrawley can sometimes be seen peering over the woods. Roads keep their distance, but at the site of Hampstall Ferry (Astley Burf) there is a small village and a riverside *pub*, with good *moorings*.

PLUMBING THE DEPTHS

It may come as something of a surprise to discover that the longest river in Britain is so little used by commercial traffic, considering its size and proximity to the industrial midlands. However its width belies its depth which throughout history has always been somewhat unreliable. Above Stourport shoals and a rocky, shelving bed have always restricted regular traffic, making it difficult for barges to penetrate above Shrewsbury, into Wales. Downstream, between Tewkesbury and Gloucester, spring tides carry silt up from the estuary which is then trapped by the weirs on the East and West Partings, unable to return with the ebb. Consequently the bottom rapidly starts to approach the top, causing considerable problems for any commercial craft still determined to exploit this navigation's potential.

This situation is further exacerbated by the exuberant performance of the Severn Bore: a spring tide *in extremis*. It shovels literally hundreds of tons of unwanted material over the weirs demanding continuous dredging to redress. Reputedly, one of its more bizarre victims was a Blue Peter camera crew, their boat swamped when overtaken by the 6ft wave, whilst filming a surfer. Boat and camera went to the bottom, as did plans for screening the event. However the BBC reckoned without the combined forces of chance and a somewhat bewildered fisherman who, some several weeks later, contacted them with news of a most unusual catch.

Pubs and Restaurants

1 The Wharf Inn Holt Heath WR6 6NN (01905 620337; www.thewharfatholt.com). North bank by caravan site. Large family pub dispensing real ale and serving food *Wed-Fri E, Sat 13.00-20.00 & Sun L*. Riverside seating and children's play area. Dog-friendly, real fires, pool table and Wi-Fi. Camping and fishing available. Mooring. B&B. *Open Mon-Fri E & Sat-Sun 12.00-23.00 (Sun 10.30). Closed Mon-Tue Nov-Easter.*

2 The Holt Fleet Hotel Holt Heath WR6 6NL (01905 620286). By the bridge. Rambling, Tudor establishment tucked in between the river and the steep bank below Holt Heath. Freehouse. Bar meals together with an à la carte and carvery restaurant serving food *L and E, daily* available. Limited moorings. Children welcome.

3 The Lenchford Inn Lenchford, Shrawley WR6 6TB (01905 620229; www.thelenchfordinn.co.uk). Riverside, upstream of Holt Lock. Real ales are served in this riverside hotel with B&B accommodation.

Restaurant meals available *L and E*. Also breakfast available *Mon-Sun 07.30-09.30 (Sat-Sun 08.00)*. Sun carvery. Children welcome at all times. Riverside garden and moorings (free to patrons *only*). Dog-friendly, traditional pub games, real fires and Wi-Fi. Camping. B&B. *Open 11.00-23.00 (Sat-Sun 00.00).*

4 The Hamstall Inn Astley Burf, Stourport DY13 0RY (01299 822600). Originally known as the Old Cider House, overlooking the river ½ mile below Lincomb Lock. Real ale together with real ciders are served in this friendly pub with good moorings and a riverside garden. Bar food available *Mon-Fri L and E, Sat 12.00-21.00 & Sun L. Also all day on B Hols*. Dog- and family-friendly. Traditional pub games, sports TV and Wi-Fi. Mooring. *Open 12.00-23.00 (Sat-Sun 00.00).*

Holt Heath

Worcs. PO, tel, stores, off-licence. One of a scattering of assorted settlements around the river, and approximately half mile to the west. The elegant narrow bridge here was built by Telford in 1828. Holt Fleet exploits the river in a most unattractive fashion, being composed of a large sprawling caravan site, whose television aerials and wires swamp the riverside. There are two large pubs. Holt Castle is up on the hill, overlooking the river. The castle is a 14th-C tower, the rest of the building is a 19th-C battlemented mansion. Nearby, set among the fruit fields, is the church, a fine late Norman building with interesting carving around the doorways, and rich in interior ornamentation. There is a shop, gas, coal and an off-licence, together with recycling facilities, immediately to the east of Holt Bridge. Also a farm shop ½ mile up the hill.

Astley Burf

Worcs. Tel. An isolated riverside settlement, comprised mainly of housing for retired persons. The word Burf is thought to mean an enclosure below a hill.

Thomas Telford's Holt Fleet Bridge dates back to 1830

Stourport-on-Severn

North of Astley Burf steep hills encroach on the east bank of the river, almost hanging over it at Lincomb Lock (01299 822887). This pretty lock is now the northernmost on the river, for signs of Stourport soon come into view. First there are the abandoned oil wharves, now frequented by the occasional fisherman. On the opposite side of the river, at the foot of a cliff, is the Redstone Rock – an unexpected outcrop of crumbling red sandstone. There was once a hermitage in caves here. Before reaching the canal junction the Severn is joined first by the River Stour and then by the little River Salwarpe, flowing in from the east, just as to the north the Staffordshire & Worcestershire Canal drops down into the Severn from the unseen basins. There are two sets of locks – narrow canal boats should use the upstream set. Just above these locks is Stourport Bridge, a heavy iron structure built in 1870. There are visitor *moorings* either side of the Broad Lock entrance leading into the basin (01299 877661) and a *floating sanitary station* and *water point Easter–Oct*. The River Severn is not officially navigable for more than a couple of hundred yards above Stourport Bridge, at which point CRT's jurisdiction as navigation authority ends. However, in suitable conditions small boats drawing not more than 1ft 9in can penetrate upstream to within a mile of Bewdley Bridge. A shoal across the river impedes further progress, and boatmen must tie up or wade ashore when they reach the shoal. Bradshaw's *Canals and Navigable Rivers Of England and Wales* (1904) stated that a few craft, in times of full water, proceeded as far as Arley Quarry, 5 miles above Bewdley, although the trade was small. There is a road into Bewdley on either side of the river (the B4194 on the west bank being the most direct). Alternatively, one can avoid all this by leaving the boat in Stourport and either walking along the riverside path (which continues to Bridgnorth) or by taking a bus to Bewdley; an excursion well worth the effort.

RIVER SEVERN ABOVE BEWDLEY

In the 19th C the Severn was fully navigable for a long way past Stourport: it was a vital trade artery right up into Wales, through Bridgnorth, Shrewsbury and Newtown. It used to connect with the Montgomery Canal north of Welshpool, and the Shropshire Canal at Shrewsbury. It is unfortunate that this upper section is unnavigable, for the river is much prettier than further south: it runs along a narrow valley, hemmed in by steep and wooded hills. However, there is a public right of way along one or both banks up to Bridgnorth and beyond, and this can form an interesting walk. Another attraction north of Bewdley is the Severn Valley Railway, a restored railway which runs a service of steam trains between Bridgnorth, Bewdley and Kidderminster (*see* page 105).

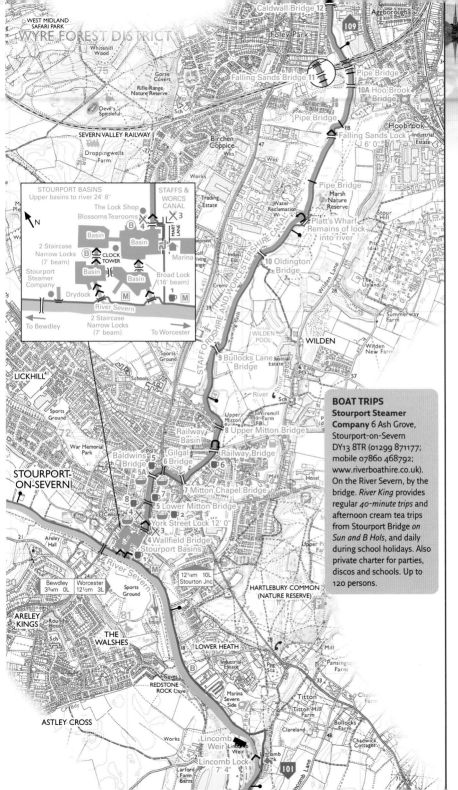

WEST MIDLAND SAFARI PARK

WYRE FOREST DISTRICT

Whitehill Wood

75

Gorse Covert

Rifle Range Nature Reserve

Devil's Spittleful

Tunnel

Sch

SEVERN VALLEY RAILWAY

Droppingwells Farm

Birchen Coppice

Wks

47

Works

Caldwall Bridge 12

Aggborough

109

Foley Park

Pipe Bridge

Falling Sands Bridge 11

10A Hoo Brook

FB

Pipe Bridge

FB

Falling Sands Lock

6' 0"

Hoobrook

Industrial Estate

Stour Hill

Pipe Bridge

Marsh Nature Reserve

Water Reclamation W

Platt's Wharf

Remains of lock into river

STOURPORT BASINS
Upper basins to river 24' 8"

N

STAFFS & WORCS CANAL

The Lock Shop

Blossoms Tearooms

3

4

B

Basin

Basin

MART LANE

2 Staircase Narrow Locks (7' beam)

B

CLOCK TOWER

Marina

Stourport Steamer Company

Basin

Basin

Broad Lock (16' beam)

Drydock

M

1

M

River Severn

To Bewdley

2 Staircase Narrow Locks (7' beam)

To Worcester

10 Oldington Bridge

Industrial Estate

Pit (dis)

The Upland

Summerway Farm

Wilden New Farm

WILDEN

WILDEN POOL

9 Bullocks Lane Bridge

Industrial Estate

Sch

PO

57

LICKHILL

Sports Ground

Schools

Sports Ground

War Memorial Park

STOURPORT-ON-SEVERN

Baldwins Bridge

5

Sch

Gilgal

Railway Basin

Railway Bridge

8 Upper Mitton Bridge

Upper Mitton Farm

Wiremill Farm

FB

River

Sch

6

21

Hotel

Mill

7 Mitton Chapel Bridge

5A

7

5 Lower Mitton Bridge

Civic Centre

4

York Street Lock 12' 0"

3

4 Wallfield Bridge

Stourport Basins

1

M

Upper

Far

Areley Hall

21

ARELEY KINGS

Round House

Sch

80

THE WALSHES

81

Bewdley 3¾m 0L

Worcester 12½m 3L

Sports Ground

12¼m 10L Stourton Jnc

HARTLEBURY COMMON (NATURE RESERVE)

82

LOWER HEATH

Industrial Estate

2B

Peg Sta

Mill

Pansington Farm

33

Titton

Titton Hill Farm

Chaston Farm

ASTLEY CROSS

REDSTONE ROCK Cave

B

Marina Severn Side

Clareland

Bullocks Farm

48

Chadwick Cottages

Works

Lincomb Weir

Lincomb Lock 7' 4"

Lincomb Lock

101

Larford Farm Barns

Larford

Boatyards

Ⓑ**CRT Stourport Yard** Stourport Basin, Stourport (0303 040 4040). 🛒🚽♿Dry dock.

Ⓑ**Stroudwater Cruisers** Engine Lane, Stourport DY13 9EP (01299 877222; www.stroudwater-cruisers.co.uk).(🛒🚽 nearby) D Pump out, gas, overnight and long-term mooring, boat building, boat sales and repairs, wet and dry docks, toilet, books and maps.

Ⓑ**Limekiln Chandlery** The Boat Shop, Mart Lane, Stourport-on-Severn (also York Street Boat Yard at Stourport Basin Marina) DY13 9ER (01299 821111; www.limekilnchandlers.co.uk). D Pump out, gas, solid fuel, maintenance, servicing, chandlery, books, maps and gifts, wet and dry dock, DIY facilities, brokerage, moorings.

Ⓑ**Starline Marine** The Basin, Engine Lane, Stourport DY13 9EP (01531 632003; www.starlinenarrowboats.co.uk). 🛒🚽♿D Pump out, gas, narrowboat hire, boat repairs, wet dock, boat building, boat sales, chandlery, toilets.

WATERWAYS UP THE SEVERN

Inevitably an arterial waterway like the Severn encouraged the construction of branch navigations at various points along its course. Near Stourport a canal was proposed to run west to the coalfields at Mamble and thence on to Leominster and Kington on the Welsh border. Only the section between the mines at Mamble and Leominster was ever completed. Further south the River Salwarpe, in conjunction with a stretch of canal, was made navigable to Droitwich, whilst the Coombe Hill Canal - just upstream of the city of Gloucester - ran eastwards 2¾ miles to aid coal transport to Cheltenham. Nearby, the Herefordshire and Gloucestershire Canal - a truly rural canal started in 1792 and completed in 1845 - linked the two cities of its title. Its 34 wandering miles followed a route via Newent, Dymock and Ledbury, required 3 tunnels and 22 locks, and appeared on the canal scene just as railway mania was taking hold. Closed in 1881 to allow part of its bed to be used as a railway (in turn axed by Dr Beeching in the 1960s), it is now firmly fixed in the sights of a very professional and dedicated canal trust, committed to its complete restoration. Equally important, the Trust now has the full policy backing of all five councils along the route who are determined to preserve the line against any future, compromising developments. Now that the comparatively easy canal restorations are complete, or at least well in hand, it is the turn of the difficult ones, considered impossible 10–15 years ago. Some 10 per cent of the canal is restored or under restoration. Work is now completed on the first phase at Over, where the canal entered the River Severn and a delightful, landscaped basin complete with the rebuilt Wharf House (*see page 85*) complements the new housing development. The lock down into the Severn will be the focus for the next phase of activity. The sheer dogged determination and tenacity shown in the face of not inconsiderable adversity, whilst meeting a demanding schedule, will surely stand as an inspiration to all those engaged in future waterway restoration. A detailed account, setting out the ups and downs of the waterway, is entitled *Rescued from Obscurity*, by Richard Skeet, and is available from the Herefordshire and Gloucestershire Canal Trust, 18 Coningsby Court, Coningsby Street, Hereford HR1 2DF – £12.00 including P&P. It can also be purchased from the Wharf House Visitor Centre at Over Basin (see Pubs and Restaurants – page 85). The Trust (www.h-g-canal.org.uk) also publish *The Wharfinger*, keeping its healthy membership abreast of progress.

● **Stourport-on-Severn**
Worcs. PO, tel, stores, chemists, takeaways, fish & chips, banks, off-licence, baker, butcher, greengrocer, laundrettes, garage. When the engineer James Brindley surveyed the line for the Staffordshire & Worcestershire Canal in the early 1760s, he chose to meet the River Severn at the hamlet of Lower Mitton, 4 miles downstream from Bewdley, where the River Stour flowed into the Severn. Basins and locks were built for the boats, warehouses for the cargoes and cottages for the workmen. In 1788 the canal company even built the great Tontine Hotel beside the locks. The hamlet soon earned the name of Stourport, becoming a busy and wealthy town. The two basins were expanded to five and the locks were duplicated. Much still remains of Stourport's former glory, for the basins are always full of moored boats, with plenty of other craft passing to and from the river. The delightful clock still functions, while the old canal maintenance yard now plays host to a boat club. Mart Lane, on the north east side of the basins, is well worth a look - the original 18th-C terrace of workmen's cottages still stands, with numbers 2, 3 and 4 listed as ancient monuments. In contrast with the basin area, the town of Stourport is not particularly interesting and, although it was built on account of the canal, the town has no relationship at all with the basins now.

- **Bewdley**

Worcs. PO, tel, stores, chemist, takeaways, fish & chips, butcher, baker, hardware, off-licence, garage. Bewdley is a magnificent small 18th-C riverside town, still remarkably intact. It is blessed with a fine river frontage and elegant bridge that make the most of the wide Severn, and a handsome main street that leads away from the river to terminate at the church. The scale of the whole town is very pleasing, a comfortable mixture of old timber-framed buildings and plainer, more elegant 17th- and 18th-C structures. Most of the town is on the west bank, and so Telford's three-arch stone bridge, built in 1798 to replace an earlier medieval structure, forms a fitting entrance to Bewdley. The Queen Elizabeth Jubilee gardens are well worth a visit and the Civic Society runs guided walks around the town. There is a good selection of pubs, cafes and restaurants in the town.

Bewdley Museum 16 Load Street, Bewdley DY12 2AE (0845 603 5699/0845 607 7819; www.bewdleymuseum.co.uk). A fascinating insight into the area and the lives of its people in a town where river trade played an important part. Interactive displays, changing exhibitions, workshops and special events. Gift shop and café. *Open daily Apr-Oct 10.00-16.30 & Nov-Mid Dec, Fri-Sun 10.00-16.30. Last admission 30 mins before closing.* Charge.

Safari Park Spring Grove, Bewdley DY12 1LF (01299 402114; www.wmsp.co.uk) Mid-way between Bewdley and Kidderminster. Whilst the park area is not accessible to the car-less boater, there are a wide range of thrilling rides and more static animals to be seen. *Open throughout the year, times vary.* Charge.

Severn Valley Railway The Station, Bewdley DY12 1BG (01299 403816; www.svr.co.uk). Arguably one of the premier restored steam line, running trains along 16 miles of one of the most beautiful sections of the Severn Valley. Trains operate *May-Sep daily* and less frequently at other times during the year. Most trains have licensed buffet cars and several stations have gift shops. Charge. Disabled facilities available by *prior booking*.

Tourist Information Centre 16 Load Street, Bewdley DY12 2AE (01299 404740; www. wyreforestdc.gov.uk). *Open daily Feb-Dec 10.00-16.30.* Information about guided town and country walks can be obtained from here.

Pubs and Restaurants (pages 102–103)

🍺 1 **The Angel** 14 Severn Side, Stourport-on-Severn DY13 9EW (01299 822661). In a fine riverside situation, this compact bar serves real ale and real cider and homemade food is available *Mon-Thu L & Fri-Sat E*. Riverside seating and moorings. Children and well-behaved dogs welcome. Traditional pub games, real fires, sports TV and Wi-Fi. Camping. B&B. *Open 11.00-23.00.*

🍺 2 **The Hollybush** 54 Mitton Street, Stourport-on-Severn DY13 9AA (01299 827435). Friendly, welcoming community pub serving real ales and real cider. Child- and dog-friendly, beer garden. Traditional pub games, newspapers, real fires, sports TV and Wi-Fi. Live music *Thu-Sat. Open Sun-Thu 12.00-23.30 (Sun 23.00) & Fri-Sat 12.00-00.00.*

✕🍽 3 **Namaste Indian Eatery** 1 Lichfield Street, Stourport-on-Severn DY13 9EU (01299 877448; www.namastestourport.com). Relaxed, contemporary restaurant, in a building listed as an ancient monument, offering Pan-Asian cuisine. Children welcome. Eat in and takeaway. *Open Tue-Sun 17.30-23.00 (Fri-Sat 23.30).*

✕ 4 **Blossoms Tea Rooms** 18 York Street, Stourport-on-Severn DY13 9EE (01299 829442). Café, adjacent to York Street Lock. Tearooms, sandwiches, ice cream and drinks, light snacks including homemade cakes. *Open Wed-Sun 09.30-16.30.*

🍺 5 **The Rising Sun** 50 Lombard Street, Stourport-on-Severn DY13 8DU (01299 822530). Canalside, between Baldwins Bridge 5A and Gilgal Bridge 6. Small, friendly pub serving real ale. Food is available *L and E (not Sun E)*. Children welcome away from the bar, and there is a garden. Dog-friendly. Traditional pub games, newspapers, real fires, sports TV and Wi-Fi. Camping. *Open 10.30-00.00 (Sun 12.30).*

🍺 6 **The Bird in Hand** 5 Holly Road, Stourport-on-Severn DY13 9BA (01299 871515). Real ale is served in this black and white canalside pub, which has a pleasant garden and a bowling green. Food is served *Mon-Sat 12.00-20.00 (Fri-Sat 21.00) & Sun L and E*. Child- and dog-friendly. Real fires, sports TV and Wi-Fi. *Open 12.00-00.00 (Fri-Sat 01.00).* Have a look at the canal company cottages next door.

🍺✕ 7 **The Black Star** Mitton Street, Stourport-on-Severn DY13 8YP (01299 488838; www. wyevalleybrewery.co.uk/the-black-star). This pub has a bright, airy feel and an attractive floral beer garden. It also dispenses a wide range of Wye Valley Brewery real ales together with real cider. Food is available *Tue-Sat 12.00-21.00 & Sun L*. Dog- and family-friendly. Real fires and Wi-Fi. Live music *Fri-Sun. Open 12.00-23.00 (Fri-Sat 00.00).*

Also try: 🍺 8 **The Swan**, 56 High Street, Stourport-on-Severn DY13 8BX (01299 877832; www.stourporttown.co.uk/the-swan).

STAFFORDSHIRE & WORCESTERSHIRE CANAL

MAXIMUM DIMENSIONS

Length: 72'
Beam: 7'
Headroom: 6' 0"

MANAGER

0303 040 4040
enquiries.westmidlands@canalrivertrust.org.uk

MILEAGE

STOURPORT to:
Kidderminster Lock: 4½ miles
Wolverley Lock: 6 miles

STOURTON JUNCTION: 12¼ miles
Swindon: 16¾ miles
Bratch Locks: 19 miles

ALDERSLEY JUNCTION: 25 miles

AUTHERLEY JUNCTION: 25½ miles

GREAT HAYWOOD JUNCTION: 46 miles

Locks: 43

Construction of this navigation was begun immediately after that of the Trent & Mersey, to effect the joining of the rivers Trent, Mersey and Severn. After this, only the line down to the Thames was necessary to complete the skeleton outline of England's narrow canal network. Engineered by James Brindley, the Staffordshire & Worcestershire was opened throughout in 1772, at a cost of rather over £100,000. It stretched 46 miles from Great Haywood on the Trent & Mersey to the River Severn, which it joined at what became the bustling canal town of Stourport. The canal was an immediate success. It was well placed to bring goods from the Potteries down to Gloucester, Bristol and the West Country; while the Birmingham Canal, which joined it halfway along at Aldersley Junction, fed manufactured goods northwards from the Black Country to the Potteries via Great Haywood. Stourport has always been the focal point of the waterway, for the town owed its birth and rapid growth during the late 18th C to the advent of the canal. It was here that the cargoes were transferred from narrowboats into Severn Trows for shipment down the estuary to Bristol and the south west. The Staffordshire & Worcestershire Canal soon found itself facing strong competition. In 1815 the Worcester & Birmingham Canal opened, offering a more direct but heavily locked canal link between Birmingham and the Severn. The Staffordshire & Worcestershire answered this threat by gradually extending the opening times of the locks, until by 1830 they were open 24 hours a day. When the Birmingham & Liverpool Junction Canal was opened from Autherley to Nantwich in 1835, traffic bound for Merseyside from Birmingham naturally began to use this more direct, modern canal, and the Staffordshire & Worcestershire lost a great deal of traffic over its length from Autherley to Great Haywood. Most of the traffic now passed along only the ½-mile stretch of the Staffordshire & Worcestershire Canal between Autherley and Aldersley Junctions. This was, however, enough for the company, who levied absurdly high tolls for this tiny length. In 1836 the B & LJ Company, therefore, cooperated with the Birmingham Canal Company to promote a parliamentary Bill for the Tettenhall & Autherley Canal and Aqueduct. This remarkable project was to be a canal flyover, going from the Birmingham Canal right over the profiteering Staffordshire & Worcestershire and locking down into the Birmingham & Liverpool Junction Canal. In the face of this serious threat to bypass its canal altogether, the Staffordshire & Worcestershire company gave way and reduced its tolls to a level acceptable to the other two companies. In later years the device was used twice more to force concessions out of the Staffordshire & Worcestershire. In spite of this set-back, the Staffordshire & Worcestershire maintained a good profit, and high dividends were paid throughout the rest of the 19th C. When the new railway companies appeared in the West Midlands, the canal company would have nothing to do with them; but from the 1860s onwards railway competition began to bite, and the company's profits began to slip. Several modernisation schemes came to nothing, and the canal's trade declined. Like the other narrow canals, the Staffordshire & Worcestershire had faded into obscurity as a significant transport route by the middle of this century, although the old canal company proudly retained total independence until it was nationalised in 1947. Now the canal is used by numerous pleasure craft – it is certainly most delightful for cruising, walking and cycling.

The Staffordshire & Worcestershire Canal, Stourport

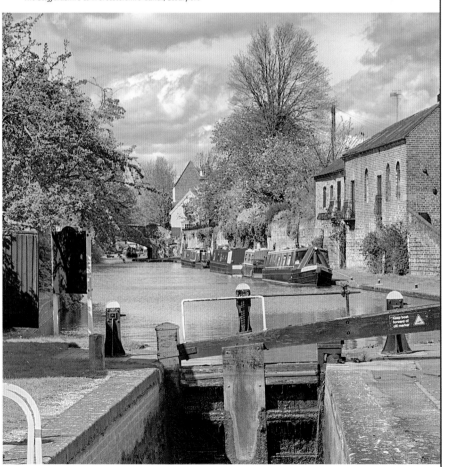

Stourport

The Staffordshire & Worcestershire Canal is, without doubt, one of the prettiest and most interesting waterways in England. The locks and basins at Stourport make for a fascinating start, having an intriguing combination of all kinds of engineering features and fine buildings, with the famous clock tower looking out over all. There are two sets of locks here, narrow and broad, as well as the usual facilities which include *toilets, showers, pump out and a laundry*. The narrow locks are those most commonly in use, and form a staircase – the lock keeper is usually around to help if you have difficulties. To reach the Staffordshire & Worcestershire Canal itself, boats should proceed to the eastern corner of the upper basins, pass under the bridge and climb the deep lock at York Street. There is a useful *tearoom* and *craft shop* by the lock, and above the lock there are good temporary *moorings*. The canal soon acquires a secluded, unspoilt character, flanked by discreet houses and walls. Keep a look out for the lovely old red-brick canalside building, with a terrace (and large tropical fish), by Gilgal Bridge, and the roller on the towpath side opposite Railway Basin, once used to pull the boats out. The navigation continues to creep through the town, soon emerging into the country. It follows the west side of a valley, the steep slopes rising sharply from the water. The River Stour approaches, and at Pratt's Wharf the towpath rises over the remains of a lock that once joined the canal to the Stour. This river used to be navigable from here for $1\frac{1}{4}$ miles down to the Wilden Ironworks. Soon the canal's surroundings change, for the hillside on the west bank becomes a dramatic cliff of crumbling red rock rising sheer from the canal. This is the southern end of a geological feature that stretches almost to Wombourn, 15 miles away. Falling Sands and Caldwall locks both enjoy delightful situations at the foot of the sandstone, and both have split iron bridges of a type usually associated with the Stratford-on-Avon Canal. Beyond Falling Sands Bridge look out for the steam trains of the Severn Valley Railway on the viaduct. There are shops by bridge 5A.

A LATE 18TH-CENTURY VIEW OF STOURPORT

'About 1766, where the river Stour empties itself into the Severn below Mitton stood a little ale house called Stourmouth. Near this Brindley has caused a town to be erected, made a port and dockyards, built a new and elegant bridge, established markets and made it a wonder not only of this county but of the nation at large.'

Nash, a Worcestershire historian.

Boatyards

See Page 104.

WILDLIFE
The *Large Skipper* favours grassy places of all kinds and flies during June and July. The upperwings are dark brown and orange-brown with pale markings. The underwings are buffish orange with paler spots. In common with most other skipper butterflies, at rest the Large Skipper often holds its wings at an angle and can look rather moth-like. The caterpillars feed on grasses.

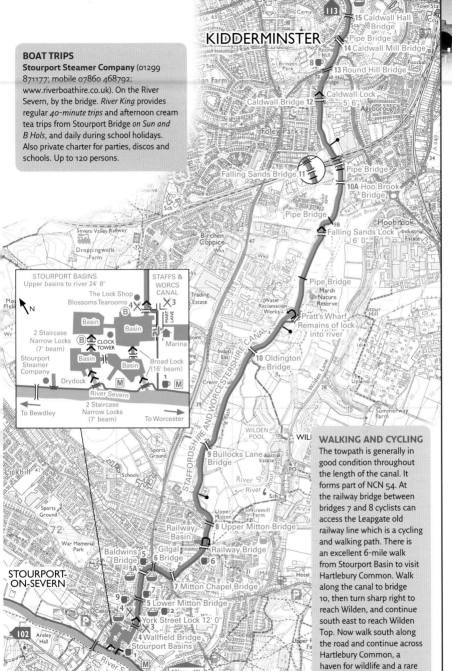

BOAT TRIPS

Stourport Steamer Company (01299 871177; mobile 07860 468792; www.riverboathire.co.uk). On the River Severn, by the bridge. *River King* provides regular *40-minute trips* and afternoon cream tea trips from Stourport Bridge *on Sun and B Hols*, and daily during school holidays. Also private charter for parties, discos and schools. Up to 120 persons.

KIDDERMINSTER

15 Caldwall Hall Bridge
Pipe Bridge
14 Caldwall Mill Bridge
13 Round Hill Bridge
Caldwall Lock
Caldwall Bridge **12**
Pipe Bridge
Falling Sands Bridge **11**
10A Hoo Brook Bridge
Pipe Bridge
Falling Sands Lock
Hoobrook
Pipe Bridge
Marsh Nature Reserve
Pratt's Wharf
Remains of lock into river
10 Oldington Bridge

STOURPORT BASINS
Upper basins to river 24' 8"

STAFFS & WORCS CANAL

The Lock Shop
Blossoms Tearooms

2 Staircase Narrow Locks (7' beam)
CLOCK TOWER
Stourport Steamer Company
Drydock
Basin
Basin
Basin
Basin
Marina
Broad Lock (16' beam)
River Severn
To Bewdley
2 Staircase Narrow Locks (7' beam)
To Worcester

WILDEN POOL

9 Bullocks Lane Bridge
River Stour
Upper Mitton Farm
Railway Basin
8 Upper Mitton Bridge
Railway Bridge
Baldwins Bridge **5**
Gilgal Bridge **6**
6
5A
7 Mitton Chapel Bridge
5 Lower Mitton Bridge
York Street Lock 12' 0"
4 Wallfield Bridge
Stourport Basins
12¼m 10L Stourton Jnc

STOURPORT-ON-SEVERN

Areley Hall
War Memorial Park
Areley Kings
Round House
The Walshes
HARTLEBURY COMMON

WALKING AND CYCLING

The towpath is generally in good condition throughout the length of the canal. It forms part of NCN 54. At the railway bridge between bridges 7 and 8 cyclists can access the Leapgate old railway line which is a cycling and walking path. There is an excellent 6-mile walk from Stourport Basin to visit Hartlebury Common. Walk along the canal to bridge 10, then turn sharp right to reach Wilden, and continue south east to reach Wilden Top. Now walk south along the road and continue across Hartlebury Common, a haven for wildlife and a rare expanse of inland sand dunes. Continue south through Titton to join the River Severn, where you turn right to return to Stourport.

● **Stourport-on-Severn**

Worcs. PO, tel, stores, chemists, takeaways, fish & chips, banks, off-licence, baker, butcher, greengrocer, laundrettes, garage. When the engineer James Brindley surveyed the line for the Staffordshire & Worcestershire Canal in the early 1760s, he chose to meet the River Severn at the hamlet of Lower Mitton, 4 miles downstream from Bewdley, where the little River Stour flowed into the Severn. Basins and locks were built for the boats, warehouses for the cargoes and cottages for the workmen. In 1788 the canal company even built the great Tontine Hotel (which has, alas, been closed for some years and now looks very sorry for itself) beside the locks. The hamlet soon earned the name of Stourport, becoming a busy and wealthy town. The two basins were expanded to five (one has since been filled in) and the locks were duplicated. Much still remains of Stourport's former glory, for the basins are always full of moored boats, with plenty of other craft passing to and from the river. The delightful clock tower still functions and there is a canal office in the old workshops by the locks. Mart Lane, on the north east side of the basins, is well worth a look – the original 18th-C terrace of workmen's cottages still stands, with numbers 2, 3 and 4 listed as ancient monuments. In contrast with the basin area, the town of Stourport is not particularly interesting, and, although it was built on account of the canal, it has no relationship at all with the basins now.

Hartlebury Common To the east of Stourport. This is regarded by naturalists as one of the most important surviving areas of heathland in the West Midlands, recognised by the Nature Conservancy Council in 1955 and designated a SSSI. Originally owned by the Church Commissioners, it was purchased by the County Council in 1968. It covers an area of 216 acres rising to a height of 184ft, and consists mainly of dry lowland or scrub heath on river terraces of sand, over a bedrock of Triassic sandstone. The sand has, in places, formed into dunes, which can shift with the wind – a feature rare so far inland. There is a pond and marshy areas which support aquatic plants, dragonflies and frogs. Birds to look out for include long-tailed tits, tree pipits and stonechats. Plants to be seen include ling and bell heather, bogbean, marsh cinquefoil, heath milkwort and shepherds purse. The particularly sharp-eyed may notice dung beetles, green tiger beetles, large skipper butterflies and common lizards. The views from the top are splendid.

Pubs and Restaurants (page 109)

⬤ 1 **The Angel** 14 Severn Side, Stourport-on-Severn DY13 9EW (01299 822661). In a fine riverside situation, this compact bar serves real ale and real cider and homemade food is available *Mon-Thu L & Fri-Sat E*. Riverside seating and moorings. Children and well-behaved dogs welcome. Traditional pub games, real fires, sports TV and Wi-Fi. Camping. B&B. *Open 11.00-23.00.*

⬤ 2 **The Hollybush** 54 Mitton Street, Stourport-on-Severn DY13 9AA (01299 827435). Friendly, welcoming community pub serving real ales and real cider. Child- and dog-friendly, beer garden. Traditional pub games, newspapers, real fires, sports TV and Wi-Fi. Live music *Thu-Sat. Open Sun-Thu 12.00-23.30 (Sun 23.00) & Fri-Sat 12.00-00.00.*

✕♀ 3 **Namaste Indian Eatery** 1 Lichfield Street, Stourport-on-Severn DY13 9EU (01299 877448; www.namastestourport.com). Relaxed, contemporary restaurant, in a building listed as an ancient monument, offering Pan-Asian cuisine. Children welcome. Eat in and takeaway. *Open Tue-Sun 17.30-23.00 (Fri-Sat 23.30).*

✕ 4 **Blossoms Tea Rooms** 18 York Street, Stourport-on-Severn DY13 9EE (01299 829442). Café, adjacent to York Street Lock. Tearooms, sandwiches, ice cream and drinks, light snacks including homemade cakes. *Open Wed-Sun 09.30-16.30.*

⬤ 5 **The Rising Sun** 50 Lombard Street, Stourport-on-Severn DY13 8DU (01299 822530). Canalside, between Baldwins Bridge 5A and Gilgal Bridge 6. Small, friendly pub serving real ale. Food is available *L and E (not Sun E)*. Children welcome away from the bar, and there is a garden. Dog-friendly. Traditional pub games, newspapers, real fires, sports TV and Wi-Fi. Camping. *Open 10.30-00.00 (Sun 12.30).*

⬤ 6 **The Bird in Hand** 5 Holly Road, Stourport-on-Severn DY13 9BA (01299 871515). Real ale is served in this black and white canalside pub, which has a pleasant garden and a bowling green. Food is served *Mon-Sat 12.00-20.00 (Fri-Sat 21.00) & Sun L and E*. Child- and dog-friendly. Real fires, sports TV and Wi-Fi. *Open 12.00-00.00 (Fri-Sat 01.00).* Have a look at the canal cottages next door.

⬤✕ 7 **The Black Star** Mitton Street, Stourport-on-Severn DY13 8YP (01299 488838; www.wyevalleybrewery.co.uk/the-black-star). This pub has a bright, airy feel and an attractive floral beer garden. It also dispenses a wide range of Wye Valley Brewery real ales together with real cider. Food is available *Tue-Sat 12.00-21.00 & Sun L*. Dog- and family-friendly. Real fires and Wi-Fi. Live music *Fri-Sun. Open 12.00-23.00 (Fri-Sat 00.00).*

⬤ 8 **The Watermill** Park Lane, Kidderminster DY11 6TL (01562 66713; www.watermillpub.co.uk). By Round Hill Bridge (13). A fine pub with gardens onto the canal. Food is served *daily 12.00-22.00 (Sun 21.00)*. Dog- and family-friendly. Wi-Fi and moorings. *Open 11.30-23.00.*

Also try: ⬤ 9 **The Swan**, 56 High Street, Stourport-on-Severn DY13 8BX (01299 877832; www.stourporttown.co.uk/the-swan).

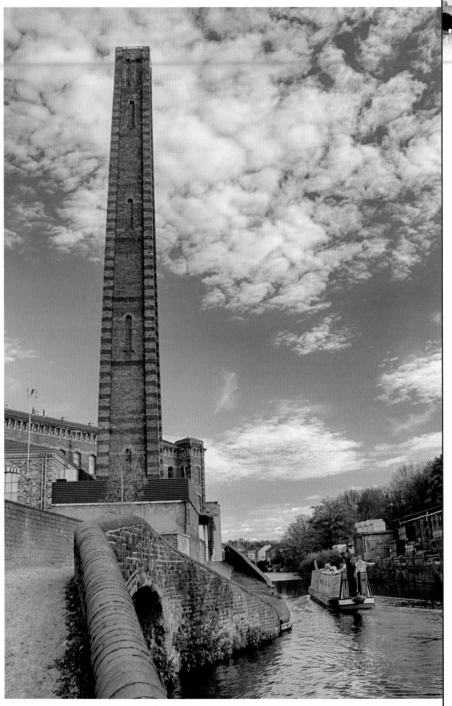

Passing Weaver's Wharf shopping centre, Kidderminster

Kidderminster

The approach to Kidderminster has changed considerably – what was once an almost claustrophobic route between red-brick mills is now smart developments, with a broad towpath, good *moorings* and *supermarkets* and *cafés* close by. The cost is the disappearance of some visible canal history. The canal still creeps under a roundabout at the centre of the town to emerge at Kidderminster Lock by the handsome church and wharf crane which overlook the moorings. But there is still traffic all around, and reaching the shopping streets, which are close by, requires the crossing of some busy roads. Nearby is a statue of Richard Baxter, the 17th-C thinker who advocated unity and comprehension in religion. Just above Kidderminster Lock the River Stour appears, and the canal crosses it on an aqueduct. There is another *supermarket* by bridge 17. Leaving the town behind, the navigation moves into an area of quiet water meadows created by the River Stour, which is now on the west side. Passing the isolated Wolverley Court Lock, the village of Wolverley on the other side of the valley is marked by its unusual Italianate church standing on a large outcrop of rock. The approach to the deep Wolverley Lock is lined by trees. There is a *pub* beside the lock, and good *moorings* above and below it. Beyond here the course of the canal becomes really tortuous and narrow as it proceeds up the enclosed and thickly wooded valley, forced into endless diversions by the steep cliffs of friable red sandstone. Vegetation of all kinds clings to these cliffs, giving the impression of jungle foliage. At one point the navigation opens out, becoming momentarily like a normal canal; but soon the rocks and trees encroach again, returning the waterway to its previous constricted width. An impressive promontory of rock compels the canal to double back on itself in a great horseshoe sweep that takes it round to the pretty Debdale Lock. A doorway reveals a cavern cut into the solid rock here; this may have been used as an overnight stable for towing horses, although access would not have been straightforward. Beyond Cookley Tunnel the steep rocks along the right bank used to culminate in a remarkable geological feature where Austcliff Rock overhung the canal. It was removed when it became unstable. Across the River Stour, 1/4 mile west of bridge 26, is the small settlement of Caunsall. There are farms here, and *two pubs*, but little else. Between bridges 26 and 27 the canal passes from Worcestershire into Staffordshire, but the surroundings of this remarkable waterway do not change: it continues through secluded woodlands, the rocky hillside on the east bank steepening as the valley narrows again. The nearby main road remains unnoticed while the canal reaches Whittington Lock, which has a pretty lock cottage beside it. The Bridge at the lock tail is typical of this navigation, its parapet curving fluently round and down to the lower water level.

● **Kidderminster**
Worcs. All services. Kidderminster once existed above all for carpet weaving. The industry was first introduced in 1735, when the town was already a prosperous cloth manufacturing centre. Rowland Hill, founder of the Penny Post, was born here in 1793. His statue, in front of the head post office, commemorates his 'creative mind and patient energy'. The best place for access to the town is from the moorings between bridges 15 & 16, or from the mooring above Kidderminster Lock, just below the church. The inner ring road unfortunately passes the door of the impressive, dark church of St Mary and All Saints, cutting it off completely from Church

Street, in which Kidderminster's few Georgian houses are situated.
Severn Valley Railway Kidderminster Town Station, Comberton Hill Kidderminster DY10 1QX (01299 403816/talking timetable; www.svr.co.uk). A fine preserved steam railway on which you can travel the 16 miles to Bewdley, Arley, Highley, Hampton Loade and Bridgnorth. Most trains have buffet and bar facilities, and you may book in advance for special dining car services on *Sun, B Hols, Gala Weekend Sats and selected evenings*. The King & Castle at Kidderminster Station is decorated in GWR style and offers a wide choice of real ales – there is also a small museum at the station. Courses are organised for prospective train drivers – telephone for details.

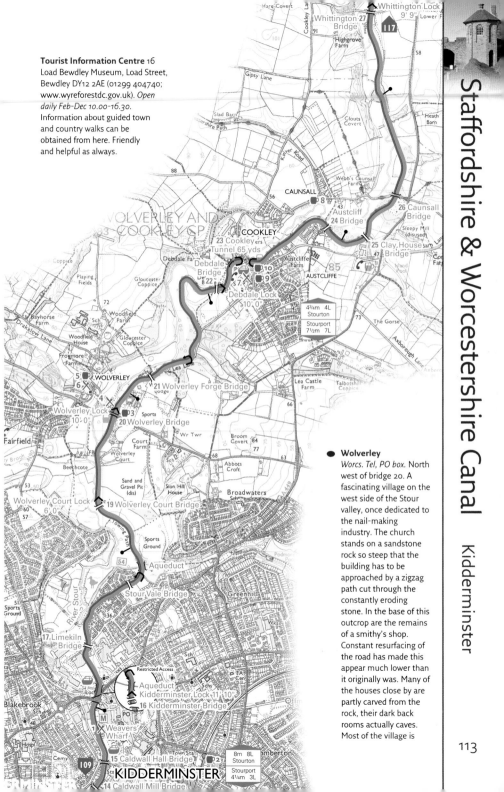

Tourist Information Centre 16
Load Bewdley Museum, Load Street,
Bewdley DY12 2AE (01299 404740;
www.wyreforestdc.gov.uk). *Open
daily Feb-Dec 10.00-16.30.*
Information about guided town
and country walks can be
obtained from here. Friendly
and helpful as always.

● **Wolverley**
Worcs. Tel, PO box. North
west of bridge 20. A
fascinating village on the
west side of the Stour
valley, once dedicated to
the nail-making
industry. The church
stands on a sandstone
rock so steep that the
building has to be
approached by a zigzag
path cut through the
constantly eroding
stone. In the base of this
outcrop are the remains
of a smithy's shop.
Constant resurfacing of
the road has made this
appear much lower than
it originally was. Many of
the houses close by are
partly carved from the
rock, their dark back
rooms actually caves.
Most of the village is

clustered just to the north of the church, near the little-used but dignified stone buildings of the Old Court House, which has also seen service as both a grammar school and council offices. The school was endowed in 1629, but most of the buildings date from 1820. Around it is the bulk of this small village, where gardens make the most of the brook that flows through. There is an attractive pub in the centre of the village, and another, with spacious gardens, up the hill. Wolverley is certainly a village worth visiting – easily accessible from Wolverley Lock.

St John the Baptist Wolverley DY11 5XD. A predominant dark red structure built in 1772 in a precise Italianate style, succeeding earlier churches which have stood on this site since Anglo-Saxon times. In legend the Lord of the Manor, a crusader called Attwood, was found in chains in the meadow, having been miraculously transported from a prison after seeing a vision of the Virgin Mary. Indeed the field by the lock is still called the Knight's Meadow. Fragments of the knight's effigy can be seen in the church.

● **Cookley**
Worcs. PO, tel, stores, fish & chips, off-licence, takeaway. The village is set well above the canal, which passes underneath it in a tunnel. Although it has an attractive situation, Cookley is a straightforward and workmanlike village, useful for supplies. Down in the valley, near the River Stour, there are older, more attractive cottages, and clearly visible are the entrances to caves in the cliff face. Moor west of Cookley Tunnel and the towpath bridge to gain eaeasy access. Stores *open 06.00-23.00.*
Cookley Tunnel Cookley. This is 65yds long and is rough hewn from the living rock. It is unusual, in having a towpath running through it, but this probably reflects the ease with which sandstone can be worked.

Pubs and Restaurants (page 113)

✕♈ 1 **Frankie & Benny's** The Pump House, Weavers' Wharf, Kidderminster DY10 1AA (01562 741333; www.frankieandbennys.com/restaurant/frankie-bennys-kidderminster) A member of the popular 'New York Italian' restaurant chain, right beside the moorings. Food served *daily 09.00-23.00 (Sun 22.30).*

● 2 **The King & Castle** Station Approach, Comberton Hill, Kidderminster DY10 1QX (01562 747505). East of bridge 15. A fine bar, decorated in GWR style and offering a wide range of real ales and real ciders, together with home-cooked meals *Mon-Sat 08.00-21.00 (Sat 10.00) & Sun 11.00-21.00.* Breakfast served *until 11.00.* Children welcome, and there are seats outside on the platform. Dog-friendly. Traditional pub games, newspapers, real fires and Wi-Fi. *Open Mon-Fri 08.00-23.00, Sat 10.00-23.30 & Sun 11.00-23.00.*

● 3 **The Lock** Wolverley Road, Wolverley DY10 3RN (01562 850581; thelockinnwolverley.co.uk). A fine canalside pub, which was previously 16th-C cottages. It was converted in stages to a pub and once had a brewhouse. There are stories of one landlord, Harry Davies, who held the licence for 55 years, taking his payment for ale in cargoes from passing boats. This resulted in drunken boatmen with their wallets still full but their boats half-empty. But the pub pre-dates the canal, and originally drew its trade from the drove road which passed between the Black Country and Wales. Real ale. Meals served *daily 12.00-21.00 (Sun 20.00).* Child- and dog-friendly. Canalside garden with moorings nearby. Newspapers, real fires and Wi-Fi. *Open Mon-Sat 11.00-23.00 (Sat 23.30) & Sun 11.00-22.30.*

✕ 4 **The Old Smithy Tearoom** Wolverley Road, Wolverley DY10 3RN (01562 850581/07964 287550; thelockinnwolverley.co.uk/tea-room). Friendly establishment serving a wide selection of teas and coffee together with appetising range of hot snacks, sandwiches, cakes and scones. Also cold drinks and ice creams. *Open daily 10.00-16.00 (Sat-Sun 09.30).*

● 5 **The Queens Head** Wolverley Village, Kidderminster DY11 5XB (01562 850433; www.queensheadwolverley.com). 17th-C pub set in the village conservation area, with an attractive stream-side terrace garden, serving real ales and food *Mon-Sun L and E (not Sun E).* Tue folk/blues and Fri live music. Children and dogs welcome. Traditional pub games, newspapers and sports TV. *Open Mon-Thu 11.00-23.00 & Fri-Sun 12.00-00.00 (Sun 23.00).*

✕ 6 **The Old Village Store** Wolverley Village, Kidderminster DY11 5XB (01562 850499; www.theoldvillagestore.co.uk). A real community hub, with pretty décor and friendly proprietors, serving an appetising selection of coffee, tea, cakes and sandwiches, tucked away in the tranquillity of the old village centre. *Open Mon-Sat 09.00-16.30 (Sat 15.00) & Sun 10.00-15.00.*

✕ 7 **Cookley Fisheries** 1 Bridge Road, Cookley, Kidderminster DY10 3SA (01562 850554). Excellent fish & chips, kebabs, burgers and chicken. *Open Mon-Sat 11.30-14.00 & 16.30-22.30.*

● 8 **The Anchor Inn** Caunsell Road, Cookley, Kidderminster DY11 5YL (01562 850254; www.theanchorinncaunsall.co.uk). A short walk west of bridge 26. Real ales and real cider in an old-fashioned pub, which has been in the same family since 1927 and was purchased by the them, 10 years later, for just £1,800. Known for its friendly welcome and well-filled cobs, this unadulterated hostelry has an outside courtyard and Wi-Fi. Children and dogs welcome. *Open L and E.*

Also try: ● 9 **The Eagle & Spur** 176 Castle Rd, Cookley DY10 3TB (01562 850184) and ● 10 **The Bulls Head** 10 Bridge Rd, Cookley, Kidderminster DY10 3SA (01562 228658).

Kinver

This stretch of the canal begins with yet another delightful scene – on both sides of the canal are cottages, pretty gardens, moored boats and a low bridge. Tall, steep, hills rising to over 250ft appear on the east bank. The canal leaves this damp, mossy area and bends round to Kinver Lock. There is a *pub* here, and a road leading round to the village, behind the bold modern waterworks, built in 1939. The waterworks pump water from the vast underground lake that lies deep below the great sandstone ridge stretching from Kidderminster to Wombourne. Beyond the particularly pretty Hyde Lock, the canal wanders along the edge of woods on the east side of the valley, where in one place the sandstone, eroded away, is supported on brick pillars – it then passes through the charmingly diminutive (25yds long) Dunsley Tunnel, a rough-hewn bore carved out of the rock, with overhanging foliage at each end. The next lock is at Stewponey, accompanied by a toll house. The Stourbridge Canal leaves at Stourton Junction, north of the wharf: the first of the many locks that carry this canal up towards Dudley and the Birmingham Canal Navigations is just a few yards away (*see* page 132). Beyond Stourton Junction, a 90-degree bend to the left takes the canal to an aqueduct over the River Stour: this river now disappears to the north east and is not seen again. Its place near the canal is taken by the Smestow Brook as far as Swindon. At the far end of the aqueduct is a curious narrowboat-house, known as the Devil's Den, cut into the rock. Prestwood Park is concealed in the woods above the east bank. The hall is now a hospital: it used to be the home of the Foleys, a family of Black Country ironmasters. Beyond Prestwood Bridge (34), now rebuilt in red brick to the original design, the canal makes a remote journey through Gothersley and Rocky locks: at Gothersley a memorial marks the site of the Roundhouse, built in 1805 as part of the ironworks, and lived in until the 1930s. After Rocky Lock, where rooms have been carved into the sandstone, the canal comes to a fork: the narrow entrance on the right leads into the long Ashwood Basin, where there is a marina. Now the outcrops of sandstone appear less frequently, and the countryside becomes flatter and more regular. The locks, however, do not disappear, for the canal continues the steady rise up the small valley of the Smestow Brook, through southern Staffordshire towards Wolverhampton. At Greensforge Lock (*toilets, showers and sanitary station*) there is an attractive *pub*, and another of the circular weirs that are found, often hidden behind a wall or a hedge, at many of the locks along this delightful canal.

● **Kinver**
Staffs. PO, tel, stores, chemist, bank, bakery, off-licence, fish & chips, takeaways, delicatessen, greengrocer, butcher. Kinver deservedly has a reputation as a very pretty village. It is surrounded by tall hills and consists of a long main street of reasonably attractive houses, but its chief glory is its situation – it nestles among tall wooded hills, a position that must strike the visitor as remarkable for a village so close to the industries of the West Midlands. Kinver Edge (National Trust), west of the village, is a tremendous ridge covered in gorse and heather, and for anyone prepared to toil up to the top from the valley it provides a splendid view of the Cotswold and Malvern Hills. The church of St Peter is near the Edge, and is reached by a steep zigzag road. It overlooks the village

and contains several items of interest, including plaques recording the Charter granted by Charles I in 1629 and the Charter granted by Ethelbad in 736, giving '10 cessapis of land to my general Cyniberte for a religious house'. If you walk up Stone Lane, close to the White Harte Hotel, until trees appear on your left, then follow the path into the trees, you will come to some superb examples of rock houses at Holy Austin Rock. Here you will see rooms, windows, cupboards, doorways and chimneys carved out of the cliffs. One of these houses, which from the inside appeared just like normal dwellings (apart from a lack of windows) was in continuous occupation for 150 years until 1935. Rock dwellings were first recorded here in 1777, and it is likely that the name, Holy Austin, originated from an Augustinian Friar who lived here prior to that time. The film *Bladys of the Stewponey* was made here in 1919 by the folklorist and novelist Sabine Baring-Gould. Take care when exploring, as the rock can be slippery underfoot.

● **Stewponey Wharf**
An interesting wharf at the head of Stewponey Lock, with a restored octagonal toll office. From near the wharf the long-abandoned Kinver Valley Light Railway used to run from Stourbridge to Kinver. From Stewponey to Kinver it followed a route close to the canal. Note also the fine circular weir by the lock. Just across the river from the wharf is the impressive bulk of Stourton Castle, while in the opposite direction – but shielded by trees – is a fast main road and a built-up area. There is an excellent tearoom just across the very busy road.

Stourton Castle Just a few yards west of Stewponey Wharf, this building is a curious mixture of building styles and materials. The castle is notable as the birthplace of Cardinal Pole in 1500. A friend of Mary Tudor, Pole became Archbishop of Canterbury in her reign after Cranmer had been burned at the stake. The castle is privately owned.

● **Ashwood Basin**
This used to be a railway-connected basin owned by the National Coal Board. After the line was closed the basin was disused for some years, but it has now been enlarged and provides a pleasant mooring site for a large number of pleasure boats in a private marina. A road is carried over the basin by a small viaduct, visible from the canal.

Boatyards

Ⓑ**Ashwood Marina Ltd** 295535/07743 667192; www.ashwoodmarina.co.uk). Just past Bridge 36 at Ashwood Basin. 🛢 Gas, overnight mooring (telephone in advance) long-term mooring, solid fuel, boat service and repair, dry dock, winter storage, bottom blacking, boat sales, outboard and inflatable sales, chandlery, books, maps. *Emergency call out. Open daily 10.00-16.00 (Sun 12.00).*

WALKING AND CYCLING
Stone Lane, Kinver makes a fine start for a walk which visits the rock houses by Holy Austin Rock, and then climbs south to Kinver Edge, Nanny's Rock and Kingsford Country Park. You can then return across Blakeshill Common to Cookley, where you join the canal and turn left.

Pubs and Restaurants (pages 117)

🍺✕ 1 **The Manor House of Whittington** Whittington, Kinver DY7 6NY (01384 872110; themanorhouseofwhittington.com). 300 yds east of bridge 28, along a footpath, and well worth the walk. Dating from 1310, this building has an impressive history. It was the home of Dick Whittington's grandfather, and much later of Lady Jane Grey, whose ghost is sometimes encountered. There are also priest holes and a tunnel to the nearby Whittington Hall. Restaurant and bar meals available *daily 12.00-22.00 (Sun 21.30).* Real ale, cocktails and an extensive wine list. Family-friendly, garden. Real fires and Wi-Fi. *Open daily 11.00-23.00 (Thu-Sat 00.00).*

✕♀ 2 **Baci Ristorante Italiano** 47-48 High St, Kinver DY7 6HE (01384 878789; www.baciristoranteitaliano.co.uk). Bright, airy establishment, with friendly attentive staff, serving classic Italian food. Children welcome. *Open Tue-Sun L and E.*

🍺 3 **The Cross Inn** Church Hill Close, Kinver DY7 6HZ (01384 878481; www.blackcountryales. co.uk/the-pubs/the-cross-inn). Traditional local's pub serving large selection of real ale

and real cider, together with bar snacks available *all day.* Children welcome *until 19.00,* dogs 'til closing time. *Regular* live music. Outside seating, traditional pub games, newspapers, sports TV, real fires and Wi-Fi. *Open daily 12.00-23.00 (Thu-Sat 00.00).*

✕♀ 4 **Basil's** 116 High Street, Kinver DY7 6HL (01384 878888; www.basilsrestaurantkinver. co.uk). Homely, popular restaurant *open Tue-Sun L and Mon-Sat E.* Booking recommended.

🍺 5 **Ye Old White Hart Hotel** 111 High Street, Kinver DY7 6HL (01384 872305; www. whitehartpub.co.uk). A large pub serving real ale, and food *daily 12.00-21.00 (Sun 20.00).* Garden and children's play area. Dog-friendly, traditional pub games and Wi-Fi. *Open daily 12.00-23.00 (Thu-Sat 00.00).*

🍺 6 **The Navigation Inn** Greenforge Lock, Kingswinford DY6 0AH (01384 273721). This pub was originally built in 1767. Log fires for the winter and canalside seating in the pretty garden for the summer. Real ale and home-made food is served *daily 12.00-21.00.* Children welcome *until 20.00.* Dog-friendly, real fires and sports TV. *Open 12.00-00.00.*

Camp
Cottages
GREENSFORGE
Greensforge Lock 9' 0"
Greensforge Bridge 37
6
119
RO
FORT

Ashwood Lodge

62
Marina
The
Gorse
ASHWOOD
Ashwood
Private Marina
Ashwoodfield
House Farm
A 449

Flatheridge
Bridge 36
Old Mill
Pond
Checkhill
Farm
Nursery
Waterworks
Cottages
Gorse Corner
63
78
ROMAN ROAD

Rocky Lock
7' 0"
62
Rumford Hill

Gothersley
Lock 7' 0"
35 Gothersley Bridge
Holloway
House
SITE OF GOTHERSLEY
ROUND HOUSE
Radway Hill
83

Gothersley
House
Gothersley
Farm
56
Gothersley
Rough
74
Yewtree
Farm

34 Prestwood Bridge
Lousy
Wood

Hampton Valley
135
Stourton Gorse
Gothersley Lane
PRESTWOOD
Nursing
Home
River Stour
MS
Newlands
132

The Slads
91
DEVIL'S DEN
Weir
Halcot
Farm
66
Prestwood Drive
Newtown Bridge
Newtown
Bridge

Clanbrook
MP
Stourton Farm
Aqueduct
Stourton
Top Lock
17
Stourbridge
Canal

56
Holly
Wood
Stourton
Junction
Monarch's
STEWPONEY
The
Hawthorns

12¾m 18L
Aldersley Jnc
Stourport
12¼m 11L
69
Stourton
Hall
Stourton
Bridge 33
19
18
Four Locks Bridge
Barratt's Coppice
Farm

Littlewood's Common
54
Stewponey Wharf
MS
20
Stourton Bottom Lock
72

Heathermoor
Farm
Gallowstree Elm
Stewponey Lock 10' 0"
Stewponey New Bridge 31A
32 Stewponey Bridge
STOURTON
Gibbet
Cottages
Barratt's
Coppice

KINVER
CP
River Stour
31
Dunsley Tunnel
(25 yds)
Dunsley Bank
Sand Pit
1S

Hyde Farm
The
Hyde
STAFFORDSHIRE AND WORCESTERSHIRE CANAL
Dunsley Hall
Dunsley
Hall
Farm
School
Plantation
Roundhill
Works

Potter's
Cross
Sch
Hyde Lock 10' 0"
30 Hyde Bridge
24
Dunsley Manor
Gibbet Wood
Gibbet Lane

56
KINVER
Manor
Farm
Dunsley
Dunsley
House
New Cottages

Miniature
Railway
DUNSLEY
2
29 Kinfare
Bridge
A 449

ber
Kinver Lock 7' 3"
5
4
3
51

Scout Camp
Site
Hill Farm
56
117
127
Cem
Whittington Horse 28
Bridge
113
1
Whittington Hall
Cottages
Whittington
Common

Hare Covert
WHITTINGTON
Whittington Hall
Whittington
Lower Farm

Whittington Lock
9' 9"
Whittington Bridge 27
Bridge
91

The Bratch

Another wooded, rocky section soon gives way to more open country. Passing through the isolated Hinksford Lock, the navigation bends round to Swindon where the canal is flanked by the tidy gardens of new houses. There are four locks hereabouts – Botterham Lock is a two-step staircase with a bridge crossing in the middle. Now the canal begins to lose its rural character as it encounters the modern outskirts of Wombourn, passing under a new bridge that, happily, retains the original cast iron name plates. There is a *pub* by this bridge (43) and a useful *range of shops* in Womborne, not far to the north east of the next one. Yet another *pub* is at the next bridge (45); and beyond it is Bumblehole Lock. The three Bratch Locks are next, raising the canal level by over 30ft. From the top there is a good view back down the valley, with the spire of Wombourn Church backed by the great ridge of the Orton Hills to the east. Leaving The Bratch, the canal wanders through open farmland parallel to a long-closed railway, now the course of the Kingswinford Railway Walk, arriving at the pleasantly situated Awbridge Lock, accompanied by a fine circular weir.

● **Swindon**
Staffs. PO, tel, store, bakery, fish & chips. A small village, once a mixture of farming and industry. The 19th-C ironworks has been demolished, replaced with a housing estate.

● **Wombourne**
Staffs. PO, tel, stores, delicatessen, bank, chemist, hardware, off-licence, bakery, library, garage. A village much expanded by housing development.

● **Bratch Locks**
With their octagonal toll office, attractive situation and unusual layout, these three locks are well known among students of canal engineering and architecture. At first sight they appear curiously illogical, with an impossibly short pound between the bottom of one lock and the top gate of the next; but the secret of their operation is the side ponds hidden behind the towpath hedge, and the culverts that connect these to the intermediate pounds. In fact, to work through these locks, boaters should simply treat each one as a separate lock, like any other. *Carefully study the operating instructions before use, and consult the lock keeper if you are in any doubt.*

NAVIGATIONAL NOTES

The Bratch Locks These are manned from *end Mar–end Oct*: first boat in lock *08.00*, last boat in lock by *19.40*. During the *winter months* the locks are not manned. Therefore, read the information boards carefully before starting to navigate the locks. In the *summer months*, the lock keeper sells Watermate keys, anti-vandal Keys (aka Handcuff Keys) and pump out tokens.

Pubs and Restaurants

● ✕ 1 **The Old Bush** High Street, Swindon DY3 4NR (01384 274852; www.theoldbushswindon. co.uk). East of bridge 40. Real ale and real cider in a homely pub where food is served *L and E (not Sun-Mon E)*. Dog-friendly, garden. Newspapers and sports TV. *Open Mon-Sat 12.00-23.00 (Fri-Sat 00.30) & Sun 12.00-22.30.*

● 2 **The Green Man Inn** High Street, Swindon DY3 4NR (01384 400532). A friendly, family-oriented traditional local, with open fires and a quiet snug with old books, serving real ale and real cider. Homemade food is available *L and E (not Sun E)*. Dog- and family-friendly, small attractive garden. Traditional pub games, real fires, sports TV and Wi-Fi. *Open Sun-Fri 12.00-23.00 & Sat 11.00-23.00.*

● ✕ 3 **The Waggon & Horses** Bridgnorth Road, Wombourne WV5 0AQ (01902 892828; www.waggonhorsespub.co.uk). Near the canal at bridge 43. Sociable real ale pub, serving food *daily 12.00-22.00 (Sun 21.00)*. Large garden with children's play area. Wi-Fi. Quiz *Mon. Open Mon-Sat 11.30-23.00 (Fri-Sat 23.30) & Sun 12.00-22.30).*

● 4 **The Round Oak** 100 Ounsdale Road, Wombourne WV5 8BU (01902 892083). Canalside at bridge 45. A real ale pub, dating from the 1800s, serving food *Mon-Thu L and E, Fri-Sat 12.00-21.00 & Sun 12.00-18.00.* Dog- and child-friendly, garden. Wi-Fi. *Open 12.00-23.00 (Fri-Sat 00.00).*

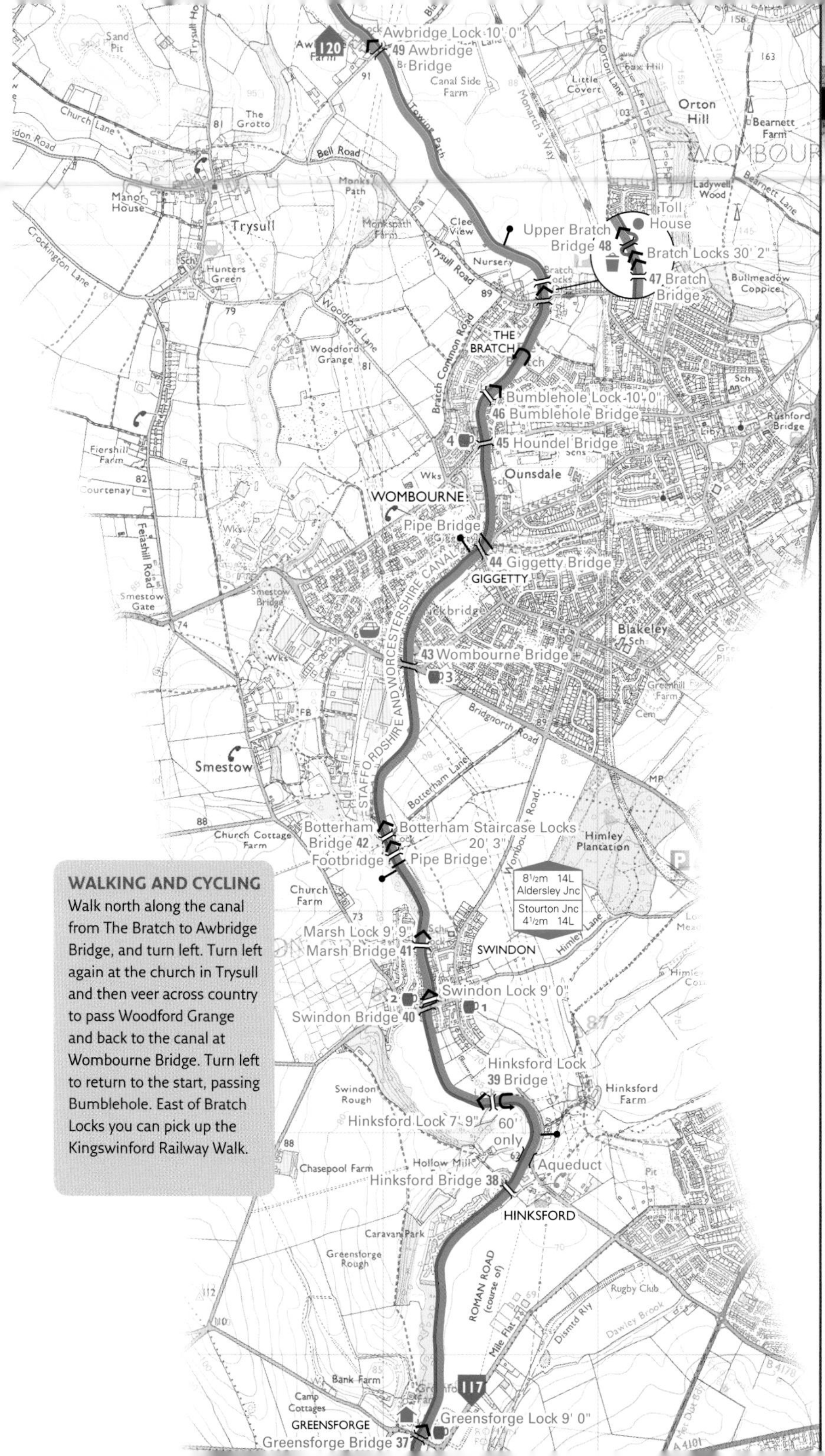

Map labels (Staffordshire & Worcestershire Canal — The Bratch):

Awbridge Lock 10' 0"
120
49 Awbridge Bridge
Aw Farm
91
Canal Side Farm
Orton Hill
Bearnett Farm
WOMBOURNE
Toll House
Upper Bratch Bridge 48
Bratch Locks 30' 2"
47 Bratch Bridge
Bullmeadow Coppice
Rushford Bridge
THE BRATCH
Trysull
Bratch Common Road
Bumblehole Lock 10' 0"
46 Bumblehole Bridge
45 Houndel Bridge
4
Ounsdale
WOMBOURNE
Pipe Bridge
44 Giggetty Bridge
GIGGETTY
Blakeley
43 Wombourne Bridge
23
Smestow
Botterham Bridge 42
Footbridge
Botterham Staircase Locks 20' 3"
Pipe Bridge
Himley Plantation
8½m 14L Aldersley Jnc
Stourton Jnc 4½m 14L
Marsh Lock 9' 9"
Marsh Bridge 41
SWINDON
2
Swindon Lock 9' 0"
1
Swindon Bridge 40
Hinksford Lock 39 Bridge
Hinksford Farm
Hinksford Lock 7' 9"
60' only
Aqueduct
Hinksford Bridge 38
HINKSFORD
ROMAN ROAD (course of)
GREENSFORGE
117
Greensforge Lock 9' 0"
Greensforge Bridge 37

WALKING AND CYCLING

Walk north along the canal from The Bratch to Awbridge Bridge, and turn left. Turn left again at the church in Trysull and then veer across country to pass Woodford Grange and back to the canal at Wombourne Bridge. Turn left to return to the start, passing Bumblehole. East of Bratch Locks you can pick up the Kingswinford Railway Walk.

Wightwick

North of Awbridge Lock the countryside gradually becomes less interesting and, although it is still quiet and remote from roads and railways, the canal is accompanied by overhead power lines for a mile as it rises through Ebstree and Dimmingsdale locks. At bridge 53 a private arm provides moorings for a fine array of traditionally painted working boats, amidst overhanging trees. Beyond the bridge a pretty lake to the west closes in – this is a canal-feeder reservoir of considerable interest to fishermen. Ahead, the hills of Wightwick overlook the navigation as it approaches a shallow valley and a busy main road. This valley – in places an artificial cutting – contains the canal right through to the flatter land at Aldersley. Houses, mostly modern, are never far away, although the canal manages to preserve its rural character all the way through what are in effect the western outskirts of Wolverhampton. Compton Lock marks the end of the 31-lock climb from the River Severn at Stourport, a rise of 294ft. There is a *supermarket* nearby. From here northwards, a 10-mile level pound takes the Staffordshire & Worcestershire on to Gailey, where the first of 12 locks begin the fall towards the Trent & Mersey Canal. At the Wildside Activity Centre, beside Hordern Road Bridge 62A, there are *boater facilities* located under the main building which include *toilets, showers, rubbish disposal and water.* Half a mile north west of here, there is a useful *parade of shops including a chemist, stores, off-licence and two pubs.*

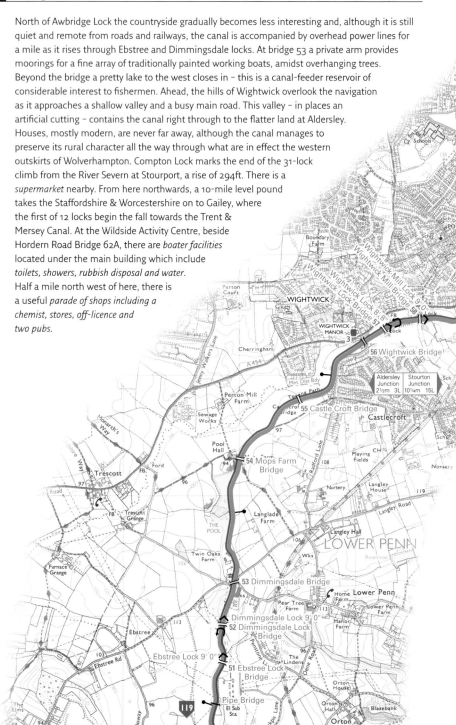

Aldersley Junction	Stourton Junction
2½m 3L	10¼m 15L

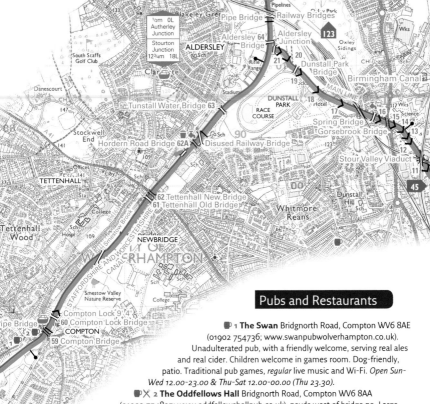

Pubs and Restaurants

🍺 1 **The Swan** Bridgnorth Road, Compton WV6 8AE (01902 754736; www.swanpubwolverhampton.co.uk). Unadulterated pub, with a friendly welcome, serving real ales and real cider. Children welcome in games room. Dog-friendly, patio. Traditional pub games, *regular* live music and Wi-Fi. *Open Sun-Wed 12.00-23.00 & Thu-Sat 12.00-00.00 (Thu 23.30).*

🍺✕ 2 **The Oddfellows Hall** Bridgnorth Road, Compton WV6 8AA (01902 754805; www.oddfellowshallpub.co.uk). 50yds west of bridge 59. Large stylish restaurant and bar serving real ale and food *L and E*. Children welcome. No dogs. Wi-Fi and garden. *Open 11.00-23.30 (Sun 22.30).*

🍺✕ 3 **The Mermaid** Bridgnorth Road, Wightwick WV6 8BN (01902 764896; www. vintageinn.co.uk/restaurants/midlands/themermaidwightwick). 100yds west of bridge 56. A large, warm and friendly pub serving real ale, and meals *all day, every day*. Children welcome, and there is a patio and Wi-Fi. *Open 11.00-23.00 (Sun 22.30).*

● **Wightwick**
Staffs. (pronounced Wittick). Once a village but now a suburb. There is a hill and plenty of trees, and in spite of the busy road it is a pleasant scene around the canal bridge and the pub. It is worth the short walk to Wightwick Manor.
Wightwick Manor Wightwick Bank, Wolverhampton WV6 8EE (01902 761400; www.nationaltrust.org.uk). *NT.* About 300yds north west of bridge 56, across the busy road and up the hill. Built between 1887 and 1893 for Theodore Mander, a paint and varnish maker, and designed by Edward Ould. The manor has an exterior that embodies many of the idiosyncrasies of the time. Inside, it is furnished with original wallpapers and fabrics by William Morris and various contributions by the Pre-Raphaelites. This certainly makes a pleasing change from the usual venerable stone or timbered buildings that are open to the public. The drawing room is perhaps the most richly decorated, with a Jacobean-style ceiling, a 16th-C alabaster carved fireplace and

William Morris Dove and Rose silk wall hangings. The Great Parlour is the main room of the house, and gives the impression of a Tudor hall, richly timbered and glowing with stained glass, tiles and porcelain. It contains what is considered to be the finest of Burne-Jones' later works *Love among the Ruins.* Other superb rooms include the kitchen and nursery. The beautiful 17-acre Edwardian gardens were laid out from plans by Alfred Parsons and Thomas Mawson drawn in 1904 and 1910. *Opening times* for the garden, tearoom and Old Manor *vary, with partial opening out of season.* It is therefore best to visit the website or to telephone. Charge.

● **Compton**
Staffs. PO, tel, stores, chemist, fish & chips, off-licence, takeaways, laundrette, garage. A busy but uninteresting village with a modern shopping centre, a pub, and a restaurant by the bridge. The canal lock here was the first that James Brindley built on the Staffordshire & Worcestershire Canal in the late 1760s, but unfortunately the cottage that accompanied it has been demolished.

121

Autherley Junction

Autherley Junction is marked by a big white bridge on the towpath side. The stop lock just beyond marks the entrance to the Shropshire Union: there is a useful boatyard just to the north of it. Leaving Autherley, the Staffordshire & Worcestershire passes new housing before running through a very narrow cutting in rock, once known as 'Pendeford Rockin', after a local farm: there is only room for boats to pass in the designated places, so **a good lookout should be kept for oncoming craft**. After passing the motorway the navigation leaves behind the suburbs of Wolverhampton and enters pleasant farmland. The bridges need care: although the bridgeholes are reasonably wide, the actual arches are rather low.

- **Autherley Junction**
A busy canal junction with a full range of boating facilities close by.

- **Coven**
Staffs. PO, tel, stores, chemist, baker, off-licence, takeaway, fish & chips. The only true village on this section, Coven lies beyond a dual carriageway north west of Cross Green Bridge. There are a large number of shops, including a *laundrette*.

Boatyards

Ⓑ**Napton Narrowboats** Autherley Junction, Oxley Moor Road, Wolverhampton WV9 5HW (01902 789942; www.napton-marina.co.uk). 🚽⛽D Pump out, gas, narrowboat hire, overnight mooring, short term mooring, slipway, limited chandlery, provisions, books and maps, boat repairs, solid fuel, gifts. *Emergency call out.*

Ⓑ**Oxley Marina** The Wharf, Oxley Moor Road, Wolverhampton WV10 6TZ (01902 789522; www.oxleymarina.co.uk). 🚽⛽DE Pump out, gas, day boat hire, over night and long-term mooring, slipway, solid fuel, winter storage, lifting facility, DIY facilities, boat sales and repairs, engine sales and repairs, welding and fabrication, toilets, car parking, *emergency call out.* Licensed bar *evenings and at weekends.* Snacks.

Pubs and Restaurants

🍺 1 **The Pendulum** 48 Blaydon Road, Wolverhampton WV9 5NP (01902 783779). North west of Blaydon Road Bridge. Rota of guest ales. *Food L and E (not Sun E).* Children welcome. Outside seating, traditional pub games, *regular* quiz and music nights. *Open Mon-Thu 12.30 23.30, Fri-Sat 12.00-00.10 & Sun 12.00-00.00.*

🍺✕ 2 **Fox & Anchor Inn** Brewood Road, Cross Green, Wolverhampton WV10 7PW (01902 798786; www.vintageinn.co.uk/restaurants/midlands/thefoxandanchorcrossgreen). Canalside by Cross Green Bridge. Large and friendly pub. Real ale, and meals available *all day.* Menu is traditional English, along with steaks and *Sun* roast. Children's menu, garden and good moorings. Wi-Fi. *Open daily 12.00-23.00 (Sun 22.30).*

WALKING AND CYCLING
The towpath is generally in good condition for both walkers and cyclists.

BIRD LIFE
The *Long-Tailed Tit* is a charming resident of woods, heaths and hedgerows. Feeding flocks of these birds resemble animated feather dusters. Their plumage can look black and white, but at close range there is a pinkish wash to the underparts and pinkish buff on the backs. The long-tailed tit has a tiny, stubby bill, a long tail, and an almost spherical body.

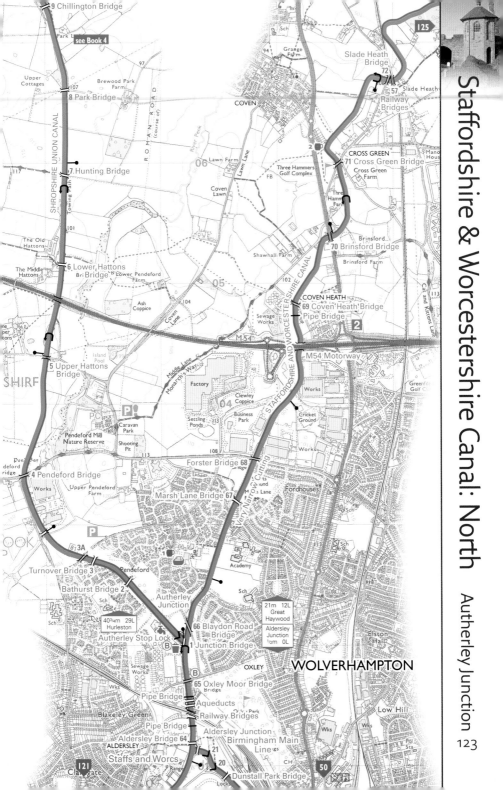

Gailey Wharf

The considerable age of this canal is shown by its extremely twisting course, revealed after passing the railway bridge. There are few real centres of population along this stretch, which comprises largely former heathland. The canal widens just before bridge 74, where Brindley incorporated part of a medieval moat into the canal. Hatherton Junction marks the entrance of the former Hatherton Branch of the Staffordshire & Worcestershire Canal into the main line. This branch used to connect with the Birmingham Canal Navigations. It is closed above the derelict second lock, although the channel remains as a feeder for the Staffordshire & Worcestershire Canal. There is a campaign for its restoration. There is a *marina* at the junction. A little further along, a chemical works is encountered, astride the canal in what used to be woodlands. This was once called the 'Black Works', as lamp black was produced here. Gailey Wharf is about a mile further north: it is a small canal settlement that includes a *boatyard* and a large, round, toll keeper's watch-tower, containing a *canal shop* and there are *toilets* nearby. The picturesque Wharf Cottage opposite has been restored as a bijou residence. Half a mile west, along the busy A5, there is a useful *shop selling all manner of combustibles, from coal to kindling, and including gas*. The canal itself disappears under Watling Street and then rapidly through five locks towards Penkridge. These locks are very attractive, and some are accompanied by little brick bridges. The M6 motorway, and the traffic noise, comes alongside for ¹/₂ mile, screening the reservoirs which feed the canal.

Pillaton Old Hall Penkridge, ST19 5RZ (01785 712200). South east of bridge 85. Only the gate house and stone-built chapel remain of this late 15th-C brick mansion built by the Littleton family, although there are still traces of the hall and courtyard. The chapel contains a 13th-C wooden carving of a saint. Visiting is by appointment only: telephone 01785 712200. The modest charge is donated to charity.

Gailey and Calf Heath reservoirs ¹/₂ mile east of Gailey Wharf, either side of the M6. These are feeder reservoirs for the canal, though rarely drawn on. The public has access to them as nature reserves to study the wide variety of natural life, especially the long-established heronry which is thriving on an island in Gailey Lower Reservoir. In Gailey Upper, fishing is available to the public from the riparian owner. In Gailey Lower a limited number of angling tickets are available on a season ticket basis each year from BW. There is club sailing on two of the reservoirs.

Boatyards

Ⓑ**Hatherton Marina** Kings Road, Calf Heath WV10 7DU (07919 466368; hathertonmarina.co.uk). Short- and long-term moorings, dry dock, boat building and repairs, engine sales and repairs, boat painting and electrical work, boat fitting out, boat sales, bottom blacking, showers, toilets. BSC Examiner.
Ⓑ**Otherton Boat Haven** Ltd Otherton Lane, Otherton, Penkridge ST19 5NX (01785 712515; 07581 459309; www.othertonboathaven.co.uk). 🛏🚿⛽D Pump out, gas, overnight and long-term mooring, boat and engine sales and repairs, toilets, coal.
Ⓑ**J D Boat Services** The Wharf, Gailey, Stafford ST19 5PR (01902 791811; www.jdboats.sharepoint. com/Pages/default.aspx). D Pump out, gas, solid fuel, narrowboat hire, boat share, winter storage, DIY facilities, boat servicing and repairs, painting, wet dock, diesel heaters, boat and engine sales, boat building. Gifts, maps, guides, souvenirs, windlass's etc opposite in the Roundhouse (01902 791617). *Open daily 09.00-17.00.*
Ⓑ**ABC Boat Hire** At J D Boat Services (01905 610660; www.abcboathire.com). Narrowboat hire.

Pubs and Restaurants

🍺 1 **Cross Keys** Filance Lane, Penkridge ST19 5HJ (07810 080668). Canalside, at Filance Bridge (84). Once a lonely canal pub, now it is modernised and surrounded by housing estates. Family orientated, it serves real ale and food *daily 11.00-21.00.* Family-friendly, garden. Traditional pub games, real fires and sports TV. *Open daily 11.00-00.00).* ⛽ There is a useful *shop and garage* ¼ mile west of Cross Keys Bridge 83A.
🍺✕ 1 **The Spread Eagle** Watling Street, Gailey ST19 5PN (01902 790212; www. spreadeaglepubgailey.co.uk). Imposing road house, with a massive garden and children's play area, serving real ale and food *all day* (breakfast from 08.00). *Daily* carvery, takeaway service and Wi-Fi. B&B. *Open 08.00-23.00 (Sun 22.00).*

84 Filance Bridge

126

Boss\nor

Moor Hall Cottages

Pillaton Farm

PILLATON

Cross Keys 83A Bridge

Lyne Hill Nursery

Lynhill Bridge 83

88

Marina

B

Depot

Otterton Lane

82 Otterton Bridge

36 Otterton Lock Helipad
10' 3"

OTHERTON

Otterton Lock

Otterton Farm

BOAT TRIPS
Truman Enterprise Narrowboat Trust
Hatherton Marina, Queens Road, Calf Heath,
Near Cannock, WV10 7DT (0121 357 2570/07971
266686; www.truman-enterprise.org.uk).
Nb A J Feldgate provides affordable residential
and day trips for youth and community groups.
Disabled access.

81 Otterton Lane Bridge
96

Rail Bridge

odbaston
tables

Micklewood Lane

102

Mick

Aqueduct

Fullmoor Wood

94

35 Rodbaston Lock
8' 6"

104

Gailey Lea Farm

97

13¼m 11L
Great Haywood

Autherley Junction
7¾m 1L

Lock 34 Bogg's Lock
8' 6"

33 Brick Kiln Lock
8' 0"

Gailey Wharf

94

Gailey Lea Lane

Plough Farm

POTTERY

GAILEY
Gailey Far

79 Gailey Bridge

32 Gailey Top Lock
8' 6"

GAILEY UPPER RESERVOIR

91

102

A5

B

WHARF

12

GAILEY LOWER RESERVOIR

Croft Farm

CALF HEATH RESERVOIR

Watling Street Plantation

Vic

107

106

Gravelly Way House

Quarry

Reservoir Plantation

FB

78A Four Ashes Bridge
Bridge

78 Gravelly Way Bridge

M6

Woodlands Lane

Oak Lane

Gravelly Way

CALF HEATH WOOD

108

Heath Farm

CALF HEATH

Woodside Farm

Vicarage Road

Pipe Bridges

Chemical Works

106

Straight Mile Farm

106

The Hollies

Works

Calf Heath Bridge

Marina

Loc

Marina

Hatherton Branch

Calf Heath Bridge 77

76

Long Moll's Bridge

FBs

B

Goldie Brook Bridge

Sewage Works

Aqueduct

Four Ashes

Industrial Estate

Deepmore Farm

75 Deepmore Bridge

Sandon Brook

Latherford

Wood

Standeford

Upper Latherford Farm

Pool House

Aqueduct

Lower Latherford Farm

108

deford Green

A449

Aspley Farm

73 Laches Bridge

Lower Laches Farm

74 Moat House Bridge

Moat House

123

Sch

The Laches

Penkridge

The navigation now
passes through Penkridge
and is soon approached
by the little River Penk: the
two water courses share
the valley for the next few
miles. The Cross Keys at
Filance Bridge (*see* page 124)
was once an isolated canal
pub – now it is surrounded by
housing, which spreads along
the canal in each direction.
Apart from the noise of the
motorway this is a pleasant
valley: there are plenty of trees,
a handful of locks and the large
Teddesley Park alongside the
canal. At Acton Trussell the M6
roars off to the north west and
once again peace returns to
the waterway. Teddesley Park
Bridge was at one time quite
ornamental, and became
known as 'Fancy Bridge'. It
is less so now. At Shutt Hill
an iron post at the bottom
of the lock is the only
reminder of a small
wharf which once
existed here. The post
was used to turn the
boats into the dock.

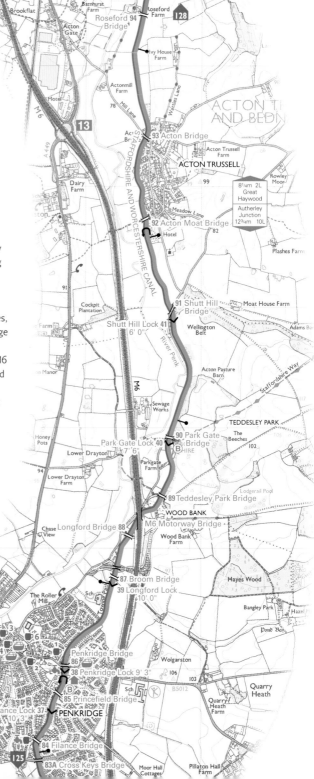

- **Penkridge**
Staffs. PO, tel, stores, chemist, delicatessen, hardware, bank, butcher, baker, takeaways, fish & chips, off-licence, garage, station. Above Penkridge Lock is a good place to tie up in this relatively old village. It is bisected by a trunk road, but luckily most of the village lies to the east of it. The church of St Michael is tall and sombre, and is well-kept. A harmonious mixture of styles, the earliest part dates from the 11th C, but the whole was restored in 1881. There is a fine Dutch 18th-C wrought iron screen brought from Cape Town, and the tower

is believed to date from c.1500. There are fine monuments of the Littletons of Pillaton Hall (*see* page 124), dating from 1558 and later.
Teddesley Park On the east bank of the canal. The Hall, once the family seat of the Littletons, was used during World War II as a prisoner-of-war camp, but has since been demolished. Its extensive wooded estate still remains.
- **Acton Trussell**
Staffs. PO box, tel. A village overwhelmed by modern housing: much the best way to see it is from the canal. The church stands to the south, overlooking the navigation. The west tower dates from the 13th C, topped by a spire built in 1562.

Boatyards

Ⓑ**Teddesley Boat Company** Park Gate Lock, Teddesley Road, Penkridge ST19 5RH (01785 714692; www.narrowboats.co.uk). 🔧 D Pump out, gas, narrowboat hire, overnight and long-term mooring, winter storage, crane (32 tonne), boat and engine sales and repairs, boat painting, books and maps. Midland Chandlers is next door, telephone 01785 712437.

Ⓑ**Tom's Moorings** Cannock Road, Penkridge ST19 5DX. Contact Streethay Wharf (01840 770128/07803 499111/07860 729522; www.bargemovers.com). Above Penkridge Lock. 🛢🔧 Overnight- and long-term mooring, electrical hook up, boat moving, cranage.

PLANT LIFE
The *Bluebell* is a familiar bulbous perennial, often carpeting whole woodland floors if the situation suits its requirements. The leaves are narrow and all basal. Bell-shaped flowers in one-sided spikes appear April–June.

Pubs and Restaurants

🍺✕ 1 **The Boat Inn** Cannock Road, Penkridge ST19 5DT (01785 715170; theboatinn.org.uk). Canalside, by Penkridge Lock. Mellow and friendly red-brick pub dating from 1779. Real ale. Food is available *Mon–Fri L and E & Sat–Sun 12.00-20.00 (Sun 19.00).* Child- and dog-friendly, garden. Sports TV. *Open Mon-Sun 12.00-23.00 (Fri-Sat 00.00).*
🍺 2 **The Star Inn** Market Place, Penkridge ST19 5DJ (01785 712513; thestarpenkridge.wixsite.com/home). Fine old pub serving real ale and bar meals *Mon–Thu L and E & Fri–Sun L.* Garden, traditional pub games and real fires. *Open Sun-Thu 12.00-23.00 (Thu 23.30) & Fri-Sat 12.00-00.00).*
🍺 3 **White Hart** Stone Cross, Penkridge ST19 5AS (01785 748598). This historic former coaching inn, visited by Mary, Queen of Scots, and Elizabeth I, has an impressive frontage, timber-framed with three gables. It serves real ale. Outside seating,

dog-friendly. Traditional pub games, real fires, sports TV and Wi-Fi. *Open 12.00-00.00.*
🍺 4 **The Horse & Jockey** Market Street, Penkridge ST19 5DH (01785 716299). Opened in 1754 and still serving real ale! Family- and dog-friendly, beer garden. Traditional pub games, real fires, sports TV and Wi-Fi. *Open daily 12.00-23.00 (Mon 15.00).*
🍺✕ 5 **The Littleton Arms** St Michael's Square, Penkridge ST19 5AL (01785 716300; www.thelittletonarms.com). Hotel, bar and restaurant. Real ale and excellent food available *Mon–Fri L and E & Sat–Sun 12.00-21.00.* Garden, dog- and child-friendly *(until 21.00). Open Mon-Sat 12.00-23.00 (Fri-Sat 00.00) & Sun 12.00-22.30.*
✕🍷 6 **Flames** Mill Street, Penkridge ST19 5AY (01785 712955). Contemporary eastern cuisine. Takeaway service. *Open daily 17.00-23.00.*

WALKING AND CYCLING
The Staffordshire Way crosses the canal between bridges 89 and 90. This 90-mile path stretches from Mow Cop in the north (near the Macclesfield Canal) to Kinver Edge in the south, using the Caldon Canal towpath on the way. It connects with the Gritstone Trail, the Hereford & Worcester Way and the Heart of England Way. A guide book is available from local Tourist Information Centres.

Tixall

Continuing north along the shallow Penk valley, the canal soon reaches Radford Bridge, the nearest point to Stafford. It is about 1¹/₂ miles to the centre of town: there is a frequent bus service. A canal branch used to connect with the town via Baswich Lock and the River Sow. If you look carefully west of bridge 101 you can just about deduce where the connection was made – some remains of brickwork are the clue. A mile further north the canal bends around to the south east and follows the pretty valley of the River Sow, and at Milford crosses the river via an aqueduct – an early structure by James Brindley, carried heavily on low brick arches. Tixall Lock offers some interesting views in all directions: the castellated entrance to Shugborough Railway Tunnel at the foot of the thick woods of Cannock Chase and the distant outline of the remarkable Tixall Gatehouse. The canal now completes its journey to the Trent & Mersey Canal at Great Haywood. It is a length of waterway quite unlike any other. Proceeding along this very charming valley, the navigation enters Tixall Wide – an amazing and delightful stretch of water more resembling a lake than a canal, said to have been built in order not to compromise the view from Tixall House (alas, no more), and navigable to the edges. The Wide is noted for its kingfisher population. Woods across the valley conceal Shugborough Hall. The River Trent is met, on its way south from Stoke-on-Trent, and is crossed on an aqueduct. There is a wharf, and *fresh produce* (see page 129) can be purchased at the *farm shop* beside Bridge 75 on the Trent & Mersey, which is entered through an elegantly arched bridge. The bridge is the subject of a very famous photograph taken by the canal historian Eric de Maré. Immediately before this bridge there is a useful *boatyard* which, amongst other services, provides *Elsan disposal* (charge).

Boatyards

ⓑ**Stafford Boat Club** Off Maple Wood, Wildwood, Stafford ST17 4SG (01785 660725/07716 960049; staffordboatclub.co.uk). At Bridge 96. 🚿🛒D Pump out, gas, solid fuel, overnight and short-term moorings, limited winter moorings, slipway, wet dock, laundry, print shop, use of clubhouse (bar *open every evening and 12.00-15.00 Sun*).

ⓑ**Anglo Welsh** The Canal Wharf, Mill Lane, Great Haywood ST18 0RJ (01889 881711; http://www.anglowelsh.co.uk/Locations/Bases/Great-Haywood). 🚿🛒D Pump out (not *Sat*), gas, narrowboat hire, day-hire craft, overnight and long-term mooring, coal, engine repairs, chandlery, toilets, books, maps and gifts, ice cream and soft drinks. *Open daily 08.30-17.00 (Sun 09.00).*

ⓑ**Great Haywood Marina** The Marina Building, Canalside Farm, Mill Lane, Great Haywood ST18 0RQ (01889 883713/07771 685731; www.greathaywoodmarina.co.uk). 🚿🛒D Pump out, gas, short- and long-term mooring, boat sales and repairs, solid fuel, slipway, chandlery, laundrette, toilets, showers, Wi-Fi, CCTV. Farm shop adjacent.

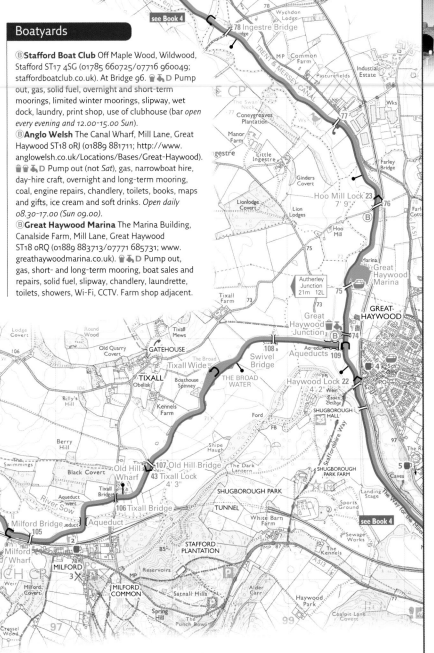

Canalside Farm Mill Lane Great Haywood ST18 0RQ (01889 881747; www.canalsidefarm.co.uk). Immediately east of Bridge 75, beside the marina. Selling an excellent selection of local (within 30 miles) seasonal, fresh produce. Butcher, baker and delicatessen. PYO strawberries and raspberries. Bedding plants and ice creams. Café. *Open Apr-Oct, daily 09.00-18.00 & Nov-Mar, Tue-Sat 09.00-18.00 & Sun 10.00-17.00.*

WALKING AND CYCLING
There is a Nature Trail at Milford Common, and visitors to Shugborough Hall can enjoy excellent walks in the park.

- **Stafford**
Staffs. All services. This town is well worth visiting, since there is a remarkable wealth of fine old buildings. These include a handsome City Hall complex of ornamental Italianate buildings, c.1880. The robust-looking gaol is nearby; and the church of St Mary stands in very pleasing and spacious grounds. There are some pretty back alleys: Church Lane contains a splendid-looking eating house, and at the bottom of the lane a fruiterer's shop is in a thatched cottage built in 1610.
Tourist Information Centre Gatehouse Theatre, Eastgate Street, Stafford ST16 2LT (01785 619619; www.staffordbc.gov.uk/stafford-visitor-information-centre). *Open Mon-Sat 09.30-17.30.*
- **The Stafford Branch**
Just west of bridge 101 there was once a lock taking a branch off the Staffordshire & Worcestershire to Stafford. One mile long, it was unusual in that it was not a canal but the canalised course of the River Sow.
- **Milford**
Staffs. PO box, tel, takeaway Best reached from Tixall Bridge (106). Milford Hall is hidden by trees.
- **Tixall**
Staffs. PO box, tel. Just to the east are the stables and the gatehouse of the long-vanished Tixall Hall. This massive square Elizabethan building dates from 1598 and is fully four storeys high. It stands alone in a field and is considered to be one of the most ambitious gatehouses in the country. The gatehouse is now available for holiday lets: telephone the Landmark Trust (01628 825925) for details.
- **Great Haywood**
Staffs. PO, tel, stores, fishmonger. Centre of the Great Haywood and Shugborough Conservation Area, the village is attractive in parts, but it is closely connected in many ways to Shugborough Park, to which it is physically linked by the very old Essex Bridge, where the crystal clear waters of the River Sow join the Trent on its way down from Stoke.

Shugborough Hall Great Haywood, Milford ST17 0XB (01889 880160; www.nationaltrust.org.uk/shugborough-estate). Walk south along the road from bridge 106 to the A513 at Milford Common. The main entrance is on your left. The present house dates from 1693, but was substantially altered by James Stuart around 1760 and by Samuel Wyatt around the turn of the 18th C. The Trust has leased the whole to Staffordshire County Council who now manage it. The house has been restored at great expense. There are some magnificent rooms and treasures inside. *Opening times vary* so telephone or visit the website for further details. Charge.

Shugborough Park There are some remarkable sights in the large park that encircles the Hall. Thomas Anson, who inherited the estate in 1720, enlisted in 1744 the help of his famous brother, Admiral George Anson, to beautify and improve the house and the park. In 1762 he commissioned James Stuart, a neo-Grecian architect, to embellish the grounds. 'Athenian' Stuart set to with a will, and the spectacular results of his work can be seen scattered round the park.

Park Farm at Shugborough (01889 880160; www.nationaltrust.org.uk/shugborough-estate/features/park-farm-at-shugborough). Within Shugborough Park. Designed by Samuel Wyatt, it contains an agricultural museum, a working mill and a rare breeds centre. Traditional country skills such as bread-making, butter-churning and cheese-making are demonstrated. *Opening times vary* so telephone or visit the website for further details. Charge.

Pubs and Restaurants (pages 128–129)

🍺 1 **Radford Bank Inn** Radford Bank, Stafford ST17 4PG (01785 242825; www.stonehouserestaurants.co.uk/nationalsearch/eastandwestmidlands/theradfordbankinnstafford/foodanddrink). Canalside at bridge 98. Real ale. Food is served *daily 08.00-22.00* (including *weekday* breakfast *08.00-11.30*). Family-friendly, garden. Traditional pub games, sports TV and Wi-Fi. Quiz *Fri.* Takeaway service. *Open 08.00-23.00.*

🍺 2 **The Barley Mow** 28 Main Road, Milford ST17 0UW (01785 665230; www.eating-inn.co.uk/house/barley-mow-stafford). Predominantly aimed at the hungry, this pub also serves ales – food *09.00-22.00 daily* (including *weekday* breakfast *09.00-11.00*). Children's 'PlayZone' *open 11.00-20.00.* Garden and Wi-Fi. Quiz *Sun. Open daily 09.00-23.00.*

✕🍷 3 **The Viceroy Indian Restaurant** 8 Brocton Road, Milford ST17 0UH (01889 663239; www.viceroyrestaurant.co.uk). With its elegant, modern interior and warm welcome, this restaurant showcases its chef/proprietor's Indian and Bangladeshi culinary heritage. Food to savour is served *daily 17.30-23.00.* Takeaway service with online ordering.

Also try: 🍺✕ 4 **The Clifford Arm** Main Road, Great Haywood ST18 0SR (01889 881321; cliffordarms.co.uk) and 🍺 5 **The Red Lion** Main Road, Little Haywood ST18 0TS (01889 881314).

STOURBRIDGE & DUDLEY CANALS

MAXIMUM DIMENSIONS
Length: 70'
Beam: 6' 10"
Headroom: 6' 0"

MANAGER
0303 040 4040
enquiries.westmidlands@canalrivertrust.org.uk

MILEAGE

Stourbridge Canal
STOURTON JUNCTION to:
Wordsley Junction: 2 miles
Stourbridge: 3¼ miles

BLACK DELPH bottom lock: 5¼ miles

Locks: 20

Dudley No. 1 and No. 2 Canals

Dudley No. 1 Canal
Delph Bottom Lock (Stourbridge Canal) *to:*
PARK HEAD JUNCTION: 2 miles
Dudley Tunnel (north end): 4 miles
TIPTON JUNCTION: 4½ miles
Locks: 12

Dudley No. 2 Canal
PARK HEAD JUNCTION to:
WINDMILL END JUNCTION: 2⅝ miles
HAWNE BASIN: 5½ miles
No locks

The Stourbridge and Dudley Canals are to some extent inseparable, being part of the same grand scheme to link the Dudley coal mines with the Stourbridge glass works, and with the Severn Navigation by means of the Staffordshire & Worcestershire Canal – indeed the Acts for the two canals were passed on the same day in 1776. Well supported by local glass masters, the Stourbridge Canal was soon under way, with Thomas Dadford as engineer. From a junction with the Staffordshire & Worcestershire at Stourton, the canal ran to Stourbridge. There was a 2-mile branch to the feeder reservoirs on Pensnett Chase, with 16 rising locks, and another level branch ran to Black Delph, where it met the Dudley Canal. Combined with the Dudley Canal, the Stourbridge was soon profitable, and it was not long before the two companies were seeking to increase their revenue. They decided to try to capture some of the rich traffic on the Birmingham Canal. A joint proposal for a junction with the Birmingham Canal line via the Dudley Tunnel was authorised in 1785, and the through route was opened in 1792. Although the two companies worked closely together, they resisted the temptation to amalgamate, relying on their mutual dependence to sort out any problems. Although the Dudley Canal became part of the BCN system, the central position of the Stourbridge made it a very profitable undertaking, and throughout the early years of the 19th C the trade steadily increased. Even the opening of the rival Worcester & Birmingham Canal in 1815 did not affect the profits. Revenues were further increased in 1840 when the Stourbridge Extension Canal, later GWR owned, was opened to capture the coal trade from the Shut End collieries.

In the middle of the 19th C railway competition began to affect the canal, first from the Oxford, Worcester & Wolverhampton Railway, and later from the Great Western Railway. Revenues began their inevitable decline, but the Stourbridge was able to maintain its profits, and thus its independence, until nationalisation in 1948, although by then it was in the same run-down state as most canals in Britain. Commercial traffic died away, and by the 1950s the canal was no longer usable.

In 1964 the Staffordshire & Worcestershire Canal Society and the BWB (now CRT) decided to restore the 16 locks and re-open the line between Birmingham and the Severn. Today these canals are both useful routes into the BCN and excellent cruising waterways in their own right, passing through a mixture of fine countryside, old industrial surroundings and extensive new development.

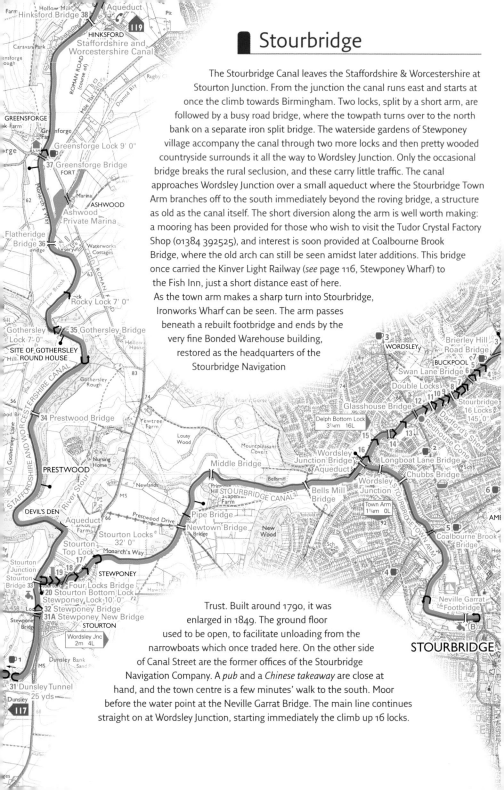

Stourbridge

The Stourbridge Canal leaves the Staffordshire & Worcestershire at Stourton Junction. From the junction the canal runs east and starts at once the climb towards Birmingham. Two locks, split by a short arm, are followed by a busy road bridge, where the towpath turns over to the north bank on a separate iron split bridge. The waterside gardens of Stewponey village accompany the canal through two more locks and then pretty wooded countryside surrounds it all the way to Wordsley Junction. Only the occasional bridge breaks the rural seclusion, and these carry little traffic. The canal approaches Wordsley Junction over a small aqueduct where the Stourbridge Town Arm branches off to the south immediately beyond the roving bridge, a structure as old as the canal itself. The short diversion along the arm is well worth making: a mooring has been provided for those who wish to visit the Tudor Crystal Factory Shop (01384 392525), and interest is soon provided at Coalbourne Brook Bridge, where the old arch can still be seen amidst later additions. This bridge once carried the Kinver Light Railway (*see* page 116, Stewponey Wharf) to the Fish Inn, just a short distance east of here.

As the town arm makes a sharp turn into Stourbridge, Ironworks Wharf can be seen. The arm passes beneath a rebuilt footbridge and ends by the very fine Bonded Warehouse building, restored as the headquarters of the Stourbridge Navigation

Trust. Built around 1790, it was enlarged in 1849. The ground floor used to be open, to facilitate unloading from the narrowboats which once traded here. On the other side of Canal Street are the former offices of the Stourbridge Navigation Company. A *pub* and a *Chinese takeaway* are close at hand, and the town centre is a few minutes' walk to the south. Moor before the water point at the Neville Garrat Bridge. The main line continues straight on at Wordsley Junction, starting immediately the climb up 16 locks.

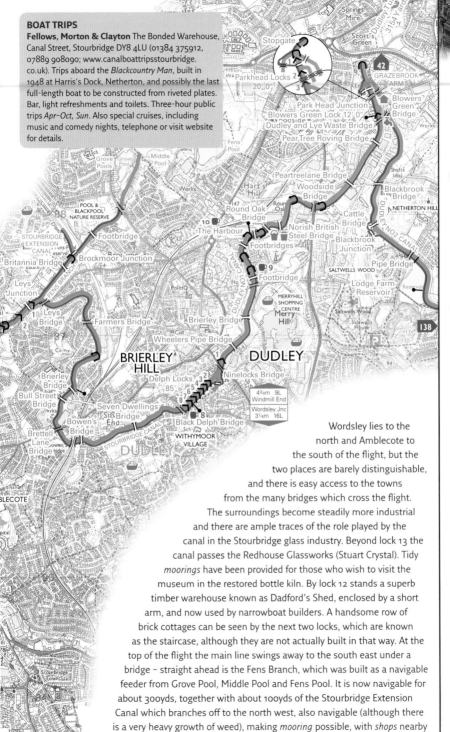

BOAT TRIPS

Fellows, Morton & Clayton The Bonded Warehouse, Canal Street, Stourbridge DY8 4LU (01384 375912, 07889 908090; www.canalboattripsstourbridge. co.uk). Trips aboard the *Blackcountry Man*, built in 1948 at Harris's Dock, Netherton, and possibly the last full-length boat to be constructed from riveted plates. Bar, light refreshments and toilets. Three-hour public trips *Apr–Oct, Sun*. Also special cruises, including music and comedy nights, telephone or visit website for details.

Wordsley lies to the north and Amblecote to the south of the flight, but the two places are barely distinguishable, and there is easy access to the towns from the many bridges which cross the flight. The surroundings become steadily more industrial and there are ample traces of the role played by the canal in the Stourbridge glass industry. Beyond lock 13 the canal passes the Redhouse Glassworks (Stuart Crystal). Tidy *moorings* have been provided for those who wish to visit the museum in the restored bottle kiln. By lock 12 stands a superb timber warehouse known as Dadford's Shed, enclosed by a short arm, and now used by narrowboat builders. A handsome row of brick cottages can be seen by the next two locks, which are known as the staircase, although they are not actually built in that way. At the top of the flight the main line swings away to the south east under a bridge – straight ahead is the Fens Branch, which was built as a navigable feeder from Grove Pool, Middle Pool and Fens Pool. It is now navigable for about 300yds, together with about 100yds of the Stourbridge Extension Canal which branches off to the north west, also navigable (although there is a very heavy growth of weed), making *mooring* possible, with *shops* nearby

133

in Bromley. The reservoirs form the Fens Pools Nature Reserve, and are a pleasant place to walk. The towpath stays on the north for the branch, but turns over to the south bank on the main line which swings south round Brierley Hill. There is a handy *fish & chip shop* and a *takeaway* next to Farmers Bridge. A more open landscape flanks the canal in the latter stages of its journey. After passing under the last bridge Delph Bottom Lock comes into sight, and here the Stourbridge Canal ends.

The Dudley No. 1 Canal joins the Stourbridge Canal at the bottom of Delph Locks. This flight, now designated a conservation area, is notable for its high waterfall overflows, which are very dramatic after a prolonged spell of wet weather. Known as the Nine Locks, seven of the original flight were rebuilt as six on the present line in 1858. Some remains of the old locks can still be seen to the east. Old stables by lock 3 have been well restored. Leaving the flight, the canal winds its way through what was once the site of Round Oak Steelworks, which ceased production in 1983 after almost two centuries of steelmaking, but is now the vast new Merryhill Shopping Centre. This massive and popular development transports those on the canal briefly into another dimension, with sparkling buildings, *restaurants, cinema and bars* lining the towpath, and extensive car parks, seemingly full to the brim, leading shoppers into a vast modern world of retailing. There are good moorings and lots of restaurants here for those who wish to stop but, if you keep going, it all suddenly ends beyond Round Oak Bridge, and you are immediately back in more familiar surroundings.

A cast iron bridge marked Horseley Co, Tipton 1858 carries the towpath over what was, until subsidence caused its closure in 1909, the old Two Lock Line – a short cut which avoided the longer route to the Dudley No. 2 Canal via Park Head Junction. Now the canal passes along a side cut embankment with good views towards Netherton Hill as it approaches Blowers Green Lock, the deepest on the BCN, built to replace two earlier locks which suffered from subsidence. Note the restored Blower's Green Pumphouse here, in the care of the Dudley Canal Trust. Park Head Junction immediately follows, where a sharp turn to the south east must be made to continue towards Windmill End. Straight ahead, the three Park Head Locks climb to the southern entrance of Dudley Tunnel (*see* note below), accompanied by a toll office and a fine lock house, and · overlooked by a railway viaduct. At the top of the flight the entrance to the long-defunct Pensnett Canal can be seen on the west side, with the more substantial remains of the Grazebrook Arm, abandoned in 1953, to the east.

Leaving Park Head Junction towards Windmill End the canal skirts Netherton Hill, which is topped by St Andrew's Church, where cholera victims were buried in mass graves. High Bridge spans a cutting which was originally Brewins Tunnel, built in 1838 but opened out only 20 years later. However, the rural feel here soon disappears as houses appear and Lodge Farm Reservoir is passed.

Boatyards

Ⓑ**ABC Marine Services** Canal Street, Stourbridge DY8 4LU (07968 508872). Opposite the Bonded Warehouse. 🚽🛒🔧 Gas, solid fuel, pump out, dry dock, boat repairs, bottom blacking, boat fitting out, basic chandlery, maps and gifts. Gas Safe registered.

WALKING AND CYCLING
The towpath is in excellent condition on both canals and as they, for the most part, wind through urban areas, it is relatively easy to devise circular walks, using a street atlas. For example, you can walk up the Stourbridge Sixteen and follow the canal to Delph. At the top of the locks turn left, and left again along the road to follow a fairly direct return route back to Brierley Hill Road Bridge. There are good short walks around the Pool & Blackpool Nature Reserve, to the west of the Fens Branch, and Saltwells Nature Reserve, to the west of the Dudley No. 2 Canal.

NAVIGATIONAL NOTES

1 Moorings at Merryhill are generally considered to be safe, but noisy (until midnight).
2 An anti-vandal (aka 'handcuff') key is required for Delph Locks.
3 An anti-vandal key is required for lock 1 of Parkhead Locks, and to access the facilities at Park Head Junction.
4 **Dudley Tunnel** All passages through the tunnel **MUST** be booked in advance with the Dudley Canal Trust, 0121 557 6265 (www.dudleycanaltrust.org.uk). Internal combustion engines must not be used in this tunnel, due to very limited ventilation. Headroom is also limited (all boats are gauged). The Dudley Canal Trust operate an electric tug, the *John C Brown*, which can be made available to either tow, or escort those wishing to leg through. A detailed leaflet is available from: The Dudley Canal Trust 501 Birmingham New Road, Dudley, West Midlands DY1 4SB, and local CRT offices. Netherton Tunnel is the most suitable route through to the Birmingham Canal Main Line (see page 42).

● **Stourbridge**
Worcs. All services. Although the origins of Stourbridge go back to the Middle Ages, there is little trace of this today and it is almost entirely a 19th-C town, reflecting the great expansion of the glass industry during that period. The first glassmakers in Stourbridge were from Lorraine in eastern France, their presence being recorded in the Kingswinford Parish Register on 26 April 1612. Attracted by rich deposits of fireclay and coal, they originally established window glass production, and it was not until the discovery of lead glass in the 1700s that the manufacture of table glass became established here. Holloway End Glassworks, near the end of the Stourbridge Arm, is one of the surviving original factories, dating from the 17th C. *Each year, at the end of August*, the Dudley Glass Festival celebrates the area's long association with this craft with events at Broadfield House, Himley Hall and other venues. Information from the Tourist Information Centre *(below)*, who also produce a fascinating Crystal Trail leaflet.
Redhouse Glass Cone High Street, Wordsley, Stourbridge DY8 4AZ (01384 812381; www.dudley.gov.uk/see-and-do/museums/red-house-glass-cone). By Glassworks Bridge on the Stourbridge Sixteen. The elegant brick cone, one of the few still surviving in the country, stands 100ft high and is right by the canal. Built 1788-94, it replaced earlier buildings on the same site, and housed a furnace around which the glass-making activities took place. Visitors can now see glassmaking, glass-blowing and cutting in progress, and visit the Stuart Crystal shop (01384 342701). *Open Mon-Fri 10.00-15.00 & Sat-Sun 11.00-16.00.* Coffee House. Good moorings for visitors only. Charge.
Tourist Information Centre Dudley Council Plus, 259 Castle Street, Dudley DY1 1LQ (0300 5552345; www.discover.dudley.gov.uk). See also The Merry Hill Centre, Brierley Hill DY5 1SR (01384 487900; visitbirmingham.com/explore-birmingham/places/merry-hill-tourist-information-centre).

● **Brierley Hill**
West Midlands. All services. A Black Country town founded on coal, iron and limestone, where no less than 12 pit pumping engines (known as whimseys) once kept the mines dry. Of course these mines are no more, and redevelopment has wrought extensive changes. There are a great many pubs, notwithstanding the decline since 1843, when it was recorded that there was one for every 143 head of population, who found refuge from their daily tasks in ale and good company. The Victorian church, when first built, had the poet Thomas Moss appointed as perpetual curate. His most notable work was a sentimental piece called *The Beggar*, which adorned many Victorian drawing rooms and was mentioned by Dickens in *Nicholas Nickleby*.

● **Dudley Tunnel**
Re-opened in 1973 with the rebuilding of Park Head Locks, Dudley Tunnel is one of the wonders of the BCN. This narrow bore, 3154yds long, was opened in 1792 after the usual delays and problems, to connect with the Birmingham Canal at Tipton. Inside there is a vast network of natural caverns, basins and branches serving old quarries and mines. In all there are over 5000yds of underground waterways, some cut off and abandoned, others still accessible. *Internal combustion engines must not be used – see* Navigational Notes, page 135. There are trips into the tunnel from the Black Country Museum *(see page 43)*.
Lodge Farm Reservoir This was built in 1838, and covers part of the old line of the canal. The new, more direct, line was instigated by Thomas Brewin, who built a new tunnel. Although still known as Brewin's Tunnel, it was opened in 1858. The reservoir is used now for sailing and fishing, and also supplies the canal.

 **1 The Vine** Vine Lane, Clent, Stourbridge, Dudley DY9 9PH (01562 882491; www.vineinnclent. com.) See mapping on page 117. Food is available *L and E*, along with real ale, traditional wines and ciders. Children and dogs welcome. Real fires. *Open 11.00–23.00 (Sun 12.00).*

2 The Glassworks Audham Road, Stourbridge DY8 4AF (01384 482699; www. glassworkspubstourbridge.co.uk). Recently refurbished pub serving real ale and food *daily 11.30–22.00 (Sun 21.00).* Family-friendly, garden and traditional pub games. Wi-Fi. *Open 11.00–23.00.*

3 The New Inn 117 High Street, Wordsley DY8 5QR (01384 295614; www.bathams.co.uk/pubs/the-new-inn-at-wordsley). A real local with a striking Victorian façade, dispensing real ales and a friendly welcome. Patio and children's play area (children in garden only *until 21.00*). Bar snacks available. Dog-friendly. Traditional pub games, newspapers, sports TV and Wi-Fi. *Open 12.00–23.00 (Sun 22.30).*

4 The Starving Rascal 1 Brettell Lane, Amblecote, Stourbridge DY8 4BN (01384 381618). Once know as as the Dudley Arms, legend has it that a bygone landlord once turned away a starving beggar, who was found dead in the street the next day. Today there is a warm welcome for all, together with real fires, real ales and food available *Fri-Sat E & Sun L*. Dog-friendly. Traditional pub games, sports TV and Wi-Fi. *Open 12.00–23.00 (Fri-Sat 00.00).*

5 The Maverick Drinking House 1 High Street, Amblecote, Stourbridge DY8 4BA (01384 824099). Imposing corner building dispensing real ales (many from local breweries) and real cider with a wild west theme. Traditional pub games and a small garden.

Regular live music, sports TV and Wi-Fi. *Open from 13.00 (12.00 Sat-Sun) until late.*

6 The Robin Hood 196 Collis Street, Amblecote, Stourbridge DY8 4EQ (07436 793462). A warm welcome, real ales and real cider makes this friendly hostelry well worth a visit. Snacks available *L*. Family-friendly, patio. Real fires and Wi-Fi. B&B. *Open Mon-Tue E & Wed-Sun 12.00–23.00 (Fri-Sat 00.00).*

7 The Samson & Lion 140 Brierly Hill Road, Wordsley, Stourbridge DY8 5SP (01384 76062; www.samsonandlion.co.uk). A fine old canal pub where the boatmen's horses were once stabled. Real ale and bar snacks and cobs are available. Dog- and child-friendly, patio. Traditional pub games (skittle alley) newspapers and Wi-Fi. *Open 12.00–23.00.*

8 The Tenth Lock 154 Delph Road, Brierley Hill, Dudley DY5 2TY (01384 79041; www.tenthlockpub. co.uk). A Homely-looking pub with an attractive canalside garden. Real ales and food available *12.00–21.00 (Fri-Sun 20.00).* Dog- and family-friendly. Traditional pub games, sports TV and Wi-Fi. Quiz *Thu*. *Open 12.00–23.00 (Fri-Sat 00.00).*

9 The Brewer's Wharf The Waterfront, Level Street, Brierley Hill, Dudley DY5 1SY (01384 483522; www.brewerswharfpub.co.uk). Built on the site of an old foundry, beside Greens Bridge. A handsome and busy canalside pub, serving real ale, together with food *daily 12.00–22.00 (Sun 21.00).* Children welcome, patio. Traditional pub games, newspapers, sports TV and Wi-Fi. Moorings nearby. *Open 12.00–23.00 (Fri-Sat 23.30).*

Also try: **10 The Blue Brick** 153 Dudley Road, Brierley Hill DY5 1HG (01384 671776).

Bridge at Windmill End junction

Windmill End

Netherton was at one time a centre for the manufacture of chains and anchors, although there is little to be seen of this activity now, with the wharves covered in the spoils of late-20th-C preoccupations. Just after Bishtons Bridge a short arm full of moored narrowboats encloses pretty gardens cared for by the Withymoor Island Trust. Visitors are welcome to *moor* here, and *pump outs* is sometimes available. Beyond Fox & Goose Bridge, the houses retreat and a fine green open space by a lake makes the perfect setting for Windmill End Junction, with cast iron canal bridges and the remains of Cobbs Engine House, its tall chimney still standing. The machine this building contained used to pump water from the local mines, to prevent flooding – it was said that if the engine ever missed a beat, a thousand women's hearts missed one also. The Bumblehole Branch, a lovely urban environment of canalside gardens and old and new houses looking out over landscaped workings, branches off to the west. This arm, which was once the main line of the canal prior to the building of Netherton Tunnel, terminates in a 'Y', overhung with willows, where stands the last surviving timber 'gallows' crane, built prior to 1882. Straight on towards Windmill End Junction and the grand entrance to Netherton Tunnel, the canal sits high on an embankment in what is now a nature reserve, rich in bird and insect life. The Bumblehole Conservation Group Visitor Centre is housed in the building by the junction. At a canal crossroads the short Boshboil Branch heads west, while to the east the Dudley No. 2 Canal continues on its way to Hawne Basin, at present a dead end, but one worthy of exploration. Straight ahead, through the tunnel, is the BCN.

The Dudley No. 2 Canal once continued in a wide loop to join the Worcester & Birmingham Canal via the notorious and claustrophobic Lappal Tunnel, which closed in 1917 due to subsidence. Some 3795yds long, this rocky tunnel was the longest in the BCN network and one of the narrowest in the country. Leaving Windmill End, there is a toll island and a disused colliery basin, one of many which once fed traffic onto the canal here, and soon the waterway is passing through houses, factories and playing fields interspersed with newly landscaped areas, the tidy legacy of these once thriving industrial areas. At the entrance to the 577yd Gosty Hill Tunnel (no towpath) the lay-by once used by the tunnel tug can be seen – regrettably the tughouse is no more. If you are walking, look out for the tunnel ventilation shaft in the front garden of 171 Station Road as you pass over the hill. The waterway then passes through what was once a steelworks, now replaced with modern factory units. Gradually it emerges from enclosing brick walls to pass a tidy trading estate and reach Hawne Basin, a canal/railway interchange until 1967 and now a friendly place full of moored narrowboats. You can *moor* here, but it is a bleak walk along Hereward Rise to the *shops and pubs*. The Lapal Tunnel Trust (www.lapal.org) campaigns for the restoration of the rest of the canal between Hawne Basin and Selly Oak on the Worcester & Birmingham – the section to the south of the A458, by Leasowes Park, is currently receiving their attention.

● **Netherton Tunnel**
Opened in 1858, Netherton was the last major canal tunnel to be built in Britain and, as such, it is suitably grand. At 3027yds long, it was built with a bore sufficient to allow a towpath on both sides, and when opened was equipped with gas lighting, later converted to electricity. Although it passes deep underground, it is 453ft above sea level, and was built to relieve congestion in the Dudley Tunnel. It runs on a parallel course, joining the Birmingham Main Line at Dudley Port.
Tourist Information Centre Dudley Council Plus, 259 Castle Street, Dudley DY1 1LQ (0300 5552345; www.discover.dudley.gov.uk). *Open Mon-Fri 08.00-17.30 & Sat 09.00-12.00.*

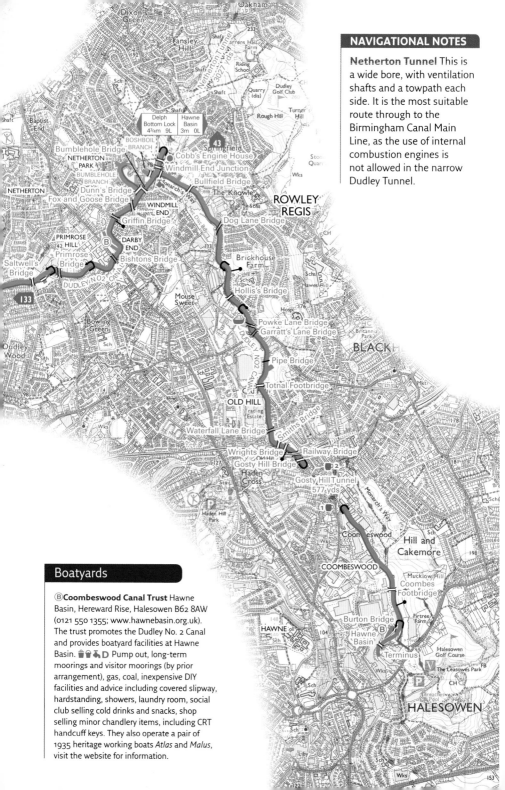

Delph Bottom Lock 4¾m 9L	Hawne Basin 3m 0L

Boatyards

Ⓑ**Coombeswood Canal Trust** Hawne Basin, Hereward Rise, Halesowen B62 8AW (0121 550 1355; www.hawnebasin.org.uk). The trust promotes the Dudley No. 2 Canal and provides boatyard facilities at Hawne Basin. ⬆⬆♣D Pump out, long-term moorings and visitor moorings (by prior arrangement), gas, coal, inexpensive DIY facilities and advice including covered slipway, hardstanding, showers, laundry room, social club selling cold drinks and snacks, shop selling minor chandlery items, including CRT handcuff keys. They also operate a pair of 1935 heritage working boats *Atlas* and *Malus*, visit the website for information.

153

Pubs and Restaurants

🍺 1 **The Lighthouse** 153 Coombs Road,
Halesowen B62 8AF (0121 602 1620;
www.sabrain.com). Real ale is served, along
with food *Mon-Sun L & Wed-Sat E*, in this
recently refurbished pub, once decorated with
a large mural of a lighthouse. Garden and Wi-Fi.
Open 12.00-00.00 (Sun 23.00).

Also try: 🍺 2 **The Bell & Bear Inn** 71 Gorsty
Hill Road, Blackheath, Rowley Regis B65 0HA
(0121 406 3556).

WALKING AND CYCLING

There is a good towpath through Netherton Tunnel so, if you have a torch and are not bothered by the dark, you can enjoy a walk deep underground. You will need a street atlas. Start by walking over the hill from Windmill End. Cross Rough Hill, pass Oakham and descend to Tividale and Dudley Port. Then follow the long (3027yds), straight and very dark towpath back through the tunnel. There are excellent short rambles around Windmill End.

THE END OF WINDMILL END

Overlooking the southern portal of Netherton Tunnel stand the gaunt remains of what is known as Cobbs Engine House. Its actual name is the Windmill End Pumping Station. Sir Horace St Paul built it in 1831 to drain his mines where, as well as coal, iron stone and clay were extracted. Boilers, blast furnaces, open cooking hearths and brick kilns stood by the canal here, each contributing to the dirty and poisonous fumes which gave their name to the Black Country. Netherton Tunnel was opened in 1858 to ease the terrible delays caused by the claustrophobic Dudley and Lapal Tunnels, and soon the engine house stood witness to another scene of water-borne congestion, where horse-drawn boats vied with each other to enter the tunnel first. To the south east of Cobbs Engine House stood a second building housing a smaller engine, which operated a lift in a second shaft. The machinery here was dismantled in 1928 and shipped to the USA by Henry Ford, who erected it in his museum at Dearborn, Detroit. What happened to the Cobbs beam engine is not entirely clear: for some years it appears to have lain derelict before being broken up for scrap. The fate of the great beam, which had a stroke of 8ft and a rate of 6 or 8 strokes each minute to operate a pump some 7ft in diameter in a shaft 522ft deep, lifting about 400,000 gallons of water each day, remains a mystery. Many believe it broke free during removal and fell down the shaft, which was subsequently infilled.

STRATFORD-UPON-AVON CANAL

MAXIMUM DIMENSIONS

King's Norton to Kingswood
Length: 70'
Beam: 7'
Headroom: 7' 3"

Kingswood to Stratford
Length: 70'
Beam: 6' 10"
Headroom: 6'

MANAGER

0303 040 4040
enquiries.westmidlands@canalrivertrust.org.uk

MILEAGE

KING'S NORTON JUNCTION to:
Hockley Heath: 9¾ miles

LAPWORTH Junction with Grand Union
Canal: 12½ miles
Preston Bagot: 16¼ miles
Wootton Wawen Basin: 18½ miles
Wilmcote: 22 miles

STRATFORD-UPON-AVON Junction with
River Avon: 25½ miles

Locks: 54

The opening of the Oxford Canal in 1790 and of the Coventry Canal throughout shortly afterwards opened up a continuous waterway from London to the rapidly developing industrial area based on Birmingham. It also gave access, via the Trent & Mersey Canal, to the expanding pottery industry based upon Stoke-on-Trent, to the Mersey, and to the East Midlands coalfield. When the Warwick & Birmingham and Warwick & Napton canals were projected to pass within 8 miles of Stratford-upon-Avon, the business interests of that town realised that the prosperity being generated by these new trade arteries would pass them by unless Stratford acquired direct access to the network. And so, after the usual preliminaries, on 28 March 1793 an Act of Parliament was passed for the construction of the Stratford-on-Avon Canal, to start at King's Norton on the Worcester & Birmingham Canal (itself a long way from completion at that time). The junction was to be less than 3 miles from the junction of the Worcester & Birmingham with the Dudley Canal, and would thus provide a direct route to a major coal-producing area without passing through Birmingham.

Progress was rapid at first, but almost the total estimated cost of the complete canal was spent in the first three years, on cutting the 9¾ lock-free miles to Hockley Heath. It took another four years, more negotiations, a revision of the route and another Act of Parliament to get things going again. By 1803 the canal was open from King's Norton Junction to its junction with the Warwick & Birmingham Canal (now part of the Grand Union main line) near Lapworth, with through traffic along the whole of this northern section. Even more delays then followed, with little enthusiasm on the part of private investors to put up more money. Cutting re-commenced in 1812, the route being revised yet again in 1815 to include the present junction with the River Avon at Stratford. From here, the Avon was navigable down to the Severn at Tewkesbury.

In its most prosperous period, the canal's annual traffic exceeded 180,000 tons, including 50,000 tons of coal through the complete canal, down to Stratford. By 1835 the canal was suffering from railway competition. This grew so rapidly that in 1845 the Canal Company decided to sell out to the Great Western Railway. There was opposition, however, and it was not until 1 January 1856 that the sale was considered complete. Thus the canal had been in full, independent operation for less than 40 years. Traffic was not immediately suppressed by the new owners, but long-distance haulage was the first to suffer as it was a more direct threat to the railway. In 1890 the tonnage carried was still a quarter of what it had been 50 years before, but the fall in ton-miles was much greater.

This pattern of decline continued in the 20th C, and by the 1950s only an occasional working boat was using the northern section; the southern section (Lapworth to Stratford) was badly silted, some locks were unusable and some of the short pounds below Wilmcote were dry. It is believed that the last boat to reach Stratford did so in the early 1930s, but there is evidence that a pleasure cruiser reached Wilmcote during the Easter holiday of 1947.

After World War II interest began to grow in boating as a recreation. In 1955 a Board of Survey had recommended sweeping canal closures, including the southern section of the Stratford-upon-Avon Canal, but public protest was such that a Committee of Enquiry was set up in 1958, and this prompted the start of a massive campaign to save the canal. The campaign was successful: the decision not to abandon it was announced by the Ministry on 22 May 1959. On 16 October of the same year the National Trust announced that it had agreed a lease from the British Transport Commission under which the Trust would assume responsibility for restoring and maintaining the southern section. The transfer took place on 29 September 1960 and restoration work began in earnest in March of the following year. The terms of the arrangement included a contribution towards the cost of restoration but a very substantial sum was provided by the Trust, which maintained the southern section at its own expense.

The reopening ceremony was performed by Queen Elizabeth the Queen Mother on 11 July 1964, after more than 4 years of hard work by prison labourers, canal enthusiasts, army units and a handful of National Trust staff. On 1 April 1988 control of the southern section of the Stratford-upon-Avon Canal was passed to the British Waterways Board (now Canal and River Trust), finally relieving canal users of the necessity to purchase a separate licence, and the National Trust of a property which, with what was certainly the best will in the world, it was not equipped to care for.

The guillotine-gated stop-lock near King's Norton Junction, start of Stratford-upon-Avon Canal

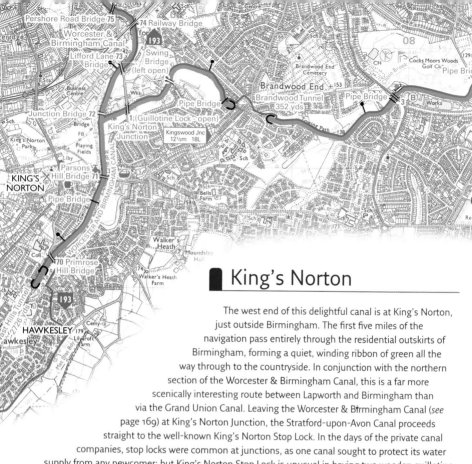

King's Norton

The west end of this delightful canal is at King's Norton, just outside Birmingham. The first five miles of the navigation pass entirely through the residential outskirts of Birmingham, forming a quiet, winding ribbon of green all the way through to the countryside. In conjunction with the northern section of the Worcester & Birmingham Canal, this is a far more scenically interesting route between Lapworth and Birmingham than via the Grand Union Canal. Leaving the Worcester & Birmingham Canal (*see* page 169) at King's Norton Junction, the Stratford-upon-Avon Canal proceeds straight to the well-known King's Norton Stop Lock. In the days of the private canal companies, stop locks were common at junctions, as one canal sought to protect its water supply from any newcomer; but King's Norton Stop Lock is unusual in having two wooden guillotine gates mounted in iron frames, balanced by chains and counterweights. The machinery, although recently fully restored, is not now used and boats pass under the two gates without stopping. The next bridge is a small swing bridge (usually left open), followed by Brandwood Tunnel. Further east is a beautiful tree-lined cutting, then a bridge with a *pub* beside it (*garage and telephone nearby*) and the remains of an old arm just beyond it. Passing over a small aqueduct, the canal reaches a steel lift bridge, which is raised and lowered electrically (see note below). Then beyond a railway bridge the canal begins to shed all traces of the suburbs, maintaining its twisting course in wooded cuttings through quiet countryside. The bridges over the navigation are mostly the generous brick-arched bridges typical of the canal between King's Norton and Lapworth Locks (in contrast to the much smaller bridges further south, and built when there were plans for a broad canal), but few roads of any significance come near the canal. At bridge 16 the canal emerges from a long cutting and is joined by a feeder from the nearby Earlswood Reservoir. Boats are moored along this, since it is the base of the Earlswood Motor Yacht Club. There are no villages along this rural stretch of canal.

NAVIGATIONAL NOTES

You will need a Watermate key to operate Shirley Drawbridge, 8. A single button completes the operation, and a line of piles guides you through.

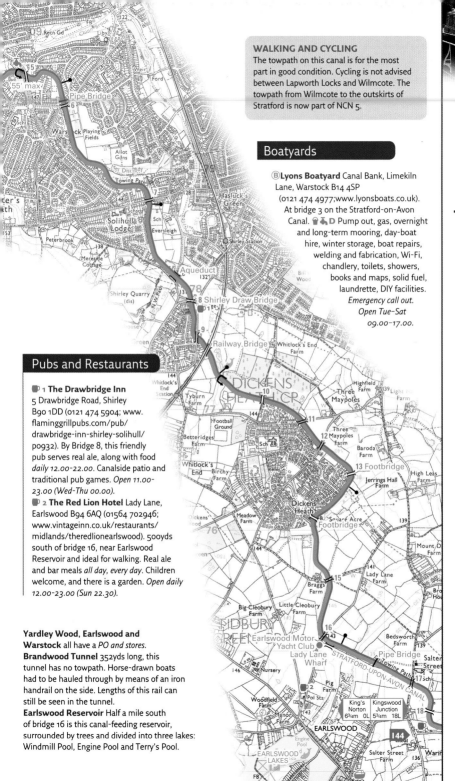

WALKING AND CYCLING

The towpath on this canal is for the most part in good condition. Cycling is not advised between Lapworth Locks and Wilmcote. The towpath from Wilmcote to the outskirts of Stratford is now part of NCN 5.

Boatyards

Ⓑ**Lyons Boatyard** Canal Bank, Limekiln Lane, Warstock B14 4SP
(0121 474 4977; www.lyonsboats.co.uk). At bridge 3 on the Stratford-on-Avon Canal. 🛒🔧 **D** Pump out, gas, overnight and long-term mooring, day-boat hire, winter storage, boat repairs, welding and fabrication, Wi-Fi, chandlery, toilets, showers, books and maps, solid fuel, laundrette, DIY facilities. *Emergency call out. Open Tue–Sat 09.00–17.00.*

Pubs and Restaurants

🍺 1 **The Drawbridge Inn** 5 Drawbridge Road, Shirley B90 1DD (0121 474 5904; www.flaminggrillpubs.com/pub/drawbridge-inn-shirley-solihull/p0932). By Bridge 8, this friendly pub serves real ale, along with food *daily 12.00-22.00*. Canalside patio and traditional pub games. *Open 11.00-23.00 (Wed-Thu 00.00)*.

🍺 2 **The Red Lion Hotel** Lady Lane, Earlswood B94 6AQ (01564 702946; www.vintageinn.co.uk/restaurants/midlands/theredlionearlswood). 500yds south of bridge 16, near Earlswood Reservoir and ideal for walking. Real ale and bar meals *all day, every day*. Children welcome, and there is a garden. *Open daily 12.00-23.00 (Sun 22.30)*.

Yardley Wood, Earlswood and **Warstock** all have a *PO and stores*.
Brandwood Tunnel 352yds long, this tunnel has no towpath. Horse-drawn boats had to be hauled through by means of an iron handrail on the side. Lengths of this rail can still be seen in the tunnel.
Earlswood Reservoir Half a mile south of bridge 16 is this canal-feeding reservoir, surrounded by trees and divided into three lakes: Windmill Pool, Engine Pool and Terry's Pool.

Lapworth Locks

The canal continues on its south easterly course, passing through quiet countryside interrupted only by the incessant roar of the M42 motorway, crossing overhead. is an excellent, *combined bakery, delicatessen and café* just north of Bridge 20. There are no locks, and the bridges – especially those in the cuttings – are still the big brick arches built when a broad canal was planned. At Hockley Heath (bridge 25) there is a tiny arm that once served a coal wharf. Nearby the Wharf Inn overlooks the canal. East of here things change dramatically, for the first of the locks down to Kingswood Junction is reached. The top lock is numbered 2, as the old stop lock at King's Norton is number 1. The surroundings of the top lock are indeed pleasant: a white house enclosed by walls and hemmed in by trees stands beside the lock, while a cottage with a delightful garden faces the towpath just below. To the south west can be seen the spire of Lapworth church. After the first four locks, there is a 1/2-mile breathing space: then the Lapworth flight begins in earnest, with each of the next nine locks spaced only a few yards from its neighbour.

The short intervening pounds have been enlarged to provide a bigger working reservoir of water, so that one side of each lock is virtually an isthmus. The locks have double bottom gates so are not heavy going, and are interspersed with the old cast iron split bridges that are such a charming feature of the Stratford-upon-Avon Canal. These bridges are built in two halves, separated by a one inch gap

Boatyards

(B)**Swallow Cruisers** Wharf Lane, Hockley Heath B94 5NR (01564 783442; www.bridge27.co.uk). 🛏🛒⛽D Pump out, gas, overnight and long-term mooring, winter storage, chandlery, books and maps, outboard engine sales and repairs, GRP repairs, wooden boat building, solid fuel, DIY facilities, boat painting, servicing and repairs. *Emergency call out. Open Mon-Fri 08.30-16.30 (Fri 16.00) & Sat 08.30-13.00.*

(B)**Knowle Hall Wharf** Kenilworth Road, Knowle, Solihull B93 0JJ (01564 778210; www.knowlehallwharf.co.uk). 🛏🛒⛽D Pump out, gas, overnight and long-term mooring, dry dock and DIY facilities, engine services, heating services, build, repair and refit of narrow boats and cruisers. *Emergency breakdown service (24 hr).*

NAVIGATIONAL NOTES

1 *Please go slowly* to minimise your wash.
2 Bridges 26 and 28 operate hydraulically, using a lock windlass.
3 Due to rebuilding, the chamber of lock 15 on the Lapworth flight is now over 2ft shorter than the other locks. Those in full-length boats should take extra care when descending.

so that the towing line between a horse and a boat could be dropped through the gap without having to disconnect the horse. There are *shops* south of bridge 34. Below lock 19 is Kingswood Junction: boats heading for Stratford should keep right here. A short branch to the left leads under the railway line to the Grand Union Canal, or you can use the Lapworth Link after lock 22 if you are heading north to the GU, avoiding unnecessary lockage. There are *toilets* and a shaded *picnic area* beside the car park adjoining the towpath at Lock 19.

Pubs and Restaurants

🍺 1 **The Blue Bell Cider House** Warings Green Road, Hockley Heath B94 6BP (01564 702328; www.thebluebellciderhouse. co.uk). A pretty, traditional cider house serving real draught cider and a range of real ales. Food available *Mon-Sat 12.00-20.30 & Sun 12.00-17.00*. Dog- and family-friendly, canalside garden. Traditional pub games, real fires, sports TV and Wi-Fi. Mooring. Quiz *Wed*. Open *Mon-Sat 11.30-23.00 (Fri-Sat 23.30) & Sun 12.00-22.30*.

✗ 2 **Wedges Bakery and Delicatessen** 495 School Road, Hockley Heath B94 6RP (01564 702542; www.wedgesbakery. co.uk). 100yds north east of Bridge 20. Set in the original bake house, dating from 1850, this café, delicatessen and bakery sells a tantalising selection of fresh food – both to eat in and take away – including breakfast, light lunches and afternoon teas. Courtyard seating. Open *Mon-Fri 08.00-17.30, Sat 07.00-17.00 & Sun 10.00-15.00*.

Also try: 🍺 3 **The Bulls Head** 7 Limekiln Lane, Earlswood B94 6BU (01564 700368; www.thwaites.co.uk/hotels-and-inns/ inns/bulls-head-at-earlswood/food-and-drink/menus/).

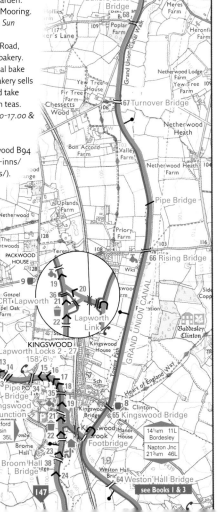

145

● **Hockley Heath**
Warwicks. PO, tel, stores, butcher, delicatessen, fish & chips, garage (1 mile distant). A featureless place, but the several shops are conveniently close to the canal bridge, and the pub is pleasant. There is also a handy cycle shop: **Dynamic Rides** 2364 Stratford Road B94 6QT (01564 783332; www.dynamicrides. co.uk) which includes the Flying Squirrel Café. *Shop open 06.00–22.00.*

● **Lapworth**
Warwicks. PO, tel, stores, off-licence, garage, station. Indivisible from Kingswood, this is more a residential area than a village. Two canals pass through Lapworth: the heavily locked Stratford-on-Avon Canal and, to the east, the main line of the Grand Union Canal. These two waterways, and the short spur that connects them, are easily the most interesting aspect of Lapworth. The canalside buildings are attractive and there are two small

reservoirs at the junction. The mostly 15th-C church is quite separate from the village and is 1¹/₂ miles west of the junction; it contains an interesting monument by Eric Gill, 1928.

Packwood House Packwood Lane, Lapworth B94 6AT (01564 782024; www.nationaltrust.org.uk/ packwood-house). ¾ mile north of Bridge 31. Timber-framed Tudor house, dating from the late 16th C and enlarged in the 17th C, where Cromwell's general, Henry Ireton, slept before the Battle of Edgehill in 1642. Owned by the Featherstones until 1869, it was eventually purchased by Alfred Ash, who repaired the house and reinstated the gardens. Collection of tapestry, needlework and furniture. Park with formal grounds and 17th-C yew garden possibly laid out to represent the Sermon on the Mount, the trees taking the place of Jesus and his followers. Café. *Opening times vary* so telephone or visit website for details.

Pubs and Restaurants (pages 144–145)

✕♀ 4 **Tagore Restaurant** 2571a Stratford Road, Hockley Heath B94 6NL (01564 784800; tagorerestaurant.com). Well-regarded Indian restaurant that will deliver a takeaway direct to your boat. *Open Mon–Sun 17.30–23.00 (Fri–Sat 23.30).*

◖✕ 5 **Miller & Carter Steak House** Stratford Road, Hockley Heath B94 6NL (01564 784137; www.miller andcarter.co.uk/millerandcarterhockley heath). Traditional steak house serving much more besides, including real ale. Family-friendly, garden and Wi-Fi. *Open daily 12.00–23.00 (Fri–Sat 00.00).*

◖✕ 6 **The Wharf Tavern** 2390 Stratford Road, Hockley Heath B94 6QT (01564 782075; www. wharftavern.co.uk). A friendly, community pub overlooking the canal serving real ales and food *daily 12.00–22.00.* Child- and dog-friendly, canalside patio. Traditional pub games, sports TV and Wi-Fi. *Open 12.00–23.00 (Fri–Sat 00.00).*

◖ 7 **The Boot Inn** Old Warwick Road, Lapworth B94 6JU (01564 782464; www.lovelypubs.co.uk/the-boot-lapworth). Cosmopolitan country pub serving real ale. Fashionable bar meals *L and E*. Children and well-behaved dogs welcome; garden. Open fires. *Open Mon–Sat 11.00–23.00 (Fri–Sat 00.00) & Sun 12.00–22.30.*

◖✕ 8 **The Navigation** Old Warwick Road, Lapworth B94 6NA (01564 783337; www.navigationlapworth. co.uk). Real ales, real cider and food available *Mon–Thu L and E & Fri–Sun 12.00–21.30 (Sun 20.00).* Breakfast *Sat–Sun from 10.00.* Family-friendly, canalside garden. Traditional pub games, real fires and Wi-Fi. Camping & Moorings. *Open 11.30–00.00.*

Also try: ◖✕ 9 **The Punchbowl** Mill Lane, Lapworth B94 6HR (01564 784564; www. thepunchbowllapworth.com).

Lowsonford Bridge

Lowsonford

The canal continues south, pursuing a fairly direct and wholly peaceful course. There is a barrel-roof cottage, typical of this part of the canal, by lock 28. At Yarningale, having followed a small stream for several miles, it crosses it on a tiny aqueduct adjoining lock 34. Preston Bagot Bottom Lock is squeezed in by the road once this has been negotiated, the canal again resumes its peaceful course through rural Warwickshire. Good moorings are available by lock 25.

● **Preston Bagot**
Warwicks. The Church of All Saints has a pretty timber bell-turret and a spire, a Norman nave and a north wall with three Norman windows.

Pubs and Restaurants

🍺 1 **The Fleur-de-Lys** Lapworth Street, Lowsonford B95 5HJ (01564 782431; www.fleurdelys-lowsonford.com). Canalside, just north of lock 31. Attractive 13th-C cottages, which once incorporated a bakehouse, converted into a beamy pub in the 15th C, with open fires and a large garden. The famous Fleur-de-Lys pies were once cooked here. Although now mass produced, they still offer a good pie menu.

Real ale is served, along with bar meals *Mon-Sat 12.00-21.00 (Fri-Sat 21.30 & Sun 12.00-19.00.* Children welcome, and a safe play area in the large canalside garden. 🛶 and moorings (*but please ask first – don't tie-up to the trees). Open Mon-Sat 11.00-22.00 (Fri-Sat 23.00) & Sun 12.00-21.00.*

🍺✕ 2 **The Crabmill Inn** Preston Bagot B95 5EE (01926 843342; www.lovelypubs.co.uk/the-crabmill-pub). A light, modern pub, influenced by continental style, serving real ale and food *L and E (not Sun E).* Dog- and family-friendly, garden. Newspapers, real fires and Wi-Fi. *Open Mon-Sat 11.00-23.00 & Sun 12.00-18.00.*

Edstone Aqueduct

The canal continues through delightfully quiet country as Austy Wood looms up on the hill to the east, with Austy Manor, a low stone hall, below. Beyond bridge 53 the canal widens into a basin – *a craft centre, coffee shop and farm shop* are just two minutes away to the west, and a basin and a *pub* are passed – then the canal immediately crosses the A3400 road on a cast iron aqueduct. This is followed by a slight cutting – rare on the southern section of this canal – and then the waterway straightens out at Bearley Lock. Further south the canal rises on an embankment and is then carried across water meadows, a road and a railway by the splendid Edstone Aqueduct. At the southern end is a very pretty cottage and garden. The navigation now winds along a secluded section to Wilmcote. Just north of the village are the remains of a bridge – this used to carry a horse tramway that served nearby quarries. The winding hole and the cottages on the towpath at this point were built for the quarry trade. Wilmcote is close to the canal, and, if you wish to visit what we know as Mary Arden's House, you must moor north of bridge 59.

● **Wootton Wawen**
Warwicks. PO, tel, stores, off-licence, hardware, station.
This scattered but pretty village is a 1/2 mile west of the basin, and has been designated a conservation area. There are plenty of timbered houses and the late 17th-C Hall looks superb across the parkland and pond; but the chief glory is St Peter's Church on its rise overlooking the whole village.
St Peter's Church Stratford Road, Wootton Wawen B95 6BD (www.saxonsanctuary.org.uk). There was originally a wooden church on this site, built c.720–740 by Earl Aethelric, but the present structure dates from 1035, when it was erected by Wagen the Thane, a local landowner, as part of an early Saxon monastic complex. Most of the tower and parts of the walls survive from this time. Later additions include the barn-like Lady Chapel, added during the 14th C, the tower-top and clerestory added in the late 15th C, and various other additions since then. This has given it a pleasantly disorderly external appearance, but inside there are rare and fascinating things to see. The church is the only one in Warwickshire that derives from Saxon times, and the original sanctuary in the centre of the 11th-C church survives intact, still the focus of the building after over 900 years. The nave is conspicuously Norman, the chancel is bare but large, with a superb 14th-C east window. The Lady Chapel is probably the oddest part of the whole building – it is like a barn in more ways than one. It is enormous, with a primitive tiled roof and a completely irregular brick floor which still has traces of family pews and their fireplaces! All around the walls are a medley of monuments, together with fine 13th- and 17th-C oak parish chests. Saxon Sanctuary exhibition. Toilets. Craft centre nearby. Open *daily during daylight hours*.
Wootton Wawen Basin This wide, embanked basin was built when construction of the canal was halted here for a while. With a nearby *pub, farm shop and craft centre*, the wharf is a popular halt with both boaters and motorists. A cast iron aqueduct carries the canal over the A3400 by the basin. Attached to the aqueduct, and visible from the road, is an original iron plaque commemorating the opening of the structure in 1813. A large sign on the southern

end relays similar information to canal and towpath users. Just down the hill is a fine brick watermill, built originally as a paper mill and still in good repair. This dates from the late 18th C.
Edstone (or Bearley) Aqueduct This major aqueduct, approaching 200yds in length, consists of a narrow cast iron trough carried on brick piers across a shallow valley. As with the two other – but much smaller – iron aqueducts on this canal (at Yarningale and Wootton Wawen), the towpath runs along the level of the bottom of the tank, so that towing horses and pedestrians get a duck's eye view of passing boats. This feature makes the aqueducts on this canal very unusual.
Yew Tree Farm Shopping Village Pettiford Lane, Wootton Wawen, B95 6BY (01564 792701; yew-tree-farm.co.uk). Sixteen barns and a coffee shop offering a range of products from around the world. Farm Shop *(open daily)*. Complex open Tue-Sun & B Hols *10.00-17.00 (winter Sun 16.00)*.
● **Wilmcote**
Warwicks. PO, tel, stores, off-licence, coal, firewood, station. A small and attractive village, typical of this part of the country. A beautiful lime tree on the green is the centre of the village: nearby are a fine old pub and the most well-known building in the village – known as Mary Arden's House *(see below)*. The school and a vicarage by the church were built by William Butterfield in 1844 and 1845, and were his first non- religious buildings. Mobile PO *open Mon, Wed & Fri 09.30-11.30 & Tue & Thu 14.00-16.00*.
Mary Arden's Farm Wilmcote CV37 9UN (01789 293455; www.shakespeare.org.uk/visit-the-houses/plan-your-visit.html). Thought for many years to be the home of Shakespeare's mother, it has now been discovered that she actually lived 30yds away at Glebe Farm. What we call Mary Arden's House was not actually built until 5 years after she had left the village. It incorporates a museum of agricultural implements and local rural bygones, and is furnished as the home of a yeoman farmer in Shakespeare's time. It is owned by the Shakespeare Birthplace Trust. Café and shop. *Open daily, mid-Mar-Oct 10.00-17.00*. Charge.

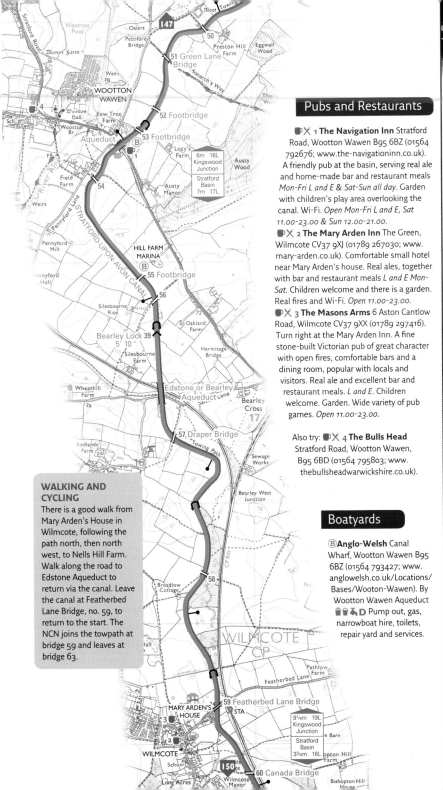

Pubs and Restaurants

◖▯✕ **1 The Navigation Inn** Stratford Road, Wootton Wawen B95 6BZ (01564 792676; www.the-navigationinn.co.uk). A friendly pub at the basin, serving real ale and home-made bar and restaurant meals *Mon-Fri L and E & Sat-Sun all day.* Garden with children's play area overlooking the canal. Wi-Fi. *Open Mon-Fri L and E, Sat 11.00-23.00 & Sun 12.00-21.00.*

◖▯✕ **2 The Mary Arden Inn** The Green, Wilmcote CV37 9XJ (01789 267030; www. mary-arden.co.uk). Comfortable small hotel near Mary Arden's house. Real ales, together with bar and restaurant meals *L and E Mon-Sat.* Children welcome and there is a garden. Real fires and Wi-Fi. *Open 11.00-23.00.*

◖▯✕ **3 The Masons Arms** 6 Aston Cantlow Road, Wilmcote CV37 9XX (01789 297416). Turn right at the Mary Arden Inn. A fine stone-built Victorian pub of great character with open fires, comfortable bars and a dining room, popular with locals and visitors. Real ale and excellent bar and restaurant meals. *L and E.* Children welcome. Garden. Wide variety of pub games. *Open 11.00-23.00.*

Also try: ◖▯✕ **4 The Bulls Head** Stratford Road, Wootton Wawen, B95 6BD (01564 795803; www. thebullsheadwarwickshire.co.uk).

Boatyards

Ⓑ **Anglo-Welsh** Canal Wharf, Wootton Wawen B95 6BZ (01564 793427; www. anglowelsh.co.uk/Locations/ Bases/Wooton-Wawen). By Wootton Wawen Aqueduct 🛁🚿⛽D Pump out, gas, narrowboat hire, toilets, repair yard and services.

WALKING AND CYCLING
There is a good walk from Mary Arden's House in Wilmcote, following the path north, then north west, to Nells Hill Farm. Walk along the road to Edstone Aqueduct to return via the canal. Leave the canal at Featherbed Lane Bridge, no. 59, to return to the start. The NCN joins the towpath at bridge 59 and leaves at bridge 63.

Stratford-upon-Avon

South of Wilmcote, the two long pounds from Preston Bagot are terminated by a dense flight of locks – there are 11 in the Wilmcote flight, in groups of 3, 5 and 3. They are, in the main, set in pleasant open country, in which Stratford can occasionally be seen to the east. Beyond a rather large road bridge the canal descends another lock and reaches the nether regions of Stratford. There is little yet, however, to suggest you are entering one of Britain's premier tourist destinations as you pass through the light industrial surroundings typical of a Midlands town. The canal then enters a residential area as it approaches the River Avon, dropping steeply through several locks, number 54 being in a particularly pretty setting. It then ducks through the lowest bridge since Lapworth and emerges at the splendid great basin in the middle of the riverside parkland beside the Shakespeare Memorial Theatre, a flower-decked area frequented by hundreds of tourists. *Ice creams and baguettes* are sold from moored narrowboats. Amidst all the relics of Shakespeare's life, have a walk over Tramway Bridge, passing the handsome timber shed of J. Cox, to stroll in parkland alongside the River Avon. If all the moorings in the basin are taken, a place can usually be found on the river above Colin P. Witter Lock for which there is a charge.

BOAT TRIPS

Countess of Evesham Bancroft Gardens, Waterside, Stratford-upon-Avon CV37 6BA (07836 769499; www.countessofevesham.co.uk). Cruises for lunch and dinner, *all year round*. Meals are freshly produced on board, and there is a bar. Also available for private hire.
See also **Boat Trips** on page 33

31

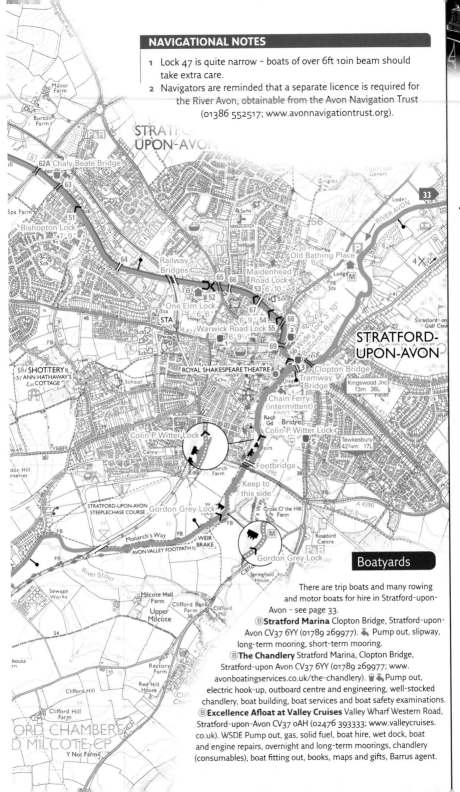

NAVIGATIONAL NOTES

1. Lock 47 is quite narrow – boats of over 6ft 10in beam should take extra care.
2. Navigators are reminded that a separate licence is required for the River Avon, obtainable from the Avon Navigation Trust (01386 552517; www.avonnavigationtrust.org).

Boatyards

There are trip boats and many rowing and motor boats for hire in Stratford-upon-Avon – see page 33.

Ⓑ**Stratford Marina** Clopton Bridge, Stratford-upon-Avon CV37 6YY (01789 269977). Pump out, slipway, long-term mooring, short-term mooring.

Ⓑ**The Chandlery** Stratford Marina, Clopton Bridge, Stratford-upon Avon CV37 6YY (01789 269977; www.avonboatingservices.co.uk/the-chandlery). Pump out, electric hook-up, outboard centre and engineering, well-stocked chandlery, boat building, boat services and boat safety examinations.

Ⓑ**Excellence Afloat at Valley Cruises** Valley Wharf Western Road, Stratford-upon-Avon CV37 0AH (02476 393333; www.valleycruises.co.uk). WSDE Pump out, gas, solid fuel, boat hire, wet dock, boat and engine repairs, overnight and long-term moorings, chandlery (consumables), boat fitting out, books, maps and gifts, Barrus agent.

Stratford-upon-Avon

Warwicks. All services. Tourism has been established for a very long time in Stratford. It was in 1789 that the first big celebrations in William Shakespeare's honour were organised by the actor David Garrick. They are now held annually on St George's Day (23 April), which is believed to have been Shakespeare's birthday. An annual Mop Fair on 12 October reminds the visitor that Stratford was already well-established as a market town long before Shakespeare's time. Indeed the first grant for a weekly market was given by King John in 1196. Today, Stratford is well used to the constant flow of charabancs and tourists, ancient charm vying with the expected commercialism that usually mars popular places like this. There are wide streets of endless low, timbered buildings that house dignified hotels and antique shops; plenty of these are also private houses. On the river, hired punts and rowing boats jostle each other while people picnic in the open parkland on the banks. The Royal Shakespeare Theatre, opened in 1932, is on an enviable site beside the Avon. Its massive industrial-style building, designed by Elizabeth Scott to replace an earlier theatre, destroyed by fire in 1926, is being re-developed by the theatre company. More in keeping with the historic Shakespearian tradition is the delightful Swan Theatre, risen phoenix-like from the ashes of the original building, thanks to the exceptional generosity of a single benefactor – for a long time anonymous. Attached to the main building, this theatre has a simple charm echoing the 16th-C Globe Playhouse.

Shakespeare Birthplace Trust Stratford-upon-Avon (01789 204016; www.shakespeare.org.uk). This Trust was founded in 1847 to look after the five buildings most closely associated with Shakespeare; four of these are in Stratford (listed below) and the other is Mary Arden's Cottage at Wilmcote (*see page* 148). Admission charge to each building. *The summer season is mid Mar–mid Oct. An all-inclusive ticket is available covering either the in-town properties, or all five Shakespeare Houses.*

Shakespeare's Birthplace Henley Street CV37 6QW (01789 204016/201822; www.shakespeare. org.uk). An early 16th-C half-timbered building containing books, manuscripts and exhibits associated with Shakespeare and rooms furnished in period style. Gardens. Next door is the Shakespeare Exhibition *open daily (except Xmas day) Apr-Oct 09.00-17.00 & Nov-Mar 10.00-16.00. Charge.*

Hall's Croft Old Town CV37 6BG (01789 292107; www.shakespeare.org.uk). A Tudor house and garden complete with period furniture – the home of Shakespeare's daughter Susanna and her husband Dr John Hall. *Open daily (except Xmas & Boxing days) Apr-Oct 10.00-17.00 & Nov-Mar 11.00-16.00. Charge.*

Nash's House and New Place Chapel Street CV37 6EP. (01789 292325; www.shakespeare.org.uk). The foundations of Shakespeare's last home set in a replica of an Elizabethan garden. *Open daily (except Xmas & Boxing days) Apr-Oct 10.00-17.00 & Nov-Mar 11.00-16.00. Charge.*

Anne Hathaway's Cottage Cottage Lane, Shottery CV37 9HH (01789 292100; www.shakespeare.org.uk). 1 mile west of Stratford. Dating from the 15th C this fine thatched farmhouse was once the home of Anne Hathaway before she married William Shakespeare in 1582. Her family, yeoman farmers, remained in occupation until 1892, when the cottage was purchased by the Shakespeare Birthplace Trust. The rooms retain their original features. The cottage was badly damaged by fire in 1969, but has since been completely restored. It has a mature, typically English garden, and long queues of visitors in the summer. *Open daily (except Xmas & Boxing days) Apr-Oct 09.00-17.00 & Nov-Mar 10.00-16.00. Charge.*

Royal Shakespeare Theatre (Tickets 0844 800 1110; www.rsc.org.uk). The home of the Royal Shakespeare Company, which produces Shakespeare plays to a very high standard *Apr–Dec every year.* The first theatre in Stratford was a temporary octagon built for Garrick's festival in 1769. A permanent theatre was not erected until 1827, with a library and art gallery being added in 1881.

Stratford-upon-Avon Butterfly Farm Swan's Nest Lane CV37 7LS (01789 299288; www.butterflyfarm. co.uk). Just south of the Tramway Bridge. Rainforest growth, fish pools and waterfalls, hundreds of butterflies and fascinating insects. For the not-so-squeamish there is Arachnoland, where you can view deadly insects (in perfect safety). Adventure playground, gift shop and refreshments. *Open 10.00–18.00 (17.00 in winter). Charge.*

Stratford Waterways Information Centre aboard *William James,* Bancroft Basin, Stratford-upon-Avon CV37 6YS (07584 086321; www.avonnavigationtrust. org/index.php?id=141). A wide range of boater and tourist information is available from the Avon Navigation Trust's boat moored in Bancroft Basin. Also licenses for the River Avon and the canal system, gifts, souvenirs and a meeting room for hire. *Open daily Apr-Oct 08.00-17.00.*

Holy Trinity Church Old Town CV37 6BG (01789 266316; www.stratford-upon-avon.org). Attractively situated among trees overlooking Colin P. Witter lock on the River Avon. Mainly of the 15th C but the spire was rebuilt in 1763. William Shakespeare is buried in the chancel. His tomb bears a curse against anyone who dares to disturb it.

Tourist Information Centre Bridgefoot CV37 6GW (01789 264293; www.discover-stratford.com). A mine of information, and lots of guide books and souvenirs for sale. *Open Mon-Sat 09.00-17.30 & Sun 10.00-16.00*

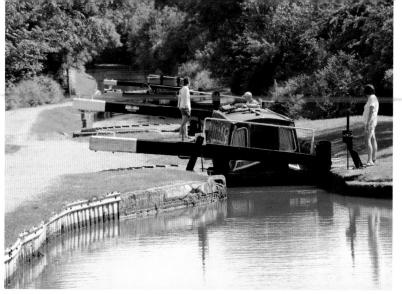

Wilmcote Locks

WALKING AND CYCLING

The Stratford Greenway is a linear country park, almost five miles long, following the old Honeybourne Railway Line and providing a traffic-free walking and cycling route, together with two picnic sites. It starts immediately to the south of Colin P. Witter Lock, finishing in Long Marston and interlinks with other riverside footpaths which can be used to form a number of circular walks. *See also* Walking & Cycling on page 159 and visit Country Parks Information Service at www.warwickshire.gov.uk.

Pubs and Restaurants (pages 150–151)

There are numerous restaurants, snack bars, fast-food outlets and pubs in Stratford-upon-Avon.

🍺 1 **The Stratford Alehouse** 12B Greenhill Street, Stratford-upon-Avon CV37 6LF (07746 807966; thestratfordalehouse.com). Totally devoid of gaming machines and loud music, this small, family-run pub serves superb real ales, ciders and wines. Dog-friendly and newspapers. Folk club *1st & 3rd Wed of month* with live music *every Wed and most Sun*. Open *Mon-Sat 13.00-23.00 & Sun 14.00-20.00*.

🍺✕ 2 **The Pen & Parchment Hotel** Bridgefoot CV37 6YY (01789 297697; www.oldenglishinns. co.uk/our-locations/the-pen-and-parchment-stratford-upon-avon). This is a pleasant beamy pub in a listed building. Good selection of real ale. Wide range of bar and restaurant meals available *daily, L and E*. There are outside seats surrounded by tubs of flowers, where you can watch the tourist sightseeing buses depart. Children welcome. Wi-Fi. B&B. Open *11.00-23.00*.

🍺 3 **Cox's Yard** Bridgefoot CV37 6YY (01789 404600; www.coxsyard.com). Pub, restaurant, theatre and teashop, this 'total leisure experience' offers food *all day, every day*, together with a selection of real ales. Children welcome, outside seating area. *Regular* live music events. Open *Mon-Sat 12.00-23.00 (Fri-Sat 00.00) & Sun 12.00-22.30*.

✕♟ 4 **Connolly's Tapas Bar** 25 Main Street, Tiddington CV37 7AN (01789 204712; www. connollystapasbar.co.uk). Family owned restaurant, fully licensed bar and deli serving fresh and locally sourced food in a relaxed and friendly atmosphere. Hearty breakfasts, takeaway coffee, sandwiches, tapas-style dishes and main courses; full complement of deli foods. Open *Wed-Sat 10.00-23.00 & Tue 10.00-15.00*.

Also try: 🍺 5 **Old Tramway Inn** 91 Shipston Road, Stratford-upon-Avon CV37 7LW (01789 297593; www.theoldtramwayinn.co.uk)

153

STROUDWATER NAVIGATION AND THAMES & SEVERN CANAL

STROUDWATER NAVIGATION

MAXIMUM DIMENSIONS

Length: 74' 0"
Beam: 15' 6"
Draught: 5' 0" (as built)
Headroom: 8' 0"

MILEAGE

FRAMILODE Junction with the River Severn to:
Saul Junction: 1 mile
Bristol Road Lock 10: 2½ miles
Ryeford Double Lock 6: 6¼ miles

WALLBRIDGE, Junction with the Thames & Severn Canal: 8 miles

Locks: 13

THAMES & SEVERN CANAL

MAXIMUM DIMENSIONS

Wallbridge to Bourne Lock (90' x 16')
Length: 74' 0"
Beam: 15' 6"

Beales Lock to Inglesham
Length: 90' 0" (many later shortened to 70' 0")
Beam: 12' 6"
Draught: 5' 0" (as built)
Headroom: 8' 0"

MILEAGE

WALLBRIDGE Junction with the Stroudwater Navigation to:
Brimscombe Port: 2½ miles
Bakers Mill Lower Lock 17: 5½ miles
Sapperton Tunnel Daneway Portal: 7½ miles
Sapperton Tunnel Coates Portal: 9½ miles
Siddington Upper Lock 29, junction with the Cirencester Branch: 15¼ miles

LATTON Junction with the North Wilts Branch of the Wilts & Berks Canal: 20 miles
Eisey Lock 41: 22½ miles

INGLESHAM LOCK Junction with the River Thames: 28¾ miles

Locks: 44

COTSWOLD CANALS TRUST

Bell House, Wallbridge Lock, Stroud, Glos. GL5 3JS
01453 752568
mail@cotswoldcanals.com
www.cotswoldcanals.com

The two waterways sitting under the umbrella title of the 'Cotswold Canals' are – running west to east – the Stroudwater Navigation and the Thames & Severn Canal. Collectively they span a distance of almost 37 miles, forming an important link between the tidal (and very treacherous) River Severn and the quiet, meandering River Thames, at its limit of navigation above Lechlade – in the heart of the Cotswolds.

Convenient though this collective title may seem to those engaged in their very active restoration, it nevertheless obscures the fact that these are two very different canals in terms of their success, their longevity and, in particular, the terrain they traverse.

Few difficulties had been encountered in the building of the Stroudwater Navigation which opened in 1779, the same year that Abraham Darby raised the first iron bridge over the Severn in Coalbrookdale and at a time when the American War of Independence was at its height. No great engineering works were required, all the constructional materials were available locally, no townships were passed through and, above all, demand for its primary cargo was burgeoning in Stroud. With the coming of the Industrial Revolution, mechanisation of the woollen mills was not confined to water power, coal also being required to drive steam engines. This was initially provided by the Midlands' mines and then from the Forest of Dean. Subsequently, the canal carried timber (and its bark for tanning), salt from Droitwich, together with chemicals used in textile dyeing processes, shipped from Bewdley.

The Company of Proprietors always benefited from sound and dedicated management throughout the life of the navigation, while shares tended to be passed down within the same families from generation to generation.

However, by the time of the Second World War it became clear that the Navigation was no longer viable and this coincided with Gloucestershire County Council's mounting concern over the state of some of the bridges. Only an official Act of Abandonment would allow the Council to adopt these structures, this being finally obtained in 1954. Intriguingly, the Company of Proprietors remained in existence: indeed they still do to this day, holding regular monthly meetings and acting as pivotal members of the Cotswold Canals Partnership.

Linking Stroud to the Thames at Lechlade – and ultimately to London – was an obvious development but the terrain, including an abrupt 241ft rise over the Cotswold scarp, within the first seven miles between Stroud and Daneway, was an entirely different engineering proposition.

28 locks are employed in elevating the waterway to its meeting with the castellated Daneway Portal, at the western end of 3817 yds-long Sapperton Tunnel, giving a theoretical spacing of ¼ mile between locks. With sensible length pounds, side ponds, intermediate reservoirs and feeds from local streams and the River Frome, this was within the realms of the possible. However, in spite of what was, by then, already fairly well understood and developed technology, received engineering wisdom was often ignored, and water shortages were the norm on this section of the navigation throughout its chequered life.

The appointment of an incompetent contractor prolonged the building of the tunnel itself which, together with further sections of the summit pound, was built on badly fissured rock leading to problems with constant leakage, which even a beam engine – delivering three million gallons of water per day – struggled at times to overcome. Further water saving measures included shortening lock chambers (between Chalford and South Cerney) by inserting a second pair of top gates but, with revenue peaking in 1841, the waterway steadily declined in the face of the usual railway competition.

Following closure in 1893, the navigation was taken over by a Trust and eventually reopened. In 1901 it passed into the hands of Gloucestershire County Council. The last fully laden boat crossed the summit level in May 1911 and by 1933 the entire length had fallen to Acts of Abandonment.

Today the focus is on connecting the completed Phase 1A restoration through Stroud to the Gloucester & Sharpness Canal at Saul and the main waterways system. To this end the Cotswold Canals Trust are joint lead partners, together with Stroud District Council, in a Heritage Lottery Fund bid identified as "Stroudwater Navigation Connect."

WALKING AND CYCLING

The restoration to navigation of the two waterways that make up the Cotswold Canals is an ambitious – and on-going – waterways project, set in some of the most charming countryside to be found anywhere within the British Isles. Access to walkers and, to a limited extent cyclists, precedes the arrival of boats by a considerable margin but this does carry some restrictions and limitations, although these are not necessarily too onerous.

The end-to-end route currently plotted in this guide – the embryo of the Thames & Severn Way – does not always follow the towpath, but makes use of public footpaths and quiet, minor roads where there is no public right of access. It aims to keep as close to the line of the navigation as is practical and, as restoration proceeds, will be modified to include new sections of reinstated towpath.

It cannot be stressed too strongly that, with the abandonment of the navigation in 1927, parts of the Thames & Severn Canal now run through private land to which there is **no public access**. Therefore, to stray off designated footpaths and bridleways, is to **jeopardise future restoration** and the painstaking efforts already put into re-establishing rights of navigation and access.

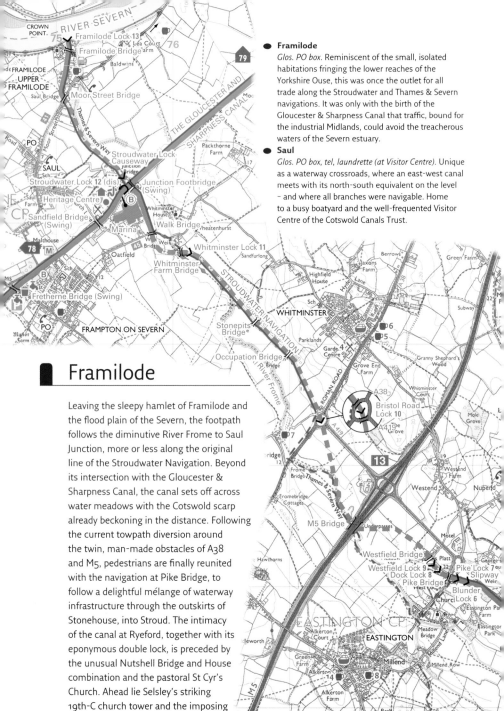

● **Framilode**
Glos. PO box. Reminiscent of the small, isolated habitations fringing the lower reaches of the Yorkshire Ouse, this was once the outlet for all trade along the Stroudwater and Thames & Severn navigations. It was only with the birth of the Gloucester & Sharpness Canal that traffic, bound for the industrial Midlands, could avoid the treacherous waters of the Severn estuary.

● **Saul**
Glos. PO box, tel, laundrette (at Visitor Centre). Unique as a waterway crossroads, where an east-west canal meets with its north-south equivalent on the level – and where all branches were navigable. Home to a busy boatyard and the well-frequented Visitor Centre of the Cotswold Canals Trust.

Framilode

Leaving the sleepy hamlet of Framilode and the flood plain of the Severn, the footpath follows the diminutive River Frome to Saul Junction, more or less along the original line of the Stroudwater Navigation. Beyond its intersection with the Gloucester & Sharpness Canal, the canal sets off across water meadows with the Cotswold scarp already beckoning in the distance. Following the current towpath diversion around the twin, man-made obstacles of A38 and M5, pedestrians are finally reunited with the navigation at Pike Bridge, to follow a delightful mélange of waterway infrastructure through the outskirts of Stonehouse, into Stroud. The intimacy of the canal at Ryeford, together with its eponymous double lock, is preceded by the unusual Nutshell Bridge and House combination and the pastoral St Cyr's Church. Ahead lie Selsley's striking 19th-C church tower and the imposing bulk of Ebley Mill. And all the while the Cotswold scarp looms closer: a prelude to the climb yet to come.

Cotswold Canal Trust Visitor Centres The Canal Towpath, Church Lane, Saul GL2 7LA (07854 026504; www.cotswoldcanals.com). A mine of information on all things to do with the ambitious restoration project that sits under the Cotswold Canals umbrella. Find out more about the phased approach to breathing new life into the Stroudwater Navigation and the Thames & Severn Canal, and see the state of current progress. Complimentary tea, coffee, hot chocolate and Severn Bore timetables. Children actively engaged and outside seating. Toilets and showers. Shop selling ice cream, soft drinks, confectionary, books, maps and gifts. *Open summer, Sat 12.30-17.00; Sun and B Hols 10.00-17.00 & winter Sat, Sun and B Hols 12.30-16.00* and whenever the green flag is flying. Also pump-out cards, Watermate keys and laundry tokens for sale.

A new **Visitor and Interpretation Centre** has been launched in the listed gatehouse at Bond's Mill (GL10 3TF). Telephone 01453 752568 or visit www.cotswoldcanals.com for details of opening times.

● **Whitminster**
Glos. PO box, tel, stores, takeaway, fish & chips, off-licence. The village is strung out along the A38 and was once known as Wheatenhurst, the name being officially changed in 1945. *The post office is in the garden centre.*

● **Eastington**
Glos. PO, tel, stores, off-licence, butcher, garage. Like Whitminster, Eastington has become a popular dormitory village sharing easy access to the M5, A38 and A419 making Bristol, the Midlands and South Wales within a comfortable hour's drive.

● **King's Stanley**
Glos. PO, tel, stores off-licence, takeaway. One of the three adjoining 'Stanleys' (Leonard

Stanley and Stanley Downton being its two companions), the village is overseen by Selsley Common – much of it a SSSI – and the oldest Baptist Chapel in Gloucestershire, erected in 1640.

● **Stonehouse**
Glos. PO, tel, stores, chemist, butchers, baker, greengrocer, hardware, fish & chips, takeaway, garage, station. The name reflects the stone-built manor recorded in the Domesday Book, at a time when nearly all dwellings were of timber frame construction. The Manor, sited close to St Cyr's Church and the canalside Stonehouse Court Hotel, burnt down in 1908. There is a useful cycle shop in the town.
St Cyr's Church Stonehouse. There has been a church of some kind on this site since Saxon times, although it was not until William the Conqueror gifted the manor to his relative William de Eu, that a simple stone building was erected. This remained in various forms until permission was granted, in 1852, for demolition due to its parlous state. Its replacement, rendered in a chaste Perpendicular style, retained the original tower and the foundations of the chancel. Copies were made of the north doorway and font.
Woodchester Mansion Nympsfield, Stonehouse GL10 3TS (01453 861541; www. woodchestermansion.org.uk). This striking building is a fascinating, unfinished, Gothic revival mansion house – designed by local architect Bejamin Bucknall – located in Woodchester Park, near Nympsfield. Tea shop *(closes at 16.00). Open Apr-Oct, Fri-Sun & B Hol Mon 11.00-17.00. Guided tours 11.45 & 14.30 (subject to availability of volunteers).* Charge.

Pubs and Restaurants (pages 156–157)

🍺 1 **The Ship Inn** Framilode, Saul GL2 7LH (01452 740260; www.shipinnframilode.co.uk). An easy walk west from Saul Junction, along the bed of the Stroudwater Navigation, beside the River Frome. An excellent hostelry serving real ales, together with an interesting selection of food *L* and *E*. Large garden with children's play area. Traditional pub games and real fires. B&B. *Open Tue-Sat L and E (not Tue L) & Sun 12.00–19.00.*

🍺 2 **The Anchor** Epney GL2 7LN (01452 740433). Beside the River Severn, dispensing real ales and good food *daily L and E* – homemade pies a speciality. Children welcome inside, dogs outside on a chain. Large garden. Very busy *in the summer.*

✗ 3 **The Stables Café** Sandfield Bridge, Canal Bank, Saul GL2 7LA (01452 741965; www.thestablescafe. co.uk). Once a stables catering for canal horses, this establishment now serves breakfasts *until 11.30*; *lunches* using fresh, locally sourced ingredients and a selection of homemade cakes, tea and coffee. Children welcome. Garden and terrace. *Open daily 09.00–16.30 (Sat & Sun 17.00).*

✗ 4 **Greenways Restaurant** Highfield Garden World, Bristol Road, Whitminster GL2 7PB (01452 741444; www.highfieldgardenworld.co.uk/restaurant.html). Breakfast; *L* (including a roast carvery *Tue, Thu & Sun*); homemade cakes, scones and tea. Children welcome. Wi-Fi. *Open Mon-Sat 08.30–17.30 & Sun 09.30–16.30.*

🍺✗ 5 **The Whitminster Inn** Bristol Road, Whitminster GL2 7NY (01452 740234; www.whitminsterinn.co.uk). Embracing English *(open daily 10.00–00.00 – Sun 23.00)*; Chinese (01452 742111; www.whitminsterinn.co.uk/food-drink/china-garden-chinese-restaurant – *open Land E daily)*; and Indian (01452 741919; www.indian-garden.co.uk – *open E daily)* restaurants, together with real ales, traditional pub games and camping. Children welcome. B&B. Online takeaway ordering service.

🍺 6 **The Old Forge Inn** Bristol Road, Whitminster GL2 7NY (01452 741306). Cosy, 16th-C, heavily beamed hostelry serving real ales and generous portions of food *Mon-Fri L and E (not Mon E in winter) & all day Sat-Sun.* Aquaria vie for space with collections of brasses and commemorative spoons. Beer garden and traditional pub games. Dog- and family-friendly. Wi-Fi and camping. B&B. *Open daily 12.00–23.00.*

🍺✗ 7 **Fromebridge Mill** Fromebridge Lane, Whitminster GL2 7PD (01452 741796; www.

oldenglishinns.co.uk/our-locations/pubs-in-whitminster-fromebridge-mill). *Open daily 11.00–23.00*, serving good value food and real ale. Riverside seating, children welcome. B&B.

✗ 8 **Old Badger Inn** Alkerton Road, Eastington GL10 3AT (01453 822892; www.oldbadgerinn.co.uk). Traditional village pub, serving an excellent range of frequently rotating real ales, together with appetising food *L and E (not Sun E)*. Log fires and garden. Friendly dogs and children welcome. Traditional pub games and Wi-Fi. *Open 12.00–23.00 (Sun 22.30).*

🍺✗ 9 **The Stonehouse Court Hotel** Bristol Road, Stonehouse GL10 3RA (0843 357 5557; www.bespokehotels.com/stonehousecourt). 17th-C manor house, overlooking the Ocean and close to St Cyr's Church, serving restaurant and bistro meals *daily L and E*. Six acres of grounds. Wi-Fi. B&B.

✗♀ 10 **The Gate of India** 8 High Street, Stonehouse GL10 2NA (01453 792525/791846; www.gateofindia.co.uk). Traditional and contemporary Indian cuisine, served in a friendly, welcoming restaurant. Children welcome. *Open daily L and E.* Takeaway service.

🍺 11 **The Woolpack Inn** 4 High Street, Stonehouse GL10 2NA (01453 822542). Locals pub serving a selection of real ales and food *L and E*. Family-friendly, garden. Traditional pub games and real fires. *Open L and E.*

🍺 12 **The Globe Inn** 42 High Street, Stonehouse GL10 2NG (01453 297691). Welcoming, modernised pub serving real ale and real cider, together with food *L*. Family-friendly, garden. Traditional pub games. *Open daily 10.00–23.00.*

✗♀ 13 **Kitsch Coffee & Wine Bar** 192 Westward Road, Ebley, Stroud (01453 297916). Great place to watch the world go by and share nibbles and tapas-style dishes with friends. Excellent tea and coffee. Outside seating close to the canal. *Open Mon-Sat 09.00–17.15 (Fri 21.00).*

Also try: 🍺✗ 14 **The Kings Head** Bath Road, Eastington GL10 3AA (01453 822277; www.thekingsheadhouse.com/contact.aspx); 🍺✗ 15 **The Kings Head** High Street, Kings Stanley GL10 3JD (01453 828293; www.eipublicpartnerships.com/run-a-pub/pubs/pages/kings-head-stonehouse.aspx) and ✗ 16 **Café At The Mill** Bond's Mill, Stonehouse GL10 3RF (01453 828042; cafeatthemill.com) – *open Mon-Fri 08.00–15.00.*

BOAT TRIPS

The Cotswold Canals Trust (www.cotswoldcanals.com) run two trip boats on this side of the Cotswolds: *nb Endeavour* from Saul Junction (01453 752568) and *nb Perseverance* from the Operations Wharf, on the towpath side of the canal, just west of Ebley Cloth Mills Bridge. *Nb Perseverance* operates *Apr-Sep, Sun & B Hol Mon 12.00-16.30* and *nb Endeavour* operates *Apr-Sep, Sat 12.00-16.30*. No booking is required for public trips. Both craft can be booked for private charter, *throughout the year*, on those days not allocated for public trips by telephoning 01453 752568

Cotswold Boatmobility Stonehouse Wharf (off Boakes Drive) Stonehouse GL10 3QW (07562 173659; www.cotswoldboatmobility.org.uk). Operating a Wheelyboat and Katakanus to provide accessible boating opportunities for all. Telephone or visit their website for further details..

The Willow Trust 11A Whiteway Court, Whiteway Farmhouse, Cirencester GL7 7BA (01285 651661; www.willowtrust.org). The Trust, a charitable organisation founded in 1989, operates two purpose-built boats (carrying up to 30 people) from Saul Junction (GL2 7LA) for seriously ill and disabled children and adults, giving them the opportunity to enjoy a day afloat totally free of charge. Telephone or visit the website for further details.

NAVIGATIONAL NOTES

Much of this section falls within the Phase 1B restoration plan, now identified as Stroudwater Navigation Connect, and a Heritage Lottery Fund bid has been submitted by the Cotswold Canals Trust and Stroud District Council, who are the joint lead partners. A decision is expected in April 2018. However, the length east from the Ocean to Ham Mill is in water. It is intended that, between A38 and Westfield Lock 9, the navigation will briefly divert into the bed of the River Frome in order to bypass the obstruction now posed by the M5 motorway.

Boatyards

Ⓑ**ACP Fuels Ltd** Frampton On Severn Industrial Park, Bridge Road, Frampton on Severn GL2 7HE (01452 741821; www.johnstonfuels.co.uk). D Gas.

Ⓑ**R.W. Davis & Son** Junction Dry Dock, Saul GL2 7LA (01452 740233; www.rwdavis.co.uk). Long-term mooring, winter storage, crane (10 tons), dry dock, boat building and fitting out, boat and engine sales and repairs (including wooden boat repairs), shot blasting, foam insulation spraying, modest chandlery stocking nautical antiques, solid fuel nearby.

Ⓑ**Saul Junction Marina** Church Lane, Frampton-on-Severn GL2 7JY (01452 740043; www.saulmarina.co.uk). 🛁🎁⚓D Pump-out, gas, slipway, boat sales, chandlery, coal, wood, launderette, toilets, showers, CRT licences, Wi-Fi.

Winter at Pike Lock

Brimscombe Port

Throughout much of the previous section, the River Frome has courted the navigation, indeed has shared its bed in parts. Through Ebley, into Stroud and in its vertiginous ascent of the Golden Valley, this intimacy never once falters. The power of much of this water, swelled by the five lateral streams that once drove this area's majestic mills, is today released into the hydro-electric scheme incorporated with Dudbridge Locks. The canal had its terminal basin at Wallbridge, immediately below Wallbridge Lower Lock and now covered by a small industrial estate. However, the imposing Headquarters for the Proprietors of the Stroudwater Navigation still stands, flanking the newly constructed Stroud Brewery Bridge, as the waterway (now metamorphosed into the Thames & Severn Canal) once again makes its triumphant entry into the town. The short dogleg, through the railway viaduct at Capel's Mill, is a man-made channel bypassing the municipal rubbish tip, as a close inspection of the concrete piling will confirm. From there on it's relentlessly upwards, in concert with the railway and the old London Road, the valley floor steadily contracting, forcing buildings, pasture and woods to straggle up the sides of the increasingly steep Cotswold scarp. Brimcombe Port is somewhere to pause, in an attempt to conjure up the scene of what was once an unremitting hive of activity: a seemingly unlikely location for a thriving inland port and busy cargo interchange.

BOAT TRIPS

The Cotswold Canals Trust (01453 752568; www.cotswoldcanals.com). *nb Perseverance* departs from the Operations Wharf, on the towpath side of the canal, just west of Ebley Cloth Mills Bridge. Operates *Apr-Sep, Sat 12.00–16.30*. No booking is required for public trips. Can be booked for private charter, throughout the year, on those days not allocated for public trips by telephoning 01453 752568.

WALKING AND CYCLING

The towpath is in excellent condition (and constantly being upgraded) throughout this section as far as Brimscombe Port. It is suitable for walkers, cyclists and, in many sections, wheelchairs.
Beyond the Port it is only suitable for walkers (and intrepid cyclists) and currently involves brief road diversions around both the Brimscombe and Chalford Industrial Estates.
An audio trail, comprising 22 stopping points, has been set up between The Ocean (near Stonehouse) and Bourne Mill at Brimscombe. Information is available via the QR codes using a smartphone or can be downloaded from www.alongthecotswoldcanals.co.uk.

NAVIGATIONAL NOTES

Much of this section falls within the Phase 1A restoration plan and the entire length between the Ocean and Ham Mill is now in water. A whole range of factors will determine when the final section into Brimscombe Port will reach completion but exciting developments are already under way.

Ebley

Glos. PO box tel, stores, fish & chips. Attractive residential area on the western outskirts of Stroud, dominated by the striking mill building, imaginatively re-invented as the District Council offices.

Selsley

Glos. PO box, tel. The striking 19th-C Church of All Saints, designed by George Frederick Bodley in the French Gothic style, is visible from the navigation for much of its journey into Stroud. Commissioned by the Marling family (owners of the nearby Elizabethan manor house – much rebuilt in the mid-18th C and now turned into flats), it's construction is modelled on a similar building in Marlengo – in the Italian Tyrol – and its intention was to play on a perceived Marling/Marlengo link. The stained glass is early William Morris work.

Stroud

Glos. All services (including launderette). Sited immediately below the western Cotswold escarpment, Stroud developed its separate identity in the 13th C as a community founded at the confluence of the River Frome and the Slad Brook, known as La Strode. It is the Slad Brook that now joins the canal underneath the new Stroud Brewery Bridge. As the meeting point of the Five Valleys, each with its own babbling stream, the town was an early participant in the Industrial Revolution, benefitting from this free source of power to turn the waterwheels that drove the cloth and woollen mills. Apart from the numerous, imposing mill buildings – dominating skylines or nestling in the valley – the only remnants of this once thriving trade, is a small textile industry producing the green baize for snooker tables, fine cloth for ceremonial military uniforms and the material encasing championship tennis balls. Once labelled 'Notting Hill with Wellies', by the London Evening Standard, today Stroud is a bustling township that thrives on independence in both thought and action.

Cotswold Canals Trust Visitor Centre Bell House, Wallbridge Lock, Stroud GL5 3JS (01453 752568/07582 286636); www.cotswoldcanals. com). A mine of information on all things to do with the ambitious restoration project that sits under the Cotswold Canals umbrella. Children actively engaged and outside seating. Toilets and baby changing facilities. Disabled access. Shop selling books, maps and gifts. *Open Mon-Fri 10.00-13.00 & Sat 10.00-16.00* and whenever the green flag is flying. Wi-Fi.

Farmers Market Cornhill Market Place & surrounding streets, Stroud GL5 2HH (01453 758060/07813 943237; www.fresh-n-local.co.uk/markets/stroud.php). *Open Sat 09.00-14.00.* Award-winning, fresh, local produce market.

Lansdown Hall & Gallery Lansdown, Stroud GL5 1BN (01453 767576; www.lansdownhall.org).

Stroud's community venue run by volunteers, housing a variety of workshops, exhibitions, performances and a *winter* film club.

Made in Stroud 16 Kendrick Street, Stroud GL5 1AA (01453 840265; www.madeinstroud. co.uk). An essential part of the thriving, local art network with close links to the Farmers Market (see above), selling homeware, gifts, edibles & wearables. Once described as 'the Covent Garden of the Cotswolds.'

Museum in the Park Stratford Park, Stratford Road, Stroud GL5 4AF (01453 763394; www.museuminthepark.org.uk). Housed on two floors of a Grade II listed, 17th-C, wool merchant's mansion, this museum celebrates the rich history and heritage of the Stroud district. Changing exhibitions. *Open Apr-Sep, Tue-Fri (& Mon in Aug) 10.00-17.00 and Sat, Sun & B Hol 11.00-17.00; Oct-Mar, Tue-Fri 10.00-16.00 and Sat & Sun 11.00-16.00. Closed throughout Dec.* Free – donations welcome.

The Shambles is one of the oldest areas in Stroud, home to the historic market and the Old Town Hall, which dates from the late 16th C. The market stalls used to be housed in the arches under the Hall. John Wesley, founder of the Methodist Church, preached from the butcher's blocks outside the nearby Church Hall on 26th June 1742.

Shambles Market The Shambles, Off the High Street, Stroud GL5 1AP (01453 755788/884320/07515 392958; www.shamblesmarketstroud.co.uk). *Open Fri & Sat 08.00-16.00.* Both indoor and outdoor markets that perpetuate an ancient and worthy tradition.

Subscription Rooms George Street, Stroud GL5 1AE (01453 760999; www.subscriptionrooms.org.uk). Built in 1833 by public subscription, this venue still plays an important part in community events. The Subscription Rooms is a handsome, late Regency building in the heart of Stroud, hosting year-round arts and entertainment, exhibitions, markets and meetings. Also Mr Twitchett's Café Bar *open Mon-Sat 10.0-17.00* (later on performance nights) with live music *last Fri of the month*. Wi-Fi.

Tourist Information Centre Subscription Rooms, George Street, Stroud GL5 1AE (01453 760960; www.cotswolds.com/plan-your-trip/stroud-tourist-information-centre-p572713). *Open Mon-Sat 10.00-18.00.*

Thrupp

Glos. PO box, tel. Location of the Phoenix Ironworks, well known as manufacturers of cloth-making machinery, steam engines and waterwheels in the early 19th C. They are credited with inventing a machine to shear surplus fibre (or nap) from the surface of cloth, using a horizontal blade. An employee, one Edwin Budding, developed this device to use a revolving cylinder – adorned by three blades – before realising its wider potential for mowing grass. Not content with making the scythe more or less redundant, he is also reputed to have invented the adjustable spanner.

- **Brimscombe**

Glos. PO, tel, stores, fish & chips. It's difficult to comprehend the layout and the extent of this once prosperous, bustling inland port and canal interchange, before its eclipse by today's sprawling industrial estate. It's 10 plus acres once embraced a substantial island (used to store easily 'portable' merchandise), a textile mill and a shipyard, together with all the trappings and accoutrements of a thriving commercial dockyard. The entire site has been purchased by Stroud District Council, for onward sale to a housing developer. It will come with a brief that provides for a renewed navigation, a marina and associated waterway infrastructure.

Pubs and Restaurants (pages 160–161)

✗♀ 1 **Upper Lock Café** Wallbridge Lock, Stroud GL5 3JS (01453 297172; upperlockcafe.co.uk). Overlooking Wallbridge Upper Lock, this friendly cafe serves fresh coffee, tea and delicious cakes, together with light snacks including hot and cold sandwiches, ciabatta, hearty salads and soup. Wines and local beers. Dog- and family-friendly, lock-side seating. Newspapers and Wi-Fi. *Open Mon-Sat 09.00-16.00 & Sun 10.00-15.00.*

🍺✗ 2 **The Clothiers Arms** 1 Bath Rd, Stroud GL5 3JJ (01453 763801; www.clothiersarms.co.uk). An attractive stone building dating from 1880, built on the site of an earlier ale house. Real ales and cider are served, together with bar meals *all day*. An à la carte menu is offered in the restaurant *Wed-Sat E and Sun L*. Children's play area and garden. Real fires and traditional pub games. *Open Mon-Sat 11.00-23.00 (Fri-Sat 23.30) & Sun 12.00-22.30.*

🍺 3 **The Crown & Sceptre** 98 Horns Road, Stroud GL5 1EG (01453 762588; www.crownand sceptrestroud.com). Real ales are dispensed in this friendly local with a real community feel while homemade bar snacks are available *L*. Terraced garden with views across to Butterow and the edge of Rodborough Common. Traditional pub games, newspapers, real fires, sports TV and Wi-Fi. Dog- and child-friendly. *Open Mon-Thu 15.00-23.00 &Fri-Sun 12.00-23.00 (Fri-Sat 23.30).*

🍺 4 **The Prince Albert** Rodborough Hill, Stroud GL5 3SS (01453 755600; www.theprincealbert stroud.co.uk). The heady mix of decoration, adorning the bar walls, does nothing to detract from a warm welcome in this popular pub, serving an excellent range of real ales. Children, dogs and walkers welcome. Bar food available *L and E* when open. Traditional pub games, a garden, newspapers, real fires and Wi-Fi. *Regular* live music. *Open Mon-Fri 16.00-23.30 (Fri 00.30) & Sat-Sun 12.00-00.30 (Sun 22.30).*

✗♀ 5 **No 23 Tapas Bar & Bistro** 23 Nelson Street, Stroud GL5 2HH (01453 298525; www. no23stroud.com). Quirky, inexpensive (both drinks and food), welcoming and friendly are just some of the comments from a very satisfied clientele, who rate the Spanish influenced cuisine very highly. *Open Mon-Fri 17.00-late & Sat-Sun 11.00-late.*

🍺 6 **The Ale House** 9 John Street, Stroud GL5 2HA (01453 755447). A pub set in an impressive 1837 town house – with high ceilings and a lantern window – serving up to 12 real ales and a couple of real ciders. The food (served *Mon-Sat L and E & Sun L*) revolves around simple, freshly prepared British pub classics, which do not disappoint. Dog- and child-friendly, garden. Newspapers, real fires, sports TV and Wi-Fi. Live music *Thu-Sat. Open Mon-Thu L and E & Fri-Sun 11.00-23.00.*

✗ 7 **Black Book Café** Unit 2 Nelson St, Stroud GL5 2HL (01453 764509; www.blackbookcafe. com). Coffee, cake, muffins, second hand books and free Wi-Fi. *Open Mon-Sat 09.00-16.00.*

✗♀ 8 **Jrool Bistro** 12 Union Street, Town Centre, Stroud GL5 2HE (01453 767123; www.jrool.co.uk). Majoring on freshly prepared food – using locally sourced, seasonal ingredients – this restaurant has a regularly changing menu. Children welcome. *Open Tue-Sat L and Thu-Sat E.*

✗ 9 **Woodruffs Organic Café** 24 High Street, Stroud GL5 1AJ (01453 759195; www.woodruffs organiccafe.co.uk). Serving a mainly vegetarian (including fish from the local fishmonger) menu that caters for all dietary requirements. Teas, coffee, juices, smoothies and homemade cakes. Healthy breakfasts. Children welcome. Outside seating. *Open Mon-Sat 08.30-17.00.*

🍺 10 **The Bowbridge Arms** London Rd, Stroud GL5 2AY (01453 298914; thebowbridgearms.co.uk). On A419 at Thrupp. An old-fashioned pub, in the best sense of the phrase, serving excellent value, home-cooked food – *Mon-Sun L and E (not Sun E)* – real ales (from their own Kennet & Avon Brewery) and real cider. Child- and dog-friendly, outside seating and children's play area. Real fires. *Open Mon-Sun 11.00-23.00 (Sun 17.00).*

🍺 11 **The Ship Inn** Brimscombe Hill, Brimscombe, Stroud GL5 2QN (01453 884388). Immediately west of Brimscombe Port. Traditional pub, dating from 17th C, serving food *daily L and E (not Sun* E). Darts and outside seating. B&B. Wi-Fi. *Open L and E.* Recently sold so details may change.

Sapperton

Superlatives are wasted in describing the true extent of Sapperton Tunnel (the longest, tallest and widest of its day) just as they fail to do justice to the sylvan stretch of canal, clawing its way up the Golden Valley towards Daneway. The deviation into the village of Sapperton itself; the amble along a quiet country lane in tandem with the navigation many feet below (as witnessed by the beech-topped spoil mounds, initially running parallel with the road); the swoop down a generously wide footpath – paved by ox-eye daisies in summer – across arable land and A419 and thence into the cool shade of Hailey Wood, are each a joy in themselves. Arriving, eventually, at the ornately decorated Coates Portal of this extraordinary tunnel, is to have the wonder reinforced as the waterway, once again fully visible, sets off purposefully in an intricate stone-lined trough, on its journey eastwards along the 9½-mile summit pound.

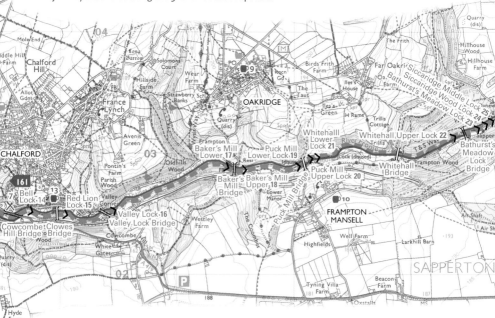

NAVIGATIONAL NOTES

This entire length falls within restoration Phase 3 and, as such, is the final section scheduled for attention.

WALKING AND CYCLING

The towpath, which is unsuitable for all but the most intrepid cyclist, continues up the north side of the navigation, before briefly crossing to the south above Puck Mill Lock 20. It returns to the north side at Bathurst's Meadow Lock Bridge, following the waterway to the Daneway Inn car park (here cycling ceases to be a practical proposition), where it is again on the south side as far as the tunnel. Here the path crosses above the castellated portal and heads due west, up the steep grassy hill, into Sapperton village.

Bear right, then right again, and on past the primary school, take the footpath left, up to the village green. Follow the minor road southeast for 1¼-miles, initially running alongside the tree-topped spoil heaps, ringing the shafts that mark the line of the tunnel.

Take the broad footpath right, across arable land and A419, to enter Hailey Wood. Continue to follow the way-marked Macmillan Way through the wood, under the railway line, to the Tunnel House Inn above the Coates Portal.

Chalford

Glos. PO box, stores, tel. Regarded as the start of the Golden Valley streets once served by donkeys zig zag their way up sylvan slopes. An ancient settlement – as demonstrated by the discovery of a Roman villa and Stone Age flints – it became home to displaced Flemish Huguenot silk and cloth weavers in 17th and 18th C. The building of the Thames & Severn Canal later encouraged the growth of broadcloth weaving, much of it supplied to the East India Company. The village is the site of one of five Round Houses built beside the canal, while the local church currently hosts the community shop.

There is a helpful cycle shop in Bourne Mills GL5 2TA: **Noah's Ark** (01453 884738; www.noahsark.co.uk).

Minchinhampton

Glos. PO, tel, stores, chemist, butcher, takeaways, fish & chips, organic dairy, garage.

Of all the charming habitations, in and around the Stroud valley this, arguably, is the most delightful. The ancient, stone-built town, features a 17th-C Market House sitting atop a maze of higgledy piggledy streets.

Oakridge

Glos. PO box, tel. The village is made up of five separate hamlets scattered haphazardly across the northern side of the Frome valley, approached up a warren of steep, narrow, tree-clad lanes.

Frampton Mansell

Glos. PO box, tel. The charming Neo-Norman Church of St Luke is perched high above the railway viaduct, overlooking the Frome valley. Built by Lord Bathurst in 1843, it was a conventicle church erected for the unofficial, unofficiated meeting of lay people to discuss religious matters in an intimate surrounding.

Sapperton

Glos. PO box, tel. Characterful cottages, straggling along the hillside, present a portrait totally lacking in uniformity. The Arts and Crafts style village hall is a reminder of the movement's connection with the village.

Tarlton

Glos. PO box, tel. A hamlet of predominantly stone cottages, some thatched, thronged around a diminutive village green shaded by a voluminous copper beech. The tiny church of St Osmund's is a gem, with its ornately carved pews, delicate stained glass and Norman chancel arch with chevron carving: in all both simple and beautiful.

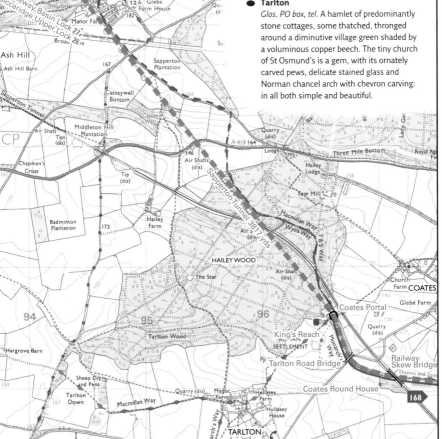

Pubs and Restaurants (pages 164–165)

✗ 1 **The Kitchen** 7 High Street, Minchinhampton GL6 9BN (01453 882655; www.thekitchenminch.co.uk). The kitchen offers cake, coffee, teas and homemade cakes, pies and tarts, together with an appetising lunch menu (using local produce), which changes *daily*. Open *Tue-Sat 09.00-16.00*.

⬤✗ 2 **The Ragged Cot** Cirencester Road, Minchinhampton, Stroud GL6 8PE (01453 884643; www.theraggedcot.co.uk). 17th-C coaching Inn on the outskirts of Minchinhampton serving real ales and food *daily L and E (not Sun E)*. Dogs, children and wellies willingly accommodated. Real fires and a garden. B&B.

✗♀ 3 **Munchinhampton Café and Restaurant** 3 West End, Minchinhampton GL6 9JA (01453 883382). Home cooking and baking served in intimate surroundings. Snacks, salads, lunches, and an array of enticing desserts are all available in this friendly, welcoming establishment *open Wed-Mon 09.00-16.00 (Sat 17.00) & Fri 18.00-22.00*.

⬤ 4 **The Crown Inn** High Street, Minchinhampton GL6 9BN. This pub was closed and undergoing refurbishment when visited but should be well worth investigating when it reopens.

✗♀ 5 **Sophie's Restaurant** 20 High Street, Minchinhampton GL6 9BN (01453 885188;www. sophiesrestaurant.co.uk). Fresh, no-nonsense French cuisine that never disappoints, from a *daily* changing menu based mainly around local produce. Fixed price menu (by course) available. Excellent 100% French wine list. *Open Wed-Fri L & E* selected *Evenings*, usually *Sat* (telephone or see website for details). Booking advisable.

⬤ 6 **The Weighbridge Inn** Longfords, Minchinhampton GL6 9AL (01453 832520; www.weighbridgeinn.co.uk). Situated on the old packhorse road, the Weighbridge once served the local mills but today dispenses real ale and real cider and is popular for its 2in1 pies. Food available *daily 12.00-21.30*. Exposed beams and open fires. Muddy boots, children and dogs welcome. Garden and Wi-Fi. *Open Mon-Sun 12.00-23.00 (Sun 22.30)*.

✗♀ 7 **Lavender Bakehouse & Coffee Shop** 20 London Road, Chalford, Stroud GL6 8NW (01453 889239; www. lavenderbakehouse.co.uk). Imaginative breakfasts *until 11.30 daily*; a mouth watering array of cakes and patisseries; *midday* snacks and meals, together with afternoon cream teas, all served in a cosy, warehouse conversion by friendly, attentive staff. Gift shop upstairs. *Open Mon-Sat 09.00-16.00 (Thu-Sat 17.00) & Sun 10.00-16.00*.

⬤✗ 8 **The Woolpack** Slad, Nr Stroud GL6 7QA (01452 813429; thewoolpackslad.com). On B4070, two miles or so north of the canal in Stroud, but well worth the detour. A favourite with Laurie Lee, who was instrumental in preventing its closure, this unadulterated hostelry has stunning views over the Slad Valley. Real ales, cider and perry, together with excellent food served *daily Mon-Sun (Not Sun-Mon E) and restaurant meals Wed-Sun L and E (not Sun E)*. Garden, real fires, traditional pub games and Wi-Fi. Children, dogs, walkers and wellies welcome. *Open daily 12.00-00.00*.

⬤✗ 9 **The Butchers Arms** Oakridge Lynch, Stroud GL6 7RH (01452 812113; www.butchersarms oakridge. com). Real ale served in an 18th-C, oak-beamed pub, together with food *Tue-Sun L and E (not Sun E)*. Open fires and a garden. Children and dogs welcome. Traditional pub games, real fires and Wi-Fi. *Regular* live music. *Open Tue-Sun L and E (not Sun E) and B Hol Mon*.

⬤ 10 **The Crown Inn** Frampton Mansell, Stroud GL6 8JG (01285 760601; www.thecrowninn-cotswolds.co.uk). Stone-built, 17th-C cider house serving real ale (often from local micro-breweries) and food *Mon-Sat L and E; Sun & B Hols 12.00-20.30*. Large garden and winter log fires. Children and dogs welcome. Traditional pub games. B&B. *Open daily 12.00-23.00*.

⬤ 11 **The Daneway Inn** Daneway, Sapperton, Cirencester GL7 6LN (01285 760297; www. thedaneway.pub). Daneway Upper Lock 28 is currently buried under the car park of this popular Cotswold hostelry, which serves real ales and hearty pub meals *Mon-Sat 12.00-21.00 & Sun L and E*. Family-friendly, garden and camping. Real Fires. *Open 10.00-23.00*.

⬤✗ 12 **The Bell** Sapperton, Cirencester GL7 6LE (01285 760298; www.bellsapperton.co.uk). Locally sourced food, some from their own vegetable garden, provides appetising meals *daily L and E (not Sun E)* together with real ales – often from local breweries. A profusion of beams, flagstone floors and open fires. Dog- and family- friendly; horses welcome. Courtyard garden. *Open Mon-Sat 11.00-23.00 & Sun 12.00-21.00*.

Also try: ⬤ 13 **The New Red Lion** High Street, Chalford, Stroud GL6 8DJ (01453 882384; newredlion. wordpress.com).

Coates Portal, southern entrance to the Sapperton Tunnel

Siddington

Leaving the cool shade of mature beech trees, the walker is rewarded by the sight of the second Round House, characteristic of this waterway and, in this remote location, originally built with an inverted, conical roof to harvest rainwater for domestic use. There are five in all and this one, in the ownership of Lord Bathurst, was saved from dereliction by the Canal Trust. From Coatesfield Bridge (where the footpath deviates from the waterway until Siddington is reached) the canal's summit pound performs a series of extravagant meanders in its efforts to occupy a single contour. Upon abandonment in 1927, parts of the navigation were sold to adjacent landowners and in places the line has totally disappeared. Siddington Locks, however, are very much in evidence and provide a fascinating opportunity to study their original construction (and subsequent modification) in detail. Passing the only permanent obstruction to restoration, throughout the entire length of the navigation (a house built close to Greyhound Bridge) the waterway wanders off across water meadows, flanked by an almost continuous ash glade, passing the site of the River Churn Aqueduct, which was blown up during WWII as part of an army training exercise.

- **Coates**
  Glos. PO box, tel. An estate village, largely swamped by contemporary housing, close to Thames head and the Fosse Way. The delightful St Matthews Church has a 13th-C nave and piscine, a simple Norman font and doorway complete with traditional chevron decoration, 15th-C Perpendicular tower and windows – some of which contain Victorian stained glass by Clayton and Bell.

- **Kemble**
  Glos. PO, tel, stores, station. A somewhat austere, Cotswold stone village, bisected by A429, with many imposing houses lurking up long driveways. The area around the station is altogether more approachable.

- **Ewen**
  Glos. PO box, tel. Virtually on the outskirts of Kemble, this is another predominantly stone-built village – though of a more homely nature than its neighbour.

- **Siddington**
  Glos. PO, tel, stores, off-licence. There is evidence of both Bronze Age and Roman settlement in this busy village on the outskirts of Cirencester. The Norman Church of St Peter's, with its distinctive spire, stands close to one of the country's oldest tithe barns, dating from the 13th C, when the manor was gifted to the Knights Hospitaler of St John. Nearby lies Roberts House, former residence of John Roberts (1619-1683), who was a founder member of the Quaker movement. There is also a disused Quaker burial ground. Shop *open Mon-Sat 07.00-19.00 & Sun 08.00-12.00.*

- **Cirencester**
  Glos. All services except station. During the Roman occupation of Britain, Corinium Dobunnorum – or Cirencester as it is known today – was the second largest town after London, with a population of around 10,000. As the self-proclaimed capital of the Cotswolds, its buildings embrace a myriad of contrasting architectural styles, all married in perfect harmony through the use of the very similar Cotswold stone. Cirencester is an historic market town, with a population of around 19,000, its past prosperity, based on the wool industry, mirrored in the richness of its buildings.

  Charter Market Market Place, Cirencester GL7 2NZ (01285 655646). Mentioned in the Doomsday Book of 1086, this is one of the oldest Charter Markets in the country. *Open Mon & Fri 09.00-15.00.*

  Chedworth Roman Villa Yanworth, Cheltenham GL54 3LJ (01242 890256; www.nationaltrust.org.uk/chedworth-roman-villa). There are well over a thousand exciting artefacts, many found during the excavation of the site, together with impressive in-situ mosaics. Costumed interpretation brings Roman history to life. You can explore the villa with a virtual tour while interactive educational games cater for children. Nymphaeum. *Weekend* events and special activity programmes during school holidays. Café and shop. *Open early Feb-Nov, 10.00-17.00.* Charge.

  Church of St John the Baptist 5 Market Place Cirencester GL7 2NX (01285 659317; www.cirenparish.co.uk). This Cotswold 'wool church', with its cathedral-like proportions and Perpendicular tower, is one of the most spacious in England. Standing next to the site of the demolished abbey, it plays host to a recently refurbished Father Willis organ, original medieval wall paintings, a striking reredos, Anne Boleyn's cup and a delicate wine glass pulpit. The magnificent south porch (built circa 1500 and therefore a more recent addition) was not originally part of the church and conjecture has it that it might have had a relationship to a guild – or even have been used for church ales. Certainly it became the Town Hall in 1672 and has recently undergone extensive restoration, finished in a coat of pigmented limewash, intended to unite the existing with the new stone and plastic repair – which is not to everyone's taste. Book and coffee shop. Tours and tower climbs. Charge. *Open daily*

Coriniun Museum Park Street, Cirencester GL7 2BX (01285 655611; coriniummuseum.org). Home to one of the largest Romano-British collections of antiquities – in direct contrast to the its assortment of work by Prehistoric metal smiths. Also Medieval sculpture, Civil War coin hoards and the opportunity to experience the elegance of Victorian Cirencester. Café. *Open Mon-Sat 10.00-17.00 & Sun 14.00-17.00. Closes at 16.00 Nov-Mar.* Charge.

Cotswold Craft Market The Corn Hall, Market Place, Cirencester GL7 2NY (01285 740641/ 07970 859703; www.cotswoldcraftmarket.co.uk). The market is held on *2nd and 4th Sat of each month.* Free.

New Brewery Arts Centre Brewery Court, Town Centre, Cirencester GL7 1HW (01285 657181; www.newbreweryarts.org.uk). Contemporary art and craft centre in a converted Victorian brewery. Café, shop and craft stalls. *Open Mon-Sat 09.00-17.00 & Sun and B Hol 10.00-16.00.*

Roman Amphitheatre Cotswold Avenue, off Bristol Road, Cirencester GL7 1XW (0370 333 1181/01285 655611; www.english-heritage.org.uk/visit/places/cirencester-amphitheatre). Built just outside the town walls in early 2nd C AD, this is the largest known example surviving in Britain and is unusual in that it is constructed on an oval plan. When the last contingents of the regular Roman army left this country in 408 AD, ditches were dug and the entrances narrowed, turning it into a fortress protecting the town against marauding Saxons. *Open at any reasonable time.* Free.

NAVIGATIONAL NOTES

The Phase 3 restoration plan covers the waterway as far east as the Cotswold Water Park, where over a mile of canal has recently been dredged. A west-east water transfer scheme, utilising the bed of the navigation, is in the early stages of consideration, and could greatly accelerate the pace of restoration.

Sundial Theatre Cirencester College, Fosse Way Campus, Cirencester GL7 1XA (01285 654228; www.sundial-theatre.co.uk). Popular community theatre, offering an exciting and varied programme. Box office *open Tue-Fri 16.30-18.00 & 1 hour before performances.*

Tourist Information Centre Corinium Museum, Park Street, Cirencester GL7 2BX (01285 654180; www.cirencester.co.uk/visitor informationcentre). *Open Apr-Oct, Mon-Sat 10.00-17.00 & Sun 14.00-17.00; Nov-Mar, Mon-Fri 10.00-16.00 & Sun 14.00-16.00.* For a snapshot of current events in the town visit www.cirencester.gov.uk/what-s-on.

Gateway Information Centre Spine Road, South Cerney GL7 5TL (01793 754413/752730; www.waterpark.org). Source of information and interpretation for the Cotswold Water Park. *Open daily 09.00-17.00.* Café, shops and toilets. There is a wealth of tourist information at the centre, which is often manned by volunteers. Further information is available by contacting the Cotswold Water Part Trust – available *Mon-Fri, 09.00-17.00* – on the telephone numbers listed above.

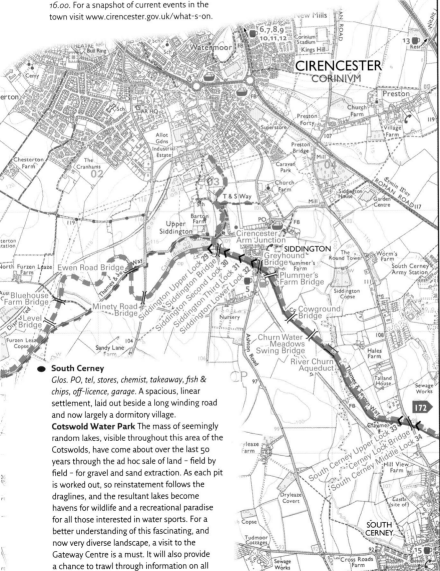

● **South Cerney**
Glos. PO, tel, stores, chemist, takeaway, fish & chips, off-licence, garage. A spacious, linear settlement, laid out beside a long winding road and now largely a dormitory village.

Cotswold Water Park The mass of seemingly random lakes, visible throughout this area of the Cotswolds, have come about over the last 50 years through the ad hoc sale of land – field by field – for gravel and sand extraction. As each pit is worked out, so reinstatement follows the draglines, and the resultant lakes become havens for wildlife and a recreational paradise for all those interested in water sports. For a better understanding of this fascinating, and now very diverse landscape, a visit to the Gateway Centre is a must. It will also provide a chance to trawl through information on all the leisure opportunities based on its 150 lakes, spreading across 40 square miles. www.cirencester.gov.uk/whats-on.

●✗ 1 **The Tunnel House Inn** Tarlton Road, Cirencester, GL7 6PW (01285 770280; www.tunnelhouse.com). In a magnificent position atop the Coates Portal of the canal, surrounded by beech trees, this welcoming hostelry serves real ales and food *daily L and E*. Children welcome, spacious garden, traditional pub games and camping. *Open L and E*.

✗ 2 **Off the Rails Café** Kemble Railway Station, Kemble GL7 6AW (07717 503872). Friendly station café, with a personal touch, selling light meals, snacks, tea and coffee, together with cards and gifts. *Open Mon-Fri 06.00–11.00*.

● 3 **The Tavern Inn** Kemble, GL7 6AX (01285 770216; www.arkells.com/the-tavern-inn-kemble.htm). Immediately west of Kemble station. Describing itself as a town pub in a country location, this establishment serves real ales and home-cooked food *L and E*. Children's play area and large garden. Skittle alley. Traditional pub games, real fires and camping. *Open L and E*.

●✗ 4 **The Wild Duck** Drakes Island, Ewen GL7 6BY (01285 770310). Set in a 16th-C stone building, surrounded by gardens, this popular hostelry serves real ales together with food from bar and restaurant menus *L and E*. Family-friendly, garden. Traditional pub games and real fires. B&B. *Open 11.00–23.00*.

● 5 **The Greyhound** Ashton Road, Siddingham, Cirencester GL7 6HR (01285 653573; www.thegreyhound-inn.co.uk). Close to the derelict Siddingham lock flight, this pub serves real ales and home-cooked food *Mon-Fri L and E & Sat-Sun 12.00–21.00 (Sun 20.00)*. Family friendly, outside seating. Traditional pub games and real fires. *Open Mon-Wed L and E & Thu-Sun 11.30–23.45 (Sun 23.00)*.

●✗ 6 **The Corinium Hotel** 12 Gloucester Street, Cirencester GL7 2DG (01285 659711; www.coriniumhotel.com). Originally an Elizabethan wool merchant's house, this agreeable hostelry now serves real ales and appetising food *L and E*. Delightful walled garden, children welcome. B&B. *Open daily 11.00–23.00 (Sun 22.30)*.

● 7 **The Black Horse** 17 Castle Street, Cirencester GL7 1QD (01285 653187; www.blackhorsepubcirencester.co.uk). Inviting, town-centre pub, serving real ales and good value food *all day, every day*. B&B.

● 8 **The Fleece Hotel** 41 Market Place, Cirencester GL7 2NZ (01285 658507; www.thwaites.co.uk/hotels-and-inns/inns/fleece-at-cirencester). Charming, timber-framed building in the centre of the town dispensing real ales and food *daily from 12.00*. Children welcome. B&B. *Open all day from 10.00*.

✗♉ 9 **Rajdoot** 35 Castle Street, Cirencester GL7 1QD (01285 652651; www.raj-doot.co.uk). Popular Indian restaurant serving authentic cuisine of a high standard *daily L and E*. Family, *Sun* buffet. Children welcome.

✗ 10 **Jacks** 44 Black Jack Street, Cirencester GL7 2AA (01285 640888). A Mecca for cake lovers with one of the finest arrays of the cake baker's art to be found in the Cotswolds. Tea, coffee and snacks too. Large portions and sensible Prices. *Open Mon-Sun 09.00–17.00 (Sun 10.30)*.

●✗ 11 **The Waggon & Horses** 11 London Road, Cirencester GL7 2PU (01285 652022). This rambling 300-year-old stone building is home to real ale, real cider and food served *L and E when open*. Garden, traditional pub games, real fires and Wi-Fi. B&B. *Open Mon-Sat 17.00–22.00 & Sun 12.00–15.00*.

● 12 **The Drillmans Arms** 34 Gloucester Rd, Cirencester GL7 2JY (01285 653892). A busy, welcoming pub just north of the town, serving real ales and homemade food *L*. Dog- and child-friendly, outside seating. Traditional pub games including a skittle alley, real fires, sports TV and Wi-Fi. *Open Sun-Fri L and E & Sat 11.00–00.00*.

●✗ 13 **The Crown of Crucis** Ampney Crucis, Cirencester GL7 5RS (01285 851806; www.thecrownofcrucis.co.uk). Just east of Cirencester, this establishment blends atmosphere and character with contemporary standards of service, providing appetising food from *12.00–22.00 daily*, together with a selection of real ales. Garden and children welcome. Wi-Fi. B&B. *Open 11.00–23.00*.

●✗ 14 **The Royal Oak** High Street, South Cerney GL7 5UP (01285 860900; www.royaloaksouthcerney.com). Highly regarded village pub serving real ales and superb food *Tue-Sun L and E (not Sun E)*. Children welcome, courtyard seating, Traditional pub games and real fires. *Open Tue-Thu L and E & Fri-Sun 12.00–00.00 (Sun 23.00)*.

●✗ 15 **The Eliot Arms** Clarks Hay, South Cerney GL7 5UA (01285 860215; www.eliotarmspub.co.uk). A 16th-C hotel serving real ales and pub food *all day*. Beer garden and skittle alley. Children welcome. B&B. *Open 11.00–23.00*.

●✗ 16 **The Old George Inn** Clarks Hay, South Cerney GL7 5UA (01285 869989; www.oldgeorgeinn.co.uk). Welcoming, family-friendly village pub serving excellent, value for money food *L and E*, together with real ales. Family friendly, outside seating, traditional pub games and camping. *Open 11.00–23.00*.

WALKING AND CYCLING

Public access to the towpath ceases at Coatesfield Bridge, ¼-mile east of Railway Skew Bridge, so turn right and follow the Wysis Way a further ¼-mile to Thames Head, picking up the Thames Path.

Follow this into Ewen (via the outskirts of Kemble), turning left at the staggered crossroads. Take the next fork right (NCR 45) and follow the minor road for 2 miles to the T-junction. Turn left, then immediately right and, after ½-mile, take the minor road on your right beside the playing fields, re-joining the towpath beside the derelict Siddington Locks.

The navigation can now be followed to Latton Junction, apart from a short (way-marked) break where the in-filled canal bed crosses a field.

Cricklade

Apart from a slightly un-nerving walk across open pasture where only a few exposed, and seemingly random, patches of stone hint at two former locks, the waterway is now very much in evidence and, for the most part, still cocooned in a delightful colonnade of mature ash trees. Lock chambers have been cleared and, in many cases, repaired; indeed the section between the Gateway Centre and the third Round House at Cerney Wick, has recently been dredged. On one side the A419 dual carriageway intrudes noisily while on the other, in stark contrast, deer can be spotted grazing amongst the water meadows of the River Churn. Throughout, the navigation plays tag with a continuous collection of man-made lakes – worked out gravel pits that now make up the Cotswold Water Park.

● **Cerney Wick**
Glos. PO box, tel. Another linear village strung out along a twisting road.

● **Ashton Keynes**
Wilts. PO, tel, stores, garage. It is reputed that there are more bridges over the infant Thames within the village, than there are over the river in the Inner London area.

● **Latton**
Wilts. PO box, tel. Sitting astride the old A419, the main feature of the village is its Grade I listed, 12th-C church dedicated to St John the Baptist. The battlements to its sturdy tower, which is adorned by gargoyles and topped by a sundial, date from the 15thC. The simple building is of local limestone and it is similarly roofed with Cotswold stone. Inside are 17th-C oak pews. There is an underpass, already formed in the new A419 dual carriageway, awaiting the resurrection of the canal here.

● **Down Ampney**
Glos. PO, tel, stores. Birthplace of Ralph Vaughan Williams (at the Old Vicarage in 1872), the village became a significant airfield during the Second World War and there is a stained glass window in the church, commemorating the aircrew that flew to the Battle of Arnhem in 1944. The community post office (01793 750385) is *open Mon-Tue & Thu-Fri 09.00-12.00* and the combined shop and café is *open daily between similar hours.*

Latton Junction A fascinating waterways junction, with excellent interpretation, where the derelict North Wilts Branch of the Wilts & Berks Canal meets its slumbering cousin – the Thames & Severn Canal. Just like Sleeping Beauty it will, one day, be returned to life.

● **Cricklade**
Wilts. PO, tel, stores, chemist, hardware, bank, baker, butcher, takeaways, off-licence, fish & chips, library. The self-styled threshold of the Cotswolds and a significant township since Saxon times. The stores *open Mon-Sat 06.00-23.00 & Sun 07.00-10.30.*

Pubs and Restaurants (pages 172–173)

🍺✕ 1 **The Crown** Cerney Wick, Cirencester GL7 5QH (01793 750369; www.thecrowncerney wick.co.uk). Close to Cerney Wick Lock 39, this village pub serves real ales and traditional pub food *L and E (not Sun E).* Outside seating and children welcome. Traditional pub games and open fires. B&B and camping. *Open daily L and E from 11.00 & 18.00.*

🍺✕ 2 **The White Hart Inn** 31 High Road Ashton Keynes SN6 6NX (01285 861247; www. thewhitehartashtonkeynes.com). Originally a cottage dating from mid 18th C, this highly regarded community local serves real ales and locally-sourced, homemade food *L and E, Tue-Sun (not Sun E).* Traditional *Sun L* – children's portions available. Beer garden and open fires. Wi-Fi. *Open Mon-Fri L and E (not Mon L) & Sat-Sun 12.00-01.00 (Sun 22.00).*

🍺✕ 3 **The Red Lion** 74 High Street, Cricklade SN6 6DD (01793 750776; www.theredlion cricklade. co.uk). Award-winning pub – dating from the early

17th C – with its own micro-brewery and pig herd, serving a very wide range of real ales and ciders. Delicious home-cooked food (each with a recommended beer accompaniment) is available *daily L and E (not Sun E).* Log fires and a beer garden where dogs are allowed. Real fires and Wi-Fi. *Booking advisable.* B&B. *Open daily 12.00-23.00 (Sun 22.30).*

🍺✕ 4 **The White Hart Hotel** The High Street, Cricklade SN6 6AA (01793 750206; www.thewhite hartcricklade.co.uk). Impossible to miss on the High Street owing to its magnificent glazed canopy spanning the pavement, this 17th-C hotel serves real ale and food *daily L and E (not Sun E).* A plethora of oak beams vie with flagstone floors, complimenting the open fires. Child- and dog-friendly. Traditional pub games, sports TV and Wi-Fi. B&B. *Open Mon-Sat 11.00-23.00 & Sun 12.00-22.30.*

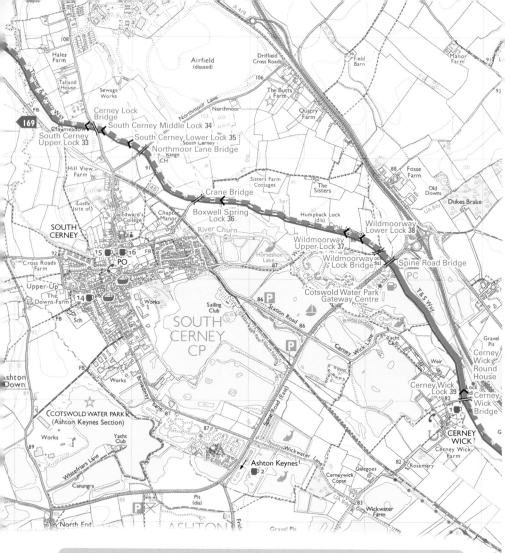

WALKING AND CYCLING

The line of the towpath can be followed from the start of this section, beginning where the minor road crosses the line of the navigation on a causeway that was once Cerney Lock Bridge – beside South Cerney Upper Lock 33 – now incorporated into the garden of a private house. Take the footpath southeast across the field to Northmoor Lane, where the canal bed is once again visible. The towpath can now be followed to Latton Junction and then, via short way-marked sections of the North Wilts Canal and the Thames Path, into Cricklade. A variation on this route – in the Cricklade area – is set out in a leaflet Cricklade – Latton Circular Walk, obtainable from the Cotswold Canals Trust (01453 752568; www.cotswoldcanals.com) or local Tourist Information Centres.

On leaving Cricklade, continue following the Thames Path east towards Castle Eaton.

NAVIGATIONAL NOTES

The section of the waterway running from the Cotswold Water Park to Cricklade falls within Phase 2 of the restoration plan – see Navigational Notes on page 174.

🍺 5 **The Old Bear Inn** 101 High Street, Cricklade SN6 6AA (01793 750005; www.theoldbearinn.com). Ancient hostelry on the main street with a cottagey feel, serving real ales. Beer garden, dog-friendly, traditional pub games and sports TV. *Open Mon-Fri E & Sat-Sun 12.00-00.00 (Sun 23.00).*

✕🍷 6 **The Jicsaw Thai Restaurant** 32 High Street, Cricklade SN6 6AY (01793 753838; www.jicsawthai.com). Highly regarded restaurant, with an open-plan kitchen, where you can see authentic Thai food being prepared and cooked. Patio seating. Takeaway service. *Open Tue-Sun L and E & B Hol Mon.*

🍺✕ 7 **The Old Spotted Cow** The Street, Marston Meysey SN6 6LQ (01285 810264; www.theoldspottedcow.co.uk). An attractive garden surrounds an old stone-built building with a wealth of flag floors and oak beams. Real ales and *food L and E (not Sun E).* Well-behaved, dry dogs are welcome in the bar area (water and dog biscuits provided) and there is a wealth of books and games for children. Also coffee and elevenses. Traditional pub games, real fires and Wi-Fi. *Open 11.00-23.00 (Sun 18.30 or sunset – whichever is the earlier).*

🍺✕ 8 **The Masons Arms** 28 High Street, Meysey Hampton GL7 5JT (01285 850164; www.themasonsarms-meyseyhampton.co.uk). Dating from 17th C, this gem of a pub, with its attentive staff, serves real ale and 'simple pub food made with locally sourced ingredients *Mon-Sun L and E (not Sun E).* Tables on the village green in *summer* and log fires in the *winter.* B&B. *Open daily L and E (not Sun E).*

🍺✕ 9 **The Red Lion** The Street, Castle Eaton SN6 6JZ (01285 810280; www.red-lion.co.uk). Reputed to be the first pub on the Thames, this imposing establishment serves real ale, bar snacks and restaurant meals *Mon-Fri L and E & Sat-Sun 12.00-21.00 (Sun 19.00).* Patio and riverside garden – children welcome. Packed lunches available for walkers and canoeists. Petanque and fishing. Camping. B&B. *Open Mon-Fri L and E & Sat-Sun 12.00-23.00.*

🍺 10 **The George** High Street, Kempsford GL7 4EQ (01285 810236; www.arkells.com/pubs_more2.php?id=617). Real ales and traditional pub food available *daily L and E (not Sun E).* Children welcome. *Open daily L and E.*

🍺 11 **The Jolly Tar** Queens Road, Hannington SN6 7RP (01793 762245; www.thejollytarinn.co.uk). A quaint, cosy pub in a peaceful, rural location, serving real ales and appetising, homemade food *daily L and E (not Mon L except B Hols).* Open fires, a conservatory dining area and garden including a children's play area. Dog-friendly and Wi-Fi. B&B. *Open Tue-Sun L and E.*

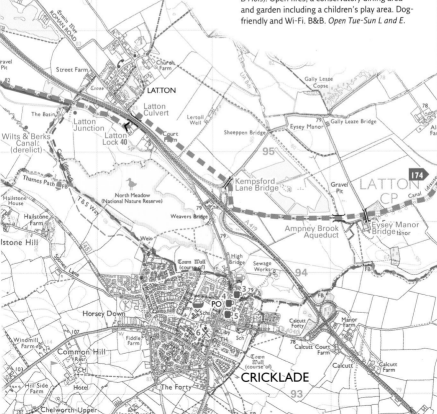

Kempsford

Quite understandably there was considerable outcry when the new, dual carriageway A419 was being constructed, without any provision for future restoration, where it crossed the line of the Thames & Severn Canal at Latton. Happily, today, there is both a culvert (and a new line for the navigation) in place and both canal and walker can rapidly retreat from the hubbub of this 20th-C intrusion alongside the more peaceful mix of gravel pits and arable land. For the time being the meandering, infant Thames – once actually navigable to Cricklade – provides an exit from this charming town, but now that the Canal Trust has completed restoration of Eisey Lock, it is to be hoped that access to stretches of the towpath will not be too far away.

NAVIGATIONAL NOTES

This stretch of the waterway falls within Phase 2 of the restoration plan and, as such, will receive attention once Phase 1B – the length from Saul to the Ocean at Stonehouse – is complete. Eisey Lock has already been restored, while Inglesham Lock and the first ¼-mile of the canal are now in CCT ownership. The navigation will certainly make an enticing destination for those currently obliged to wind at the navigable head of the Thames, beside Inglesham Round House.

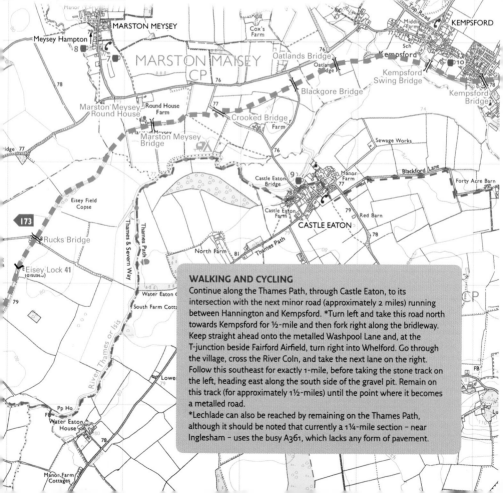

WALKING AND CYCLING

Continue along the Thames Path, through Castle Eaton, to its intersection with the next minor road (approximately 2 miles) running between Hannington and Kempsford. *Turn left and take this road north towards Kempsford for ½-mile and then fork right along the bridleway. Keep straight ahead onto the metalled Washpool Lane and, at the T-junction beside Fairford Airfield, turn right into Whelford. Go through the village, cross the River Coln, and take the next lane on the right. Follow this southeast for exactly 1-mile, before taking the stone track on the left, heading east along the south side of the gravel pit. Remain on this track (for approximately 1½-miles) until the point where it becomes a metalled road.

*Lechlade can also be reached by remaining on the Thames Path, although it should be noted that currently a 1¼-mile section – near Inglesham – uses the busy A361, which lacks any form of pavement.

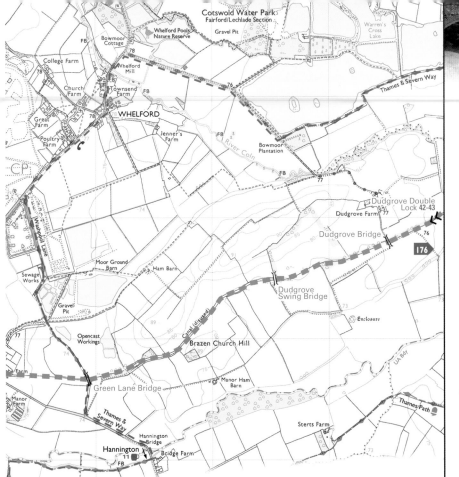

Marston Meysey
Wilts. PO box, tel. The attractive Grade II listed school building, closed in 1924 when the roll fell to 18, is now the village hall in the ownership of the community.

Meysey Hampton
Glos. PO box, tel. Comprised largely of appealing ivy-clad, stone buildings, this settlement lies under the shadow of Fairford Airfield. The compact village green sports an ancient water pump, in an elevated position, accessed by a rustic flight of stone steps.

Castle Eaton
Wilts. PO box, tel. At the west end of the village there is a large, new housing development incorporating an original Thames watermill. The community-run post office combines with a coffee morning, which takes place in the village hall *Thu 09.30-11.30*.

Second Chance Campsite Castle Eaton SN6 6SZ (01285 810675; www.secondchance touring.co.uk/). Small family-owned touring park, close to the Thames and the canal, that welcomes tents.

Kempsford
Glos. PO box, tel. Taking its cue from nearby Castle Eaton, there is a community post office in the village hall on *Thu morning*, combining with a café.

Hannington
Wilts. PO box. There is a small library in the redundant telephone box, while the pretty, retiring Church of St John the Baptist is somewhat distant, down a gated farm road.

Whelford
Glos. PO box, tel. A quiet, agricultural village, flanked by the River Coln and watched over by the pocket-sized Church of St Anne. Completed in 1864, this building is a fine example of G. E. Street's elemental geometry, reflecting the Victorian Gothic Revival style. It is of stone construction, with a tiled roof, simple wooden south porch, a round apse with three slender lancet windows, all topped off with a lead-covered pyramidal bellcote. The simple interior furnishings remain very much as their designer intended.

175

Inglesham

Dudgrove Double Locks share their isolation with a single farmhouse, in what is still a sparsely populated area of Gloucestershire. Interestingly, while the upper chamber has a fairly typical rise of 9ft, the lower chamber lifts craft a mere 2' 6". This inequality of effort is somewhat unusual in the design of a staircase lock and suggests that the second chamber is something of an afterthought. Indeed, the upper chamber is built of neat ashlar, while its companion is roughly constructed of un-mortared stones. At the time of its construction, the canal proprietors were still debating the waterway's ultimate junction with the Thames and the additional drop may well have been necessitated by their final choice of a more easterly (downstream) option. The blend of gravel pits (both active and worked-out) and mixed farming firmly defines the landscape, punctuated by mature hedgerows and diminutive copses. The navigable Thames begins at the Round House, just below Inglesham Lock 44, at its junction with the canal. The hamlet of Inglesham itself is an attractive group of buildings by the river's edge. Moored craft, together with all the activities of a riverside park, are present as the Thames passes Lechlade on its leisurely, 146-mile journey – via Oxford and Reading – into the very heart of the Capital.

See Book 7

BOAT TRIPS
The Cotswold Canals Trust offers public trips on the classic Thames river launch *Inglesham* from the south bank of the river in Riverside Park. Trip and Charter details from 01453 752568 www.cotswoldcanals.com.

● **Inglesham**

Wilts. A marvellous architectural group around the church. Although of late Saxon origin, the present building is largely 13th C. William Morris was responsible for the remarkable original state of the building – he loved it and saved it from 19th-C restoration. There are the remains of a rare painted 13th-C reredos, box pews, and an ancient carving of the Mother and Child. The adjoining farm was once the priory. On the north bank the Inglesham Round House – the last of five along the Thames & Severn Canal – is a notable landmark, announcing to river users that they have reached the effective limit of navigation. It was once home to the canal lock keeper and is now incorporated into a private dwelling.

● **Lechlade**

Glos. PO, tel, stores, chemist, fish & chips, *takeaway.* A golden grey market town dominating the river in all directions and best seen from St John's Bridge, with the tall spire of the Perpendicular wool church rising above the surrounding cluster of buildings. Shelley's Walk leads from the river to the church, where his *Stanzas in a Summer Churchyard* is quoted on a plaque in the churchyard wall. Shelley, Peacock, Mary Godwin and Charles Clairmont stayed in Lechlade in 1815, after rowing from Windsor.

WALKING AND CYCLING

Where the track makes a sharp turn to the left, becoming a metalled road, take the footpath on the right, following the driveway to Inglesham Round House. At the river, follow the pathway to the footbridge and, once again, pick up the Thames Path on the south side of the river.

Walking the River itself begins with the start of the Thames Path near Kemble and full details, including sections available to cyclists, can be downloaded at www.nationaltrail.co.uk/ThamesPath. The path is in good shape throughout the length of the river, on its journey east to London. However, it should be noted that currently a 1¼-mile section, running upstream from here to Upper Inglesham, uses the busy A361, which lacks any form of pavement.

Pubs and Restaurants

🍺 1 **The Riverside Inn** Park End Wharf, Lechlade GL7 3AQ (01367 252234; www.riverside-lechlade.com). This pub sits amidst a pleasant mix of boats and antiques, beside Ha'penny Bridge. Food is available *daily 12.00-20.00.* Real ales. Riverside terrace. Camping and traditional pub games. B&B. *Open daily 11.00-23.00.*

🍺✕ 2 **The Old Swan Inn** 7 Burford Street, Lechlade GL7 3AP (01367 253571; www.swaninnlechlade.co.uk). Peaceful and cosy, stone-built pub, the oldest in Lechlade. Real ale. Food served *L and E (not Sun E).* Children welcome. B&B. *Open 11.00-23.00.*

🍺 3 **The Crown Inn** High Street, Lechlade GL7 3AE (01367 252198; www.crownlechlade.co.uk). Popular 16th-C coaching Inn, with open fires, serving a range of real ales including several from its own micro-brewery. *Sun L* only. Children, dogs and muddy boots are welcome. Garden. Live bands *Fri and Sat.* Wi-Fi. B&B. *Open 12.00-00.00.*

✕♈ 4 **Colleys** High Street, Lechlade GL7 3AE (01367 252218; www.colleyslechlade.co.uk). Brasserie, grill and restaurant in a 16th-C coaching inn, serving appetising meals *Tue-Sun L & Tue-Fri E. Booking advisable. Open Mon-Sun L and E (not Mon L or Sun E).*

🍺✕ 5 **The New Inn Hotel** Market Place, Lechlade GL7 3AB (01367 232296; www.newinnhotel.com). Attractive pub between the church and the river dispensing real ale. Bar meals and an à la carte menu – featuring a range of food from the traditional to the exotic – are available *L and E.* Children over 5 years old are welcome and there is a large garden with play area. B&B. There are shower facilities available here. *Open daily L and E.*

🍺 6 **The Keeper's Arms** Church Road, Quenington GL7 5BL (01285 750349; thekeepersarms.co.uk). Formerly a gamekeepers' cottage, in part dating back 300 years, this bright airy pub now dispenses real ales and food *Wed-Sun L and E (not Sun E) together with B Hol Mon L.* Dog- and family-friendly, outside seating. Real fires and Wi-Fi. B&B. *Open daily L and E (not Mon-Tue L).*

🍺 7 **The Rose & Crown** 19 The Green, Highworth, Swindon SN6 7DB (01793 764699; roseandcrownhighworth.co.uk). Happy and friendly staff and a pleasant atmosphere make this pub well worth straying away from the Thames for a visit. Real ales and real cider are available, as is breakfast *Mon-Fri 09.00-11.00 and lunch Mon-Sat 12.00-15.00.* Dog- and child-friendly, together with a garden and play area. Real fires, newspapers and Wi-Fi. Boules and *monthly* live music. *Open Mon-Fri 09.00-23.30 (Fri 00.00) Sat 11.00-00.00 & Sun 12.00-23.00.*

WORCESTER & BIRMINGHAM CANAL

MAXIMUM DIMENSIONS

Length: 72' 0"
Beam: 7'
Headroom: 8'

MANAGERS

0303 040 4040

Diglis Basin to Wast Hills Tunnel south portal:
enquiries.southwalessevern@
canalrivertrust.org.uk

Wast Hills Tunnel south portal to Kings Norton
Junction enquiries.westmidlands@
canalrivertrust.org.uk

MILEAGE

WORCESTER, Diglis Basin to:
Tibberton: 5¾ miles
Dunhampstead: 7½ miles
Hanbury Wharf: 9¼ miles
Stoke Wharf: 12¾ miles
Tardebigge Top Lock: 15½ miles
Bittell Reservoirs: 20½ miles
KING'S NORTON JUNCTION: 24½ miles
BIRMINGHAM Gas Street Basin: 30 miles

Locks: 58

The Bill for the Worcester & Birmingham Canal was passed in 1791 in spite of fierce opposition from the Staffordshire & Worcestershire Canal proprietors, who saw trade on their route to the Severn threatened. The supporters of the Bill claimed that the route from Birmingham and the Black Country towns would be much shorter, enabling traffic to avoid the then-notorious shallows in the Severn below Stourport. The Birmingham Canal Company also opposed the Bill and succeeded in obtaining a clause preventing the new navigation from approaching within 7ft of their water. This resulted in the famous Worcester Bar separating the two canals in the centre of Birmingham (replaced by a stop lock in 1815).

Construction of the canal began at the Birmingham end following the line originally surveyed by John Snape and Josiah Clowes. Even at this early stage difficulties with water supply were encountered. The company was obliged by the Act authorising the canal to safeguard water supplies to the mills on the streams south of Birmingham. To do this, and to supply water for the summit level, ten reservoirs were planned or constructed. The high cost of these engineering works led to a change of policy: instead of building a broad canal, the company decided to build it with narrow locks, in order to save money in construction and water in operation.

Work in Wast Hills Tunnel, described at the time as 'a stupendous undertaking', began in 1794; by 1807 boats could get from Birmingham to Tardebigge Wharf. Here work came to a standstill for several years while the company considered alternative cheaper ways of completing the line down to the Severn. Work eventually started again under a new engineer, John Woodhouse, a great exponent of boat lifts. He proposed reducing the number of locks down to Worcester from 76 to 12, using lifts to descend most of the fall. The company were less enthusiastic and limited his enterprises to one experimental lift at Tardebigge. This seems to have worked reasonably well but the company were still sceptical. They called in the famous canal engineer John Rennie, who decided that the mechanism would not withstand the rough treatment it would doubtless receive from the boatmen. Consequently locks were built but reduced in number to 58. The site of the lift became the top lock of the Tardebigge flight, reputedly the second deepest narrow lock in the country.

After this, work proceeded steadily and the canal was completed in 1815. In the same year an agreement with the Birmingham Canal proprietors permitted the cutting of the stop lock through Worcester Bar. The canal had cost £610,000, exceeding its original estimate by many thousands of pounds. Industrial goods and coal were carried down to Worcester, often for onward shipping to Bristol, while grain, timber and agricultural produce were returned to the growing towns of the Midlands. The canal basins in Worcester became important warehousing and transhipment points: Diglis Basin had warehousing for general merchandise, grain and wine, and Lowesmoor Basin specialised in coal and timber. Prosperous businesses were conducted from these wharves and they were an important port of call for the main canal carriers. However the opening of railways in the area in the 1840s and 1850s reduced this traffic considerably and had a profound effect on the fortunes of the canal.

In an attempt to win back salt carrying, the canal company cut the Droitwich Junction Canal in 1852 to connect the Droitwich Barge Canal and the town of Droitwich with their main line at Hanbury Wharf. Toll income and profits continued their relentless decline and, after 1864, the company was unable to pay a dividend. In 1874 the canal was bought by the Sharpness New Docks Company. The new management commenced a programme of works to improve the canal in the hope of attracting trade but, in effect, the canal was subsidised by the Gloucester & Berkeley Ship Canal for the rest of its working life.

The animals that used to draw the boats along the Worcester & Birmingham Canal were mainly donkeys worked in pairs, instead of the more usual horse – the donkeys could easily be carried on the boat while it was being towed by tug on the river. Both horse and donkey were unsatisfactory on the summit level with its four tunnels, for only the short Edgbaston Tunnel has a towpath through it. To overcome the delays caused by the need to leg boats through the other tunnels, steam tugs were introduced in the 1870s and successfully hauled trains of boats through the tunnels for many years.

By the early 1900s the commercial future of the canal was uncertain, although the works were in much better condition than on many other canals. Schemes to enlarge the navigation as part of a Bristol–Birmingham route came to nothing. Commercial carrying continued until about 1964, the traffic being mostly between the two Cadbury factories of Bournville and Blackpole (closed in the 1920s), to Frampton on the Gloucester & Sharpness Canal, and to Worcester Porcelain. It is now a dramatically interesting route, relatively unspoiled but exceedingly hard work!

THE EXTRA PADDLE

Sugar, cocoa beans, soap, tea, metal ingots and tinned food, unloaded at Avonmouth into barges and trans-shipped into narrowboats at Gloucester, were regular cargoes bound for the Midlands in the early years of the 20th C. Narrowboats, often in groups of 12, would lock down into the River Severn to be towed by one of the Severn & Canal Carrying Company's tugs as far as Worcester, and sometimes on to Stourport.

Those that had booked the tow were arranged in a double line behind the tug, perhaps it would be the *Alert*, with the tow ropes leading from one stern quarter of the boat ahead to the opposite forequarter of the boat following, thereby allowing each craft steerage.

The narrowboats, on arrival at Diglis, then locked up onto the Worcester & Birmingham Canal, collecting donkeys or mules from the stables to complete their journey to the Midlands.

Tardebigge Locks presented a formidable challenge to the crews, who would often urge the donkeys on at the locks, partially opening the gates while the water was still two foot off the level. A block of wood was then inserted between the gates to create an unofficial extra paddle – *a practice we would not even contemplate today.*

Worcester

The Worcester & Birmingham Canal begins at Diglis, on the south side of Worcester. It leaves the River Severn a few hundred yards north of Diglis Locks, climbs two wide (18ft) locks and opens out into one of the two Diglis Basins, where a large number of pleasure boats are moored, some of them seagoing. In its recent, complete rebuilding, it attempts to compete (successfully) with the bland modern housing foisted upon its sister basin, at Stourport, further up the Severn. Gone now for good is the charming hotch, potch of craft, which seemed to capture all of the elements of the cartoonist Giles' view of boating – ramshackle

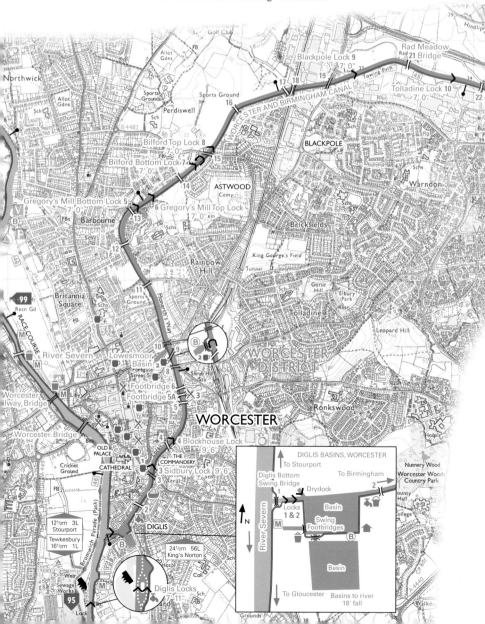

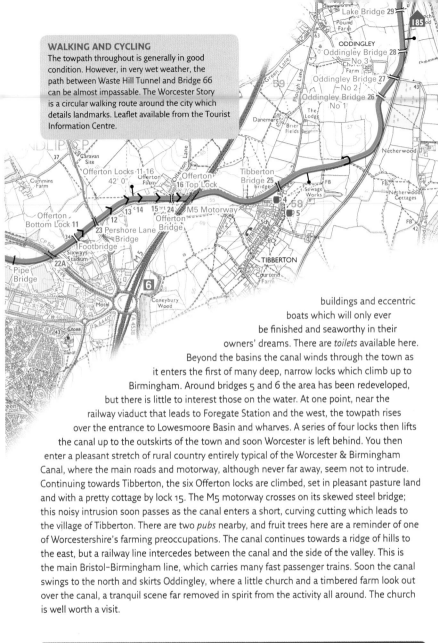

WALKING AND CYCLING
The towpath throughout is generally in good condition. However, in very wet weather, the path between Waste Hill Tunnel and Bridge 66 can be almost impassable. The Worcester Story is a circular walking route around the city which details landmarks. Leaflet available from the Tourist Information Centre.

buildings and eccentric boats which will only ever be finished and seaworthy in their owners' dreams. There are *toilets* available here. Beyond the basins the canal winds through the town as it enters the first of many deep, narrow locks which climb up to Birmingham. Around bridges 5 and 6 the area has been redeveloped, but there is little to interest those on the water. At one point, near the railway viaduct that leads to Foregate Station and the west, the towpath rises over the entrance to Lowesmoore Basin and wharves. A series of four locks then lifts the canal up to the outskirts of the town and soon Worcester is left behind. You then enter a pleasant stretch of rural country entirely typical of the Worcester & Birmingham Canal, where the main roads and motorway, although never far away, seem not to intrude. Continuing towards Tibberton, the six Offerton locks are climbed, set in pleasant pasture land and with a pretty cottage by lock 15. The M5 motorway crosses on its skewed steel bridge; this noisy intrusion soon passes as the canal enters a short, curving cutting which leads to the village of Tibberton. There are two *pubs* nearby, and fruit trees here are a reminder of one of Worcestershire's farming preoccupations. The canal continues towards a ridge of hills to the east, but a railway line intercedes between the canal and the side of the valley. This is the main Bristol–Birmingham line, which carries many fast passenger trains. Soon the canal swings to the north and skirts Oddingley, where a little church and a timbered farm look out over the canal, a tranquil scene far removed in spirit from the activity all around. The church is well worth a visit.

NAVIGATIONAL NOTES

1 Diglis Locks 1 & 2 are *open summer 08.00–19.30 daily, winter 08.00–16.00 daily. Last locking 30 minutes before closing.* Diglis Basin Office: 01905 358758/0303 040 4040. Out of hours emergencies: 0800 4799947. Maximum craft size from the river into the basins: 72ft x 18ft 6 ins *(7ft only on the canal).*
2 The top gates of Offerton Locks can be difficult to open when the pounds above are full.

Battle of Worcester, 3 September 1651 On 22 August 1651, Charles Stuart (later Charles II), having been proclaimed king by the rebels at Scone, reached Worcester with his Scottish army of 17,000 men. The Roundhead General Lambert was sent off in pursuit with his northern cavalry, and captured the Severn Bridge at Upton upon Severn, cutting off Charles' retreat. Meanwhile, another army of 28,000 under Cromwell advanced on Worcester from Nottingham. Charles, realising that he would have to fight at Worcester, organised his defences around the rivers Severn and Teme. After receiving further reinforcements from Banbury, the Roundhead armies advanced across the Severn, using a pontoon made of boats; meanwhile their cavalry crossed by a ford south of Powick Bridge, on the Teme. Heavy fighting broke out, and Charles' Scottish infantry, taken by surprise, were soon driven back. Charles tried to redeem the battle by leading a brave charge out of the east gate of Worcester; supported by cavalry this might have succeeded, but by this time the Scottish cavalry had fled. Cromwell held his ground and forced the Royalists back into the town, killing many in the narrow streets. This Roundhead victory ended the Royalist hopes; Charles fled with a few followers, and after the famous Boscobel Oak episode he made his way back to France.

● **Worcester**

Worcs. All services. A bishopric was founded in the Saxon town of Wigorna Ceaster around the year 680, and a castle was built here following the Norman conquest. During the Civil War the city was the first to declare for Charles I, and the last place where the Royalists rallied around Charles II. They were subsequently defeated in 1651 by Cromwell's army. These days Worcester has plenty to offer the visitor, although the enjoyment is lessened by the constant flow of heavy traffic through the city. A railway bridge at Foregate Street does not intrude, for the girders are suitably decorated and trains are infrequent. However the best area is around Friar Street, and of course the splendid cathedral.

The Commandery Sidbury, Worcester WR1 2HU (01905 361821; www.worcestershire.gov.uk/museums/info/1/the_commandery). By Sidbury Lock. Founded as a small hospital just outside the city walls by Bishop Wulstan in 1085: from the 13th C the masters of the hospital were referred to as commanders, hence the building's name. The present timbered structure dates from the reign of Henry VII in the 15th C, and served as Charles II's headquarters before the Battle of Worcester in 1651. The glory of the building is the superb galleried hall with its ancient windows and Elizabethan staircase. The museum explains in detail various points of time in the building's history, including the monastic hospital and the Battle of Worcester. *Open Feb-Dec, Tue-Sat 10.00-17.00 & Sun 13.30-17.00.* Charge.

Diglis Basin This is a fascinating terminus at the junction of the River Severn and the Worcester & Birmingham Canal. It consists of basins, old warehouses and a dry dock, much of which has undergone considerable redevelopment. Commercial craft have been entirely replaced by a mixture of pleasure boats designed for narrow canals, rivers and the sea. The locks will take boats up to 72ft by 18ft 6in, although obviously only narrowboats can proceed along the canal. The locks are under the supervision of the basin attendant, who is available *from 08.00-19.30 (16.00 winter) with breaks for meals.* Craft are not permitted to use the locks outside these times. The CRT basin attendant can be contacted on (01905) 358758, or enquire through the Waterways Unit Office (0303 040 4040; enquiries. southwalessevern@canalrivertrust.org.uk). Near the first lock is a small pump-house that raises water from the river to maintain the level in the basin.

George Marshall Medical Museum Charles Hastings Education Centre, Worcester Royal Hospital, Worcester WR5 1DD (01905 760738; www.medicalmuseum.org. uk). Meet the past heros of medicine and see how its developing science has transformed our lives. *Open Mon-Fri 09.00-17.00.* Free. Regular bus service from Crowngate Bus Station

The Greyfriars Friar Street, Worcester WR1 2LZ (01905 23571; www.nationaltrust.org.uk/greyfriars-house-and-garden). Dating from 1480, this was once part of a Franciscan priory and is one of the finest half-timbered houses in the country. Charles II escaped from this house after the Battle of Worcester on 3 September 1651. It has a delightful walled garden. *Opening times vary* so visit the website or telephone for details.

The Guildhall High Street, Worcester WR1 2EY (01905 723471). Built in 1721-3 by a local architect, Thomas White, this building has a splendidly elaborate façade with statues of Charles I and Charles II on either side of the doorway and of Queen Anne on the pediment. It contains a fine assembly room.

Worcester Live Huntingdon Hall, Crowngate, Worcester WR1 3LD (01905 611427; www.worcesterlive.co.uk). For information on all events at the Swan Theatre, Huntingdon Hall, the Worcester Festival, as well as Shakespeare at The Commandery and the Historic Ghost Walk of Worcester.

Worcester Porcelain Museum Severn Street, Worcester WR1 2ND (01905 21247; www. museumofroyalworcester.org). Here, where it should be, is the most comprehensive collection of Worcester porcelain in the world, from 1751 to the present day. Visitor Centre. *Open Mar-Oct 10.00-17.00 & Nov-Feb 10.00-16.00.* Tours of the porcelain works. Shop. Charge.

Swan Theatre The Moors, Worcester WR1 3ED. Year-round drama, music and dance from local and national companies. *see* Worcester Live above.

Worcester Cathedral 8 College Yard, Worcester WR1 2LA (01905 732900; www.worcestercathedral.co.uk). An imposing building which dates from 1074 (when Bishop Wulstan started to rebuild the Saxon church), but has work representative of the five subsequent centuries. There is a wealth of stained glass and monuments to see - including the tomb of King John, which lies in the chancel. Carved out of Purbeck marble in 1216, this is the oldest royal effigy in England. When he was dying at Newark, King John demanded to be buried at Worcester Cathedral between two saints: but the saints have gone now. The best way into the cathedral is from the Close with its immaculate lawns and houses, passing through the cloisters where one may inspect five of the cathedral's old bells, two of which were cast in 1374. The gardens at the west end of the building look out over the Severn and on to the Malvern Hills – a particularly fine sight at sunset. Gift shop, tours and tearoom. *Open daily 07.30-18.00*. Donations. **The Three Choirs Festival** is held annually in rotation at the cathedrals of Worcester, Gloucester and Hereford, during the last week in *Aug*. This famous festival has inspired some fine music, one notable composer being Vaughan Williams. For further information about the festival, contact the Tourist Information Centre in any of the three cities. **Worcester City Art Gallery and Museum** Foregate Street, Worcester WR1 1DT (01905 25371; www.worcestershire.gov.uk/museums/info/2/ city_art_gallery_and_museum). Opened in 1896, it contains collections of folk life material and natural history illustrating man and his environment in the Severn valley. In the Art Gallery are a permanent collection and loan exhibitions. Children's activities. Also the Worcestershire Soldier Gallery. Balcony Café. Open *Mon-Sat 10.30-16.30*. Free. **Tourist Information Centre** The Guildhall, High Street, Worcester WR1 2EY (01905 726311; www.visitworcester.com). Enquire here about local guided walks (www.worcesterwalks.co.uk). *Open Mon-Sat 09.30-17.00; B Hols 10.00-16.00*.

● **Tibberton**
Worcs. PO, tel, stores, off-licence. A small but expanding canalside village. There is a fine old rectory by the Victorian church.

● **Oddingley**
Worcs. The church and farm overlook the canal. The Church of St James was originally a depen-dent chapel of the church of St Helen, Worcester, and was first mentioned in 1288. The present building of lias limestone is mainly 15th-C, with 17th-C additions, and has been well restored. There is some fine 15th-C stained glass, and a wooden arch of the same period in the south transept opening. Set into the floor of the sanctuary is a memorial to George Parker, a rector of St James who was murdered in his fields in 1806. He had demanded a rise in the church tithes from his parishioners, which were at that time paid in money, rather than in kind. When his parishioners refused, he built a barn with the intention of collecting the tithes in kind, but this was met with violent protest, and he was shot.

Boatyards

Ⓑ**Worcester Dry Dock** Diglis Basin, Worcester WR1 2BF (07734 500490). Dry dock, boat building and repairs, engineering, bottom blacking.
Ⓑ**Diglis Basin Marina** Diglis Road, Worcester WR5 3BW (01905 356314; bwml.co.uk/diglis-basin-marina). 🛢🔧. Long-term and visitor moorings (contact in advance), boat sales, chandlery, toilets, showers. *Open Tue & Sun 09.00-12.00; Thu 09.00-15.00*.

Ⓑ**Grist Mill Boatyard** Diglis Basin, Diglis Dock Road, Worcester (01905 350814/07956 084107).
Ⓑ**Worcester Marina** Lowesmoor Wharf, Lowesmoor, Worcester WR1 2RS (01905 734160/0330 333 0590; www.worcestermarina. com). 🛢🔧D Pump out, gas, narrowboat hire, overnight and long-term mooring, boat sales, chandlery, books, maps and gifts, dry dock, boat servicing, boat painting, bottom blacking, Wi-Fi. *Open daily 08.30-17.00*.

Pubs and Restaurants (pages 180–181)

🍺 1 **The Kings Head** 67 Sidbury, Worcester WR1 2HU (01905 726025; www.kingsheadsidbury. co.uk). Lockside, Sidbury Lock. Bar and restaurant serving modern British cooking – *daily 12.00-21.00 (Sun 20.00)* – along with real ales. Breakfast available *from 09.00 daily*. Courtyard seating beside the lock. Children and dogs welcome. Traditional pub games. *Open Mon-Sat 09.00-23.00 (Sat 00.00) & Sun 10.00-22.30*.

🍺 2 **The Bridge Inn** 1 Lowesmoor Terrace, Worcester WR1 2RX (01905 23980). Friendly, welcoming local serving real ale. Traditional pub games including a skittle alley. Poker nights and live music *Sat-Sun*. *Open Mon-Fri 15.00-23.30 (Fri 00.30) & Sat-Sun 12.00-00.30 (Sun 23.30)*.

🍴🍷 3 **Pizza Hut** Shrub Hill Retail Park, George Street, Worcester WR1 2DD (01905 610066; www.pizzahut.co.uk/restaurants/find-a-hut/ worcester/worcester-shrub-hill). Canalside by bridge 5A. Part of the multi-national chain offering freshly cooked pizza.Terrace overlooking the canal. Takeaway service. *Open 12.00-22.00*.

🍺🍴 4 **The Bridge Inn** Plough Road, Tibberton WR9 7NQ (01905 345874; bridgeinntibbertondroitwich.co.uk). Handsome traditional canalside village local serving real ale and home-made food *daily 12.00-20.00*. Child- and dog-friendly, canalside garden and play area. Mooring. *Open daily 11.00-00.00*.

🍺 5 **Speed the Plough** Plough Road, Tibberton WR9 7NQ (01905 345146; www.speedtheplough-tibberton.co.uk). Up the road from bridge 25. An attractive 17th-C country pub named after the agricultural well-wishing 'God speed the plough', with a fine collection of clocks. No jukebox or gaming machines. Real ale and bar meals *L and E*. Children welcome *until 21.00*. Small garden with children's play area. *Open daily 12.00-00.00*.

Hanbury Wharf

A wooded cutting beyond the crowded moorings at Dunhampstead leads to Dunhampstead Tunnel, the first of five between here and Birmingham. There is no towpath in the tunnel; horses used to walk over the hill while boatmen pulled the boats through using the handrail along each side. Leaving the tunnel, the canal enters flatter countryside as the hills recede to the east. The pretty, residential settlement of Shernal Green flanks the canal, while Hadzor Hall, built in the late 18th C in the classical tradition, is visible in the trees on the west side of the canal. This straight stretch is terminated by the very busy area of Hanbury Wharf, where an old arm encloses boatbuilders and a lighthouse. There is a *pub* by the main road bridge, and the Droitwich Junction Canal joins just to the north. Navigators should now cherish this 5½-mile level – it is easily the longest pound between Worcester and Tardebigge Top Lock. As the canal passes under the railway to take up position on its east side, the ridge of hills nears again, accompanied by attractive parkland around Hanbury Hall. Ahead are the six locks of the Astwood flight, set in pleasant open pastureland – take time to admire the flower and vegetable gardens around lock 18. A short walk west from the top is a *pub*, beside the railway line.

Boatyards

Ⓑ**Brookline Narrowboat Holidays** Dunhampstead Wharf, Trench Lane, Dunhampstead WR9 7JX (01905 773889; www.brookline.co.uk). Narrowboat hire, boat sales.

Ⓑ**Bridge 35 Chandlers** Unit 3, Canal Village, Hanbury Wharf Droitwich WR9 7DU (07748 408245). D Gas, chandlery, refreshments, ice cream. *Open Thu-Tue 09.00-17.00 (Sun 10.00).*

Ⓑ**Hanbury Wharf Canal Village** Hanbury Road, Droitwich WR9 7DU (01905 794445; www.newand usedboat.co.uk). 🛢🚿🔧D Gas, long-term mooring, winter storage, boat building, boat sales and repairs, chandlery, toilets, showers, books, maps and gifts, solid fuel.

Pubs and Restaurants

🍺✗ 1 **The Fir Tree Inn** Trench Lane, Oddingley, Dunhampstead WR9 7JX (01905 774094; www.thefirtreeinn.co.uk). A smart and comfortable pub near the canal, serving food at the bar or à la carte *L and E Mon-Fri and all day Sat and Sun.* Children welcome, and there is a fine garden with plenty of seats. Wi-Fi and mooring. *Open Mon-Fri L and E & Sat-Sun 12.00-23.00 (Sun 22.30).*

🍺✗ 2 **The Eagle & Sun** Hanbury Wharf, Hanbury Rd, Droitwich WR9 7DX (01905 799266; www.eagleandsundroitwich.com). Busy pub, overlooking Hanbury Junction, serving real ales and a selection of inexpensive, fixed price menus *daily 12.00-21.00*

(Sun 20.30). Children welcome. Canalside seating. Mooring close by – use the Droitwich Canal. *Open 10.00-23.00 (Sun 22.30).*

🍺 3 **The Bowling Green Inn** Shaw Lane, Stoke Works B60 4BH (01527 861291; www.marstonspubs.co.uk). Beside the railway bridge, 200yds west of bridge 41. Attractive pub with a real fire, serving real ale and bar meals *L and E (not Sun)* with a children's menu. The garden has a play area and a bowling green. *Occasional* live music, suitable for families. Dog-friendly. Traditional pub games, real fires and Wi-Fi. *Open 12.00-23.30.*

Hanbury Hall School Road, Hanbury WR9 7EA (01527 821214; www.nationaltrust.org.uk). *NT.* Access is via the public footpath leading south east from lock 17. A red-brick house built in 1701 in the style of William and Mary and little altered since then. On show are the long room and main staircase with painted ceilings by Thornhill, c.1710, along with porcelain and Dutch flower paintings. The original gardens have been re-created and contain an Orangery, c.1740, and an 18th-C ice house. *Opening times are seasonal* so telephone or visit the website for further details.

WALKING AND CYCLING

The Wychavon Way crosses the canal at Shernal Green. This 42-mile route runs from Holt Fleet, on the River Severn, to join the Cotswold Way near Winchcombe. Details from the TIC in Droitwich.

Wychbold

Shaw Lane

Redhouse Farm

186

Astwood Bridge 41
Astwood Meadows Farm
3

Astwood Locks 17-22 42' 0"
22 Astwood Top Lock
21
20
19
18
40 Astwood Lane Bridge

Astwood Manor Farm

ASTWOOD

17 Astwood Bottom Lock

HANBURY PARK

Hanbury Hall

Summerhill Farm
Summerhill Wood

38

Hanbury Bottom Lock 10' 9"
Hanbury Middle Lock 11' 0"
Hanbury Top Lock 11' 0"

Westfields Bridge 1
Ashtrees Coppice
37

Footbridge 3
DROITWICH CANAL

Footbridge
West

B
35

36 SUMMER HILL

Belt Covert

Lady Wood

Lodge

Footbridge 3

Staircase Locks 4-5 17' 1"
Lock 6 7' 9"
Footbridge 4

71

2 Rugby club Bridge
B

HANBURY JUNCTION

WORCESTER AND BIRMINGHAM CANAL

35
2

Lock

Sandal Lodge
Oak 56

15¼m 40L King's Norton
Diglis 9¼m 16L

B4090 SALT WAY
ROMAN ROAD
Gallows Green
Cross-in Hand
Salt-Way
Crowle View

Howning's Farm

59

Home Farm

34 Coffin Bridge

33 Hadzor Bridge

Church Hadzor Hall

Ash Coppice
Court Farm

HADZOR

Manor Farm

HADZOR CP

48

Top Barn

Hazel Wood

32 Hammond's Bridge
Lane Farm

Huntingdrop Farm

Huntingdrop Common

Foot Bridge

Lilac Cottage 47

47

61

46

31 Shernal Green Bridge
Pipe Bridge

SHERNAL GREEN

Hay Lane

Goose Green

Dean Farm

DUNHAMPSTEAD

59

Nursery

Tunnel Farm

Wychavon Way

9

B

61

Dunhampstead Tunnel (230 yds)

52

30 Dunhampstead Bridge 51
Lower Saleway

Park Farm

51

Meadow Farm
Trench Farm

Saleway

ODDINGLEY CP

Pineapple Farm

29 Lake Bridge

181

63

Pound Farm
Oddingley Bridge

Trench Wood

44

185

Tardebigge Locks

Ryefield Road shops (*PO, stores, butcher, fish & chips*) can be accessed from bridge 42. The canal now passes quietly through Stoke Works and approaches Stoke Wharf, from where the hills to the north east can be seen. Just through the bridge is the first lock for over a mile, and beyond it are *moorings*, and then more locks, flanked by trees and pastureland. These locks, numbers 23–28, form the Stoke flight, but in fact there is only a breathing space of a few hundred yards, with a well-placed *pub*, before the first of the 30 Tardebigge Locks is reached just after Stoke Pound. Forward progress becomes a crawl as this great flight is climbed, but the pleasures of the surroundings make the effort worthwhile. The locks wind up through pretty, folding countryside, leaving the busy railway behind in the west. There are attractive, well-cared-for cottages scattered along the flight, generally near the bridges; their gardens overlook the canal. One of these cottages, between locks 31 and 32, by bridge 49, is available for holiday lets from the Landmark Trust (01628 825925), an organisation which was founded as a result of the demolition of Telford's handsome Junction House at Hurleston, on the Shropshire Union Canal. The locks themselves have great charm, being equipped throughout with traditional wooden gates and balance beams. Large paddles speed up locking, and so a reasonably well-co-ordinated crew of two can work through each lock quite quickly. The remote rural course of the canal takes it well wide of Bromsgrove, but Bromsgrove station is only 1 mile north west of bridge 51. Between locks 50 and 54 Tardebigge Reservoir can be seen behind an embankment on the east bank. This feeder reservoir is particularly popular with fishermen. As the reservoir is about 50ft below the summit level, a steam engine was installed to pump water up the hill. The engine house still stands near the canal. Tardebigge Top Lock, with a rise of 11ft, marks the end of the hard work. When the canal was built, there was a vertical boat lift here, but technical problems caused it to be replaced by the lock, and there is no trace of it now.

Above the lock is Tardebigge Wharf, overlooked by the elegant spire of Tardebigge church, up on the hill to the east. At the wharf is an attractive CRT maintenance yard and a large *mooring site* with *toilets and showers*. There is also an interesting interpretation board, depicting the tugs that used to be operated to tow unpowered boats through the tunnel. Leaving the wharf and its cottages behind, the canal vanishes into Tardebigge Tunnel, passing under a main road at the tunnel mouth. There now follows a most delightful stretch of canal, which winds through the hilly Worcestershire countryside: the flat Severn Valley now seems very distant as the canal plunges into Shortwood Tunnel.

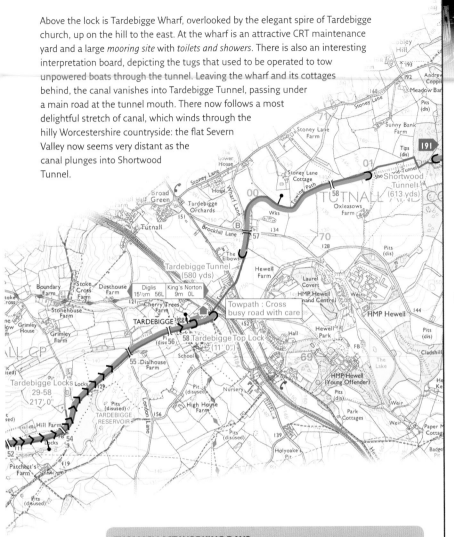

THOMAS' LAST WORKING DAYS

It was in May 1955 that the last load of coal was carried from the mines at Anglesey Basin to Townsends Flour Mill at Diglis Basin in Worcester in the *nb Thomas*, skippered by Ray White and pulled by Bob, the horse. The round trip of 103 miles was via Tardebigge, the New Main Line to Pudding Green and onto the Wednesbury Old Canal, then through Ryders Green Junction and down the eight locks to make a right turn at Doebank onto the Tame Valley Canal. A left turn at Rushall Junction brought the climb to Catshill, passing the Travellers Rest pub, once a popular overnight stop, but alas no longer there. After bearing right at Catshill Junction and left at Ogley a whole clutch of moored narrowboats, some full and some empty, would come into view at Anglesey Basin.

Loading at the basin was swift and efficient (some remains of the chutes can still be seen today), with an average of a little under 30 boats being filled daily. *Thomas* carried 27 tons of coal back to Diglis, being towed through Wast Hills Tunnel by the tug, and worked through the Tardebigge flight 'like a bat out of hell'.

187

- **Stoke Works**

  Worcs. Now closed, this establishment was built in 1828 to pump brine (salt) from underground sources for industrial use, and provided much of the canal's trade (later gained by the railways). Now an industrial estate, where housing fronts the tree-lined canal.

- **Stoke Wharf**

  Worcs. A pretty canal settlement in the best tradition – a lock, a wharf, a boatyard and a warehouse – and a pleasant line of houses facing the canal. Stoke Wharf is the only compact element of Stoke Prior – perhaps the heart of the village was drawn to the canal when the latter was built, and has remained there ever since. Stoke Prior church, which is mainly of the 12th C, stands by itself a ¹/₂ mile north of the wharf, the other side of the busy railway junction. Stoke Prior is not a good place for shopping; it is better to obtain supplies at the settlement near bridge 42. There is a decent pub, however.

  Avoncroft Museum of Historic Buildings, Stoke Heath Bromsgrove B60 4JR (01527 831363; www.avoncroft.org.uk). 1 mile north of Stoke Wharf, off the B4091. Old buildings rescued from demolition are re-erected and displayed here. Exhibits include an 18th-C post mill, a local nail and chain works, a 15th-C timber-framed house from Bromsgrove, a fully furnished post-war prefab and the 14th-C roof of Guesten Hall, Worcester. There is also a reconstruction of an Iron Age hut and the National Telephone Kiosk Collection, along with a three-seater earth closet from Leominster. Sensory garden. *Open Mar-Jun & Sep-Oct, Tue-Sun 10.30-17.00; Jul-Aug, daily 10.30-17.00; Nov-Dec, Tue-Sun 10.30-16.00 & Jan-Feb, Sat-Sun 10.30-16.00.* Charge. Gift shop and café. Full programme of events.

- **Tardebigge**

  Worcs. A small farming village flanking the main road. Apart from the settlement near the canal, the best part of the village is up on the 531ft hill, around the fine 18th-C church of St Bartholomew. Its delicate spire sits atop an airy Baroque bell-chamber and slender tower, designed by Frances Hiorn, who seemed not to bother with such inspirational ideas on the rest of the building. At the top of the locks, on the non-towpath side, a plaque commemorates the founding of the Inland Waterways Association in 1946 by L. T. C. Rolt and Robert Aickman, aboard the *nb Cressy*, which was moored here.

  Tardebigge and Shortwood Tunnels 580yds and 613yds long respectively, these are two of the four tunnels on the 14-mile summit level of the Worcester & Birmingham Canal. Neither contains a towpath, and until the turn of the century a company tug used to pull all boats through Tardebigge, Shortwood and the great Wast Hills Tunnel. Navigators will find Shortwood Tunnel extremely wet.

BOAT TRIPS

Dream Catcher New Wharf, Alcester Road, Tardebigge B60 1NF (01384 562358). Public and private cruises and special events all year round from Tardebigge Wharf. Lunch, afternoon tea or buffets can be provided. Refreshments, fully licensed bar and sound system. Telephone or visit website for details.

Pubs and Restaurants (pages 186–187)

🛥✕ **1 The Boat & Railway** Shaw Lane, Stoke Works B60 4EQ (01527 877610). Canalside, just south of bridge 42. Traditional pub with a fine terrace onto the canal. Real ale and meals all day. Between Locks 22 & 23, opposite the pub, there are handy ⚓ points. Children welcome. Traditional pub games, real fires, sports TV and Wi-Fi. *Open 12.00-00.00.*

🛥✕ **2 The Navigation** 57 Hanbury Road, Stoke Prior B60 4LB (01527 837992; thenavigationbromsgrove.co.uk). Traditional pub serving real ale, real cider and food *Mon-Fri 12.00-21.00 (Fri 22.00), Sat 10.00-22.00 & Sun 10.00-17.00.* Traditional pub games, canalside seating and moorings. *Open 12.00-23.00 (Fri-Sat 00.00).*

✕ **3 The Priory Café** 138 Hanbury Road, Stoke Prior B60 4JZ (01527 880660; www.thepriorycafe. co.uk). Serving tea, coffee, sandwiches and tasty platters. Takeaway service. *Open Mon-Sat 08.00-15.00 Sat 12.00.*

🛥✕ **4 The Queens Head** Sugarbrook Lane, Stoke Pound B60 3AU (01527 557007; www.lovelypubs. co.uk/venues/queens-head). Canalside at bridge 48. Popular and busy pub with food available *daily 12.00-21.30 (Sun 19.30)* together with real ales. Children welcome, garden and moorings. Newspapers, real fires and Wi-Fi. *Open Mon-Sat 11.00-23.00 (Thu-Sat 00.30) & Sun 12.00-22.30.* Handy for Avoncroft Museum of Historic Buildings (see above). *Open all day from 11.00.*

Boatyards

Ⓑ**Tardebigge Dry Dock** JL Pinder & Sons Unit 8-11 Metal & Ores Industrial Estate, Hanbury Road, Stoke Prior B60 4JZ (01527 876438; www. jlpinderandsons. co.uk). **D** Chandlery, coal, gas, engine repairs, boatbuilding and fitting out, boat maintenance, repairs and alterations, hull blacking and cabin painting, engineering services, dry dock, wet dock, toilets.

ⒷBlack Prince Holidays Hanbury Road, Stoke Prior B60 4LA (01527 575115; www.black-prince. com/hire-bases/stoke-prior-hire-base). **D** Pump out, gas, narrowboat hire, boat sales, books, maps and gifts.

Ⓑ**Anglo-Welsh Narrowboats** Tardebigge Old Wharf, Tardebigge B60 1LR (01527 873898; www. anglowelsh.co.uk/Locations/Bases/Tardebigge). **D** Pump out, gas, narrowboat hire, day-hire craft, long-term mooring, boat repairs, books, maps and gifts.

WALKING AND CYCLING

The Tourist Information Centre, Bromsgrove Museum, 26 Birmingham Road B61 0DD (01527 831809; tic@bromsgrove.gov.uk) has four leaflets giving details of 2-hour circular walks from Stoke Prior.

Emerging from the 580 yard Tardebigge Tunnel, Worcester & Birmingham Canal

Alvechurch

East of Shortwood Tunnel and the surrounding fruit plantations, the canal emerges high up on the side of a low wooded hill, overlooking the modest valley of the River Arrow. The canal continues northward, winding steadily through this tranquil landscape until the small town of Alvechurch is reached. The town is set below the canal in a hollow, its church up on a hill; the canal winds tortuously along the steep hills round the outskirts, passing a *boatyard* and a canalside *pub*. Ahead, in the distance, is the ridge of hills that is pierced by Wast Hills Tunnel. To the north of Alvechurch the Crown Meadow Arm branches off to the east – *no boats are allowed to enter* and it remains a quiet haven for wildlife. A little further north an aqueduct carries the canal over a little lane that leads to Barnt Green. Beyond the aqueduct and through bridge 65, Lower Bittell Reservoir comes into view, beside and below the navigation – with moored craft here it is a charming scene. The canal crosses the valley on an embankment; at the north end of this is a pretty cottage, which stands at the point where the feeder from Upper Bittell Reservoir enters the canal. With these on two sides and an overflow weir and the lower reservoir on the third, the house seems to be virtually surrounded by water. Leaving the reservoirs, the canal curves through a slight cutting to Hopwood, where there is a *pub* and a busy main road crossing. To the north the canal enters a grander cutting, and, after passing under a fine, big, arched bridge, the mighty Wast Hills Tunnel beckons. The ridge of hills that this tunnel penetrates serves as an important geographical boundary: to the south of it is the rolling open countryside of rural Worcestershire, while to the north of the tunnel is Warwickshire, and the southernmost extremities of the Black Country.

● **Alvechurch**
Worcs. PO, tel, stores, chemist, greengrocer, off-licence, butcher, fish & chips, takeaways, station. A pleasant, large village, with some fine half-timbered houses, Alvechurch is situated at the bottom of a hollow and surrounded by folds of green hills. The church stands alone on a hill; it is of Norman origin but was largely rebuilt by Butterfield in 1861. There are some interesting monuments inside.

● **Bittell reservoirs**
These two reservoirs were built by the canal company, the upper to feed the canal, the lower being a compensation to local mill owners for the loss of water resulting from construction of the canal. The reservoirs are now popular with both anglers and bird watchers.

● **Hopwood**
West Midlands. Provisions are available at the mobile home site, 200yds north west of bridge 67. More a name than a village, Hopwood is merely a small settlement. A fast main road bisects the area.

> **WALKING AND CYCLING**
> The North Worcestershire Path crosses the northern tip of Upper Bittell Reservoir and continues over the top of Wast Hill, and can be reached by walking north from bridge 66. This is a 40-mile route which stretches from Kinver Edge (Staffordshire & Worcestershire Canal) to Shirley. It also links with the Staffordshire Way, the Worcestershire Way, the Heart of England Way and the Centenary Way.

Pubs and Restaurants

▮✕ 1 **The Weighbridge** Alvechurch Marina, Scarfield Wharf, Alvechurch B48 7SQ (0121 445 5111; www.the-weighbridge.co.uk). Traditional style pub, built around part of an old weighbridge. Real ale. Food is served at *breakfast (by prior arrangement 08.30–10.00), L and E (not Tue–Wed).* Children welcome, and there is a garden. Wi-Fi. *Open daily L and E.*

▮ 2 **The Crown Inn** Withybed Green, Alvechurch B48 7PN (0121 445 2300). Canalside, at bridge 61. Pleasant country pub serving real ale. Bar meals are available *L and E (not Mon–Tue).*

Children welcome, and there are seats outside. *Open all day from 11.00.*

▮✕ 3 **Hopwood House** Redditch Road, Hopwood, Alvechurch B48 7AB (0121 445 1716; www.hopwoodhousepub.co.uk). Canalside, at bridge 67. Spacious and tasteful, serving real ale. Bar meals *all day, every day.* Children welcome *until 21.00.* Large grassy garden and an enclosed play area. Wi-Fi. *Open 11.00-23.00.*

Also try: ▮ 4 **The Swan Inn** 12 Swan Street, Alvechurch B48 7RP (0121 445 6679).

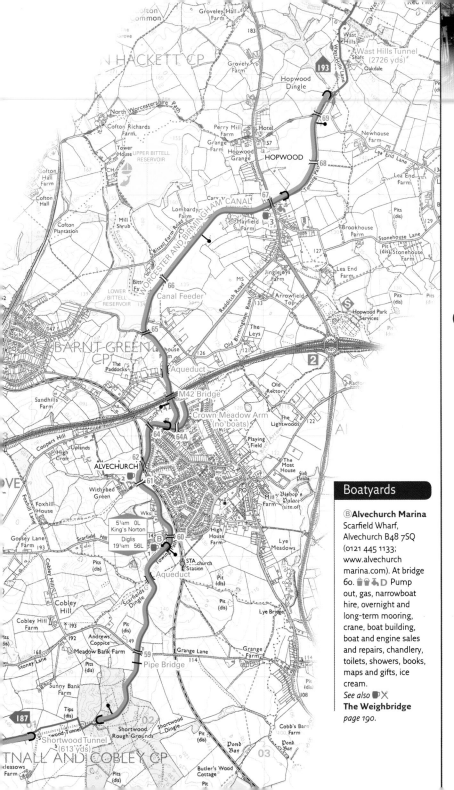

Boatyards

Ⓑ **Alvechurch Marina**
Scarfield Wharf,
Alvechurch B48 7SQ
(0121 445 1133;
www.alvechurch
marina.com). At bridge
60. 🚽🚿⛽D Pump
out, gas, narrowboat
hire, overnight and
long-term mooring,
crane, boat building,
boat and engine sales
and repairs, chandlery,
toilets, showers, books,
maps and gifts, ice
cream.
See also 🍺✕
The Weighbridge
page 190.

Wast Hills Tunnel

The built-up area is revealed as soon as the canal leaves the cutting at the north end of Wast Hills Tunnel: to the west is King's Norton, while all around are housing and light industry. Bridge 71 is the best access point for its *shops*; just past it is the old canal house at King's Norton Junction. Here the Stratford-on-Avon Canal joins at right angles – the disused guillotine mechanism of the celebrated King's Norton Stop Lock, recently restored, can be seen a short way along it. Boats heading south east should turn off along the Stratford-upon-Avon Canal here (*see* page 142). To the north of the junction, the Worcester & Birmingham passes through an industrial area, but thankfully seems to hold the factories at bay on one side, while a railway, the main line from Worcester and the south west to Birmingham, draws alongside on its west flank. Canal and railway together drive through the middle of Cadbury's Bournville works, which is interesting rather than oppressive. Beyond it is Bournville *station*, followed by a cutting. It is inadvisable to leave your boat unattended in this area.

WALKING AND CYCLING
There is no direct route for walkers and cyclists over Wast Hills Tunnel. Heading north, follow Wast Hills Lane, and turn right at Redhill Road. Take the first left into Bracken Way, and then turn right at Longdales Road. Follow this road for almost 1 mile as it bends to the left, then turn left at Primrose Hill and continue down to rejoin the canal at bridge 70.

King's Norton
West Midlands. PO, tel, stores, chemist, takeaway, fish & chips, off-licence, bank, station. The village still survives as a recognisable entity, for the suburbs of Birmingham have now extended all around it, and the small village green, the old grammar school buildings (now converted into flats) and the soaring spire of the church ensure that it will remain so. The church is set back a little from the green in an attractive churchyard, and is mainly of the 14th C, although two Norman windows can still be seen. The grammar school is even older – it was probably founded by King Edward III in 1344. An interesting puzzle is that the upper storey is apparently older than the ground floor. The school declined during the last century and was closed in 1875. Now restored, it is an ancient monument. The shop is *open daily 08.00-21.00.*

Wast Hills Tunnel Once referred to as King's Norton Tunnel, this 2726yd bore is one of the longest in the country. It is usually difficult to see right through, and there are plenty of drips from the roof in even the driest weather. A steam-powered – and later a diesel-powered – tunnel tug service used to operate in the days of horse-drawn boats, as there is no towpath. The old iron brackets and insulators that still line the roof were installed to carry telegraph lines through the tunnel. Grandiose bridges (nos. 69 and 70) span the cuttings at either end.

Bournville Garden Factory Bournville, Birmingham B30 1UB. The creation of the Cadbury family, who moved their cocoa and chocolate manufacturing business south from the centre of Birmingham. The Bournville estate was begun in the late 1800s and is an interesting example of controlled suburban development. There were once old canal wharves here, which became disused when most of the ingredients travelled by rail – but the sidings closed in the late 1960s and now regrettably everything comes by road. There is a circular walking tour around Bournville village, visit www.bvt.org.uk for details.

Cadbury World Bournville, Birmingham (0844 880 7667; www.cadburyworld.co.uk). The ultimate chocoholic's dream come true – the chance to see it; feel it, smell it and taste it and then do it all over again. Restaurant, shops, snack bar, picnic and play areas. *Open all year, daily.* Opening times vary, so telephone for details. Charge.

Selly Manor and Minworth Greaves Maple Road, Bourneville B30 2AE (0121 472 0199; www.sellymanormuseum.org.uk/explore-visit-us/minworth-greaves). Two half-timbered Birmingham houses of the 13th- and early 14th-C re-erected in the 1920s and 1930s in Bournville. They contain a collection of old furniture and domestic equipment. *Open all year Tue-Fri 10.00-17.00, also Apr-Sep, Sat and Sun 14.00-17.00; closed Nov-Mar, Sat-Mon.* Charge. The nearest point of access from the canal is at Bournville station: walk west to the Cadbury's entrance. There is a public right of way (Birdcage Walk) through the works: bear right at the fork, then turn right at the village green. The two houses are close by, on the left. Selly Oak and Bournville both have a *PO*. For more information contact the Bournville Village Trust, Estate Office, Oak Tree Lane, Bourneville B30 1UB (0844 686 1164; www.bvt.org.uk).

Pubs and Restaurants

🍺✕ **1 The Navigation Inn** 1 Wharf Road,
King's Norton B30 3LS (0121 458 1652;
www.johnbarras.com/pub/navigation-
inn-kings-norton-birmingham/p0754).
About 100yds west of bridge 71. Guest real
ales change regularly in this large rambling
pub, which offers food *daily 12.00-22.00*.
Family-friendly, garden and sports TV.
Open Mon-Sun 11.00-23.00 (Fri 22.30).

🍺 **2 The Red Lion** 229 Vicarage Road,
Kings Heath B14 7LY (0121 444 2803;
www.ember pubanddining.co.uk/the-
red-lion-kings-heath). ½ mile east of
Bridge 75, along A4040 Pershore Road.
An imposing piece of early 20th-C Grade
II listed, Neo-Gothic architecture, this
family pub serves real ales and classic
pub fare, which is available *Mon-Sat
11.30-22.00 & Sun 11.00-22.00*. Outside
drinking area and a folk club *Wed*. Quiz
Thu & Sun. Family-friendly, outside
seating, newspapers, sports TV and
Wi-Fi. *Open Mon-Fri 11.30-23.00 (Fri
00.00) & Sat-Sun 10.00-00.00 (Sun
23.00).*

✕ **3 The Greens Tea Room**
St Nicholas Place, 81 The Green,
Kings Norton B38 8RU (07812
741883; thegreenscatering.
wixsite.com/tearoom). Set in a
historic complex of medieval
buildings, overlooking the
picturesque village green, this
is a sea of tranquillity and an
excellent source of coffee,
cakes and light snacks –
including paninis, sandwiches,
wraps, jacket potatoes –
together with speciality and
cream teas. *Open Mon-Sat
09.00-16.00*. Within these
beautifully restored buildings
there is plenty more to see
including a gallery which
keeps the *same opening
hours.*

Birmingham

Soon the railway vanishes briefly behind the buildings of Selly Oak. Between bridge 80 and the next, skewed, railway bridge is the site of the junction with the Dudley Canal, but currently little trace remains here now of either the junction or the canal itself. North of here the canal and railway together shrug off industry and town, and head north on an embankment towards Birmingham in splendid isolation and attractive surroundings. Below on either side is the green spaciousness of residential Edgbaston, its botanical gardens and woods. A hospital is on the west side. The University of Birmingham is on the east side; among its many large buildings the most conspicuous is the Chamberlain Campanile Tower, which was erected in 1900. At one of the bridges near the University, two Roman forts used to stand; but most of the evidence of them was obliterated by the building of the canal and railway. Only a reconstructed part of the larger fort now exists. There is a useful *supermarket* just south of bridge 80. Past the University's *moorings*, canal and railway enter a cutting, in which their enjoyable seclusion from the neighbourhood is complete; the charming old bridges are high, while the cutting is steep and always lined by overhanging foliage. It is a remarkable approach to Birmingham. The railway is the canal's almost constant companion, dipping away here and there to reappear a short distance further on; but trains are not too intrusive and in a way their appearance heightens the remoteness that attaches to this length of canal. At one stage the two routes pass through short tunnels side by side: the canal's tunnel, Edgbaston, is the northernmost of the five on this canal and the only one with a towpath through it. It is a mere 105yds long. The Worcester & Birmingham Canal now completes its delightful approach to Birmingham. The railway disappears underneath in a tunnel to New Street station, while the canal makes a sharp left turn to the basin. The terminus of the Worcester & Birmingham Canal is the former stop lock at Gas Street Basin; this is known as Worcester Bar: originally there was a physical barrier here between the Worcester & Birmingham Canal and the much older Birmingham Canal. The latter refused to allow a junction, and for several years goods had to be transhipped at this point from one canal to the other. This absurd situation was remedied by an Act of Parliament in 1815, by which a stop lock was allowed to be inserted to connect the two canals. Nowadays the stop gates are kept open and one can pass straight through, on to the Birmingham Canal (*see* page 39). Don't leave your boat unattended in this area, although Gas Street Basin should be OK.

The Dudley No 2 Canal This canal used to join the Worcester & Birmingham Canal at Selly Oak, thus providing a southern bypass round Birmingham. The eastern end of the canal is currently being restored under the auspices of the Lapal Canal Trust (www. lapal.org.uk) and will be partly re-opened in the not too distant future. The tremendously long (3795yds) Lapal Tunnel, now collapsed, emerged 2 miles from Selly Oak. This bore was more like a drainpipe than a navigable tunnel – it was only 7ft 9in wide, a few inches wider than the boats that used it, and headroom was limited to a scant 6ft. Boats were assisted through by a pumping engine flushing water along the tunnel, but it must still have been a nightmarishly claustrophobic trip for the boatmen.

● **Edgbaston**
West Midlands. All services. A desirable residential suburb of Birmingham, Edgbaston is bisected by the canal.
Birmingham Botanical Gardens and Glasshouses Westbourne Road, Edgbaston, Birmingham B15 3TR (0121 454 1860; www.birminghambotanicalgardens. org.uk). Fifteen acres of beautiful gardens and four exotic glasshouses together with the National Bonsai

Collection and a range of colourful birds and wildfowl. Gallery, sculptures and playground. Gift shop, plant sales and tearoom. *Open Apr-Sep Mon-Fri 10.00-18.00 & Sat-Sun 10.00-19.00 and Oct-Mar 10.00-17.00. Closed Xmas & Boxing Day.* Last admission *30 mins before closing.* Charge.
Perrott's Folly 44 Waterworks Road, Edgbaston B16 9AL (www.perrottsfolly.co.uk). About ¾ mile west of bridge 86, not far from the Plough & Harrow Hotel. This seven-storey tower was built in 1758 by John Perrott and claims to be Birmingham's most eccentric building. One theory as to its origin is that Mr Perrott could, from its height, gaze upon his late wife's grave 10 miles away. One of the Two Towers of Gondor, featured in J.R.R. Tolkien's *Lord of the Rings,* is thought to have been based upon this building. Tolkien's last address in Birmingham was at 4 Highfield Road, opposite the Plough & Harrow. From 1884–1984 the folly was used as a weather station and was subsequently renovated. For further insight into its more contemporary application visit www.theguardian.com/society/2013/jan/29/tower-inspired-tolkien-bought.
For more information on Birmingham, *see* page 64.

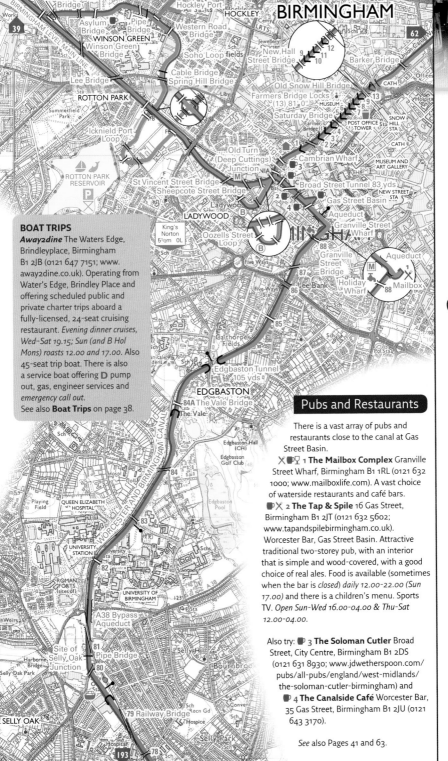

BOAT TRIPS

Away2dine The Waters Edge, Brindleyplace, Birmingham B1 2JB (0121 647 7151; www. away2dine.co.uk). Operating from Water's Edge, Brindley Place and offering scheduled public and private charter trips aboard a fully-licensed, 24-seat cruising restaurant. *Evening dinner cruises, Wed–Sat 19.15; Sun (and B Hol Mons) roasts 12.00 and 17.00*. Also 45-seat trip boat. There is also a service boat offering **D** pump out, gas, engineer services and *emergency call out.*
See also **Boat Trips** on page 38.

Pubs and Restaurants

There is a vast array of pubs and restaurants close to the canal at Gas Street Basin.

✕ ▮🍷 1 **The Mailbox Complex** Granville Street Wharf, Birmingham B1 1RL (0121 632 1000; www.mailboxlife.com). A vast choice of waterside restaurants and café bars.

▮✕ 2 **The Tap & Spile** 16 Gas Street, Birmingham B1 2JT (0121 632 5602; www.tapandspilebirmingham.co.uk). Worcester Bar, Gas Street Basin. Attractive traditional two-storey pub, with an interior that is simple and wood-covered, with a good choice of real ales. Food is available (sometimes when the bar is *closed*) daily *12.00–22.00 (Sun 17.00)* and there is a children's menu. Sports TV. *Open Sun–Wed 16.00–04.00 & Thu–Sat 12.00–04.00.*

Also try: ▮ 3 **The Soloman Cutler** Broad Street, City Centre, Birmingham B1 2DS (0121 631 8930; www.jdwetherspoon.com/pubs/all-pubs/england/west-midlands/the-soloman-cutler-birmingham) and ▮ 4 **The Canalside Café** Worcester Bar, 35 Gas Street, Birmingham B1 2JU (0121 643 3170).

See also Pages 41 and 63.

A rather ferocious looking craft, finally at rest

INDEX